palgrave macmillan law masters

# legal method

palgrave macmillan law masters

# legal method

## ian mcleod
*Associate Senior Research Fellow*
*Institute of Advanced Legal Studies*
*University of London, UK*
*Visiting Professor of Law*
*School of Social Sciences and Law*
*University of Teesside, UK*

### Sixth Edition

**Series editor:** Marise Cremona
*Professor of European Law*
*European University Institute*
*Florence, Italy*

This edition first published 2005 by
PALGRAVE MACMILLAN
Houndmills, Basingstoke, Hampshire RG21 6XS and
175 Fifth Avenue, New York, N.Y. 10010
Companies and representatives throughout the world

PALGRAVE MACMILLAN is the global academic imprint of the Palgrave Macmillan division of St. Martin's Press LLC and of Palgrave Macmillan Ltd. Macmillan® is a registered trademark in the United States, United Kingdom and other countries. Palgrave is a registered trademark in the European Union and other countries.

ISBN 13: 978–0–230–01334–6
ISBN 10: 0–230–01334–1

This book is printed on paper suitable for recycling and made from fully managed and sustained forest sources.

A catalogue record for this book is available from the British Library.

10   9   8   7   6   5   4   3   2   1
16   15   14   13   12   11   10   09   08   07

Printed and bound in Great Britain by
Creative Print & Design (Wales), Ebbw Vale

# Contents

Preface to the sixth edition     *xv*

Acknowledgments     *xvi*

Table of cases     *xvii*

**Part 1**    **Ideas and institutions**     **1**

| 1 | **An introduction to law and legal reasoning** | **3** |
|---|---|---|
| 1.1 | Introduction | 3 |
| 1.2 | Legal method as a creative process | 3 |
| 1.3 | The form of legal reasoning | 7 |
| 1.4 | Propositions and processes: truth and validity | 9 |
| 1.5 | Methods of reasoning: *induction*, *deduction* and *analogy* | 10 |
| 1.5.1 | Introduction | 10 |
| 1.5.2 | Inductive reasoning | 10 |
| 1.5.3 | Deductive reasoning | 11 |
| 1.5.4 | Reasoning by analogy | 11 |
| 1.5.5 | The legal context | 11 |
| 1.6 | Legal practice and legal scholarship | 13 |
| 1.6.1 | Legal practice | 13 |
| 1.6.2 | Legal scholarship | 14 |
| 1.7 | Law and Justice | 15 |
| 1.7.1 | Introduction | 15 |
| 1.7.2 | Law and justice: some judicial perspectives | 16 |
| 1.7.3 | The need for a real dispute | 18 |
| 1.8 | The political element in judicial decision-making | 20 |

| 2 | **The classifications of English law** | **23** |
|---|---|---|
| 2.1 | Introduction | 23 |
| 2.2 | The possible meanings of *common law* | 23 |
| 2.2.1 | Introduction | 23 |
| 2.2.2 | Common law and statute law | 23 |
| 2.2.3 | Common law and equity | 24 |
| 2.2.4 | Common law and civil law | 29 |
| 2.3 | The possible meanings of *civil law* | 30 |
| 2.3.1 | Introduction | 30 |
| 2.3.2 | Civil law and criminal law | 31 |
| 2.4 | Public law and private law | 32 |

| | | |
|---|---|---|
| 2.5 | Substantive law and procedural law | 33 |
| 2.6 | Classification by subject matter | 34 |
| 2.7 | The distinction between matters of fact and matters of law | 34 |

**3    The jurisdictions of the principal English courts    43**

| | | |
|---|---|---|
| 3.1 | Introduction | 43 |
| 3.2 | The hierarchy of the courts as a diagram | 44 |
| 3.3 | Magistrates' courts | 44 |
| 3.3.1 | Introduction | 44 |
| 3.3.2 | Magistrates' courts as courts of first instance | 44 |
| 3.3.3 | Magistrates' courts as appeal courts | 45 |
| 3.3.4 | Judicial personnel in magistrates' courts | 45 |
| 3.4 | The Crown Court | 46 |
| 3.4.1 | Introduction | 46 |
| 3.4.2 | The Crown Court as a court of first instance | 46 |
| 3.4.3 | The Crown Court as an appeal court | 46 |
| 3.4.4 | Judicial personnel in the Crown Court | 47 |
| 3.5 | County Courts | 48 |
| 3.5.1 | Introduction | 48 |
| 3.5.2 | County Courts as courts of first instance | 48 |
| 3.5.3 | County Courts as appeal courts | 48 |
| 3.5.4 | Judicial personnel in County Courts | 48 |
| 3.6 | The High Court | 49 |
| 3.6.1 | Introduction | 49 |
| 3.6.2 | The High Court as a court of first instance | 49 |
| 3.6.3 | The High Court as an appeal court generally | 49 |
| 3.6.4 | The High Court as an appeal court in criminal cases | 50 |
| 3.6.5 | The High Court as an appeal court in civil cases | 51 |
| 3.6.6 | The High Court as a supervisory court | 51 |
| 3.6.7 | Judicial personnel in the High Court | 51 |
| 3.7 | The Court of Appeal | 52 |
| 3.7.1 | The Court of Appeal | 52 |
| 3.7.2 | Court of Appeal (Criminal Division) | 53 |
| 3.7.3 | Court of Appeal (Civil Division) | 54 |
| 3.7.4 | Judicial personnel in the Court of Appeal | 54 |
| 3.8 | The House of Lords | 55 |
| 3.8.1 | Introduction | 55 |
| 3.8.2 | The House of Lords as a court of first instance | 55 |
| 3.8.3 | The House of Lords as an appeal court | 55 |
| 3.8.4 | Judicial personnel in the House of Lords | 56 |
| 3.9 | The Judicial Committee of the Privy Council | 56 |
| 3.9.1 | Introduction | 56 |
| 3.9.2 | The jurisdiction of the Judicial Committee of the Privy Council | 57 |
| 3.9.3 | Judicial personnel of the Judicial Committee of the Privy Council | 57 |
| 3.10 | The new Supreme Court | 57 |
| 3.11 | Administrative tribunals and statutory inquiries | 58 |
| 3.12 | Rights of appeal and permission to appeal | 58 |

## 4 The constitutional context of legal method 61
4.1 Introduction 61
4.2 The rule of law 61
4.3 The legislative supremacy of Parliament 61
4.3.1 A statement of the doctrine 61
4.3.2 The origins and evolution of Parliament 63
4.3.3 The problem of the royal prerogative 64
4.3.4 The revolution and its outcome 65
4.3.5 The significance of the role of the courts after the revolution 67
4.3.6 A modern example of the legislative supremacy of Parliament 68
4.3.7 The nature and status of delegated legislation 68
4.4 The separation of powers 69
4.5 Balancing the constitutional doctrines 70

## 5 European Community law and English law 73
5.1 Introduction 73
5.2 The two European communities 73
5.3 The European *Union* and the European *Community* 74
5.4 The principal Community institutions 75
5.4.1 Introduction 75
5.4.2 The European Commission (arts 211–219 [ex 155–163] EC) 75
5.4.3 The Council of the European Union (art. 202 [ex 145]) 75
5.4.4 The European Parliament (arts 187–201 [ex 137–144] EC) 76
5.4.5 The Court of Justice of the European Communities
(art. 220–244 [ex 188–245] EC) 77
5.4.6 The Court of First Instance (art. 225 [ex 168a] EC) 78
5.4.7 The European Council 78
5.5 The Enforceability of European Community Law in the
United Kingdom 79
5.5.1 Introduction 79
5.5.2 The status of treaties in English law 79
5.5.3 Direct applicability and direct effect of Community law 80
5.5.4 Direct applicability and direct effect of different types of
Community legislation and the *Francovich* doctrine 82
5.6 Indirect effect of Community law 85
5.7 European Community law and national sovereignty 86
5.7.1 Introduction 86
5.7.2 The Community Law view of national sovereignty 86
5.7.3 The English view of sovereignty in the Community context 87

## 6 The protection of human rights and fundamental
freedoms 90
6.1 Introduction 90
6.2 The English legal system and the protection of human
rights before the Human Rights Act 1998 90
6.3 The European Convention for the Protection of Human
Rights and Fundamental Freedoms 93

| | | |
|---|---|---|
| 6.3.1 | Introduction | 93 |
| 6.3.2 | Interpretation | 93 |
| 6.3.3 | Precedent | 94 |
| 6.3.4 | Some Convention case-law and some English responses | 95 |
| 6.3.5 | Procedure | 98 |
| 6.3.6 | Remedies | 98 |
| 6.3.7 | The English presumption of compliance with international law | 98 |
| **6.4** | **The Human Rights Act 1998** | **100** |
| 6.4.1 | The aims of the Act | 100 |
| 6.4.2 | How the Act achieves its aims | 100 |
| 6.4.3 | Is the Act retrospective as to matters of fact? | 105 |
| 6.4.4 | The *vertical* and *horizontal* effect of the Act | 106 |

| | | |
|---|---|---|
| **7** | **Finding, citing and using the sources of law** | **108** |
| 7.1 | Introduction | 108 |
| 7.2 | Conventions in case names | 109 |
| 7.3 | Textbooks and periodicals | 110 |
| 7.4 | Law reports | 114 |
| 7.4.1 | Introduction | 114 |
| 7.4.2 | The range of law reports | 114 |
| 7.4.3 | Neutral citation of cases | 116 |
| 7.4.4 | The citability of law reports in court | 117 |
| 7.4.5 | Editorial discretion in law reporting | 119 |
| 7.4.6 | The problem of delay in law reporting | 120 |
| 7.4.7 | Computer databases | 121 |
| 7.5 | Statutes | 121 |
| 7.6 | European Community law | 123 |
| 7.7 | Reports of the European Court of Human Rights | 123 |
| 7.8 | Miscellaneous sources | 124 |
| 7.9 | Keeping up-to-date | 124 |

| | | |
|---|---|---|
| **Part 2** | **Case-law and precedent** | **127** |

| | | |
|---|---|---|
| **8** | **An introduction to the doctrine of binding precedent** | **129** |
| 8.1 | Introduction | 129 |
| 8.2 | Bindingness, flexibility and the rule of law | 129 |
| 8.3 | A wide view of precedent | 130 |
| 8.4 | A narrow view of precedent: the doctrine of *stare decisis* | 130 |
| 8.5 | The distinction between binding precedent and *res judicata* | 131 |
| 8.6 | Retrospectivity and prospectivity in the operation of binding precedent | 133 |
| 8.6.1 | Introduction | 133 |
| 8.6.2 | The idea of prospective overruling | 138 |
| 8.6.3 | Judicial attitudes to prospective overruling | 140 |

8.7    Are the decisions of the courts actually the law or
       merely evidence of the law?                                    144

9   *Ratio decidendi* and *obiter dictum*                            **148**
    9.1    Introduction                                              148
    9.2    The concept of *ratio decidendi*                          148
    9.2.1  Introduction                                              148
    9.2.2  Goodhart's view                                           148
    9.2.3  Descriptive and prescriptive *ratios*                     150
    9.2.4  Identifying the appropriate level of generality of the facts  151
    9.2.5  The possibility of multiple *ratios*                       153
    9.2.6  Does every case have a *ratio*?                           155
    9.3    Techniques used in handling *ratios*                      155
    9.3.1  Introduction                                              155
    9.3.2  Following, approving and applying                         156
    9.3.3  Not following, doubting, disapproving and overruling      156
    9.3.4  Distinguishing                                            156
    9.3.5  The *per incuriam* doctrine                               157
    9.3.6  The changed circumstances doctrine                        159
    9.4    The concept of *obiter dictum*                            160

10  Vertical and horizontal dimensions of precedent                 **163**
    10.1   Introduction                                              163
    10.2   The vertical dimension of precedent                       163
    10.2.1 The House of Lords and the Court of Appeal                163
    10.2.2 The Court of Appeal and Divisional Courts                 167
    10.2.3 Divisional Courts and the Crown Court                     167
    10.3   The horizontal dimension of precedent                     168
    10.4   Precedent in relation to the Judicial Committee of the
           Privy Council                                             168

11  Does the House of Lords bind itself?                             **172**
    11.1   Introduction                                              172
    11.2   The historical perspective                                172
    11.3   The current position                                      173
    11.3.1 The Practice Statement of 1966                            173
    11.3.2 The leading civil cases                                   176
    11.3.3 The leading criminal cases                                186
    11.4   Is the use of the Practice Statement predictable?         189
    11.5   Departure from previous decisions without relying on
           the Practice Statement                                    190

12  Does the Court of Appeal bind itself?                           **193**
    12.1   Introduction                                              193
    12.2   The position in civil cases                               193
    12.3   The position in criminal cases                            196

12.4    Should the Court of Appeal and the House of Lords
        apply the same principles?                                    200
12.5    The relevance of the leapfrog procedure                       203

13  Does the High Court bind itself?                                  205
13.1    Introduction                                                  205
13.2    The first instance jurisdiction                               205
13.3    The appellate jurisdiction                                    205
13.4    The supervisory jurisdiction                                  206

14  Arguments for and against judicial law-making                     208
14.1    Introduction                                                  208
14.2    Perceived strengths of judicial law-making                    208
14.2.1  Speed                                                         208
14.2.2  Judicial decisions deal with real situations                 209
14.2.3  Precedent operates outside the party-political arena          210
14.3    Perceived weaknesses of judicial law-making                   210
14.3.1  The process is haphazard                                      210
14.3.2  Judges are ill-equipped for the work of law-making           215
14.4    Constitutional constraints on judicial law-making             218
14.4.1  Introduction                                                  218
14.4.2  The party-political context                                   218
14.4.3  Public policy                                                 218
14.4.4  Moral issues                                                  219
14.4.5  The relevance of Parliamentary action and inaction           221
14.5    Conclusion                                                    222

15  Precedent and principle in the European Court of
    Justice                                                           223
15.1    Introduction                                                  223
15.2    Reading European Court of Justice reports                     223
15.3    Precedent in the European Court of Justice                    224
15.4    Principles of Community law                                   226
15.4.1  Introduction                                                  226
15.4.2  Proportionality                                               226
15.4.3  Legal certainty and legitimate expectation                   227
15.4.4  Equality                                                      228
15.4.5  Fundamental rights                                            229
15.4.6  Procedural propriety                                          230
15.5    Subsidiarity                                                  230
15.6    To what extent does the Court of Justice differ in
        practical terms from the English courts with regard to
        precedent?                                                    231

**Part 3** **Legislation and legislative interpretation** **233**

16 An introduction to statute law and statutory
    interpretation                                                     235
    16.1    Introduction                                               235
    16.2    Drafting, interpretation and communication                 235
    16.2.1  Introduction                                               235
    16.2.2  *Interpretation* and *construction*                        235
    16.3    The classification of Acts of Parliament                   236
    16.4    Precedent in relation to decisions on statutory
            interpretation                                             237

17 Statutory drafting                                                  241
    17.1    Introduction                                               241
    17.1.1  The origins of Parliament                                  241
    17.1.2  The origins of the Office of the Parliamentary Counsel     242
    17.2    The modern Office of the Parliamentary Counsel             243
    17.2.1  Introduction                                               243
    17.2.2  The functioning of the Office of the Parliamentary Counsel 244
    17.3    The drafting process                                       247
    17.4    Consolidation and statute law revision                     250
    17.5    *Tilling's Rules* for the drafting of legislation          252

18 Plain meanings, mischiefs and purposes                             255
    18.1    Introduction                                               255
    18.2    Simple literalism in practice                              256
    18.3    The mischief rule                                          260
    18.3.1  The mischief rule itself                                   260
    18.3.2  How the mischief rule is applied                           261
    18.4    The purposive approach to interpretation                  263
    18.4.1  Introduction                                               263
    18.4.2  The power of purposivism                                   264
    18.4.3  Identifying the purpose                                    266
    18.5    The problem of statutory nonsense                          269
    18.6    Are there any 'rules' of interpretation?                   270

19 The idea of legislative intention                                  272
    19.1    Introduction                                               272
    19.2    Different types of intention                               273
    19.2.1  Direct and indirect intentions                            273
    19.2.2  Particular and general intentions                         273
    19.3    The speaker's meaning theory                              274
    19.4    Particular intention: delegation to the drafters          276
    19.5    General intention: delegation to the judges               276
    19.5.1  Introduction                                               276

19.5.2 The idea of political integrity 277
19.5.3 Does the delegation model give the judges too much power? 282
19.5.4 Conclusion 283

## 20 Modern statutory interpretation in practice 285
20.1 Introduction 285
20.2 The basic rule of interpretation 285
20.3 Ordinary and technical meanings 286
20.4 Analysing the context: matters of language 287
20.4.1 Dictionaries 287
20.4.2 The immediate textual context 288
20.4.3 Reading an Act as a whole 290
20.5 Analysing the context: matters of law 291
20.5.1 Introduction 291
20.5.2 The anatomy of a statute 291
20.5.3 Reference to extrinsic materials 297
20.6 Presumptions 307
20.6.1 Introduction 307
20.6.2 Presumption against injustice 307
20.6.3 Presumption against absurdity 308
20.6.4 Presumption against retrospectivity 308
20.6.5 Presumption of strict interpretation of penal provisions 312
20.6.6 Presumptions relating to 'and' and 'or' 318
20.6.7 Presumptions relating to consolidating and codifying statutes 319
20.6.8 Presumption of compliance with international law 320
20.6.9 Presumption of compliance with Community law 321
20.6.10 Presumption against gaining advantage from wrongdoing 322
20.6.11 Presumption against binding the Crown 323
20.7 The Interpretative Obligation under s. 3, Human Rights Act 1998 325
20.8 Change of meaning with the passage of time 327
20.8.1 Introduction 327
20.8.2 The problem of social change 328
20.8.3 The problem of technological change 329
20.8.4 Conclusion 330

## 21 Legislative interpretation in the European Court of Justice 336
21.1 Introduction 336
21.2 Characteristics of Community law which are relevant to its interpretation 336
21.3 The teleological approach to interpretation 338
21.4 Literal meaning, clear meaning and legal meaning 341
21.5 Retrospectivity 342

## Appendix 1 Law reports and journals (some useful references) 344

Appendix 2    Extracts from the Interpretation Act 1978    347

Appendix 3    Articles 2–12 and 14 of, and Articles 1–3 of
              the First Protocol and Articles 1 & 2 of the
              Sixth Protocol to, the European Convention
              for the Protection of Human Rights and
              Fundamental Freedoms 1950    351

Selected further reading    357

Index    360

# Preface to the sixth edition

This book continues to provide an introduction to the techniques of handling legal sources. Some comment on the nature of introductions may therefore be useful.

Introductions may appear to be simple but they must not be simplistic: 'With all its surface simplicity, an introduction must cut as deep as its author has wit and strength to see the way. It must cut for that deepest simplicity which is true meaning'. (Karl Llewellyn, *The Bramble Bush*, revised edn, 1950, p. 7.) One important consequence of this is that I have been unable to avoid the fact that legal method is open-ended, which means that on many occasions I have been unable to offer the comfort of neat conclusions and reliable rules.

Except when writing about the European Community, in which context it often seems most natural to think in terms of 'Britain' or the 'United Kingdom', I have generally written in terms of 'England' and 'English' law and practice. In doing so, I have intended to include 'Wales' and 'Welsh'.

Some of what I have written may also apply in Scotland and Northern Ireland, but how much and to what extent is beyond my knowledge. It follows that readers in those jurisdictions should proceed with caution.

I continue to agree with Lord Goodman (the late senior partner of Messrs Goodman Derrick & Co, the London solicitors) that 'a lawyer who is only a lawyer isn't much of a lawyer', and therefore I continue to urge students to read widely. In the much-quoted words of Sir Walter Scott, 'a lawyer without history or literature is a mechanic, a mere working mason: if he possesses some knowledge of these, he may venture to call himself an architect' (*Guy Mannering*). Furthermore, possession of a well-furnished mind may minimize the truth of the old gibe that 'the study of law sharpens the mind by narrowing it'.

For this edition, in addition to routine updating which is more or less evenly distributed throughout the text, I have substantially amended the material on the retrospectivity of precedent (in order to take account of the House of Lords' decision in *Re Spectrum Plus Ltd*), as well as developing the material on precedent in relation to the Judicial Committee of the Privy Council (in order to take account of the Court of

Appeal's decision in *R v James*). I have also rewritten the material on the self-bindingness of the Criminal Division of the Court of Appeal in the hope that it now makes more sense. I have renamed Chapter 14. I have pruned Chapter 17 by omitting some of the detail, as well as some of the more dated material, but I remain of the opinion that some treatment of legislative drafting is worth including in a book on *Legal Method* because of the context which it provides for the study of legislative interpretation. Throughout the whole process, I have tried to bear constantly in mind the simple fact that neither students nor their teachers have any more time at their disposal than they have previously had.

I remain indebted to the many friends, colleagues and students who have, in varying ways, had their impact on this book in general, and the improvements which have been incorporated into this edition in particular. It would be impossible to name them all and invidious to name only some. I am also grateful to Ian Kingston who has now been copyediting and typesetting editions of this book for more than 10 years.

Finally, and above all, I am indebted to my wife, Jacqui, who is always willing to function as an editorial assistant and to read drafts and proofs as occasion requires. Her patient good humour continues to amaze me.

I have tried to be up to date to 8 October 2006.

IAN MCLEOD
October 2006

# Acknowledgments

The author and publishers wish to thank the following for permission to use copyright material: Institute of Advanced Legal Studies for extracts from *British and French Statutory Drafting* (1987); Oxford University Press for extracts from Engle, 'Bills are Made to Pass as Razors are Made to Sell', *Statute Law Review* (1983), pp. 7, 9, 12, 13–14, 15.

Every effort has been made to trace all copyright holders, but if any have been inadvertently overlooked the publishers will be pleased to make the necessary arrangements at the first opportunity.

# Table of cases

*Adams v Bracknell Forest Borough Council* [2004] UKHL 29, [2004] 3 All ER 897   39

*Addie (Robert) & Sons (Collieries) Ltd v Dumbreck* [1929] AC 358   180

*Aden Refinery Co Ltd v Ugland Management Co* [1986] 3 All ER 737   121

*Aello, The* [1960] 2 All ER 578   181

*Agnew v Commissioners of Inland Revenue* [2001] UKPC 28; [2001] 2 AC 710   169

*Ainsbury v Millington* [1987] 1 All ER 929   18, 19

*Air Canada v Secretary of State for Trade (No 2)* [1983] 1 All ER 910   16, 211

*Amministratzione delle Finanze dello Stato* [1981] ECR 2735   227

*Anderson (W B) & Sons Ltd v Rhodes* [1967] 2 All ER 850   141, 161

*Anderton v Ryan* [1985] 2 All ER 355   114, 187, 188

*Anns v Merton London Borough Council* [1977] 2 All ER 492   149, 185

*Antonelli v Secretary of State for Trade and Industry* [1998] 1 All ER 997   310

*Arcaro* [1997] 1 CMLR 179   86

*Arrowsmith v Jenkins* [1963] 2 QB 561   314

*Arthur JS Hall & Co (a firm) v Simons, Barratt v Ansell (t/a Woolf Seddon (a firm)), Harris v Scholfield Roberts & Hill (a firm)* [2000] 3 All ER 673   142

*Artico v Italy* (1980) 3 EHRR 1   94

*Assam Railways and Trading Co v Commissioners of Inland Revenue* [1935] AC 445   297

*Aswan Engineering Establishment Co v Lupdine Ltd (Thurgar Bolle Ltd, Third Party)* [1987] 1 All ER 135   211

*Atalanta* [1979] ECR 2137   226

*Attorney-General v Butterworth* [1962] 3 All ER 326   144

*Attorney-General v Lamplough* (1878) 3 ExD 214   291, 295

*Attorney-General v Prince Ernest Augustus of Hanover* [1957] 1 All ER 49 — 255, 292

*Attorney-General's Reference (No 1 of 1988), Re* [1989] 1 AC 971 — 287

*Attorney-General's Reference (No 3 of 1994), Re* [1997] 3 All ER 936 — 54

*Attorney-General's Reference (No 5 of 1980), Re* [1980] 3 All ER 816 — 329

*Attorney-General for Hong Kong v Reid* [1994] 1 AC 324 — 169

*Attorney-General for Jersey v Holley* [2005] UKPC 23, [2005] 3 All ER 371 — 170, 312

*Australian Consolidated Press Ltd v Uren* [1967] 3 All ER 523 — 171

*Automatic Telephone and Electric Co Ltd's Agreement, Re* [1965] 1 All ER 206 — 120, 134

*B (A Minor) v Director of Public Prosecutions* [2000] 1 All ER 833 — 317

*Baker v Willoughby* [1970] AC 467 — 157

*Bakhshuwen v Bakhshuwen* [1952] AC 1 — 170

*Bank of England v Vagliano Brothers* [1891] AC 107 — 320

*Barker v Wilson* [1980] 2 All ER 647 — 329

*Barretto, Re* [1994] 1 All ER 447 — 311

*Bastin v Davies* [1950] 1 All ER 1095 — 112

*Bater v Bater* [1951] P 35 — 40

*Beamish v Beamish* (1861) 11 ER 735 — 153, 172

*Behrens v Bertram Mills Circus Ltd* [1957] 1 All ER 583 — 153

*Bellinger v Bellinger* [2003] UKHL 21, [2003] 2 All ER 593 — 327

*Berkeley v Berkeley* [1946] AC 555 — 132

*Berkovits v Grinberg (Attorney-General Intervening)* [1995] 2 All ER 681 — 305

*Beswick v Beswick* [1967] 2 All ER 1197 — 301, 319

*Birtwistle v Tweedale* [1953] 2 All ER 1598 — 118

*Black-Clawson International Ltd v Papierwerke Waldhof-Aschaffenburg AG* [1975] 1 All ER 810 — 263, 272, 292, 297, 298, 300, 301

*Boaler, Re* [1915] 1 KB 21 — 293

*Bokhari v Mahmood* (1988, unreported) — 194

*Bolton Metropolitan District Council v Secretary of State for the Environment* [1995] 1 WLR 1176 — 217

*Bombay Province v Bombay Municipal Corporation*  324
  [1947] AC 58
*Bonham's Case* (1610) 8 Co Rep 114  64
*Bourne v Keane* [1919] AC 815  149
*Bourne v Norwich Crematorium Ltd* [1967] 1 All ER 576  4, 255
*Bowman v Fels* [2005] EWCA Civ 226, [2005] 4 All ER  19
  609
*Boys v Chaplin* [1968] 1 All ER 283  195
*Bracegirdle v Oxley* [1947] 1 All ER 126  37
*Brasserie du Pêcheur v Germany* [1996] 2 WLR 506  85
*Bremer Vulkan, The* [1981] AC 909  181, 182, 185
*Brennwein Case* – see *Germany v Commission*
*Brentnall & Cleland Limited v London County Council*  116
  [1945] 1 KB 115
*Brickman's Settlement, Re* [1982] 1 All ER 336  290
*Bridges v Hawkesworth* (1851) LJ 21 QB 75  156
*Bridlington Relay Ltd v Yorkshire Electricity Board*  39
  [1965] 1 All ER 264
*Bright v Hutton* (1852) 3 HLC 341  172
*Brightlife, Re* [1986] 3 All ER 673  221
*Brind v Secretary of State for the Home Department*  96, 99, 221, 301
  [1991] 1 All ER 720
*British Launderers' Research Association v Central*  36, 39
  *Middlesex Assessment Committee and Borough of*
  *Hendon Rating Authority* [1949] 1 All ER 21
*British Leyland Corporation v Armstrong Patents Co Ltd*  298
  [1986] 1 All ER 850
*British Railways Board v Herrington* [1972] 1 All ER 749  180, 215
*British Railways Board v Pickin* [1974] 1 All ER 609  68, 236
*Britt v Buckinghamshire County Council* [1964] 1 QB 77  113
*Broekmeulen* [1981] ECR 2311  340
*Broome v Cassell & Co Ltd* [1971] 2 All ER 187  164
*Brutus v Cozens* [1972] 2 All ER 1297  35, 36, 38, 236, 237
*Buchanan (James) & Co Ltd v Babco Forwarding and*  321
  *Shipping (UK) Ltd* [1977] 3 All ER 1048
*Bulmer (HP) Ltd v Bollinger SA* [1974] 2 All ER 1226  336
*Burgess v McCracken* (1986) 150 JP 529  238, 288
*Burmah Oil Ltd v Lord Advocate* [1964] 2 All ER 348  68

*C, Re* [1937] 3 All ER 783  119
*C (A Minor) v Director of Public Prosecutions* [1995] 2  218
  All ER 43

*C R v United Kingdom* see *S W v United Kingdom*

*Carter v Bradbeer* [1975] 3 All ER 158     238, 263

*Cartledge v Jopling and Sons Ltd* [1963] 1 All ER 341     184

*Case of Proclamations* (1611) 12 Co Rep 74     65

*Casher v Holmes* (1831) 109 ER 1263     290

*Cassell & Co Ltd v Broome* [1972] 1 All ER 801     27, 164

*Castioni, In re* [1981] 1 QB 149     248, 249

*Celtic, The* – see *Ellerman Lines Ltd v Murray*

*Chancery Lane Safe Deposit Co Ltd v Inland Revenue Commissioners* [1966] 1 All ER 1     179

*Chaplin v Hicks* [1911–13] All ER Rep 224     26

*Chief Adjudication Officer v Foster* [1993] 1 All ER 705     217, 304

*Church of Scientology v Johnson-Smith* [1972] 1 All ER 378     302

*CILFIT v Ministry of Health* [1982] ECR 3415     224, 337

*City of London Corporation v Bovis* (1988) 153 LG Rev 166; [1992] 3 All ER 697     121

*Colchester Estates (Cardiff) Ltd v Carlton Industries plc* [1984] 2 All ER 601     205

*Coltman v Bibby Tankers Ltd* [1987] 3 All ER 1068     308

*Commission for the New Towns v Cooper (GB) Ltd* [1995] 2 All ER 929     113, 123, 290

*Congreve v Inland Revenue Commissioners* [1948] 1 All ER 948     179

*Conway v Rimmer* [1967] 2 All ER 1260     163, 164, 176, 177, 200

*Cooke v Adatia and Others* (1989) 153 JP 129     118

*Cooper v Hawkins* [1904] 2 KB 164     324

*Copeland v Smith* [2000] 1 All ER 457     124

*Cordell v Second Clanfield Properties* [1968] 3 All ER 746     112

*Cossey v United Kingdom* (1990) 13 EHRR 622     94

*Cotterill v Penn* [1936] 1 KB 53     314

*Courtauld v Legh* (1869) LR 4 Exch 126     290

*Cremin v Thomson* (1941) 71 Ll Rep 1 and see *Thomson v Cremin*     121

*Crosley v Arkwright* (1788) 100 ER 325     239

*Croxteth Hall The; Celtic, The* – see *Ellerman Lines Ltd v Murray*

*Customs & Excise Commissioners v Top Ten Promotions Ltd* [1969] 1 WLR 1163     287

*Da Costa* [1963] ECR 31     224

*Daraydan Holdings Ltd v Solland International Ltd*     169
    [2004] EWHC 622 (Ch), [2005] Ch 119
*Davis v Johnson* [1978] 1 All ER 1132     201, 203
*de Freitas v Permanent Secretary of Ministry of Agricul-*     96
    *ture, Fisheries, Land and Housing* [1999] 1 AC 69
*Defrenne v Sabena (No 2)* [1976] 2 CMLR 98     82, 228
*Derby & Co Ltd v Weldon (No 3)* [1989] 3 All ER 118     167
*Derbyshire County Council v Times Newspapers Ltd*     99
    [1993] 1 All ER 1011
*Deuka* [1975] 2 CMLR 28     227
*Dickenson v Fletcher* (1873) LR 9 CP 1     312
*Dillenkofer v Germany* [1996] 3 CMLR 469     85
*Director of Public Prosecutions v Merriman* [1972] 3 All     197, 200
    ER 42
*Director of Public Prosecutions v Schildkamp* [1969] 3 All     294
    ER 1640
*Donoghue v Stevenson* [1932] AC 562     152
*Doody v Secretary of State for the Home Department*     305
    [1993] 3 All ER 92
*Doughty v Rolls-Royce plc* [1992] IRLR 126     84
*Douglas v Hello Ltd (No 3)* [2005] EWCA Civ 596,     107
    [2005] 4 All ER 128
*Dowling, Re* [1967] AC 725     177
*Dudgeon v United Kingdom* (1982) 4 EHRR 149     95
*Duke v Reliance Systems Ltd* [1987] 2 All ER 858     157
*Duncan v Cammell Laird & Co Ltd* [1942] 1 All ER 587     163, 176, 200
*Duport Steels Ltd v Sirs* [1980] 1 All ER 529     218, 282
*Dyson Holdings Ltd v Fox* [1975] 3 All ER 1031     328

*Ealing London Borough Council v Race Relations Board*     272
    [1972] 1 All ER 105
*Eastman Photographic Materials Co Ltd v Comptroller of*     297
    *Patents* [1898] AC 571
*Edwards v Bairstow* [1955] 3 All ER 48     37, 38
*Ellerman Lines Ltd v Murray* [1930] All ER Rep 503     109, 320
*Elliott v C (A Minor)* [1983] 2 All ER 1005     151
*Energy Conversion Devices Incorporated's Applications*     35, 236
    [1982] FSR 544
*Evans v Amicus Healthcare Ltd* [2004] EWCA 727,     97
    [2004] 3 All ER 1025
*Export Credits Guarantee Department v Universal Oil*     116
    *Products Co* [1983] 2 All ER 205

*Faccini Dori v Recreb srl* [1994] ECR I-3325     225

*Factortame Ltd v Secretary of State for Transport (No 2)*     87
    [1991] 1 All ER 70

*Farrell v Alexander* [1976] 2 All ER 721     320

*Fellinger* [1980] ECR 535     341

*Firstpost Homes Ltd v Johnson* [1995] 4 All ER 355     293

*Fisher v Bell* [1960] 3 All ER 731     262, 263, 286

*Fitzleet Estates Ltd v Cherry* [1977] 3 All ER 996     179, 182

*Fitzpatrick v Sterling Housing Association* [1997]     92, 279, 280, 281, 282
    4 All ER 991 (CA); [1999] 4 All ER 705 (HL)

*Food Corporation of India v Anticlizo Shipping Corpora-*     185
    *tion* [1988] 2 All ER 513

*Foster v British Gas plc* [1991] 2 WLR 258     84

*Foster v Diphwys Casson Slate Co* (1887) 18 QBD     288
    428

*Fothergill v Monarch Airlines Ltd* [1980] 2 All ER 696     320, 321

*Fowler v Padget* (1798) 101 ER 1103     319

*Francovich v Italian State* [1991] IRLR 84     84, 85, 225, 228

*Gallie v Lee* [1969] 1 All ER 1062     201, 202, 203

*Galloway v Galloway* [1954] P 312     154

*Gammans v Ekins* [1950] 2 KB 328     328

*Gammon (Hong Kong) Ltd v Attorney-General for Hong*     314
    *Kong* [1984] 2 All ER 503

*Garland v British Rail Engineering Ltd* [1982] 2 All ER     322
    402

*Germany v Commission* [1963] ECR 63     338

*Ghaidan v Mendoza* [2004] [2004] UKHL     92, 104, 281, 282, 325, 326
    30, [2004] 3 All ER 411

*Gill v Lewis* [1956] 1 All ER 844     29

*Godden v Hales* (1686) 11 St Tr 1165     65, 66

*Gold v Essex County Council* [1942] 1 KB 293     153

*Goudrand Frères* [1981] ECR 1931     227

*Gough and Another v Chief Constable of Derbyshire*     103
    [2001] 4 All ER 289

*Gouriet v Union of Post Office Workers* [1977] 3 All ER     210
    70

*Grad v Finanzamt Traustein* [1971] CMLR 1     83, 85

*Grant v Australian Knitting Mills* [1936] AC 85     152

*Greenlands (Limited) v Wilmshurst and Others* (1913) 29     111
    TLR 685

*Grocock v Grocock* [1920] 1 KB 1     154

*H and Others (Minors), Re* [1996] 1 All ER 1 — 41

*Hadmor Productions Ltd v Hamilton* [1982] 1 All ER 1042 — 212, 301

*Halford v Brookes* [1991] *The Independent*, 1 October — 40, 41

*Handyside v United Kingdom* (1979–80) 1 EHRR 737 — 95, 97

*Hanfstaengl v W H Smith & Sons* (1905) 92 LT 676 — 26

*Hannah Blumenthal, The* [1983] 1 All ER 34 — 181

*Harrogate Borough Council v Simpson* (1986) 2 FLR 91 — 278, 279, 280

*Hart v Riversdale Mill Ltd* [1928] 1 KB 176 — 154

*Hawes v Evendon* [1953] 1 WLR 1169 — 328

*Hazell v Hammersmith & Fulham London Borough Council* [1991] 1 All ER 545 — 134

*Hedley Byrne & Co Ltd v Heller & Partners Ltd* [1963] 2 All ER 575 — 152, 160, 213

*Henty v Wrey* (1882) 21 ChD 332 — 112

*Hetherington, Re* [1989] 2 All ER 129 — 149

*Heydon's Case* (1584) 76 ER 637 — 261, 263

*Hilder v Dexter* [1902] AC 474 — 272

*Hill v East & West India Dock Co* (1884) 9 App Cas 448 — 257

*Hillsdown Holdings plc v Pensions Ombudsman* [1997] 1 All ER 862 — 305

*Holmes and Bradbury v Bradford Metropolitan City Council* (1994) 158 LG Rev 561 — 113

*Home Office v Dorset Yacht Co Ltd* [1970] 2 All ER 294 — 11

*Hornigold v Chief Constable of Lancashire* [1985] Crim LR 792 — 206

*Horton v Sadler* [2006] UKHL 27, [2006] 2 WLR 1346 — 174

*Huth v Clarke* (1890) 25 QBD 39 — 283

*Inland Revenue Commissioners v Hinchy* [1960] 1 All ER 505 — 259, 260

*Inland Revenue Commissioners v Plummer* [1979] 3 All ER 775 — 190

*Internationale Handelsgesellschaft mbH* [1974] 2 CMLR 540 — 86, 226

*J S (A Minor), Re* [1980] 1 All ER 1061 — 41, 109

*Jacobs v Booth's Distillery Co* (1901) 85 LT 262 — 174

*Jobling v Associated Dairies Ltd* [1981] 2 All ER 752 — 157

*Johanna Oldendorff, The* [1974] AC 479 — 174, 181

*Jones v Conway & Colwyn Bay Joint Water Supply Board* [1893] 2 Ch 603 — 308

*Jones v Department of Employment* [1988] 1 All ER 725    166

*Jones v Secretary of State for Social Services*    141, 177, 178, 179, 181
   [1972] 1 All ER 145

*Jones v Tower Boot Co Ltd* [1997] 2 All ER 406    240

*Kammins Ballrooms Co Ltd v Zenith Investments Ltd*    34, 264, 265
   [1970] 2 All ER 871

*Kay v Lambeth London Borough Council* [2006] UKHL    103
   10, [2006] 4 All ER 128

*Keck* [1993] ECR I-6097    224

*Kleinwort Benson Ltd v Lincoln City Council* [1998] 4    134, 141
   All ER 513

*Knocker v Youle* [1986] 2 All ER 914    286

*Langley v North West Water Authority* [1991] 3 All ER    195
   610

*Latless v Holmes* (1792) 100 ER 1230    209, 296

*Leader v Duffy* (1888) 13 App Cas 294    266

*Letang v Cooper* [1964] 2 All ER 929    297

*Lim Chin Aik v R* [1963] 1 All ER 223    313

*Lister & Co v Stubbs* (1890) 45 ChD 1    169

*Livingstone v Rawyards Coal Co* (1880) 5 App Cas 25    25

*Lloyd v McMahon* [1987] 1 All ER 1118    291

*L'Office Cherifien des Phosphates and Another v*    310
   *Yamashita-Shinnihon Steamship Co Ltd: The Boucraa*
   [1994] 1 All ER 20

*London, Chatham and Dover Railway Co v South Eastern*    185
   *Railway Co* [1893] AC 429

*London County Council v Central Land Board* [1958] 3    307
   All ER 676

*London Street Tramways Ltd v London County Council*    172
   [1898] AC 375

*Longford, The* (1889) 14 PD 34    327, 330

*Lord Advocate v Dumbarton District Council and*    324
   *Another* [1990] 1 All ER 1

*Lyde v Barnard* [1835–42] All ER Rep 690    269

*Lynch v Director of Public Prosecutions for Northern*    188
   *Ireland* [1975] 1 All ER 913

*Magnhild SS v McIntyre Bros & Co* [1921] 2 KB 97    288

*Magor & St Mellons Rural District Council v Newport*    258
   *Corporation* [1951] 2 All ER 839

*Malone v Metropolitan Police Commissioner (No 2)* [1979] 2 All ER 620 — 90

*Manton v Brighton Corporation* [1951] 2 All ER 101 — 283

*Manuel v Attorney-General* [1982] 3 All ER 822 — 63

*Marleasing SA v La Comercial Internacional de Alimentacion SA* [1992] 1 CMLR 305 — 86, 322

*Marshall v Southampton & South West Hampshire Area Health Authority* [1986] 1 CMLR 688 — 84

*Marshall v Southampton & South West Hampshire Area Health Authority (No 2)* [1993] 3 CMLR 293 — 228

*Maunsell v Olins* [1975] 1 All ER 16 — 261, 270, 286

*Melluish v BMI (No 3) Ltd* [1995] 4 All ER 453 — 305

*Meroni & Co* [1957–58] ECR 157 — 340

*Miliangos v George Frank (Textiles) Ltd* [1975] 3 All ER 801 — 141, 158, 159, 165, 175, 182, 208, 209, 216

*Miller v Minister of Pensions* [1947] 2 All ER 372 — 40

*Moodie v Inland Revenue Commissioners* [1993] 2 All ER 49 — 190

*Morelle v Wakeling* [1955] 1 All ER 708 — 194, 195

*Morgans v Launchbury* [1972] 2 All ER 606 — 216

*Mostyn, The* [1928] AC 57 — 155

*Murphy v Brentwood District Council* [1990] 2 All ER 908 — 149, 185, 210

*Myles v Director of Public Prosecutions* [2004] EWHC 594 (Admin), [2004] 2 All ER 902 — 103

*Nash v Tamplin & Sons Brewery (Brighton) Ltd* [1951] 2 All ER 869 — 155

*Netherlands v Commission* [1979] ECR 245 — 341

*New Bullas Trading, Re* [1994] 1 BCLC 485 — 169

*Newman v Lipman* [1950] 2 All ER 832 — 238, 288

*Nold v Commission* [1974] 2 CMLR 338 — 229

*Nye v Niblett* [1918] 1 KB 23 — 39

*Olsson v Sweden* (1988) 11 EHRR 259 — 95

*O'Reilly v Mackman* [1982] 3 All ER 1124 — 32

*Osborne to Rowlett* (1880) 13 ChD 774 — 151

*O'Sullivan v Herdmans Ltd* [1987] 3 All ER 129 — 13

*Parliament v Council (Chernobyl)* [1990] ECR I-2041 — 225

*Parliament v Council (Comitology)* [1988] ECR 5615 — 225

*Paton v British Pregnancy Advisory Service* [1978] 2 All ER 987 — 28

*Pepper v Hart* [1993] 1 All ER 42 — 105, 217, 298, 303, 304, 305, 306

*Percy v Hall* [1996] QB 924 — 135

*Petch v Gurney* [1994] 3 All ER 731 — 304

*Pharmaceutical Society of Great Britain v Storkwain Ltd* [1986] 2 All ER 635 — 316

*Pickstone v Freemans plc* [1988] 2 All ER 803 — 302, 306

*Pierce v Bemis* [1986] 1 All ER 1011 — 302

*Pirelli General Cable Works Ltd v Oscar Faber and Partners* [1983] 1 All ER 65 — 184, 209

*Pittalis v Grant* [1989] 2 All ER 622 — 166

*Podbery v Peake* [1981] 1 All ER 699 — 194

*Police Authority for Huddersfield v Watson* [1947] 1 KB 842 — 167, 205

*Polydor v Harlequin Records* [1982] ECR 329 — 341

*Poole Borough Council v B&Q (Retail) Ltd* [1983] *The Times*, 29 January — 205

*Powell v Cleland* [1947] 2 All ER 672 — 239

*Practice Direction (Court of Appeal: Procedure)* [1995] 3 All ER 850 — 217

*Practice Direction (House of Lords: Preparation of Case)* [1971] 2 All ER 159 — 174, 197

*Practice Direction (Judges: Mode of Address)* [1982] 1 WLR 101 — 47

*Practice Direction (Judgments: Form and Citation (Supreme Court))* [2001] 1 WLR 194 — 117, 119

*Practice Direction (Judgments: Neutral Citation)* [2002] 1 WLR 346 — 117

*Practice Note* [1995] 1 All ER 234 — 306

*Practice Note* [1995] 3 All ER 256 — 119

*Practice Note* [1997] 4 All ER 830 — 217

*Practice Statement (Judicial Precedent)* [1966] 3 All ER 77 — 157, 164, 173

*Prescott v Birmingham Corporation* [1954] 3 All ER 698 — 208

*President of India v La Pintada Compania Navigacion SA* [1984] 2 All ER 773 — 185

*Prophett v Platt Brothers & Co Ltd* [1961] 2 All ER 644 — 286

*Prudential Assurance Co Ltd v London Residuary Body* [1992] 3 All ER 504 — 137

*Pyx Granite Co Ltd v Ministry of Housing and Local Government* [1959] 3 All ER 1 — 237

*Qualcast (Wolverhampton) Ltd v Haynes* [1959] 2 All ER 38 — 35

*Quillotex Co Ltd v Minister of Housing and Local Government* [1965] 2 All ER 913 — 238

*Quinn v Leathem* [1901] AC 495 — 150

*R v A (No 2)* [2001] UKHL 25, [2001] 2 WLR 1546 — 104, 105, 325, 326

*R v Allen* (1872) LR 1 CCR 367 — 290

*R v Allen* [1985] 2 All ER 641 — 298

*R v Bow Street Metropolitan Stipendiary Magistrate ex parte Pinochet Ugarte (No 2)* [1999] 1 All ER 577 — 191

*R v Broadcasting Complaints Commission ex parte British Broadcasting Corporation* (1995) 7 Admin LR 575 — 298

*R v Broadcasting Complaints Commission ex parte Owen* [1985] 2 All ER 522 — 266

*R v Brown* [1993] 2 All ER 75 — 220

*R v Browne* [1970] 3 All ER 455 — 199

*R v C* [2004] 3 All ER 3 — 137, 174

*R v Caldwell* [1981] 1 All ER 961 — 188

*R v Cambridge Health Authority ex parte B* [1995] 2 All ER 129 — 69

*R v Clegg* [1995] 1 All ER 334 — 219

*R v Cleveland County Council ex parte Cleveland Care Homes Association* [1994] COD 221 — 207

*R v Colyer* [1974] Crim LR 243 — 167, 168

*R v Commissioner Rowe QC (Mr) ex parte Mainwaring* [1992] 4 All ER 821 — 40, 41

*R v Cook* (1995, unreported) — 198

*R v Cunningham* [1981] 2 All ER 863 — 187, 218

*R v Customs and Excise Commissioners ex parte EMU Tabac srl* [1998] *The Times*, 9 April — 237

*R v Cuthbertson* [1980] 2 All ER 401 — 289, 340

*R v G* [2003] 4 All ER 765 — 188

*R v Galvin* [1987] 2 All ER 851 — 292

*R v Gould* [1968] 1 All ER 849 — 197, 200

*R v Governor of Her Majesty's Prison, Brockhill ex parte Evans (No 2)* [1998] 4 All ER 993; on appeal [2000] 4 All ER 15 — 134, 141

*R v Governors of Haberdasher Aske's Hatcham Schools ex parte Inner London Education Authority* (1989) 153 LG Rev 809 — 303

*R v Greater Manchester Coroner ex parte Tal* [1984] 3 All ER 240 — 206

*R v Greater Manchester North District Coroner ex parte Worch* [1987] 3 All ER 661 — 291

*R v Hampden* (1637) 3 St Tr 825 — 64, 65

*R v Her Majesty's Treasury ex parte British Telecommunications plc* [1996] 2 CMLR 217 — 85

*R v Higher Education Funding Council ex parte Institute of Dental Surgery* [1994] 1 All ER 651 — 92

*R v Horseferry Road Metropolitan Stipendiary Magistrate ex parte Siadatan* [1991] 1 All ER 324 — 299

*R v Howe* [1987] 1 All ER 771 — 188

*R v James* [2006] EWCA Crim 16, [2006] 1 All ER 759 — 170, 312

*R v Judge of the City of London Court* [1892] 1 QB 273 — 257

*R v K* [2001] 3 All ER 897 — 317

*R v Kansal (No 2)* [2002] 1 All ER 257 — 106, 178

*R v Khan* [1997] AC 558 — 217

*R v Knuller* [1972] 3 WLR 143 — 186, 187

*R v Kuxhaus and Others* [1988] 2 All ER 75 — 213

*R v Lambert* [2001] 3 WLR 206 — 100, 106

*R v Leaney* [1995] Crim LR 669 — 198, 200

*R v London Boroughs Transport Committee ex parte Freight Transport Association Ltd and Others* [1991] 3 All ER 916 — 84

*R v Lord Chancellor ex parte Witham* [1997] 2 All ER 779 — 90

*R v McFarlane* [1994] 2 WLR 494 — 212

*R v Ministry of Defence ex parte Smith* [1996] 1 All ER 257 — 96, 280

*R v Montila* [2005] UKHL 50, [2005] 1 All ER 113 — 294

*R v Newcastle-upon-Tyne City Council ex parte Dixon* [1994] COD 217 — 207

*R v Newcastle-upon-Tyne Justices ex parte Skinner* [1987] 1 All ER 349 — 239

*R v Newsome – see R v BrowneR v Oakes* [1959] 2 All ER 92 — 318

*R v Oxford Crown Court and Another ex parte Smith* (1990) 2 Admin LR 395 — 113

*R v Palmer* (1785) 168 ER 279 — 239

*R v Parole Board and Another ex parte Wilson* (1992) 4 Admin LR 525 — 71, 99, 196

*R v Pigg* [1983] 1 All ER 56 — 264, 265

*R v Preddy* [1996] 3 All ER 481 — 208

*R v R (Rape: Marital Exemption)* [1991] 4 All ER 481 — 6, 135, 136

*R v Registrar-General ex parte Smith* [1991] 2 All ER 88 — 323

*R v Reynolds* [1981] 3 All ER 849 — 265

*R v St Margaret's Trust Ltd* [1958] 2 All ER 289 — 315

*R v Secretary of State for Foreign and Commonwealth Affairs ex parte Rees-Mogg* [1994] 1 All ER 457 — 304

*R v Secretary of State for Social Security ex parte B and Another* [1996] 4 All ER 385 — 91

*R (Alconbury Developments Ltd) v Secretary of State for the Environment, Transport and the Regions* [2001] 2 WLR 1389 — 102

*R (Anderson) v Secretary of State for the Home Department* [2002] UKHL 46, [2002] 4 All ER 1089 — 102, 326

*R (Daly) v Secretary of State for the Home Department* [2001] 2 WLR 1622 — 96

*R (Gillan) v Metropolitan Police Commissioner* [2005] EWCA Civ 1067, [2005] 1 All ER 970 — 39

*R (Jackson) v Attorney-General* [2005] UKHL 56, [2005] 4 All ER 1253 — 69

*R (Lord Chancellor) v Chief Land Registrar (Barking and Dagenham London Borough Council, interested party)* [2005] EWHC 1706, [2005] 4 All ER 643 — 289

*R (S) v Chief Constable of South Yorkshire* [2004] UKHL 39, [2004] 4 All ER 193 — 300

*R v Secretary of State for the Home Department and Another ex parte Norney and Others* (1995) 7 Admin LR 861 — 99

*R v Secretary of State for the Home Department ex parte Al-Mehdawi* [1989] 1 All ER 777; [1989] 3 All ER 843 — 195

*R v Secretary of State for the Home Department ex parte Brind* – see *Brind v Secretary of State for the Home Department*

*R v Secretary of State for the Home Department ex parte Cheblak* [1991] 2 All ER 319 — 16, 18

*R v Secretary of State for the Home Department ex parte Chinoy* [1992] 1 All ER 317 — 51

*R v Secretary of State for the Home Department ex parte Fire Brigades Union and Others* (1995) 7 Admin LR 473 — 296

*R v Secretary of State for the Home Department ex parte Gunnell* (1984, unreported) — 196

*R v Secretary of State for the Home Department ex parte*     41, 183, 190
    *Khawaja* [1983] 1 All ER 765

*R v Secretary of State for the Home Department ex parte*     19
    *Salem* [1999] 2 All ER 42

*R v Secretary of State for the Home Department ex parte*     183
    *Zamir* [1980] 2 All ER 768

*R v Secretary of State for Trade and Industry ex parte*     301
    *Anderson Strathclyde plc* [1983] 2 All ER 233

*R v Secretary of State for Transport ex parte Factortame*     85
    *Ltd (No 4)* [1996] 2 WLR 506

*R v Sheppard* [1980] 3 All ER 899     314

*R v Shivpuri* [1986] 2 All ER 334     111, 114, 187

*R v Shoult* [1996] RTR 298     198, 200

*R v Simpson* [2003] EWCA Crim 1499, [2003] 3 All ER     158, 199, 200
    531

*R v Smith (Morgan)* [2004] 4 All ER 289     170, 312

*R v Spencer* [1985] 1 All ER 673     197, 198, 200, 203

*R v Spens* [1991] 4 All ER 421     36

*R v Taylor* [1950] 2 All ER 170     197, 200

*R v Terry* [1983] RTR 321     193

*R v W* (1991, Crown Court, unreported)     135, 136

*R v Walsall Justices ex parte W* [1989] 3 All ER     70
    460

*R v Wandsworth London Borough Council ex parte*     307
    *Beckwith* [1996] 1 All ER 129

*R v Warner* [1968] 2 All ER 356     301, 303

*R v Wells Street Magistrate ex parte Westminster City*     316
    *Council* [1986] 3 All ER 4

*R v West Dorset District Council ex parte Poupard* (1987)     5, 307
    19 HLR 254; on appeal (1988) 20 HLR 295

*Rakhit v Carty* [1990] 2 All ER 202     158

*Ramsay (W T) Ltd v Inland Revenue Commissioners*     190
    [1981] 1 All ER 865

*Read v Joannon* (1890) 25 QBD 300     167

*Rees v United Kingdom* (1987) 9 EHRR 56     94

*Reid v Metropolitan Police Commissioner* [1973] 2 All ER     110
    97

*Restick v Crickmore* [1994] 2 All ER 112     304

*Richardson v Pitt-Stanley* [1995] 1 All ER 460     305

*Rickards v Rickards* [1989] 3 All ER 193     194, 195

*Ridgeway Motors (Isleworth) Ltd v ALTS Ltd* [2005]     217
    EWCA Civ 92, [2005] 2 All ER 304

*River Wear Commissioners v Adamson* (1877) 2 App Cas 743    257

*Roberts Petroleum Ltd v Bernard Kenny Ltd* [1983] 1 All ER 564    121

*Robinson v Barton-Eccles Local Board* (1883) 8 App Cas 798    296

*Rookes v Barnard* [1964] 1 All ER 367    164

*Rosgill Group Ltd v Commissioners of Customs & Excise* [1997] 3 All ER 1012    338

*Royal College of Nursing v Department of Health and Social Security* [1981] 1 All ER 545    330

*Royal Scholten-Honig Holdings Ltd* [1979] 1 CMLR 675    228, 229

*Ruse v Read* [1949] 1 KB 370    167

*Ruther v Harris* (1876) 1 ExD 97    257

*S (Minors) (Care Orders: Implementation of Care Plan), Re* [2002] UKHL 10, [2002] 2 All ER 192    325, 326

*S W v United Kingdom* and *C R v United Kingdom* (1995) 21 EHRR 363    137

*Saloman v Saloman & Co Ltd* [1897] AC 22    273

*Salomon v Commissioners of Customs and Excise* [1966] 3 All ER 871    321

*Saunders v Anglia Building Society* [1970] 3 All ER 961    155

*Scherer v Counting Instruments Ltd* [1986] 2 All ER 529    120

*Schorsh Meier GmbH v Henning* [1975] 1 All ER 152    165, 166

*Schweppes Ltd's Agreement, Re* [1965] 1 All ER 195    120, 134

*Scruttons Ltd v Midland Silicones Ltd* [1962] 1 All ER 1    152

*Secretary of State for Social Services v Tunnicliffe* [1991] 2 All ER 712    228, 309

*Shaw v Director of Public Prosecutions* [1961] 2 All ER 446    186

*Sherras v de Rutzen* [1895] 1 QB 918    313, 314

*Shipmoney Case* – see *R v Hampden*

*Shylock v Antonio*, William Shakespeare, *The Merchant of Venice*, Act IV, Sc 1    289

*Siebe Gorman & Co Ltd v Barclays Bank Ltd* [1979] 2 Lloyd's Rep 142    142, 169

*Sigsworth, Re* [1934] All ER Rep 113    322, 323

*Simon v Court of Justice* [1961] ECR 115    342

*Simpson v Edinburgh Corporation* 1961 SLT 17    102

*Siu Yin Kwan v Eastern Insurance Co Ltd* [1994] 1 All ER 213    299

*Smith v Baker & Sons* [1891–94] All ER Rep 69 — 166

*Smith v Hughes* [1960] 1 WLR 830 — 262, 263

*Solicitor's Clerk, Re A* [1957] 3 All ER 617 — 309, 310

*South Staffordshire Water Company v Sharwood* [1896] 2 QB 44 — 156

*South Staffordshire Waterworks Co v Barrow* (1896–97) 13 TLR 549 — 237

*Southern Pacific Co v Jensen* (1917) 244 US 205 — 91

*Spectrum Plus Ltd, Re, National Westminster Bank plc v Spectrum Plus Ltd* [2005] UKHL 41, [2005] 4 All ER 209 — 140, 142, 169, 170

*Spiliada Maritime Corporation v Cansulex Ltd* [1987] AC 460 — 112

*Stanley v International Harvester Co Ltd* [1983] *The Times*, 7 February — 121

*Stauder v City of Ulm* [1969] ECR 419 — 229, 337

*Stephens v Cuckfield RDC* [1960] 2 QB 373 — 294

*Stock v Frank Jones (Tipton) Ltd* [1978] 1 All ER 948 — 273

*Stockport Ragged, Industrial and Reformatory Schools, Re* [1898] 2 Ch 687 — 288

*Stokes v Sayers* [1987] *The Times*, 16 March — 124

*Sudbrook v Eggleston* [1982] 3 All ER 1 — 138

*Sun Life Assurance Co of Canada v Jervis* [1944] 1 All ER 469 — 19, 186

*Sussex Peerage Case* (1884) 8 ER 1034 — 256, 266

*Sweet v Parsley* [1969] 1 All ER 347 — 313, 316, 317

*Thoburn v Sunderland City Council* [2002] 3 WLR 247 — 62

*Thomson v Cremin* [1953] 2 All ER 1185, and see *Cremin v Thomson* — 121

*Three Rivers District Council v Bank of England* [1996] 2 All ER 363 — 306

*Town Investments Ltd v Department of the Environment* [1977] 1 All ER 813 — 323

*Transocean Marine Paint Association v Commission* [1979] 2 CMLR 459 — 230

*UNECTEF v Heylens* [1987] ECR 4097 — 230

*United Railways of Havana and Regla Warehouses Ltd, Re* [1960] 2 All ER 332 — 165, 182 *van Gend en Loos v Nederlandse Administratie der Belastingen* [1963] ECR 1 — 82, 86, 224, 339

*Vera Cruz, The* (1880) 9 PD 96 — 154

*Vestey v Inland Revenue Commissioners (Nos 1 & 2)* [1979] 3 All ER 976 — 179

*von Colson v Land Nordrhein-Westfalen* [1986] 2 CMLR 702 — 85

*W (A Minor) (Adoption: Homosexual Adopter), Re* [1997] 3 All ER 620 — 220

*Wagner Miret* [1995] 2 CMLR 469 — 86

*Walkley v Precision Forgings Ltd* [1979] 2 All ER 548 — 174

*Walter Rau* [1987] ECR 2289 — 228

*Warburton v Loveland* (1832) 2 D & Cl 480 — 277

*Ward v Holman* [1964] 2 All ER 729 — 293

*Ward v James* [1965] 1 All ER 563 — 11, 15

*Waring, Westminster Bank v Awdrey and Others, Re* [1942] 1 Ch 425 — 132

*Waring, Westminster Bank v Burton-Butler, Re* [1948] 1 Ch 221 — 132

*Watkins v Secretary of State for the Home Department* [2006] UKHL 17, [2006] 2 All ER 353 — 62

*Watson v Lucas* [1980] 3 All ER 647 — 328

*Watson v Thomas S Witney & Co Ltd* [1966] 1 All ER 122 — 113

*Wellingborough Borough Council v Gordon* (1991) 155 JP 494 — 118

*Wemhoff v Federal Republic of Germany* (1979–80) 1 EHRR 55 — 94

*Whiteley v Chappell* (1868–69) LR 4 QB 147 — 256, 257

*Williams v Fawcett* [1985] 1 All ER 787 — 194

*Willis v Baddeley* [1892] 2 QB 324 — 145

*Wings Ltd v Ellis* [1984] 3 All ER 577 — 315

*Wood v Commissioner of Police for the Metropolis* [1986] 2 All ER 570 — 288

*Woolwich Equitable Building Society v Inland Revenue Commissioners* [1992] 3 All ER 737 — 184, 210

*X (A Minor) (Adoption Details: Disclosure), Re* [1994] 3 All ER 372 — 265

*Yew Bon Tew v Kenderaan Bas Mara* [1982] 3 All ER 833 — 308

*Yorke Motors v Edwards* [1982] 1 All ER 1024      174, 216
*Young v Bristol Aeroplane Co Ltd*      193, 194, 195, 196, 197,
     [1944] 2 All ER 293      201, 202, 206

# Part 1

# Ideas and institutions

Having read this Part you should understand the nature of legal reasoning and have a basic knowledge of the structure of the English and European Community legal systems, as well as appreciating the growing importance of human rights in English legal method. You should also know how to find, cite and use the principal sources of law.

# Chapter 1

# An introduction to law and legal reasoning

## 1.1 Introduction

This book is about the techniques that are available to lawyers when they are handling the law. In broad terms, the law itself may be found easily enough in *Acts of Parliament* (otherwise known as *statutes*), which are *primary legislation*; certain things done under the authority of Acts of Parliament, which are *secondary* (or *delegated* or *subordinate*) *legislation*; the decisions of the courts themselves, which collectively make up the common law; the system of European Community law; and, increasingly, the law developed in the European Court of Human Rights. However, the underlying theme of this book is that, whatever sources of law are being used, legal method, when properly understood, is a creative process. More particularly, legal method provides a stimulating mixture of relatively abstract reasoning and the use of language in order to achieve practical results.

## 1.2 Legal method as a creative process

If legal method involved nothing more sophisticated than finding the right page of the right textbook in order to apply the rule to the facts, there would be no disputes beyond those as to what the facts were in each case. Plainly, however, arguments as to the law are commonplace. (Indeed, if they were not, no one would need to learn the skills of legal argument, and books such as this one would be neither written nor read.) While it is true, of course, that many important aspects of legal argument centre on the actual words of legal texts (legislation, cases, and so on), it will also be obvious that the argument may sometimes go beyond the texts themselves and include a variety of extrinsic materials. (See, in particular, page 297 in relation to English legislative interpretation.) What is less obvious, but no less important, is that legal reasoning may, in practice, also depend upon other factors which lie beyond the scope of what most people would consider to be law at all. A brief consideration of the views of two legal theorists will illustrate the point.

Oliver Wendell Holmes (1841–1935) was one of the founders of the school of thought known as American Realism, the central tenet of which is that what actually happens in the courts is what really matters. Placing the emphasis on 'law in action' rather than 'law in books', Holmes says, 'the prophecies of what the courts will do in fact, and nothing more pretentious, are what I mean by the law'. (*The Path of the Law* (1897) 10 Harv LR 457.)

Furthermore, having stated what is probably his most famous maxim ('the life of the law has not been logic, it has been experience', which is found on the first page of his textbook *The Common Law*, published in 1881), he puts the relationship between logic and experience thus:

> 'The training of lawyers is a training in logic ... The language of judicial decision is mainly the language of logic. And the logical method and form flatter that longing for certainty and for repose which is in every human mind. But certainty generally is an illusion, and repose is not the destiny of man. *Behind the logical form* lies a judgment as to the relative worth and importance of competing legislative grounds, often an inarticulate and unconscious judgment it is true, and yet the very root and nerve of the whole proceeding. You can give any conclusion a logical form.' (Emphasis added. *The Path of the Law* (1897) 10 Harv LR 461.)

In other words, behind any *explicit* formulation of judicial reasoning there lies an *implicit* attitude on the part of the judge. For reasons which will become apparent when you have read pages 8 and 9, this implicit attitude may be called the *inarticulate major premise*. The difficulty in identifying inarticulate major premises is simply that they are inarticulate, and therefore their precise formulation involves guesswork. Nevertheless, there are cases in which the judges have obligingly articulated that which could easily have remained inarticulate. Two cases are instructive.

In *Bourne v Norwich Crematorium Ltd* [1967] 1 All ER 576, the issue was whether expenditure on a furnace chamber and chimney tower built by the crematorium company qualified for a tax allowance. This depended upon whether it was 'an industrial building or structure' for the purposes of the Income Tax Act 1952, and this in turn depended upon whether it was used

> 'for a trade which consists in the manufacture of goods or materials or the subjection of goods or materials to any process.'

Stamp J said:

> 'I would say at once that my mind recoils as much from the description of the bodies of the dead as "goods or materials" as it does from the idea that what is done in a crematorium can be described as "the subjection of" the human corpse to a "process". Nevertheless, the taxpayer so contends and I must examine that contention.'

Given this as the judge's starting point, it is not surprising that the taxpayer lost.

In *R v West Dorset District Council ex parte Poupard* (1987) 19 HLR 254, Mr and Mrs Poupard had capital assets, but they were meeting their weekly living expenses by drawing on an overdrawn bank account. They applied to the council for housing benefit. This benefit was subject to a means test, and therefore the question arose as to whether the drawings were 'income'. If they were, the amounts involved were sufficient to disqualify the applicants from receiving assistance under the relevant Regulations. The council's Housing Review Board concluded that the drawings were income.

The High Court held that in each case it was a question of *fact* whether specific sums of money were 'income', and that this question was to be decided on the basis of all that the council and their Review Board knew of the sources from which an applicant for benefit was maintaining himself and paying his bills. The conclusion was that on the present facts the local authority and their Review Board had made no error of *law*, and had acted reasonably in reaching their decision.

In reaching his decision, Macpherson J, adopting an argument advanced by counsel for the local authority, said:

> 'The scheme [of Housing Benefit] is intended to help those who do not have the weekly resources to meet their bills, or their rent, and it is not intended to help comparatively better-off people (in capital terms) to venture into unsuccessful business and not to bring into account moneys which are regularly available for day-to-day spending, albeit that the use of moneys depletes their capital.'

Although the Court of Appeal upheld this decision (see (1988) 20 HLR 295), it will nevertheless be apparent that a court with different sympathies could have upheld, with equal or greater logic, the argument that the weekly drawings were outgoings, rather than income, because each drawing increased the drawer's indebtedness to the bank.

Many people find that one of the most enduring pleasures of studying law is playing the game of 'hunt the inarticulate major premise', and you may often find that your reading of even the dullest of cases can be enlivened by trying to get behind the words and the doctrine in order to penetrate the mind of the judge as an individual human being.

The second theorist whose views may usefully be considered by way of an introduction to legal method is Ronald Dworkin (b. 1931). Dworkin shares a common starting point with Holmes, to the extent that both agree that the concept of rules provides an inadequate model of law in practice. However, he proceeds down a different route, placing great emphasis on what he calls 'standards', by which he means ideas which exist outside the texts containing the rules, but which go into the melting pot, together with those rules, when it is necessary to identify the law which is to be applied to a given situation. More particularly, Dworkin calls these standards 'policies' and 'principles'.

> 'I call a "policy" that kind of standard that sets out a goal to be reached, generally an improvement in some economic, political or social feature of the community (though some goals are negative, in that they stipulate that some present feature is to be protected from adverse change). I call a "principle" a standard that is to be observed, not because it will advance or serve an economic, political or social situation deemed desirable, but because it is a requirement of justice or fairness or some other dimension of reality.' (*Is Law a System of Rules?* in *The Philosophy of Law*, 1977, p. 43.)

An example of something which Dworkin would call a principle is the presumption against gaining advantage from wrongdoing, which is discussed at page 322.

Expanding on the idea of principles, and the way in which they work, Dworkin says:

> 'All that is meant, when we say that a particular principle is a principle of our law, is that the principle is one which officials must take into account, if it is relevant, as a consideration inclining in one direction or another ...
>
> 'Principles have a dimension that rules do not – the dimension of weight or importance. When principles intersect ... one who must resolve the conflict has to take into account the relative weight of each. This cannot, of course, be an exact measurement, and *the judgment that a particular principle or policy is more important than another will often be a controversial one*. Nevertheless, it is an integral part of the concept of a principle that it has this dimension, that it makes sense to ask how important or how weighty it is.' (Emphasis added. *Op. cit.*, p. 47.)

Dworkin's concession that 'the judgment that a particular principle or policy is more important than another will often be a controversial one' is important in terms of the creativity of legal method. For example, in *R v R (Rape: Marital Exemption)* [1991] 4 All ER 481 (see page 135), the court had to choose between the principle which prohibits retrospective penalization, and the interest of a wife in preserving her own physical integrity by rejecting her husband's sexual advances. The court prioritized the latter, but in a less emotive context it may well have relied upon the former.

Since the insights offered by Holmes and Dworkin clearly diminish the significance of the plain words of the legal texts which are commonly thought to determine legal disputes, many people coming to the study of law for the first time are reluctant to acknowledge their truth.

However, mature consideration makes it plain that (whether or not you find Holmes, Dworkin, or any other legal theorist convincing) *something* beyond the legal texts must come into play in legal reasoning, if only because a legal text (or, at least, a legal text which has generated sufficient disagreement to bring the parties to court) will seldom have a single plain, or literal, meaning.

> 'The literal meaning is a *potential meaning rather than an actual usage*; it is a conventional meaning within a system of such meanings (dictionary) rather than an actual use of the word in combination with other words. The dictionary definition of a word is independent of any linguistic or empirical context ... no word has a single simple literal meaning except in certain instances in the dictionary itself or more frequently in the mind of the judge.
>
> '*A literal meaning is, at the end of the day, always an interpretative meaning.* A selection has to be made – consciously or unconsciously – to prefer *one of several possible literal meanings in the context of the phrase or clause or statutory rule to be interpreted.*' (Emphasis added. Goodrich, *Reading the Law*, 1986, p. 108.)

Of course, interpretation is not unique to legal texts: we all do it all the time. Two examples from non-legal situations will illustrate the point.

First, consider two shops, one displaying a sign saying 'Pork Butcher', and the other displaying a sign saying 'Family Butcher'. You know, of course, that the first butcher specializes in pig meat, while the second does *not* butcher families. Yet *why* does one adjective qualify the activities of the butcher in terms of the meat sold, while the other does so in terms of the market served? The answer, as Goodrich says, is that the context is all-important.

Secondly, suppose a university is worried about the possibility of being held liable for breaches of copyright by staff using photocopiers when they prepare teaching materials. Accordingly, every photocopier in the university bears a warning notice, which explains the relevant aspects of the law of copyright, and is headed 'For the Attention of Every Single Member of Staff'. Are married members of staff entitled to ignore the notice?

We will return to the problem of *plain meaning* in Chapter 18, but at this stage we must consider the form of legal reasoning.

## 1.3 The form of legal reasoning

The classic pattern of legal reasoning follows what is known technically as a syllogism. Syllogistic reasoning takes the following form:

If $A = B$
And $B = C$
Then $A = C$

The first line is known as the *major premise*, the second as the *minor premise*, and the third as the *conclusion*. Taking a legal example, therefore, the pattern becomes:

> It is an offence to exceed the speed limit
> Exceeding the speed limit is what the defendant has done
> It is an offence to do what the defendant has done

or, expressing the conclusion more directly, the defendant is guilty of speeding.

Essentially, therefore, syllogistic reasoning is perfectly straightforward. However, syllogisms assume that the major and minor premises exist, without giving any assistance as to how they may be formulated. Returning to the speeding example, it is apparent that we have: a statement of law (the major premise), a statement of fact (the minor premise) and a conclusion (which results from applying the major premise to the minor premise), but it is equally apparent that we must establish both of the premises before we can reach the conclusion. Taking the minor premise first, the facts of a case will either be proved to the satisfaction of the court or agreed between the parties. In terms of professional practice, far more disputes involve questions of fact than involve questions of law. Therefore all competent practitioners need a good grasp of the law of evidence, so that they know how to go about trying to prove the facts on which they rely, and how to try to prevent their opponents from proving other facts. For the moment, however, we need say no more about the minor premise, although at the end of Chapter 2 we will return to some of the problems surrounding the distinction between 'law' and 'fact'.

The major premise will be formulated from those sources which the legal system accepts as being authoritative. In English terms, and for almost all practical purposes, this means Acts of Parliament and delegated legislation (see pages 62 and 68); case-law (see Part 2); European Community law (see Chapters 5, 15 and 21), and, to some extent, under the Human Rights Act 1998, parts of the European Convention for the Protection of Human Rights and Fundamental Freedoms (see Chapter 6). Handling those sources, in such a way as to be able to produce a convincing formulation of the law, is a highly developed intellectual skill, which cannot be acquired quickly, easily or painlessly. However, one of the major purposes of this book is to ensure that those who are willing to persevere may equip themselves with a critical foundation on which to develop that skill.

In passing you will notice that you are now in a position fully to understand the Holmesian concept of the 'inarticulate major premise' (see page 4). Holmes' point is simply that the formal syllogism is all very well as far as it goes, but that the most important factor in determining the result of a case comes before the formal statement of the major premise, and is the judge's personal starting-point or *inarticulate* major premise.

At this stage it will be useful to examine some more generalized aspects of intellectual argument, so that legal method can be seen within the context of the broader field of intellectual endeavour, rather than as a thing apart.

## 1.4 Propositions and processes: truth and validity

It is useful to observe and to maintain the key distinction between the *truth of a proposition or conclusion* on the one hand, and the *validity of the process of argument* on the other. Some examples will illustrate the point. These examples will use incontrovertible scientific facts, simply because no one can feel strongly about such subject matter, and therefore no one will be distracted by considerations of what they think the position *ought* to be.

Speaking in round figures, it is true to say that the Sun is 93,000,000 miles from the Earth, and that light travels at 186,000 miles a second. It is also logically valid to say that if we know the distance between two points, and the speed at which something is travelling, we can work out the time taken for the journey by dividing the distance by the speed. Thus if $A$ and $B$ are 100 miles apart, something travelling at 100 miles an hour will take one hour to make the journey. Applying this to the figures given at the start of this paragraph, we can say that dividing 93,000,000 by 186,000 will give us the number of seconds which light takes to travel from the Sun to the Earth, namely 500. In this example we have applied a process of reasoning that is valid to facts that are true, and therefore we have inevitably come to a conclusion that is true.

However, it is also possible to produce a conclusion which happens to be true by applying valid reasoning to premises which are false. If I tell you that the Sun is 1,000,000 miles from the Earth, and that light travels at 2000 miles a second, dividing 1,000,000 by 2000 still produces the figure of 500 seconds. In this example the premises are false, but the process of reasoning (dividing one figure by the other) is valid. *Quite by chance* the conclusion happens to be true.

A third example shows that applying invalid reasoning to false premises may also produce a conclusion which happens, *purely by chance*, to be true. Suppose I tell you not only that the Sun is 5000 miles from the Earth, and that the speed of light is 0.1 mile a second, but also that the way to do the calculation is to multiply one figure by the other, rather than by dividing one by the other. This calculation still produces the figure of 500 seconds for the time taken by light to travel from the Sun to the Earth. As we know, this happens to be true. However, the premises are false and the argument is invalid.

In practical terms, the second and third examples illustrate a very common danger. If you see an argument which ends with a conclusion that you either know to be true or want to be true, it is easy to fall into the trap of assuming that the premises are true and that the argument is valid. Falling into this trap is particularly easy if the premises are drawn from a field in which you lack expertise, and if you are less than skilled in identifying invalid arguments. In the vast majority of cases, of course, there will be no problem. Premises which are true will be used as the basis of arguments which are valid, and the conclusions which are reached will, therefore, also be true. However, good lawyers are constantly on the lookout for cases which embody false premises or invalid arguments, or both.

We must now consider three common methods of reasoning, and the limitations of each.

## 1.5　Methods of reasoning: *induction*, *deduction* and *analogy*

### 1.5.1　Introduction

*Induction*, *deduction* and *analogy* are all methods of reasoning which are commonly employed in a variety of contexts. We will look at each method in turn, and then place them in a legal context.

### 1.5.2　Inductive reasoning

The process of *inductive reasoning* involves making a number of observations and then proceeding to formulate a principle which will be of general application. This form of reasoning is typified by the methods of experimental science, where if the same thing happens repeatedly it is assumed that there is a principle which ensures that it will always do so. So, if I drop a heavy object and a light object from the same height at the same time, and they reach the ground together, *and this happens on a large number of occasions*, I can conclude that the acceleration due to gravity is a constant, and does not depend on the weight of the objects concerned.

The potential weakness of inductive reasoning is that, however many observations support the conclusion, there remains the possibility that some other observations may refute it. In terms of legal method, this weakness is represented by the doctrine of *per incuriam*, which deals with the situation where a relevant legal authority is overlooked. This doctrine is discussed at page 157.

### 1.5.3    Deductive reasoning

The process of *deductive reasoning* involves stating one or more propositions and then reasoning your way to a conclusion by applying established principles of logic. Deductive reasoning is typified by the mathematical method, where propositions are asserted and then used as the basis of reasoning. Thus, if $A = B$ it follows that $2A = 2B$, and that $A-B = 0$, and so on.

There are two potential weakness of deductive reasoning: the premises may be false and the reasoning itself may be invalid, as illustrated in the examples previously given, based on the speed of light. A specifically legal example of invalid deductive reasoning may be found in *Ward v James* [1965] 1 All ER 563 (see page 15).

### 1.5.4    Reasoning by analogy

The process of reasoning by analogy involves saying that, if a number of different things are similar to each other in a number of different specific ways, they are, or should be, similar to each other in other ways as well. This process may be seen operating in the doctrine of precedent, which requires that cases with similar facts should be treated as being similar in law.

The problem with reasoning by analogy is to identify which points need to be similar, and how similar they need to be. This is pursued at some length in Chapter 9 in the context of identifying the *ratio* of a case.

### 1.5.5    The legal context

Judges seldom use technical vocabulary such as *induction* and *deduction*, but a notable exception may be found in the speech of Lord Diplock in *Home Office v Dorset Yacht Co Ltd* [1970] 2 All ER 294. The case raised the question of whether one party owed a duty of care to another in the law of negligence, which explains some of Lord Diplock's precise observations. However, the general tone of the passage is clearly of more general application.

> 'The justification of the courts' role in giving the effect of law to the judges' conception of the public interest in the field of negligence is based on the cumulative experience of the judiciary of the actual consequences of lack of

care in particular instances. And the judicial development of the law of negligence rightly proceeds by seeking first to identify the relevant characteristics that are common to the kinds of conduct and relationships which have been held in previous decisions of the courts to give rise to a duty of care.

'The method adopted at this stage of the process is analytical and inductive. It starts with an analysis of the characteristics of the conduct and relationships involved in each of the decided cases. But the analyst must know what he is looking for; and this involves his approaching his analysis with some general conception of conduct and relationships which *ought* to give rise to a duty of care. This analysis leads to a proposition which can be stated in the form: "In all the decisions that have been analysed a duty of care has been held to exist wherever the conduct and the relationship possessed each of the characteristics A, B, C, D, *etc.*, and has not been found to exist when any of these characteristics were absent".

'For the second stage, which is deductive and analytical, that proposition is converted to: "In all cases where the conduct and relationship possess each of the characteristics A, B, C, D, *etc.*, a duty of care arises". The conduct and relationship involved in the case for decision is then analysed to ascertain whether they possess each of these characteristics. If they do the conclusion follows that a duty of care does arise in the case for decision.

'But since *ex hypothesi* the kind of case which we are now considering offers a choice whether or not to extend the kinds of conduct or relationships which give rise to a duty of care, the conduct or relationship which is involved in it will lack at least one of the characteristics A, B, C, D, *etc.* And the choice is exercised by making a policy decision whether or not a duty of care ought to exist if the characteristic which is lacking were absent or redefined in terms broad enough to include the case under consideration. The policy decision will be influenced by the same general conception of what ought to give rise to a duty of care as was used in approaching the analysis. The choice to extend is given effect to by redefining the characteristics in more general terms so as to exclude the necessity to conform to limitations imposed by the former definition which are considered to be inessential. The cases which are landmarks in the common law ... are cases where the cumulative experience of the judges has led to a restatement in wide general terms of characteristics of conduct and relationships which give rise to legal liability.

'Inherent in this methodology, however, is a practical limitation which is imposed by the sheer volume of reported cases. The initial selection of previous cases to be analysed will itself eliminate from the analysis those in which the conduct or relationship involved possessed characteristics which are obviously absent in the case for decision. The proposition used in the deductive stage is not a true universal. It needs to be qualified so as to read: "In all cases where the conduct and relationship possess each of the characteristics A, B, C and D, *etc.*, *but do not possess any of the characteristics Z, Y or X, etc. ... which were present in the cases eliminated from the analysis*, a duty of care arises". But this qualification, being irrelevant to the decision of the particular case, is generally left unexpressed.' (Original emphasis.)

## 1.6 Legal practice and legal scholarship

### 1.6.1 Legal practice

In practical terms the legal enterprise often consists of advising clients how they may best use the law to achieve their objectives. These objectives vary widely, but it is worth identifying some of the more common possibilities, spanning a range from the wholly non-contentious, in the sense that they are highly unlikely ever to go to court, to the wholly contentious, in the sense that they are already the subject of legal proceedings in court.

Matters such as making a will are almost always non-contentious, as are straightforward conveyancing transactions. Even matters such as these, however, are potentially contentious, in the sense that the court may subsequently have to adjudicate upon the validity or effect of the will, or on the rights and obligations of the parties to the conveyancing transaction. Conversely, the parties often settle contentious matters by agreement, because they perceive it to be in their best interests to do so. As Jesus said in the Sermon on the Mount:

> 'If someone sues you, come to terms with him promptly while you are both on your way to court; otherwise he may hand you over to the judge, and the judge to the constable, and you will be put in jail. I tell you, once you are there you will not be let out till you have paid the last farthing.' (*The Gospel according to St. Matthew*, Ch. 5, vv. 25–26.)

Although this passage does not reflect the English distinction between civil and criminal law (see page 31), the sentiment remains clearly applicable. More recently, and more authoritatively from a legal point of view, Lord Mackay LC said: 'The interests of justice are, in my opinion, served by the promotion of early settlements'. (*O'Sullivan v Herdmans Ltd* [1987] 3 All ER 129.) Furthermore, the Woolf reforms of civil procedure, which came into effect in April 1999, are based on the principle that the parties to a dispute will regard legal proceedings as a last resort.

Of course, if you are cynical, you may recall the famous *Punch* cartoon of two farmers arguing over ownership of a cow. One farmer was pulling at the head and the other was pulling at the tail, while the lawyer was sitting happily in the middle, milking the cow. On the basis of this you may concede that early settlements may be in the interests of the parties and even in the interests of justice, but still harbour a lurking suspicion that they may not be in the interests of the lawyers. However, there are two reasons why virtually all practising lawyers would agree that this would be taking cynicism too far.

First, the outcome of litigation is never cut and dried, so clients may well be wise to settle, thus avoiding the element of chance.

Secondly, competent lawyers offering the sort of expertise which the market demands should seldom be short of work, and a case which is settled provides an opportunity for the lawyers to devote time and energy to the affairs of their other clients. In practice, therefore, many lawyers spend much of their time on work which neither the lawyers nor their clients think will ever go anywhere near a court, or on work which is directed at resolving disputes without the necessity of court proceedings. Bearing this in mind, you may well wonder why this book, along with the vast majority of other legal textbooks, places so much emphasis on what the courts will and will not do. The answer is straightforward.

One element which contributes to the advice which any lawyer gives to any client is the lawyer's perception of how, *if it ever comes to it*, the court will look at the legality of the client's position. This comment is not intended in any way to underestimate the importance of the many other elements, such as identifying the client's objectives and relating them to relevant legal possibilities, which go to make up good lawyering in practice, but it is intended to recognize the harsh fact of life that where the law is involved the courts are always at least potentially involved as well. And it follows that a good grounding in the techniques which the judges use is an invaluable foundation on which to build the habit of thinking like a lawyer.

### 1.6.2   Legal scholarship

There are many different models of legal scholarship, reflecting substantial variations in the degree of emphasis placed on sociological, economic and political factors. However, Feldman provides a useful version of a traditional model of scholarship in general:

> 'It is the attempt to understand something, by a person who is guided by certain ideals, which distinguishes scholarship both from the single-minded pursuit of an end and from dilettantism.
>
> 'The ideals include: (1) a commitment to employing methods of investigation and analysis best suited to satisfying that curiosity; (2) self-conscious and reflective open-mindedness, so that one does not assume the desired result and adopt a procedure designed to verify it, or even pervert one's material to support a chosen conclusion; and (3) the desire to publish the work for the illumination of students, fellow scholars or the general public and to enable others to evaluate and criticize it.' (*The Nature of Legal Scholarship* (1989) 52 MLR 498.)

While it is important to recognize that a willingness to indulge in self-criticism is an integral part of scholarship, it is equally essential to emphasize the need for self-confidence. More particularly, it is important to be willing to criticize received wisdom where its foundations are, and can be demonstrated to be, defective. The judgment of the Court of Appeal in *Ward v James* [1965] 1 All ER 563 provides a suitable example.

The background to the case was a general feeling among lawyers that juries were not making a very good job of assessing damages in personal injuries cases. This led Lord Denning MR, with the full agreement of the other members of the court, to two conclusions. First, juries should not normally hear personal injuries cases. Secondly, where there are special circumstances which justify the participation of a jury in such a case, the jury's role should be restricted to determining the facts, rather than extending to the assessment of damages.

However, if we remind ourselves of the premise from which the argument starts (juries are not very good at assessing damages in personal injuries cases), the only conclusion we can validly draw is that they should not assess damages in such cases. In other words, the court's conclusion that they should normally have no role at all is simply illogical. For example, in a typical case arising from a road traffic accident, a jury composed of ordinary motorists may be particularly well equipped to decide whether the quality of the defendant's driving was up to the standard required of the reasonable driver. Admittedly, if the defendant is found liable it may well be better for damages to be assessed by the judge rather than by the jury, but this is a long way from excluding juries altogether.

## 1.7 Law and Justice

### 1.7.1 Introduction

Having seen that there are wide variations of approach to the question of the nature of *law*, you will not be surprised to discover that there are also wide variations to the question of the nature of *justice*. Let us take two comments from opposite ends of the spectrum.

Alf Ross, a member of the Scandinavian Realist school of jurisprudence, says: 'To invoke justice is the same thing as banging on the table: an emotional expression which turns one's demand into an absolute postulate'. (*On Law and Justice*, 1958, p. 274.)

More optimistically, Tenzin Gyatso, the fourteenth Dalai Lama of Tibet, regards it as an inescapable truth that: 'In the end, the innate desire of all people for truth, justice and human understanding *must* triumph over ignorance and despair'. (Emphasis added. *Freedom in Exile*, 1991, pp. 88–9.) The heart of the matter, of course, is that in many cases there will be different views as to what actually are the requirements of justice.

Suppose, for example, that a thief steals my property and sells it to you. Suppose also that you acted in good faith, with no suspicion that the property was stolen. Does justice require that you return the property to me, on the basis that the act of theft cannot have destroyed my legal title to it? Or should you be allowed to keep the property, on the basis that you paid for it? Theoretically, the parties who suffer loss in such cases will be able to sue the thieves, but this is only realistic if the thieves are found and they have enough money to enable them to pay damages. Both these conditions will seldom be satisfied, and typically neither of them will be. It follows, therefore, that the law has to choose who stands the loss, and that the facts present no self-evident conception of justice to assist in the making of that choice.

Nevertheless, judges do commonly speak of justice, even if only in Ross's table-banging, justificatory sense. This leads us to the question: *what is the relationship between law and justice?*

### 1.7.2 Law and justice: some judicial perspectives

There are many ways of thinking about justice and deciding what we will (or will not) be willing to count as being just in any given situation. To take but two examples, some theories of justice emphasize the importance of economic efficiency (with the most efficient outcomes being those which are labelled 'just'), while others emphasize the importance of safeguarding the position of the weakest members of society. However, most practising lawyers will, for most of the time at least, be content to rely on the *due process* model of justice. According to this approach, provided the relevant law has been administered impartially, by the appropriate court, it follows that justice has been done.

In *Air Canada v Secretary of State for Trade (No 2)* [1983] 1 All ER 910, Lord Wilberforce said:

> 'In a contest purely between one litigant and another ... the task of the court is to do ... justice between the parties ... There is no higher or additional duty to ascertain some independent truth. It often happens, from the imperfection of evidence, or the withholding of it, sometimes by the party in whose favour it would tell if presented, that an adjudication has to be made which is not and is known not to be, the whole truth of the matter; yet if the decision has been in accordance with the available evidence, and with the law, justice will have been fairly done.'

In *R v Secretary of State for the Home Department ex parte Cheblak* [1991] 2 All ER 319, Lord Donaldson MR put his view of the matter thus:

'And it is the law and the rule of law which governs all. Judges take a judicial oath "to do right by all manner of people after the laws and usages of this Realm without fear or favour, affection or ill will" ... Justice is not an abstract concept. It has to have a context and a content. The context is provided by the facts underlying particular disputes. The content is the law.

'In individual cases injustice can arise from two quite different sources – human fallibility on the part of the judges or tribunal members and defects in the law. Human fallibility can never be eliminated, but its effects can be and are reduced by dedicated professionalism and by the system making provision for appeals. Defects in the law can be remedied by changing the law, but not by departing from it, an approach which would end by producing far more injustices than it cured. Judges are exhorted by commentators to be "robust". If what is meant is that judges should be very ready to re-examine the law in novel or changed circumstances, I agree that judges should indeed be "robust" and I hope that we are. But if what is meant is that in cases which arouse their sympathy, of which the present could well be one, they should depart from the law, I must disagree.'

The doctrine of the rule of law is outlined at page 61, and its significance is a major theme implicit throughout this book. However, for the moment we must put judicial comments such as these into context.

One important aspect of the problem is that the concept of justice functions at two very different levels. Both Lord Wilberforce and Sir John Donaldson MR were concentrating on justice at the level of decisions in individual cases. (This may be thought of as being the *micro* level.) But justice also operates at the level of the legal system as a whole. This may be thought of as the *macro* level. Crucially, the interests of justice at these two levels may conflict with each other. So, for example, while it may be desirable to give judges an element of discretion in individual cases, it is also desirable that legal outcomes should be predictable. Yet it is obvious that any significant element of predictability reduces the potential scope for the exercise of discretion in individual cases. This simple truth needs to be fully understood, because it underlies many of the problems which arise in legal method.

If I ask you whether the law should be rigid, or whether the courts should have the power to do what they think is right in the circumstances of each case, most of you will probably opt for the courts doing what they think is right in the circumstances of each case. (You may find yourself in some difficulty if I then ask you how the courts are to decide what they think is right in the circumstances of each case, but for the moment we will let that pass.) However, if I ask you whether people should be able to know the legal consequences of their conduct in advance, so that they may modify their conduct accordingly, or should they have to wait until after the court has decided the case arising from their conduct, most of you will probably opt for being able to know the legal outcome in advance. The problem is, as a moment's thought will show, that the two answers which I have indicated as being probable are in fact self-contradictory.

If each answer considered individually appears to be right, but both cannot co-exist, the most obvious solution is to seek a compromise in terms of finding a balance which combines an acceptable degree of predictability with an acceptable degree of flexibility to deal with individual cases. The focus, therefore, is simply on what 'acceptable' means in this context. There is, of course, no definitive answer to this question, since it involves matters of judgment and, as Alexander Pope said, albeit in a different context and before the substantially levelling effects of quartz technology:

> "Tis with our watches as our judgments, none
> Go just alike, yet each believes his own.'
>
> (*An Essay on Criticism*, 1711.)

Nevertheless, what we can do is to explore how the courts seek to strike the balance. What must be understood at the outset is that in any situation where two legitimate interests are competing but incompatible, both cannot be fully satisfied.

### 1.7.3    The need for a real dispute

You will recall (from page 16) that, in *R v Secretary of State for the Home Department ex parte Cheblak* [1991] 2 All ER 319, Lord Donaldson MR said that 'the facts underlying particular disputes' provide a context for the administration of justice. This comment is important not only for itself, but also because it reflects a very deep-seated idea of English law.

The courts are not happy unless they are dealing with real disputes, based on real facts, where the outcome will actually matter to someone in real terms. Two kinds of case are likely to fall foul of this attitude. First, there are cases which involve purely hypothetical points. This category is of little significance in practice because, even if anyone tried to start proceedings, it is extremely unlikely that the court would allow the matter to proceed to a hearing. Secondly, and more importantly in practice, there are those cases where there has been a real dispute but the parties have been overtaken by events in such a way that the dispute has effectively evaporated.

The dispute in *Ainsbury v Millington* [1987] 1 All ER 929 involved rights of access to a council house. After the proceedings had started, the council terminated the tenancy, and so there ceased to be any real substance to the dispute. Lord Bridge cited with approval the words of

Viscount Simon LC in *Sun Life Assurance Co of Canada v Jervis* [1944] 1 All ER 469:

> 'I do not think that it would be a proper exercise of the authority which this House possesses to hear appeals if it occupies time in this case in deciding an academic question, the answer to which cannot affect the respondent in any way. If the House undertook to do so, it would not be deciding an existing *lis* [i.e. a piece of litigation] between the parties who are before it, but would merely be expressing its view on a legal conundrum which the appellant hopes to get decided in his favour without in any way affecting the position between the parties ... I think it is an essential quality of an appeal fit to be disposed of by this House that there should exist between the parties a matter in actual controversy which the House undertakes to decide as a living issue.'

Returning to *Ainsbury v Millington* itself, Lord Bridge went on to say:

> 'It has always been a fundamental feature of our judicial system that the courts decide disputes between the parties before them; they do not pronounce on abstract questions of law when there is no dispute to be resolved.
>
> 'Different considerations may arise in relation to what are called "friendly actions" and conceivably in relation to proceedings instituted as a test case ... Again litigation may sometimes be properly continued for the sole purpose of resolving an issue as to costs when all other matters in dispute have been resolved.'

It is clear, however, that Lord Bridge's indication of the types of cases in which 'different considerations may arise' is not exhaustive. More particularly, in *R v Secretary of State for the Home Department ex parte Salem* [1999] 2 All ER 42, Lord Slynn added cases involving public authorities and questions of public law, before going on to say that in such cases a court has

> 'a discretion to hear the appeal... The decisions in the *Sun Life* case and *Ainsbury v Millington* ... must be read accordingly as limited to disputes concerning private law rights between the parties to the case.'

But even in these cases

> 'the discretion ... must ... be exercised with caution and appeals which are academic should not be heard unless there is a good reason in the public interest for doing so, as, for example (but only by way of example) where a discrete point of statutory construction arises which does not involve detailed consideration of facts and where a large number of similar cases exist or are anticipated, so that the issue will most likely need to be resolved in the near future.'

Subsequently, in *Bowman v Fels* [2005] EWCA Civ 226, [2005] 4 All ER 609, the Court of Appeal added a further category of exceptional cases, namely those involving matters of private law where it is in the public interest for the court to decide important and difficult questions as to the interpretation of recent statutes, even though the parties have settled their dispute without the need for a court hearing.

The issue in the case was whether the Proceeds of Crime Act 2002 imposed upon solicitors a duty to disclose to the authorities their suspicions that their clients had been involved in money laundering. The court was influenced by the fact that the issue involved a matter of law which did not depend upon a detailed consideration of the facts, and which was, moreover, of general concern to the solicitors' profession at large (and was, therefore, destined to come before the court relatively soon).

## 1.8    The political element in judicial decision-making

Judges are appointed by the state in order to perform certain public functions within the body politic. Nobody could sensibly dispute, therefore, that their activities are, in a broad sense of the word, political. However, the practical consequences of this statement are less clear. More particularly, as Chapter 14 shows, a variety of factors may come into play when a judge is deciding whether it is appropriate to develop the law by means of judicial decision-making.

John Griffith, a distinguished academic with avowedly left-wing sympathies, gave one view of the judicial role in a book which first appeared in 1977:

> 'Judges are concerned to preserve and to protect the existing order. This does not mean that no judges are capable of moving with the times, or adjusting to changed circumstances. But their function in our society is to do so belatedly
>
> ...
>
> 'That this is so is not a matter for recrimination. It is idle to criticize institutions for performing the task they were created to perform and have performed for centuries.' (*The Politics of the Judiciary*, 5th edn, 1997, p. 342.)

To describe judicial shifts of opinion as 'belated' is somewhat pejorative. Lord Devlin, a former Law Lord, writing long after his retirement, put substantially the same point, but rather more positively:

> 'I am not one of those who believe that the only function of law is to preserve the *status quo*. Rather I should say that law is the gate-keeper of the *status quo*. There is always a host of new ideas galloping around the outskirts of a society's thoughts. All of them must each first win its spurs; the law at first resists, but will submit to a conqueror and become its servant. In a changing society (and free societies that are composed of two or more generations are always changing because it is their nature to do so) the law acts as a valve. New policies must gather strength before they can force entry; when they are admitted and absorbed into the consensus, the legal system should expand to hold them, as also it should contract to squeeze out old

policies which have lost the consensus they once obtained.' (*The Judge*, 1981, p. 1.)

Finally, and pausing only to repeat the comment that the role of the judges in developing the law generally is discussed in Chapter 14, a word of caution may be appropriate. The judges are not uncommonly criticized for being drawn from a relatively small pool of people, many of whom have similar social backgrounds, as a result of which it is suggested that they all think alike. Take for example, the following passage, which is emphasized by the use of italics in the original:

> '[The judges of the Divisional Court, the Court of Appeal and the House of Lords] have by their education and training and the pursuit of their profession as barristers, acquired a strikingly homogeneous collection of attitudes, beliefs and principles, which to them represent the [public] interest.' (Griffith, *op. cit.*, p. 295.)

What comments such as this leave wholly unexplained are the common occurrences of appeals being allowed and dissenting judgments being delivered.

## Summary

- Legal method involves using reasoning and language to achieve practical results. When properly understood, it may be seen to be a creative process.

- Legal method involves factors drawn from outside the legal texts themselves.

- Legal reasoning is syllogistic in nature, involving propositions in the form of a *major premise* (which is a statement of *law*) and a *minor premise* (which is a statement of *fact*) leading to a *conclusion* (which is a statement of the *legal outcome*). Legal method is concerned with formulating the major premise.

- In legal reasoning, as elsewhere, propositions and conclusions may be true or false. Reasoning may be valid or invalid. In general, valid reasoning will produce a conclusion which is true, and invalid reasoning will produce a conclusion which is false. However, a conclusion which is true may appear to result from reasoning which is invalid; and a conclusion which is false may appear to result from reasoning which is valid.

- The process of *inductive reasoning* involves making a number of observations and then proceeding to formulate a principle which will be of general application. The process of *deductive reasoning* involves stating one or more propositions and then reasoning your way to a conclusion by applying established principles of logic. The process of *reasoning by analogy* involves saying that if a number of different things are similar to each other in a number of different specific ways, they are, or should be, similar to each other in other ways as well.

▶ Seeking to achieve the clients' objectives is the principal aim of legal *practice*. However, in legal *scholarship* the emphasis falls on developing a critical understanding of legal principles.

▶ There are many views of justice as a concept. In practical terms, however, justice needs both a context and a content. According to Lord Donaldson MR, the context is the factual situation giving rise to the case, and the content is the law which is applicable to that factual situation.

▶ The courts are generally reluctant to entertain cases where there is – or where there no longer is – a dispute between the parties, but they will sometimes do so.

▶ Since law is an inescapable aspect of the body politic, it necessarily follows that law is political in nature.

# Exercises

1  What is Griffith's view of the way judges function? Contrast this with Lord Devlin's view.

2  What is meant by an *inarticulate major premise*?

3  What does Dworkin mean by *standards*?

4  Distinguish between *truth* and *validity*.

5  What does each of the following mean: *syllogism*; *induction*; *deduction*?

6  How is the idea of 'due process' relevant to the relationship between law and justice?

7  What is the English courts' approach to hypothetical disputes involving abstract questions of law?

# Chapter 2

# The classifications of English law

## 2.1 Introduction

You will rapidly discover that when lawyers have analysed their material they proceed to classify it in various ways. Unfortunately, some of the most basic terms used by lawyers in the classifying process have a variety of meanings, depending on the context in which they are used. However, this chapter explains most of the major variations, at least to the extent of sketching an overall context within which specific topics may be placed, and introduces some of the technical terminology which you need to master. The chapter concludes with a discussion of the distinction between those matters which are regarded as being issues of fact and those which are regarded as being issues of law, and explains why the distinction matters.

## 2.2 The possible meanings of *common law*

### 2.2.1 Introduction

The phrase *common law* may be contrasted with *statute law*, *equity* and *civil law*. We will consider each of these contrasts in turn.

### 2.2.2 Common law and statute law

When *common law* is contrasted with *statute law*, it means that part of law which is contained in the decisions of the courts, rather than having been enacted by Parliament. The explanation of the use of the word common in this context is historical. In the centuries after the Norman Conquest, the King's judges travelled round the country deciding cases in various places. This meant that the judges built up an overall picture of the law in various areas, and by extending the area of operation of sensible principles and allowing less sensible ones to lapse, they were able to unify the law of the entire country. Another way of saying that the law was unified was to say that it was common to the whole country, and so it became known as the common law.

Common law and equity

*The origins and nature of equity*

The heart of the common law was originally the writ system. Writs were documents issued in order to start an action in the courts. The court office which issued writs was called the chancery, and its head was the Lord Chancellor. In the early stages, the common law was flexible and responded to new situations as they arose by issuing new forms of writ. In the 14th century the common law became more rigid. The attitude of the office of chancery came to be that, if a potential litigant asked for a writ, and there was no existing form to cover the facts which were alleged, this could only be because there was no right capable of legal protection.

Even in those cases where the common law was willing to provide an appropriate writ, an additional problem could arise. If a case was proved by evidence, the courts would regard themselves as being bound to make the order for which the proceedings had been brought. Normally this would be unobjectionable, but sometimes it would cause injustice. Take, for example, a case where there was written evidence of a debt, but the debtor repaid the money without ensuring that the documentary evidence was cancelled by the creditor. In these circumstances, if the creditor sued the debtor alleging non-payment, the courts would say, 'what better evidence could we have that the debt remains outstanding than the uncancelled document which the creditor has produced to us?' Accordingly the courts would order the debtor to repay the money for a second time. To be fair to the courts, it must be emphasized that they were not saying that double repayment was just. What they were saying was that the overriding principle was that disputes should be decided according to the best evidence which could be produced, and in this case the best evidence was the uncancelled document.

This combination of general stagnation and individual injustice gave rise to the emergence of equity. What happened was that litigants who were unable to obtain satisfaction from the King's courts developed the practice of petitioning the King himself, asking for an exception from the general rules to be made in their cases. Before deciding what to do about individual petitions, the King would take advice. One of his principal advisers was the Lord Chancellor, who not only had expert knowledge of the common law through his headship of the office of chancery, but also, at this stage of legal history, was perceived as having the additional advantage of being a clergyman. This latter qualification meant that he could be presumed to have an informed conscience as to what ought to be done. It was for this reason that the Lord Chancellor was often called 'the keeper of the King's conscience'.

Although the King originally made his own decisions in the light of advice which he received, he soon developed the practice of delegating to the Lord Chancellor the whole of the task of making decisions on individual petitions. As this practice became established, litigants began to present petitions directly to the Lord Chancellor, by-passing the King altogether. In the initial stages the Lord Chancellor issued decrees in the King's name. By the end of the 15th century he was issuing them in his own name. Thus the *office* of chancery had evolved into the *court* of chancery and the basis on which it made its decisions were known as *equity*, as distinct from the *common law*.

The existence of the court of chancery alongside the courts of common law had real advantages for the development of the law and the working of justice in individual cases, but it also gave rise to the possibility of conflict when two courts – one of chancery and one of common law – made conflicting orders in relation to the same facts. The details of the way in which this conflict was resolved are a fascinating piece of legal history. Briefly, however, in the early part of the seventeenth century it became established that, where equity and the law conflict, equity prevails. Furthermore, the enactment of the Judicature Acts 1873–75 merged the administration of the systems of law and equity, laying the foundations of the present arrangement whereby both systems are applied by the same courts. Nevertheless, the historical origins of the two systems remain relevant, especially as an aid to understanding the differences between legal and equitable remedies.

*Remedies at common law and in equity*

A discussion of the principles governing the granting of remedies at common law and in equity is a particularly useful way of emphasizing some of the distinctions between the two ways of thinking. Where there has been an infringement of the civil law, such as a breach of contract, the victim may well think of claiming damages. Damages are a common law remedy, and the basic principle, sometimes called the *compensation principle*, is:

> '[Damages] should as nearly as possible ... put the party who has suffered in the same position as he would have been in if he had not sustained the wrong for which he is ... getting ... compensation.' (*Livingstone v Rawyards Coal Co* (1880) 5 App Cas 25.)

Of course, the court may experience real difficulty in putting a financial value on the plaintiff's loss, but, unless the extent of the loss is a matter of pure speculation, the court must do its best to quantify it.

Many cases are relatively routine. For example, the courts have developed a set of financial values for various kinds of physical harm, and these values are routinely used as the basis for assessing damages in personal injury cases. The courts keep these values under constant review and they are varied from time to time. The effect of this is that in most cases, once liability has been established or admitted, the area of dispute between the parties can be narrowed down to such variables as loss of future earning capacity. Other cases may be more challenging. In *Chaplin v Hicks* [1911–13] All ER Rep 224, the court put a financial value on the loss of an opportunity to take part in a beauty contest, even though the plaintiff might not have won anything anyway. The court took the view that the chance itself had a value.

In some cases the courts will deviate from the compensation principle and award a sum other than that which a genuine quantification of the loss requires. These are cases involving *contemptuous, nominal* and *punitive* – also known as *exemplary* – damages. Damages quantified according to the compensation principle are known as *substantial* damages, but this merely means that they are more than nominal, and not that a large sum is necessarily involved.

An award of *contemptuous damages* is the court's way of showing that it regards the plaintiff with contempt for having brought the action, even though it has been successful. A typical case for contemptuous damages would be a libel action where the plaintiff has not actually suffered harm, and the bringing of the case has generated more publicity for the libel than its original publication had achieved. Traditionally, they are the smallest coin of the realm, so currently they are one penny. Bearing in mind how contemptuous damages work, it may seem somewhat artificial to call them a remedy at all. However, they are still damages, even though only of a trifling amount. The point of principle which they illustrate is that, as you will remember from the origins of equity, the common law has no discretion to refuse a remedy to a successful litigant.

*Nominal damages* are essentially different from contemptuous damages, even though they too are awarded where the plaintiff cannot prove actual loss. The difference is that by awarding nominal damages the court accepts that the plaintiff was acting reasonably in bringing the case. For example, in *Hanfstaengl v WH Smith & Sons* (1905) 92 LT 676, the defendants had infringed the plaintiff's copyright. Even though he proved no loss, the plaintiff was awarded nominal damages to mark the fact that his rights had been infringed and to discourage others from undertaking more serious infringements in the future. Traditionally, nominal damages are £2, although both smaller and larger sums have been known. If there appears to be little difference between nominal and contemptuous damages the appearance is deceptive. The real significance of the distinction lies in the parties' liability in costs.

The basic principle is that the court always has a discretion as to the award of costs. However, this discretion is exercised according to well-established principles. Normally an unsuccessful party will be ordered to pay the legal costs of the successful party, and this will be applied in the case of nominal damages. In the event of contemptuous damages, however, there is a refinement to the usual practice, which results in the plaintiff paying the defendant's costs, even though the plaintiff has won. The plaintiff's victory, therefore, is Pyrrhic.

Liability for costs is not, however, always limited to the parties. Since the amendment of s. 51 of the Supreme Court Act 1981 by s. 4 of the Courts and Legal Services Act 1990, the court has power to make a *wasted costs order* against a legal or other representative whose 'improper, unreasonable or negligent act or omission' has resulted in costs being incurred.

*Punitive* or *exemplary* damages are the third exception to the compensation principle. Here the court is deviating from the compensation principle by self-consciously awarding more than the plaintiff has lost, in order to punish the defendant and make an example of him. As the House of Lords made clear in *Cassell & Co Ltd v Broome* [1972] 1 All ER 801, punitive damages are available in three situations only. The first situation where punitive damages may be appropriate is where the defendant calculated to make more from the wrongdoing than the plaintiff would lose, and therefore more than the plaintiff could recover on a purely compensatory basis. The second situation is oppressive, arbitrary or unconstitutional action by servants of the government. In this context it is worth noticing that in *Cassell* Lord Diplock emphasized that the phrase 'servants of the government' should be interpreted widely, and it clearly includes, among others, local government employees and police officers. The third situation in which punitive damages are available is where they are authorized by statute, but this is extremely rare, and of no real significance.

Despite the exceptions, it is important to remember that the usual basis for damages is compensatory. We have seen that there may be cases where damages are difficult to quantify, but these cases must be carefully distinguished from cases where damages are wholly inappropriate. In the latter type of case equity will recall its origins as an exceptional jurisdiction, created to fill the gaps left by the law, and will try to make a distinctively equitable contribution to the righting of wrongs.

The entire range of equitable remedies cannot be covered here, but it is possible to give an indication of how they work.

The equitable remedy of specific performance is the order of the court which compels the defendant actually to perform the contract, rather than paying damages for failing to do so. For example, where there is a contract for the sale of a second-hand example of a popular car, if the seller fails to perform the contract, the purchaser can easily buy a similar car elsewhere. The measure of the purchaser's damages will be the difference (if any) between the price originally agreed and the price actually paid. Because any loss will be capable of being compensated by money, damages will be an adequate remedy. On the other hand, if there is a contract for the sale of an 'old master' painting, and the seller fails to perform the contract, no amount of money will enable the purchaser to acquire the practical equivalent of that painting elsewhere, simply because it has no practical equivalent. Therefore the court may decide to compel the seller to perform his contract.

Similarly, a neighbour who erects a garden shed partly on my garden commits the tort of trespass. If the court allows the shed to remain in position on payment of damages, the effect would be the same as compelling me to sell my land to my neighbour. Since this would clearly be an unjust outcome, it follows that damages would be an inadequate remedy, and therefore the court could grant me the equitable remedy of an injunction to restrain my neighbour from continuing the trespass. However, one of the maxims of equity is that 'equity like nature does nothing in vain', and therefore the court will not grant a remedy which it would be unwilling or unable to enforce.

In *Paton v British Pregnancy Advisory Service* [1978] 2 All ER 987, the facts were that a woman wanted to have an abortion. Her husband, who was the father of the child in the womb, did not agree. He asked the court for an injunction to prevent his wife from having the abortion. An injunction is an order of the court which, if breached, is enforceable by means of committal to prison for contempt of court. Sir George Baker P decided that the case really came down to whether the father had a legal right in the matter, in which context he said:

> 'I ask the question, "If an injunction were ordered, what could be the remedy?" and I do not think I need say any more than that no judge could even consider sending a husband or wife to prison for breaking such an order. That, of itself, seems to me to cover the application here; this husband cannot by law stop his wife by injunction from having what is ... a lawful abortion.'

We have already noted that equity began as a court of conscience, attempting to work justice where it thought the common law had failed to do so. This tradition still endures. One aspect of this is that equity does not bestow its favours indiscriminately, but may well find relevance in the conduct of those who are seeking its aid. As one of the equitable maxims puts it, 'he who comes to equity must come with clean hands'. The operation of this principle can be illustrated by the case of *Gill v Lewis* [1956] 1 All ER 844. The defendant was the tenant of a house. He fell behind with the rent, and the landlord obtained an order for possession. The tenant then found the money to pay the arrears. As the debt could now be paid, the tenant asked equity to prevent the landlord from enforcing the possession order. While in the house, however, the tenant had indecently assaulted two boys. As a result, the landlord argued that the tenant had not come with clean hands. The court rejected this argument because the indecent assaults were unconnected with the rent arrears.

In other words, the fact that the modern court exercising the equitable jurisdiction is the direct descendant of a court which came into being as a court of conscience does not entitle it to act as a general arbiter of morals, as distinct from the morality of the individuals concerned in the case in relation to each other. However, all equitable remedies remain discretionary.

### Equity and trusts

It would be wrong to discuss equity as if it dealt only with remedies. One of the most important aspects of equitable doctrine deals with the law of trusts. A trust may be described as the situation which exists when one person (a trustee) holds property on behalf of another person (a beneficiary). There is a very substantial body of law dealing with the way in which such relationships can be created and terminated, and the rights and duties of the parties while the relationship exists.

### 2.2.4   Common law and civil law

Another way in which the phrase *common law* is used is by way of contrast to *civil law*. In this context, the distinction which is being drawn is basically between the English legal system (together with those countries whose legal systems are derived from it, such as Australia, New Zealand and the USA) on the one hand and the legal systems of most of the states of Western Europe on the other.

The historical origin of this distinction is that continental Europe was heavily influenced by Roman law, and the modern European systems still show this heritage to a marked degree. In England, on the other hand, Roman law and its concepts have had no lasting impact. One of the most important aspects of the distinction is that the basic principles of law in a civil law country will be found in an enactment, or a series of enactments, called a *code*, whereas in the common law countries the basic principles have evolved through the decisions of the courts. Admittedly, as the rate of social change has accelerated from the time of the Industrial Revolution onwards, legislation has overtaken the common law as the main vehicle of legal change even in common law countries, but the historical perspective continues to influence the way in which lawyers from different traditions approach what are basically similar problems. An unfortunate terminological confusion also arises when dealing with codification, because even in the English legal system some comprehensive pieces of legislation are referred to as being codes, but all this means is that, when enacted, they contained all the English law on the topic concerned. The fundamental point remains that much of the basis of English law emerged piecemeal over the centuries as and when suitable cases came before the courts, rather than being formulated as a coherent whole.

It is worth noting that the early political union between England and Wales has resulted in the latter being part of the English legal system, and generally the same law applies throughout England and Wales. By way of contrast, Scotland, having retained its political independence for rather longer, and having previously been a civil law country, now finds itself with a curiously hybrid system. Many Scots lawyers regard themselves as enjoying the best of both the common law and civil law worlds, but English lawyers are sometimes less convinced. For example, Evershed LJ recorded Lord Maugham as having spoken of 'those interesting relics of barbarism, tempered by a few importations from Rome, known to the world as Scots law'. (Cited in Megarry, *Miscellany-at-Law*, 1955, revised impression 1958, p. 323.) Northern Ireland is basically a common law jurisdiction, but for a variety of reasons it is not unusual to find that some pieces of English legislation apply only to that Province, and that others do not apply there.

## 2.3    The possible meanings of *civil law*

### 2.3.1    Introduction

Quite apart from its use in contradistinction to *common law*, the phrase *civil law* has a variety of distinct and proper usages even within the English legal system. Here, the alternatives to *civil law* are variously *criminal law*, *ecclesiastical* (or *canon*) *law* and *military law*. Only the distinction between *civil law* and *criminal law* need be considered here, since the legal affairs of neither the Church nor the armed forces are likely to concern most law students.

Civil law and criminal law

The essence of the distinction between civil law and criminal law is that in civil law (which involves matters such as breach of contract, and torts such as trespass, libel, slander, negligence and many others) the focus is on compensating and/or protecting the victim, whereas in criminal law (which involves matters such as theft, murder, motoring offences, and so on) the focus is on punishing the offender.

Closer examination of the relevant law shows that this version of the distinction, although a useful starting-point, is something of an over-statement. This is so partly because, in modern times, the range of powers available to the courts exercising criminal jurisdiction has in-creased substantially, with some possible options (such as probation) being intended to help the offender rather than to punish him. Further-more, quite apart from such rehabilitative possibilities, there are circumstances in which a court can use the Powers of Criminal Courts (Sentencing) Act 2000 to compensate the victim of crime at the same time as it sentences the offender.

Similarly, as we saw at page 27, there are circumstances in which the court in a civil case can punish the wrongdoer by awarding damages over and above the sum required for compensation. Nevertheless, the basic point remains that in a criminal case, once guilt has been proved, the fundamental question for the court is 'what should be done with the offender?', whereas in a civil case the corresponding question, on proof of liability, is 'what should be done for the victim?'.

One of the most immediately apparent practical distinctions between civil law and criminal law lies in the basic terminology. A typical civil case will be concerned with proof of *liability*, and will be called an *action*, although there are other terminological possibilities, including an *appli-cation* and a *petition*. A criminal case will be concerned with proof of *guilt*, and will be called a *prosecution*. The legal descriptions of the parties also vary. In a typical civil case a *claimant* (who was called a *plain-tiff* before the Woolf reforms of civil procedure came into effect in April 1999) will *sue* a *defendant*. In a criminal case a *prosecutor* will *prosecute* the other party, who may be called either the *defendant* or the *accused*. The only context in which it is proper to use the term *prosecution* in a civil context is where the plaintiff has started, but failed to pursue, proceed-ings, in which case the defendant may apply to the court to have the case 'struck out for want of prosecution'.

Secondly, the standard of proof is often said to differ between civil and criminal cases, with facts necessary to establish civil liability needing to be proved only *on the balance of probabilities*, and facts establishing guilt in criminal cases needing to be established *beyond reasonable doubt*. (This is discussed more fully at page 40.)

Finally, there are various other distinctions between civil and criminal cases, including detailed matters of procedure and evidence, liability as to costs and the availability of legal aid.

## 2.4 Public law and private law

In many legal systems the distinction between public law and private law is regarded as fundamental, but in the English legal system the distinction did not come to prominence until the 1980s. This was largely as a result of the House of Lords' interpretation of certain technical changes to the procedure by which cases (which were then called *applications for judicial review*, and are now called *claims for judicial review*) were brought before the court. Briefly, in *O'Reilly v Mackman* [1982] 3 All ER 1124, the House of Lords held that judicial review was, generally, the only way in which challenges could be brought before the court in cases involving public law. Clearly, this made it essential to be able to draw the line between *public* and *private* law. Unfortunately, even now the distinction remains less than totally clear-cut, but a useful perspective can be derived from the fact that some areas of law involve public bodies or public officials doing things which, by their very nature, could not be done by private individuals. It seems that these cases, at least, involve matters of public law.

For example, if a local authority trespasses on land owned by someone else, the landowner can sue the local authority, in the same way as any other landowner can sue any other trespasser. However, the position is different if, for example, a local authority refuses to issue a licence for some activity in respect of which it is a statutory licensing authority. In this case, the local authority has power to make the decision only because it is a local authority: no private individual could have made it. In other words, the trespass example falls within the sphere of private law, and the licensing example falls within the sphere of public law.

Wherever the courts draw the line between public and private law, it is possible to make two general points arising from the distinction.

First, a court which is hearing a claim for judicial review in respect of a public law matter will, being mindful of the doctrine of the separation of powers (see page 69), be conscious that its role is to supervise the way in which the decision was made, rather than imposing its own view as to what the decision itself should have been. In other words, the court acknowledges that some kinds of decision – such as whether a local authority wishes to grant or withhold a licence – remain at all times within the discretion of the decision-makers to whom Parliament has allocated the decision-making function, because such decisions are inextricably linked with questions of policy and assessments of the merits of the situations giving rise to individual decisions. (If Parliament had wanted the court to have power to substitute its own decision, rather than merely supervising the legality of the decision-making process, it would have given challengers a *right of appeal*, rather than leaving them to rely on judicial review, where the most that the court can do, in practically all cases, is to quash a decision which has resulted from a legally defective decision-making process, and compel the decision-maker to remake the decision in a lawful manner.)

Admittedly, Part 54, Civil Procedure Rules, provides one exception to this by enabling the court to substitute its own decision where it is satisfied that there would be no point in sending the matter back to the decision-maker. In general, however, there is a clear distinction between *review* as a means of challenging the *legality* of a *decision-making process* on the one hand, and *appeal* as a means of challenging the *merits of a decision* on the other. In passing, it may be said that, quite apart from the very limited exception contained in Part 54, the distinction between *review* and *appeal* will become less clear-cut as the courts increasingly apply the case-law of the European Court of Human Rights (see page 102), but in most cases the distinction is likely to remain clear enough.

Secondly, certain aspects of procedure apply only to public law cases. These are thought to be necessary to protect public decision-makers from the constant risk of petty, vexatious and frivolous challenges made by people wanting to use the judicial process as a means of making political points. One of the most important of these safeguards is that no private individual has the right to challenge a matter of public law without first making a preliminary application to the court, asking for permission to make the full application. One factor which must be established is that the challenger has 'a sufficient interest' in the matter, and is not merely a busybody. This is known technically as the requirement of *standing*.

## 2.5 Substantive law and procedural law

Some rules of law deal with substantive rights and duties, while others deal with the procedural aspects of enforcing the substantive rules.

Procedural law is sometimes known by the alternative name of adjectival law. Judges who distinguish between matters of substance and matters of procedure will usually say why, in the context in question, the distinction is relevant. No exhaustive catalogue can be given here, but by way of example it can be said that time limits are often – though not always – procedural. The case of *Kammins Ballrooms Co Ltd v Zenith Investments Ltd* [1970] 2 All ER 871 (see page 264) illustrates the significance of classifying a time limit as procedural. Section 21(2) of the Firearms Act 1968, under which it is an offence to possess firearms or ammunition within five years of release from a custodial sentence of between three months and three years, involves a substantive time limit, since the period of five years is part of the definition of the offence.

## 2.6 Classification by subject matter

The classifications which have been outlined are all part of the conceptual structure of the legal system. However, the classifications which are referred to most frequently are those which are formulated according to the subject matter under consideration. As a matter of convenience, lawyers often refer to identifiable bodies of law, such as those dealing with contract, tort and crime. These usages may be convenient shorthand, but in reality one set of facts may give rise to many different legal relationships, and in any event the legal concepts which are placed within each of these so-called text-book unities do not always occupy watertight compartments. Attempts to force legal material to fit such predetermined schemes will often result in a seriously blinkered approach, and lead to misunderstanding.

## 2.7 The distinction between matters of fact and matters of law

One of the most vexed questions in the whole topic of legal classification is the distinction between matters of law and matters of fact. The distinction arises in many contexts, and even within a single context there may well be competing policy motives, each supporting the drawing of the line in different places.

As you will see in Part 2, the doctrine of binding precedent deals only with propositions of law; therefore one motive for classifying certain matters as being matters of fact may be the purely practical desire to avoid a multiplicity of authorities: otherwise 'the precedent system will die from a surfeit of authorities' and the judges might be 'crushed under the weight of [their] own reports'. (Lord Somervell and Lord

Denning respectively, in *Qualcast (Wolverhampton) Ltd v Haynes* [1959] 2 All ER 38.)

Looking at it more positively, classifying a question as being a matter of law, and therefore as being subject to the doctrine of binding precedent, is one way of seeking to establish uniformity of decision-making across a large number of similar cases. (How far such uniformity is actually achieved, rather than merely desired, is something you may wish to think about when you have digested Part 2.) On the other hand, there may be situations in which open flexibility of decision-making is seen to be desirable. For example, in *Brutus v Cozens* [1972] 2 All ER 1297, the facts were that anti-apartheid activists disrupted the Wimbledon tennis tournament with a political demonstration. The magistrates acquitted them of 'insulting behaviour whereby a breach of the peace was likely to be occasioned'. In due course the House of Lords took the view that the question of whether specific conduct was 'insulting' was a matter of fact to be determined by the tribunal of fact, and was not a question of law to be taken on appeal. Lord Reid said: 'The meaning of an ordinary word of the English language is not a question of law'.

*Brutus v Cozens* may be defensible on the basis that the magistrates would know their own area and the climate of opinion within it, and could make their decisions accordingly, but the flexibility which this attitude promotes may undermine the rule of law (see page 61 for a discussion of the meaning of *the rule of law*) by making it very difficult for the individual to predict the legal outcome of proposed conduct. This consideration led the House of Lords to adopt a staunchly constitutionalist stance in the patents case of *Energy Conversion Devices Incorporated's Applications* [1982] FSR 544, where Lord Diplock, expressing the unanimous opinion of the House, said:

'Your Lordships should, however, in my view take this opportunity of stating once again the important constitutional principle that questions of construction of all legislation, primary or secondary, are questions of law to be determined authoritatively by courts of law; that errors in construing primary or secondary legislation made by inferior tribunals that are not courts of law, however specialized and prestigious they may be, are subject to correction by judicial review; no tribunal and no court of law has any discretion to vary the meaning of the words of primary or secondary legislation from case to case in order to meet what the tribunal or court happens to think is the justice of the particular case. Tempting though it might sound, to do so is the negation of the rule of law. If there are cases in which the application of the Patents Rules leads to injustice, the cure is for the Secretary of State to amend the Rules. If what is thought to be the injustice results from the terms of the Act itself, the remedy is for Parliament to amend the Act.'

Although the importance of the rule of law cannot be doubted, the fact remains that in practice the dividing line between *law* and *fact* can be difficult to draw.

In *R v Spens* [1991] 4 All ER 421, the Court of Appeal held that the construction of the City Code on Take-overs and Mergers was a matter of law for the trial judge, rather than a matter of fact for the jury. Watkins LJ, giving the judgment of the Court, acknowledged that generally speaking the construction of documents raises questions of fact. However, the court asserted that contractual and legislative documents constitute exceptions to this general principle, with the need for consistency between cases being asserted as an 'almost overriding' consideration to justify the conclusion. In the result therefore it was for the judge to decide what the Code meant, and then for the jury to decide whether the defendant's conduct fell within the requirements of the Code.

Although Watkins LJ in *R v Spens* expressed himself to be perfectly well satisfied that that decision was consistent with *Brutus v Cozens*, observers possessing a greater degree of detachment may feel less certain. In particular, it may be thought that the application of the principle in *R v Spens* to the situation which arose in *Brutus v Cozens* would require the concept of 'insult' to be defined as a matter of law, before determining, as a matter of fact, whether the conduct alleged in the case fell within that concept.

The distinction between fact and law has also prompted judicial comment in Administrative Law, where a decision-maker's errors of law are often more easily challengeable than errors of fact. Here again the courts are unable to offer definitive guidance as to the nature of the distinction, but the following extract from the judgment of Denning LJ, in *British Launderers' Research Association v Central Middlesex Assessment Committee and Borough of Hendon Rating Authority* [1949] 1 All ER 21, provides some framework within which the question can be considered:

'It is important to distinguish between primary facts and the conclusions from them. *Primary facts are facts which are observed by witnesses and proved by oral testimony or facts proved by the production of a thing itself, such as original documents*. Their determination is essentially a question of fact for the tribunal of fact, and the only question of law that can arise on them is whether there was any evidence to support the finding. *The conclusions from primary facts are, however, inferences deduced by a process of reasoning from them. If, and in so far as, those conclusions can as well be drawn by a layman (properly instructed on the law) as a lawyer, they are conclusions of fact for the tribunal of fact*: and the only questions of law which can arise on them are whether there was a proper direction in point of law; and whether the conclusion is one which could reasonably be drawn from the primary facts: see *Bracegirdle v Oxley* [1947] 1 All ER 126. *If, and in so far, however, as the correct conclusion to be drawn from primary facts requires, for its correctness, determination by a trained lawyer – as for instance, because it involves the interpretation of documents or because the law on the point cannot properly be understood or applied except by a trained lawyer – the conclusion is a conclusion of law.'* (Emphasis added.)

In *Edwards v Bairstow* [1955] 3 All ER 48, the Inland Revenue had assessed the taxpayers to income tax on profit made from the purchase and sale of certain machinery, on the basis that the transaction was an 'adventure in the nature of trade'. The taxpayers succeeded on appeal to the General Commissioners, but both the High Court and the Court of Appeal held that the matter was one of fact, which meant that the General Commissioners' finding could not be overturned. Finally, however, the House of Lords decided that the meaning of 'adventure in the nature of trade' for the purposes of the income tax legislation was a question of law. More particularly, Lord Radcliffe said:

'The law does not supply a precise definition of the word "trade" ... In effect it lays down the limits within which it would be permissible to say that a "trade" ... does or does not exist. But the field so marked out is a wide one and there are many combinations of circumstances in which it could not be said to be wrong to arrive at a conclusion one way or the other. If the facts of any particular case are fairly capable of being so described, it seems to me that it necessarily follows that the determination ... that "trade" does not exist is not "erroneous in point of law" ... All these cases in which the facts warrant a determination either way can be described as questions of degree and therefore as questions of fact.'

On the other hand:

'If the Case [that is the case stated by the General Commissioners – for appeals by way of case stated, see page 50] contains anything *ex facie* which is bad law and which bears on the determination, it is, obviously, erroneous in point of law. But without any such misconception appearing *ex facie* it may be that the facts found are such that *no person acting judicially and properly instructed as to the relevant law could have come to the determination under appeal*. In these circumstances, too, the court must intervene. It has no option but to assume that there has been some misconception of the law, and that this has been responsible for the determination. So, there, too, there has been an error in point of law. I do not think it much matters whether this state of affairs is described as one in which there is no evidence to support the determination, or as one in which the evidence is inconsistent with, and contradictory of, the determination, or as one in which the true and only reasonable conclusion contradicts the determination. Rightly understood, each phrase propounds the same test. For my part, I prefer the last of the three.' (Emphasis added.)

On the central question in the instant case, Lord Radcliffe asked:

'What detail does [this purchase and sale] lack that prevents it from being an adventure in the nature of trade, or what element is present in it that makes it capable of being aptly described as anything else?'

Comparing *Brutus v Cozens* with *Edwards v Bairstow*, however, it is difficult to see any distinction in principle between having to decide whether the factual conduct of demonstrating amounts to 'insulting behaviour' for the purposes of one statute, and having to decide whether the factual conduct of buying and selling amounts to 'an adventure in the nature of trade' for the purposes of another statute.

It is not altogether surprising, therefore, that academic commentators tend to be sceptical as to whether the law/fact distinction has any practical utility as a basis for predicting judicial outcomes. For example, in the context of judicial review, where the distinction between matters of law and matters of fact is often the basis for deciding whether or not the court can intervene, Wade and Forsyth say:

'The truth is ... that there can hardly be a subject on which the courts act with such total lack of consistency as the difference between fact and law ... It may be that judges instinctively agree with an American comment:*
   "No two terms of legal science have rendered better service than 'law' and 'fact' ... They are the creations of centuries. What judge has not found refuge in them? The man who could succeed in defining them would be a public enemy." *Leon Green, *Judge and Jury*, p. 270.' (*Administrative Law*, 9th edn, 2004, p. 944.)

The distinction between matters of law and matters of fact is further complicated by judicial references to questions of 'mixed law and fact'. Turning again to material drawn from Administrative Law for elucidation, the following comment of Laws J, writing extra-judicially as Sir John Laws, is instructive:

'The judges have frequently had recourse to the notion of "a mixed question of law and fact" in dealing with cases where an issue arises whether a particular set of facts falls within a particular category. However, taken literally, no such notion can exist. There can be no *single* question which is both a question of law and a question of fact: elementarily, factual propositions are proved by evidence, and legal propositions are established by reference to statutory provisions or common law principles; thus anything that is apparently a mixed question of law and fact will always on analysis prove to involve at least two questions, *viz.* what are the facts and what is the law. The difficulty arises where, these questions having received answers, there still remains a further question whether in the end the facts lie within the legal category identified. This happens where the category ... is elastic; as for instance when the issue is whether or not a particular person is a servant or an independent contractor ... In principle, therefore ... there is ... on analysis no such legal construct as a mixed question of law and fact; rather ... the assignment of the facts to their correct legal category depends not only on the tribunal's ascertainment of the primary facts, but also – and critically – on its judgment as to what weight should be given to one aspect of the facts over another: and this latter exercise will be treated by the court as within the tribunal's fact-finding sphere [and not as a matter of law].' (Emphasis added. Supperstone and Goudie (eds), *Judicial Review*, 2nd edn, 1997, para. 4.39. This passage does not appear in the 3rd edition of the book (published in 2005 under the editorship of Goudie, Walker, Himsworth and Supperstone), but Chapter 6, which corresponds roughly to Chapter 4 of the 2nd edition, adopts a different structure because much of the material it contains is new. This is no reflection on the quality of the insight which the passage provides.)

All in all, therefore, it may seem that we can do little more than note the difficulty of drawing the distinction between matters of law and matters of fact. However, it may be appropriate at this point to develop one matter which Laws J mentioned when discussing mixed questions of law and fact, namely the question of how the parties can establish each kind of matter to the satisfaction of the court.

Establishing matters of law is, of course, the major theme of the whole of this book in general, and of Parts 2 and 3 in particular. Before moving on to those matters, however, some practical aspects of establishing matters of fact will be dealt with here in outline. Broadly speaking, there are three major possibilities: the facts may be agreed; the court may take judicial notice of the facts; and the facts may be proved by evidence. We will consider each of these in turn.

First, where the parties to a dispute agree some or all of the facts between themselves, these facts can then be either formally admitted or proved without challenge in subsequent legal proceedings.

Secondly, the court may take judicial notice of matters of fact. The basic idea underlying the doctrine of judicial notice is that some matters are so well known that a requirement of proof would be superfluous. For example, in *Nye v Niblett* [1918] 1 KB 23, the court took judicial notice of the fact that cats are kept for domestic purposes. In *Bridlington Relay Ltd v Yorkshire Electricity Board* [1965] 1 All ER 264, the court took judicial notice of the fact that the reception of television broadcasts is a common feature of English domestic life. In *Adams v Bracknell Forest Borough Council* [2004] UKHL 29, [2004] 3 All ER 897, Lord Hoffmann noted, with no adverse comment, that the trial judge appeared to have taken judicial notice of 'the generally inhibiting effect of untreated dyslexia'. Finally, in *R (Gillan) v Metropolitan Police Commissioner* [2005] EWCA Civ 1067, [2005] 1 All ER 970, Lord Woolf CJ said 'the scale of terrorist incidents around the globe is so well known that it hardly requires evidence to establish that this country is faced with a real possibility of terrorist incidents'. Thirdly, as Denning LJ pointed out in the *British Launderers'* case (see page 36), the court will receive evidence on disputed matters before deciding matters of fact.

Finally, it is often said that there are different standards of proof in *criminal* cases (*proof beyond reasonable doubt*) and *civil* cases (*proof on the balance of probabilities*). For example, in *Miller v Minister of Pensions* [1947] 2 All ER 372, Denning LJ said, in relation to criminal cases:

> 'That degree is well settled. It need not reach certainty, but it must carry a high degree of probability. Proof beyond a reasonable doubt does not mean proof beyond the shadow of a doubt. The law would fail to protect the community if it admitted fanciful possibilities to deflect the course of justice. If the evidence is so strong ... as to leave only a remote possibility ... which can be dismissed with the sentence "of course it is possible but not in the least probable" the case is proved beyond reasonable doubt, but nothing short of that will suffice.'

Contrasting this with the civil standard of proof, he said:

> 'That degree is well settled. It must carry a reasonable degree of probability, but not so high as is required in a criminal case. If the evidence is such that the tribunal can say: "we think it more probable than not", the burden is discharged, but if the probabilities are equal it is not.'

However, it is clear that, in relation to each standard of proof, the court is looking at a bracket of possibilities rather than an absolute standard. As Denning LJ put it in *Bater v Bater* [1951] P 35:

> 'It is ... true that ... a higher standard of proof is required in criminal cases than in civil cases. But ... there is no absolute standard in either case. In criminal cases the charge must be proved beyond reasonable doubt, but there may be degrees of proof within that standard ... So also in civil cases the case must be proved by a preponderance of probability, but there may be degrees of probability within that standard. The degree depends on the subject-matter. A civil court, when considering a charge of fraud, will naturally require ... a higher degree of probability than that which it would require when asking if negligence is established. It does not adopt so high a degree as a criminal court, even when considering a charge of a criminal nature; but still it does require a degree of probability which is commensurate with the occasion.'

Experience shows that even this statement of principle is a little over-cautious, since there have occasionally been civil cases where the criminal standard of proof has been explicitly applied. For example, *Halford v Brookes* [1991] *The Independent*, 1 October, involved a claim for damages arising out of an alleged murder. Because a conclusion that the defendant was liable in damages would amount to a finding that he was guilty of murder, the court specifically required that the plaintiff should satisfy it on the criminal standard. Similarly, in the undoubtedly civil case of *R v Commissioner Rowe QC (Mr) ex parte Mainwaring* [1992] 4 All

ER 821, the Court of Appeal said that the criminal standard of proof must be satisfied in order to establish allegations of malpractice by a candidate during an election campaign.

Even courts which have been unwilling to go as far as those in *Halford v Brookes* and *R v Commissioner Rowe QC (Mr) ex parte Mainwaring* may still find reason to remind themselves of the variable standard of proof. In the immigration case of *R v Secretary of State for the Home Department ex parte Khawaja* [1983] 1 All ER 765, where the issue was whether facts existed which would justify restraining the liberty of the individual, Lord Scarman said:

> 'The reviewing court will ... require to be satisfied that the facts which are required for the justification of the restraint put on liberty do exist. The flexibility of the civil standard of proof suffices to ensure that the court will require the high degree of probability which is appropriate to what is at stake.'

Whatever possibilities each standard of proof may embrace, however, in the civil case of *Re H and Others (Minors)* [1996] 1 All ER 1, Lord Nicholls made it plain that the law recognizes no intermediate standard of proof, falling between the civil and criminal possibilities. Having repeated the conventional wisdom that 'the more serious the allegation ... the stronger should be the evidence before the court concludes that the allegation is established on the balance of probability', he went on to say:

> 'Although the result is much the same, this does not mean that where a serious allegation is in issue the standard of proof required is higher. It means only that the inherent probability or improbability of an event is itself a matter to be taken into account when weighing the probabilities and deciding whether, on balance, the event occurred.'

Finally, as an all-embracing summary of the law on standards of proof, there is much to be said for the test suggested by Ormrod LJ in *Re J S (A Minor)* [1980] 1 All ER 1061:

> 'The plaintiff (or the party on whom the burden rests) must satisfy the court that it is *reasonably safe* in all the circumstances of the case *to act on the evidence* before the court, *bearing in mind the consequences which will follow.*' (Emphasis added.)

## Summary

▷ Lawyers classify their material in various ways. The terms they use may have a variety of meanings, depending on the context in which they are used.

▷ *Common law* may be contrasted with *statute law*, *equity* and *civil law*.

▷ *Civil law* may be contrasted not only with *common law*, but also with *criminal law*, *ecclesiastical law* and *military law*.

▷ *Public law* may be contrasted with *private law*.

▷ *Substantive law* may be contrasted with *procedural* (or *adjectival*) *law*.

▷ Law may be classified by reference to its subject matter.

▷ There is an important distinction between matters of *law* and matters of *fact*. However, there is very little in the way of principle offering reliable guidance as to how this distinction should be drawn. When facts have to be proved, the degree of proof which is required varies according to the circumstances of the case.

## Exercises

1 How and why did equity come into existence?

2 What does *specific performance* mean?

3 What does the term *civil law* mean when used in contradistinction to (a) *criminal law*; (b) *common law*?

4 Why may it be important to know whether an issue is one of *fact* or *law*?

5 'The civil law standard of proof is *on the balance of probabilities*; the criminal law standard of proof is *beyond reasonable doubt*.' Explain (a) what this statement means, and (b) how it can be misleading.

# Chapter 3

## The jurisdictions of the principal English courts

### 3.1 Introduction

This chapter outlines the jurisdictions of the principal English courts, and the correct way to refer to their judicial personnel. (Chapter 5 deals with the jurisdiction of the European Court of Justice.)

The principal statutes include the Magistrates' Courts Act 1980, the Supreme Court Act 1981, the County Courts Act 1984, the Courts and Legal Services Act 1990, the Civil Procedure Act 1997 and the Criminal Justice Act 2003 (all as amended). The mass of detail contained in these statutes, and the Rules made under them, need not be pursued here, but the most important points are summarized in the remainder of this chapter.

The first point to notice is that there are two principal types of jurisdiction, namely jurisdiction *at first instance*, which means that the court will be finding the facts and trying the issue between the parties, and *appellate* jurisdiction, which means that another court has already heard the case and the decision of that court is being appealed.

Secondly, the summary begins with a diagrammatic representation in which arrows indicate the principal avenues of appeal, and continues with textual explanation. Before turning to the summary, however, there is one matter which requires emphasis. As the arrows in the diagram show, there are often two avenues of appeal. It is essential to grasp that these avenues do not simply present aspiring appellants with a choice in each case: the availability of one avenue rather than another will depend on the circumstances, with the *avenue* of appeal being generally dictated by the *ground* of appeal. You will need to read the textual explanation carefully if you are to understand how this works in practice.

Finally, the arrows on the diagram deal only with avenues of *appeal*. Therefore they do not indicate the possibility of *reference* to the European Court of Justice (see page 78), nor the possibility of *judicial review* (see page 51), both of which are conceptually quite distinct from *appeal*. The European Court of Human Rights, and the changing status of its decisions within the English legal system, are dealt with in Chapter 6, but for the moment perhaps it should be said that access to this court is by way of *application* and not by way of appeal against a decision if an English court.

## 3.2 The hierarchy of the courts as a diagram

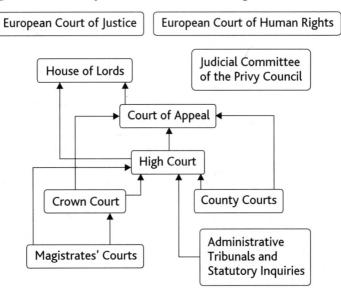

It cannot be emphasized too strongly that the diagram shown above is intended only as a visual aid. *Unless you give careful attention to the rest of this chapter, you will not understand the hierarchy of the courts.*

## 3.3 Magistrates' courts

### 3.3.1 Introduction

The magistrates' courts' jurisdiction has both civil and criminal elements, and is exercisable both at first instance and on appeal.

### 3.3.2 Magistrates' courts as courts of first instance

*Criminal jurisdiction*

Virtually all criminal cases begin in magistrates' courts, and well over 90 per cent also end there. Where the magistrates do not dispose of the case entirely, there are two possibilities.

One possibility arises in respect of defendants who have not yet been convicted. These cases will be transferred to the Crown Court for trial under a procedure introduced by the Criminal Justice Act 2003. (This process is the successor to a procedure which involved formal committal proceedings. The transfer arrangements under the current procedure are more administrative in nature, although there does remain the important issue of whether the defendant should be in custody or on bail while awaiting trial.) The other possibility involves committing defendants to the Crown Court for sentence. This arises where the magistrates convict defendants but feel that their own powers of sentencing (which are very much more limited than those of the Crown Court) are insufficient to enable them to dispose of the case appropriately. Magistrates sitting as youth courts exercise criminal jurisdiction over those between 10 and 18 years of age.

### Civil jurisdiction

Magistrates have an enormously wide-ranging civil jurisdiction. Much of it relates to local government aspects of Administrative Law, including certain aspects of the law of highways and public health and licensing. This jurisdiction represents the residue of those functions which the magistracy exercised before the creation of elected local authorities in the 19th century. Other civil matters within the jurisdiction of the magistrates include, by way of examples from a vast range of possibilities, the power to make orders for the destruction of dangerous dogs and for the disposal of property which is in the hands of the police and the ownership of which is disputed.

The civil jurisdiction of youth courts includes care proceedings in respect of children and young persons. Magistrates sitting as family proceedings courts have extensive jurisdiction in family law, but this does not extend to divorce.

### 3.3.3  Magistrates' courts as appeal courts

The magistrates' appellate jurisdiction, which is principally civil, is very diverse but of little practical significance. To take only two examples, the magistrates can hear appeals against refusals to issue driving licences, and in certain cases arising out of the making of compulsory purchase orders by public authorities.

### 3.3.4  Judicial personnel in magistrates' courts

Magistrates are technically known as *justices of the peace*. The expressions *the magistrates* and *the justices* are interchangeable. Most magistrates are lay, in the sense of not being qualified lawyers, and will therefore rely heavily on their legal advisers. Additionally, there are *district judges (magistrates' courts)*, formerly known as *stipendiary magistrates*, who work on a full-time, salaried basis. They generally sit in the busiest courts because they can deal with the weight of business more efficiently than lay magistrates can.

## 3.4 The Crown Court

### 3.4.1 Introduction

The Crown Court's jurisdiction has both civil and criminal elements, and is exercisable both at first instance and on appeal.

### 3.4.2 The Crown Court as a court of first instance

#### Criminal jurisdiction

As we saw at pages 44 and 45, the magistrates may send defendants to the Crown Court for either sentence or trial. Strictly speaking, it may be argued that the prior involvement of the magistrates means that neither of these jurisdictions is at first instance, but on the other hand neither is appellate. They are best regarded as being effectively a stage in the first instance procedure.

#### Civil jurisdiction

It would be misleading to give the impression that the Crown Court has any generally significant civil jurisdiction at first instance, but, for example, the Highways Act 1980 does confer upon it jurisdiction to adjudicate in certain disputes as to the status of highways and whether they are in disrepair.

### 3.4.3 The Crown Court as an appeal court

#### Criminal jurisdiction

The defendant has a right of appeal to the Crown Court against conviction or sentence or both in magistrates' courts. An appeal to the Crown Court against conviction is an appeal on the facts. The prosecution has no corresponding right of appeal against an acquittal, nor against a sentence which it considers to be too lenient. An appeal against conviction is a full re-hearing, which means that the witnesses are called again, and their evidence is assessed afresh. Where there is an appeal against sentence only, no witnesses are called, but the prosecution presents an outline of the facts.

If the defendant is appealing from the magistrates on a point of law, the appropriate route is to the High Court, using a procedure known as 'appeal by way of case stated' (see page 50). In this situation the defence loses the advantage which it has in relation to appeals on the facts and appeals against sentence, because here the prosecution does have a corresponding right of appeal.

In addition to its genuinely appellate jurisdiction, the Crown Court has a quasi-appellate jurisdiction under s. 11 of the Criminal Appeal Act 1995. Section 11 of the Act enables the Criminal Cases Review Commission, which was created by s. 8 of the Act, to refer to the Crown Court cases where there has been a conviction in a magistrates' court. The reference may be in respect of conviction or sentence or both, and the proceedings will be treated as if they were by way of appeal. Strictly speaking, however, the proceedings are not appellate because they are instituted by someone other than the person who is affected by the original decision. Although the Act does not say so, the procedure is intended to enable cases to be reopened where it is thought that there has been a miscarriage of justice. As we shall see, at page 53, the Criminal Cases Review Commission has an equivalent power to refer cases to the Court of Appeal following conviction on indictment.

### Civil jurisdiction

The Crown Court has a very wide-ranging appellate jurisdiction in respect of decisions of magistrates' courts in civil cases, but unlike the position in relation to criminal cases, no general distinction is drawn between the parties in terms of their rights of appeal. As with criminal cases, however, if the appeal is on a point of law, the appropriate route is to the High Court by way of case stated.

### 3.4.4    Judicial personnel in the Crown Court

Cases in the Crown Court are presided over by either a High Court judge, a circuit judge, a deputy circuit judge, a recorder, or an assistant recorder, the last three of which hold office on a part-time basis. Additionally, in trials there will be a jury. In committals for sentence and appeals of any kind, there will be no jury but the bench will include a number of magistrates.

The matter of the correct description of judicial personnel in the Crown Court is dealt with by a *Practice Direction (Judges: Mode of Address)*, issued by Lord Lane CJ and reported at [1982] 1 WLR 101. A circuit judge is referred to as 'His (or Her) Honour Judge A', which may be abbreviated in writing to 'HH Judge A'. A deputy circuit judge is referred to as 'His (or Her) Honour BC sitting as a deputy circuit judge'. Recorders are referred to as 'Mr (or Mrs) Recorder D'. Assistant recorders are referred to as 'Mr (or Mrs or Miss or Ms) EF sitting as an assistant recorder'.

## 3.5    County Courts

### 3.5.1    Introduction

The County Courts' jurisdiction is entirely civil, and is exercisable both at first instance and on appeal.

### 3.5.2    County Courts as courts of first instance

To a very large extent the jurisdiction of the County Courts makes them into a sort of mini-High Court. They have jurisdiction in respect of contractual disputes and almost all torts. They also have jurisdiction in relation to probate and divorce, and may have an Admiralty jurisdiction. Under the Woolf reforms of civil procedure, which came into effect in April 1999, the judges have very considerable powers of case management, including the power to allocate cases between the County Court and the High Court, and to give detailed directions on procedural matters. In very general terms, however, the most complex matters are more likely to be dealt with by the High Court, as are those involving large sums of money.

### 3.5.3    County Courts as appeal courts

The appellate jurisdiction of the County Courts is very limited, but one notable field of activity is in relation to appeals arising out of certain types of action taken by local authorities in respect of substandard housing, and certain decisions made by such authorities in cases of alleged homelessness. It is impossible to discern any basis of principle underlying the statutes which allocate such cases to the County Court rather than to magistrates' courts. Historical accident appears to have been the major determining factor.

### 3.5.4    Judicial personnel in County Courts

The principal judges in the County Court are circuit judges from the Crown Court, but the Courts and Legal Services Act 1990 recognized the status of the officials who were formerly known as *registrars* by redesignating them as *district judges*. A district judge called Smith is referred to as 'Mr (or Mrs) District Judge Smith'.

## 3.6  The High Court

### 3.6.1  Introduction

The High Court's jurisdiction has both civil and criminal elements, and i exercisable both at first instance and on appeal. It also has a supervisory jurisdiction. Although the High Court is nominally one court, for administrative purposes it is split into three units, namely the *Queen's Bench Division*, the *Chancery Division* and the *Family Division*.

### 3.6.2  The High Court as a court of first instance

*Criminal jurisdiction*

None of the Divisions has a criminal jurisdiction at first instance, other than the power to deal with criminal contempts of court.

*Civil jurisdiction*

The *Queen's Bench Division* deals with civil matters such as claims in contract and tort without any limit as to value. In addition to this mainstream work, it also has a number of specialist subdivisions, including the *Administrative Court*, the *Admiralty Court* and the *Commercial Court*. The third of these is designed to be particularly closely attuned to the needs of the commercial community. In practice, this means that the procedure is speedy, which is achieved by placing greater reliance on documentary evidence, and by giving the judge the more active role of an arbitrator, rather than the more passive one of an adjudicator.

The *Chancery Division* deals with matters such as land law, trusts, the administration of estates, bankruptcy, partnerships, companies, revenue cases and contentious probate, without limit as to value.

The *Family Division* deals with matters such as defended divorces, as well as some matters relating to children, and some probate cases.

### 3.6.3  The High Court as an appeal court generally

Two or more judges, sitting together, may constitute a Divisional Court of the Queen's Bench Division. The Divisional Court has both appellate and supervisory functions. (The concept of *supervisory* jurisdiction is discussed at page 51.) A minor terminological complication arises because the modern practice is for a single-judge court to exercise the supervisory jurisdiction in many civil cases, with multi-judge courts tending to be reserved for criminal cases. Although as a matter of definition a single-judge court cannot be a Divisional Court, in practice that phrase is not uncommonly applied to such courts. The other Divisions of the High Court also have Divisional Courts, but since those Divisions have no appellate jurisdiction in criminal matters, it follows that the split between their single-judge courts and Divisional Courts (using the latter phrase strictly), cannot be as straightforward as it is in the Queen's Bench Division. Accordingly, there are detailed provisions as to the jurisdiction of a single judge in the other Divisions.

### 3.6.4    The High Court as an appeal court in criminal cases

#### Queen's Bench Division

The Queen's Bench Division has an important appellate jurisdiction relating to appeals by way of case stated from magistrates' courts, and from the Crown court sitting without a jury (for example, when hearing an appeal from a magistrates' court). These appeals are available only on points of law, and not on questions of fact. Appeal by way of case stated is a procedure whereby the court whose decision is being challenged prepares a document ('states a case') asking for the opinion of the High Court. The 'case' will contain an account of the facts which the court found to have been proved, a statement of the relevant law as the court understood it, and an application of that law to those facts. The court stating the case then formally asks the High Court whether it was right on the law and on the application of the law to the facts.

If the High Court disagrees with the lower court, it may remit the case to the lower court, but it does not always do so. A typical reason for refusing to remit a case would be lapse of time since the facts giving rise to the case or since the hearing in the lower court, especially when the case is relatively trivial and the appeal has been brought principally to clarify the law for the future. In these cases the delivery of the court's judgment alone will be thought to be sufficient to serve the real purpose of the appeal. In the more usual situation where the case is remitted, the High Court may direct either that the lower court must find the case proved or not proved, or that the hearing should continue in the light of the law as stated by the High Court.

Appeal by way of case stated is somewhat anomalous, being an appeal in name, but having some of the characteristics of the court's supervisory jurisdiction (see below), at least to the extent that the court may be unable to dispose of the matter fully, but may have to remit it to the lower court. The explanation for this is historical and need not be explored here.

Appeal by way of case stated is generally available to any party to any proceedings in magistrates' courts. It is also generally available in the Crown Court except in respect of matters relating to trials on indictment.

This exception is, of course, very common in practice, and appeals by way of case stated from the Crown Court are rare. However, they may be brought against, for example, a decision made on appeal from a magistrates' court.

### Chancery Division and Family Division

Neither the Chancery Division nor the Family Division has any appellate jurisdiction in criminal cases.

**3.6.5    The High Court as an appeal court in civil cases**

### Queen's Bench Division

The Queen's Bench Division deals with appeals by way of case stated in civil matters, as it does in criminal matters.

### Chancery Division

The Chancery Division deals with a variety of appeals from County Courts, including those in insolvency cases.

### Family Division

The Family Division deals with appeals in domestic cases from magistrates' courts and the Crown Court, the latter being by way of case stated.

**3.6.6    The High Court as a supervisory court**

The Queen's Bench Division has a supervisory jurisdiction, which is exercisable by way of the procedure known as a *claim for judicial review*. (See page 32 for the nature of judicial review and the distinction between this concept and the concept of *appeal*.)

Claims for judicial review in civil cases are usually heard by a single judge of the Queen's Bench Division, while those arising from criminal cases are usually heard by two, or sometimes three, judges sitting as a Divisional Court. There appears to be no magic in the distinction between a single judge and a Divisional Court. In *R v Secretary of State for the Home Department ex parte Chinoy* [1992] 1 All ER 317, Bingham LJ, sitting in a two-member Divisional Court, said: 'We exercise, for all practical purposes, the same jurisdiction as a single judge'.

**3.6.7    Judicial personnel in the High Court**

The head of the Queen's Bench Division is the President of the Queen's Bench Division. Moreover, and curiously when it is remembered that the Queen's Bench Division's jurisdiction has both civil and criminal elements, the President has the title of Head of Criminal Justice. The President of the Queen's Bench Division (who, somewhat confusingly, will have been a Lord Justice of Appeal) is referred to in writing as, for example, either Smith LJ or, sometimes, Sir John Smith P (although this latter usage creates the potential for confusion with the President of the Family Division – see below – and may, therefore not enter widespread usage.

The head of the Chancery Division is the Chancellor of the High Court, who is referred to in writing as, for example, Sir John Brown C. Before the changes introduced by the Constitutional Reform Act 2005, the senior judge of the Chancery Division was known as the Vice-Chancellor, and was referred to in writing as, for example, Sir John Brown V-C. (It is important to distinguish between *V-C* and *VC*. The former, as we have just seen, means Vice-Chancellor, while the latter indicates that the person whose name it follows is the holder of the Victoria Cross, which is the highest British award for military gallantry.)

The head of the Family Division is the President of the Family Division, and is referred to in writing as, for example, Sir David White P. The President of the Family Division is also the Head of Family Justice.

Ordinary judges of the High Court, who are technically termed *puisne judges* (*puisne* is pronounced *puny* and merely means *junior*), are referred to orally as, for example, Mr (or Mrs) Justice Green. The written form of the title – Green J – is sexually non-specific. Judges of the Court of Appeal may sit in the High Court, but they will usually do so only where that court is exercising its appellate and supervisory jurisdictions.

On retirement from the High Court, judges sometimes return to judicial work on a part-time basis to help out with heavy workloads. Under these circumstances they will simply be referred to, both orally and in writing, in terms of the knighthood (or damehood) which they already possessed before retirement: for example Sir John Brown.

## 3.7 The Court of Appeal

### 3.7.1 The Court of Appeal

Although the Court of Appeal is nominally one court, it is divided into the Criminal Division and the Civil Division. The principal jurisdiction of both Divisions is appellate, but the Criminal Division also has a limited quasi-appellate jurisdiction.

## 3.7.2     Court of Appeal (Criminal Division)

*Appellate jurisdiction*

The appellate jurisdiction of the Court of Appeal (Criminal Division) relates to appeals against conviction, sentence or both from the Crown Court. (Criminal appeals from the High Court go directly to the House of Lords: see page 56.) In the case of an appeal against conviction, the Court of Appeal has power to hear witnesses, but seldom does so because most appeals against conviction turn on an analysis of the quality of the trial judge's summing-up to the jury. A major function of the Criminal Division is the issuing of guidelines on sentencing for the assistance of lower courts.

*Quasi-appellate jurisdiction*

In addition to the genuinely appellate jurisdiction outlined above, there are three provisions which enable cases to be referred to the Court of Appeal (Criminal Division), namely s. 9 of the Criminal Appeal Act 1995, s. 36 of the Criminal Justice Act 1972, and s. 36 of the Criminal Justice Act 1988.

Section 9 of the Criminal Appeal Act 1995, which is intended to provide a mechanism for correcting miscarriages of justice, enables the Criminal Cases Review Commission, which was created by s. 8 of the Act, to refer to the Court of Appeal cases where there has been a conviction on indictment. The reference may be in respect of either conviction or sentence or both, and the proceedings will be treated as if they were by way of appeal. Strictly speaking, however, the proceedings are not appellate because they are instituted by someone other than the person who is affected by the original decision. The procedure under s. 9 replaces the Home Secretary's power to refer cases to the Court of Appeal under s. 17 of the Criminal Appeal Act 1968. (Curiously, it is the High Court which exercises the somewhat similar, though decidedly more restricted, power under s. 54 of the Criminal Procedure and Investigations Act 1996 to quash an acquittal. The exercise of this power, which exists only where someone committed an offence against the administration of justice in the proceedings leading to the acquittal, does not result in a conviction being substituted, but does create the possibility of a second prosecution.)

Section 36 of the Criminal Justice Act 1972 provides that, following an acquittal on indictment (where the prosecution has no avenue of appeal), the Attorney-General can refer a point of law to the Court of Appeal. This procedure does not amount to an appeal by the prosecution, because the result of the Court of Appeal's deliberations has no effect on the defendant, who remains acquitted, and therefore there is a sense in which this provision requires the court to embark upon an academic exercise. However, in line with the general reluctance of the English courts to deal with anything other than real disputes (see page 18), the court should be astute enough to restrict the procedure to its proper ambit. As Lord Mustill said, in *Attorney-General's Reference (No 3 of 1994)* [1997] 3 All ER 936, the point of law referred to the Court of Appeal must have arisen in the case, which means that the Attorney-General must not, even with 'the best of intentions ... use an acquittal to set in train a judicial roving commission ... with the aim of providing clear, practical and systematic solutions for problems of current interest. And if the reference asks questions which did not arise, the court will refuse to answer them'.

Under s. 36 of the Criminal Justice Act 1988 the Attorney-General can refer a case to the Court of Appeal if he considers that a sentence imposed by the Crown court is too lenient. Although this provision is cast in terms of a reference by the Attorney-General, rather than an appeal by the prosecution, the court can vary the actual sentence, either upwards or downwards. This is, of course, in clear contradistinction to the Attorney-General's Reference procedure under s. 36 of the Criminal Justice Act 1972 following an acquittal, where the opinion of the Court of Appeal does not affect the outcome of the individual case.

### 3.7.3 Court of Appeal (Civil Division)

The Court of Appeal (Civil Division) deals almost entirely with appeals from County Courts and the High Court. Appeals are said to be by way of rehearing, but in the vast majority of cases only documentary evidence, supported by the oral arguments of counsel, is received in practice. The procedure, therefore, is not the same as the full rehearing which takes place on an appeal from a magistrates' court to the Crown Court (see page 46).

### 3.7.4 Judicial personnel in the Court of Appeal

The Lord Chief Justice is not only the Head of the Court of Appeal (Criminal Division), but is also both the Head of the Judiciary and the President of the Courts of England and Wales. The Lord Chief Justice is referred to in writing as, for example, Lord Green CJ or, with a hint of tautology, as Lord Green LCJ.

The head of the Court of Appeal (Civil Division) is the Master of the Rolls, who is also the Head of Civil Justice. The Master of the Rolls is referred to in writing as, for example, Sir James Brown MR (or Lord

Brown MR after receiving the peerage which customarily follows appointment as Master of the Rolls). An ordinary judge of the Court of Appeal will have the title of Lord or Lady Justice of Appeal. The written form of the style is, of course, sexually non-specific, and appears as, for example, Grey LJ. On retirement from the Court of Appeal, judges sometimes return to judicial work on a part-time basis to help out with heavy workloads. Under these circumstances they will simply be referred to, both orally and in writing, in terms of the knighthood (or damehood) which they already possessed before retirement: for example Dame Jane Grey.

Circuit judges may also sit in the Criminal Division of the Court of Appeal, where their day-to-day experience of conducting criminal trials can be useful.

## 3.8 The House of Lords

### 3.8.1 Introduction

The House of Lords (or more accurately an Appellate Committee of the House of Lords, because the committee which hears any given appeal is convened for that purpose, with its membership being drawn from the Law Lords as a whole), has jurisdiction in both civil and criminal cases. In practice, as its title suggests, a Committee's jurisdiction is almost entirely appellate, although there is a residual and very limited jurisdiction at first instance. As a minor point of terminology, it is worth noticing that an *Appeals* Committee (as distinct from an *Appellate* Committee) of the House of Lords is the body which deals with applications for leave to appeal to the House. In practice, it is also frequently, but inaccurately, called the Judicial Committee, presumably by analogy with the Privy Council (see below).

### 3.8.2 The House of Lords as a court of first instance

The House of Lords' jurisdiction at first instance is almost non-existent, but it includes disputed succession to peerages.

### 3.8.3 The House of Lords as an appeal court

The House of Lords has appellate jurisdiction in both criminal and civil cases.

### Criminal jurisdiction

The criminal jurisdiction of the House of Lords relates to appeals by either the prosecution or the defence from the Court of Appeal (Criminal Division) and the High Court.

### Civil jurisdiction

This jurisdiction covers, principally, appeals from the Court of Appeal (Civil Division), but additionally there is the leapfrog procedure, governed by ss. 12 and 13 of the Administration of Justice Act 1969, under which cases may progress directly from the High Court to the House of Lords. In other words, they 'leapfrog' over the Court of Appeal. This procedure, which is considered in more detail at page 203, is intended to save time and money in certain cases which are likely to end up in the House of Lords anyway.

### 3.8.4   Judicial personnel in the House of Lords

In practice, virtually all members who sit on Appellate Committees of the House of Lords are appointed specifically to do so. Commonly known as 'Law Lords', they are technically known as 'Lords of Appeal in Ordinary'. Law Lords are simply referred to by their titles, for example Lord Bounderby, either with or without the appropriate geographical designation (e.g. Lord Bounderby *of Coketown*). The Lord Chancellor, who is a member of the Government, and who, before the Constitutional Reform Act 2005, could, technically speaking, sit in Appellate Committees of the House of Lords (although in practice he had not done so for a number of years), is referred to in writing as, for example, Lord Henchard LC. Many older law reports show the Lord Chancellor of the time sitting as a Law Lord, in which case the letters LC after his name will indicate this status.) As with other Law Lords, the use of the geographical designation (e.g. Lord Henchard *of Casterbridge*) was optional.

One Law Lord is always designated as the Senior Law Lord. This designation is almost – but not quite – always a reflection of length of service as a Law Lord.

## 3.9   The Judicial Committee of the Privy Council

### 3.9.1   Introduction

The constitutional function of the Privy Council as a whole is to advise the Crown, and therefore, theoretically at least, its Judicial Committee does not actually determine cases but merely offers advice. In practice, however, the advice is always accepted, so it is not uncommon to speak of decisions of the Judicial Committee of the Privy Council, or simply of the Privy Council.

Before the Judicial Committee (Dissenting Opinions) Order 1966, the Judicial Committee's decisions always took the form of a single opinion, but thereafter dissents have been permitted. (The Order does not expressly permit a multiplicity of assenting opinions, but these are now sometimes delivered.)

### 3.9.2    The jurisdiction of the Judicial Committee of the Privy Council

The Judicial Committee is principally concerned with both civil and criminal appeals from certain Commonwealth countries, although the number of countries preserving this avenue of appeal has diminished over the years. Additionally, it has jurisdiction in a wide range of appeals relating to disciplinary proceedings brought by various professional bodies. Finally, it has a relatively new jurisdiction, under the Northern Ireland Act 1998, the Scotland Act 1998, and the Government of Wales Act 1998, in respect of certain constitutional disputes concerning devolution issues.

### 3.9.3    Judicial personnel of the Judicial Committee of the Privy Council

The Committee's membership overlaps to a large extent with the membership of the Appellate Committee of the House of Lords, although members from overseas may sometimes sit as well.

## 3.10    The new Supreme Court

Under the terms of the Constitutional Reform Act 2005, the House of Lords will cease to function as a court, being replaced by a new Supreme Court. The existing Law Lords will become Justices of the Supreme Court.

The timing of this change depends on the availability of the Supreme Court's accommodation (in the form of the old Middlesex Guildhall, on the opposite side of Parliament Square from the Palace of Westminster). This, in turn, depends on the progress of the building works which are necessary in order to enable the building to fulfil its new role. (Towards the end of 2006, completion of the works was scheduled for 2009, having previously slipped from 2008.)

The Supreme Court will take over the judicial functions of the House of Lords, as well as those of the Judicial Committee of the Privy Council in relation to devolution matters arising from Northern Ireland, Scotland and Wales.

Despite the name of the new court, its jurisdiction will not in any way challenge the existing constitutional doctrine of the legislative supremacy of Parliament (see page 61).

## 3.11 Administrative tribunals and statutory inquiries

As their names suggest, administrative tribunals and statutory inquiries are not courts and therefore cannot be part of the hierarchy of the courts. Nevertheless, they are generally subject to control by the courts, by way of either appeal, where statute so provides, or supervisory review. A major difference between tribunals and courts is that the members of a tribunal will usually have extensive practical knowledge of the type of cases which come before them. Additionally, tribunals tend to be less formal, cheaper and generally more accessible than courts. Examples of tribunals include Employment Tribunals (which were called Industrial Tribunals before being renamed by the Employment Rights (Dispute Resolution) Act 1998), dealing with certain types of dispute between employers and employees, and Social Security Appeal Tribunals, whose jurisdiction is self-evident.

Inquiries are also usually conducted by people with technical expertise. Examples of inquiries include appeals to the Secretary of State for the Environment against the refusal of planning permission by a local authority. Inquiries tend to be less formal, cheaper and more accessible than the courts. Nevertheless, they are essentially different from tribunals, as indicated by the following comment from the Council on Tribunals Annual Report for 1960:

'Tribunals, generally speaking, exercise an independent jurisdiction: they decide particular cases by applying rules and regulations and sometimes by using their own discretion. Inquiries, on the other hand, form part of the process by which a Minister exercises his discretion – discretion for which he is answerable to Parliament.'

## 3.12 Rights of appeal and permission to appeal

There have been various references throughout this chapter to rights of appeal. Whether there is any right of appeal in a given situation will always depend on the relevant statutory provisions. However, as a very general proposition, where there is a right of appeal there will often be one appeal on the facts and the law, but with the possibility of further appeal on the law only. It is also worth noticing that some rights of appeal are conditional, in the sense that permission to appeal must be obtained before the right is exercised. Depending on the detailed statutory provisions in question, permission may be obtainable either from the court whose decision is being challenged or from the court which will deal with the appeal if it proceeds.

# Summary

- The structure of the courts' system within the English legal system is hierarchical.

- The principal classification of the jurisdictions of the courts is into *first instance* and *appellate*, and into *civil* and *criminal.*

- The magistrates' courts' jurisdiction has both civil and criminal elements. It is exercisable at first instance and, in some civil matters, on appeal.

- The Crown Courts' jurisdiction has both civil and criminal elements, and is exercisable both at first instance and on appeal.

- The County Courts' jurisdiction is entirely civil, and is exercisable principally at first instance but also to some extent on appeal.

- Although the High Court is nominally one court, for administrative purposes it is split into three parts, namely the Queen's Bench Division, the Chancery Division and the Family Division. As a whole, the High Court's jurisdiction comprises both civil and criminal matters, and is exercisable both at first instance and on appeal. The Queen's Bench Division also has a supervisory jurisdiction.

- Although the Court of Appeal is nominally one court, it is divided into the Criminal Division and the Civil Division. The principal jurisdiction of both Divisions is appellate, but the Criminal Division also has a limited quasi-appellate jurisdiction.

- The Appellate Committee of the House of Lords has jurisdiction in both civil and criminal cases. In practice the jurisdiction is almost entirely appellate, although there is a residual and very limited jurisdiction at first instance.

- The Judicial Committee of the Privy Council, which has jurisdiction in both civil and criminal cases, is principally concerned with appeals from certain Commonwealth countries. Additionally, it has jurisdiction over a wide range of appeals relating to disciplinary proceedings brought by various professional bodies, as well as certain constitutional disputes arising out of devolution to Northern Ireland, Scotland and Wales.

- In 2008, or shortly thereafter, a new Supreme Court will come into being. It will exercise the judicial functions currently exercised by the House of Lords and the functions which are currently exercised by the Judicial Committee of the Privy Council in respect of devolution matters.

- Administrative tribunals and statutory inquiries are not courts and therefore cannot be part of the hierarchy of the courts. Nevertheless, they are generally subject to control by the courts, by way of either appeal or supervisory review.

▶ The system of appeals is governed entirely by statute, which means that in each case the existence and extent of any right of appeal depends on the relevant statute. However, it is common to find a more extensive right to appeal against rulings of law than against findings of fact.

## Exercises

1 Apart from the Court of Appeal (Civil Division), which court has only civil jurisdiction?

2 Distinguish between *appeal* and *review*.

3 In what sense can it be said that the Judicial Committee of the Privy Council does not give *judgments*?

4 Distinguish between *tribunals* and *inquiries*.

5 Generally speaking, are the rights of appeal more extensive in relation to matters of *fact* or matters of *law*?

# Chapter 4

# The constitutional context of legal method

## 4.1 Introduction

One of the major concerns of legal method is to identify the scope of the courts' power to develop the law. It follows from this that, although the study of constitutional law is a substantial exercise in its own right, the study of legal method must include at least an overview of the legal basis of the constitution as the foundation of any real understanding. This chapter, therefore, considers the legal framework of the British constitution generally, while Chapter 5 considers various aspects of the European Community context, and Chapter 6 deals with the growing importance of an awareness of the place of human rights within legal method.

Although the British constitution is often described as being un-written, there are some underlying ideas (or doctrines) which are of enduring influence. These are the rule of law, the legislative supremacy of Parliament and the separation of powers.

## 4.2 The rule of law

The rule of law may be seen in two ways. One, known as the *formal view*, merely requires that the appropriate formalities required by the legal system are observed, so that the legal system functions according to identifiable rules and government operates according to law rather than whim. The other, known as the *substantive view*, goes further by requiring the law to possess at least some substantive qualities. An example of the latter view within the English legal system may be found in the presumption against gaining advantage from wrong-doing, which is discussed at page 322.

## 4.3 The legislative supremacy of Parliament

### 4.3.1 A statement of the doctrine

According to Dicey, whose influential book *The Law of the Constitution* was first published in 1885, 'the very keystone of the law of the Constitution' is that

'Parliament ... has ... the right to make or unmake any law whatever; and further, that no person or body is recognized by the law of England as having a right to override or set aside the legislation of Parliament.'

Furthermore, it is clear that Parliament may set aside or override (or, to use the technical term, repeal) its own legislation, either expressly or impliedly. Express repeal is obvious. Implied repeal occurs where a later statute is inconsistent with an earlier one, because the court will conclude that Parliament knew what it was doing and, therefore, must have intended the later statute to prevail over the earlier one. However, following the decision of the High Court in *Thoburn v Sunderland City Council* [2002] 3 WLR 247, it seems that there may be one exception to the doctrine of implied repeal. More particularly, Laws LJ said that the doctrine could apply only to 'ordinary' statutes, and not to 'constitutional' ones, such as the European Communities Act 1972. In other words, where a later statute conflicts with the 1972 Act, it cannot be argued that the 1972 Act has been impliedly repealed to the extent which would be necessary in order to give effect to the later statute. (There has been little further judicial consideration of the idea that there is a distinct category of 'constitutional statutes', but in *Watkins v Secretary of State for the Home Department* [2006] UKHL 17, [2006] 2 All ER 353, Lord Rodger cast serious doubt on its very existence, albeit when approaching the matter from the perspective of whether the law of tort recognizes a distinct category of 'constitutional rights':

'[62] The term "constitutional right" works well enough, alongside equivalent terms, in the field of statutory interpretation. But, even if it were otherwise suitable, it is not sufficiently precise to define a class of rights whose abuse should give rise to a right of action in tort without proof of damage. Moreover, any expansion to cover abuse of rights under 'constitutional statutes', as defined by Laws LJ in *Thoburn* ... would carry with it similar problems of deciding which statutes fell within the definition. Even supposing that these could be resolved, it is by no means clear that the abuse of 'constitutional rights' or rights under 'constitutional statutes' should necessarily attract a remedy which would be denied for the abuse of other important rights. Is the prisoner who suffers no material harm from abuse of his right to correspond with his solicitor necessarily more deserving of a remedy than the patient who is actually perfectly healthy but whose general practitioner maliciously refuses to see him? Or than the applicant who is not actually entitled to a social security benefit but who is maliciously denied the appropriate hearing by the relevant official?'

Whether it is possible to develop a coherent theory of 'constitutional statutes' remains to be seen. But the assertions of Laws LJ in *Thoburn* are plainly inadequate for this purpose, and are not even necessary for the decision in that case. There is no jurisprudential reason why the

European Communities Act 1972 cannot be regarded as being in a category of its own.

There is, however, a logical conundrum lurking within the concept of the legislative supremacy of Parliament, namely the question of whether one Parliament can enact legislation in such a way that a later Parliament cannot repeal it, even by an express provision purporting to do so. The classic reply to this is that such unrepealable provisions are impossible, because their effect would be to destroy the supremacy of later Parliaments. As Sir Robert Megarry said, in *Manuel v Attorney-General* [1982] 3 All ER 822, 'As a matter of law the courts of England recognize Parliament as being omnipotent in all save the power to destroy its own omnipotence'. We will return to this question of whether one Parliament can prevail over its successors when we consider the impact of Community law on English law and national sovereignty in Chapter 5. For the moment, however, it will be useful to consider the origins of Parliament as a basis for understanding the doctrine of legislative supremacy generally.

Finally, it must be emphasized that the doctrine of the legislative supremacy of Parliament applies only to Acts *of Parliament*. In other words, it does not apply to statements or decisions made by government ministers (which may or may not be lawful, depending on whether they conform to the principles of administrative law), nor to delegated legislation. (See page 68 for the nature and status of delegated legislation.)

<h2>4.3.2    The origins and evolution of Parliament</h2>

The details of the origins of Parliament are shrouded in a good deal of historical uncertainty. Nevertheless, in broad outline, the period between the Norman Conquest and the so-called Glorious Revolution of 1688 clearly witnessed a transition from absolute monarchy to constitutional monarchy. Even in the early days of absolute monarchy, however, the Kings of England kept in touch with political reality through the *Curia Regis* (or *King's Council*), which consisted of advisers who helped the King to govern the country. At this stage, Parliament was, as the Norman-French root of the word indicates, merely a talking-shop.

In time, however, Parliament came to be a legislative body. In other words, statutes, having been made originally by the King, started to be made by Parliament. Thus it was that statutes changed from being Acts of the King into being Acts of Parliament. Similarly, the constitutionally correct form of words to describe the legislature is the King (or Queen) in Parliament, as reflected in the standard form of words used at the beginning of the vast majority of statutes:

> 'Be it enacted by the Queen's most Excellent Majesty, by and with the advice and consent of the Lords Spiritual and Temporal, and Commons, in this present Parliament assembled, and by the authority of the same, as follows: ...'

Admittedly the final stage of the legislative process was, and indeed still is, the giving of the Royal Assent, but this is now merely a formality, and is certainly not a mark of Royal initiative.

### 4.3.3    The problem of the royal prerogative

As we have seen, the power of making statutes devolved from the King alone to the King in Parliament. However, there remained two questions. First, did the process of devolution to Parliament totally extinguish the King's personal legislative power? Secondly, if the King did retain any personal power, what were its limits? In other words, rolling both questions into one: what, if anything, remained of the *royal prerogative*? In order to answer this question we must survey, albeit briefly, the political history of the 17th century.

The starting point is that at the beginning of the 17th century Parliamentary legislation enjoyed much lower status than it does now. For example, in *Bonham's Case* (1610) 8 Co Rep 114, Coke CJ said: 'When an Act of Parliament is against common right and reason, or repugnant, or impossible to be performed, the common law will control it, and adjudge such Act to be void'. In this context, therefore, it is not altogether surprising that the courts were willing to listen to arguments presented on behalf of the King and against Parliament. A classic example is to be found in *R v Hampden* (1637) 3 St Tr 825 (also known as the *Shipmoney Case*). Charles I claimed to have the right to raise a tax to pay for ships for the defence of the realm, without the consent of Parliament, even though the Petition of Right 1628 required such consent. Sir John Hampden refused to pay, although he conceded that he would have had no choice if there had been an actual emergency, rather than merely a threatened one. The court decided against Hampden, holding not only that in the case of an emergency did the King have the power he claimed, but also that the King was the sole judge of whether there was a sufficient emergency to justify such a tax. The King was also held to be the sole judge of how much the tax should be. In passing, it is interesting to note that, whatever constitutional significance *R v Hampden* may have, Sir John's lasting fame is probably due more to Thomas Gray, who, in his *Elegy Written in a Country Churchyard* (1751), wrote:

'Some village Hampden that with dauntless breast
The little tyrant of his fields withstood;
Some mute, inglorious Milton here may rest;
Some Cromwell, guiltless of his country's blood.'

Despite the decisions in some of the cases concerning the royal prerogative in the early part of the 17th century, it would be a mistake to conclude that the courts were simply an agency to enforce royal whims: they certainly did control the power of the King where they thought it appropriate to do so. For example, in the *Case of Proclamations* (1611) 12 Co Rep 74, the court said:

'1.  The King by his proclamation cannot create any offence which was not one before; for then he might alter the law of the land in a high point; for if he may create an offence where none is, upon that ensues fine and imprisonment.
'2.  The King hath no prerogative but what the law of the land allows him.'

*R v Hampden* was, of course, decided before the Civil War. Even after the restoration of the monarchy, however, the new King claimed rights which seemed to be out of line with the spirit of the age. The classic case here is *Godden v Hales* (1686) 11 St Tr 1165. Hales, a Roman Catholic, was appointed as a colonel in the army. Contrary to the law, he refused to take holy communion in the Anglican church and to take the usual form of oath of allegiance. King James II, also a Roman Catholic, claimed to have the power to dispense with the ordinary legal requirements, so that Hales would suffer no adverse consequences as a result of his refusal to obey the law. The court accepted that the King did have the power which he claimed.

### 4.3.4  The revolution and its outcome

The departure of King James II in 1688 caused a fundamental break in the legitimacy of constitutional power, which was resolved as follows.

First, in 1688 an informal group, consisting of peers, former members of the House of Commons (which had not met since 1685) and leading citizens of the City of London, invited William of Orange to summon a Convention.

Secondly, the Convention met, declared the throne to be vacant, and invited William and Mary to occupy it jointly. The offer was, however, conditional on William and Mary accepting the terms of a document which was drawn up and called the Declaration of Right. Thirdly, William and Mary accepted the offer of the throne, on the terms indicated. (In passing, it is interesting to note that, despite Shelley's view that poets are 'the unacknowledged legislators of the world', Dryden was dismissed from the post of Poet Laureate for refusing to take an oath of allegiance to William and Mary.)

Finally, the Convention passed the Crown and Parliament Act 1689, declaring itself to be a properly constituted Parliament, and it then enacted the Bill of Rights 1689, which restated the terms of the Declaration of Right. The most important terms of the Bill of Rights (in modernized spelling) are:

'(1) That the pretended power of suspending* of laws or the execution of laws by regal authority without consent of Parliament is illegal.

'(2) That the pretended power of dispensing* with laws or the execution of laws by regal authority as it hath been assumed and exercised of late is illegal.

...

'(4) That the levying of money for or to the use of the crown by pretence of prerogative without grant of Parliament for longer time or in other manner than the same is or shall be granted is illegal.

...

'(6) That the raising or keeping of a standing army within the kingdom in time of peace unless it be with the consent of Parliament is against the law...

...

'(8) That election of members of Parliament ought to be free.

'(9) That the freedom of speech and debates or proceedings in Parliament ought not to be impeached or questioned in any court or place out of Parliament.

'(10) That excessive bail ought not be required nor excessive fines imposed nor cruel and unusual punishments inflicted.

'(11) That jurors ought to be duly impanelled and returned...

...

'(13) And that for redress of all grievances and for the amending, strengthening and preserving of the laws Parliaments ought to be held frequently.'

(*The distinction between suspending and dispensing is that the former had the effect of preventing the operation of a law generally, whereas the latter was personalized, as in *Godden v Hales*.)

Although the intrinsic legitimacy of this process involved the Convention in nothing more sophisticated than lifting itself up by its own bootstraps, two points are basic. First, the idea of the legislative supremacy of Parliament was fundamental to the intentions of the drafters of the Bill of Rights. Secondly, and it is at this stage that any revolutionary process progresses beyond mere bootstrapping, the courts accepted not only the legitimacy of statutes passed by the post-1689 Parliaments. Moreover, they also accepted, by implication, their own newly defined status as being subordinate to Parliament. However, the revolutionary establishment of a constitutional monarchy did nothing to endow the new structure with anything which could, in modern terms, be regarded as democratic legitimacy. Indeed, G K

Chesterton, in his poem *The Secret People*, expresses a more cynical view of the revolution:

'We saw the King as they killed him and his face was proud and pale;
And a few men talked of freedom, while England talked of ale.'

It was not until the passing of the Great Reform Act in 1832 that the House of Commons started to become genuinely representative, and this process was not completed until 1928, with the extension of the franchise to women on equal terms with men. Historically, therefore, the question of the royal prerogative cannot accurately be seen in terms of exemption from democratic control, but simply as a straightforward power struggle between two legislative institutions: the King on the one hand and Parliament on the other.

**4.3.5**    The significance of the role of the courts after the revolution

Although we have just seen that an integral part of the post-revolution settlement was the courts' acceptance of their own subordinate position, it is worth reflecting on the significance of this. For example, if *A* claims a particular right, and *B* agrees when it is open to *B* to disagree and *B*'s disagreement would have the practical consequence of preventing *A* from enforcing the right, it can be argued that in reality *B* is exercising the greater power, because *B* could frustrate *A*'s alleged right. Thus, if the courts had withheld their recognition of post-revolution statutes, on the basis that they were the invalid acts of an illegitimate Parliament, the revolution would not have been resolved in the way that it was. (What would have happened instead must, of course, remain speculative.)

This leads to the somewhat paradoxical statement that the legislative supremacy of Parliament, which is the most fundamental constitutional doctrine of English Law, is effectively the creation of the courts, rather than of Parliament itself. Two consequences flow from this.

First, and in the abstract, supremacy which is held on sufferance is clearly a peculiar kind of supremacy.

Secondly, and more practically, arguments sometimes arise as to the extent to which, if at all, one Parliament can bind future Parliaments. However, as we have seen, a technically more accurate way of expressing this problem would be to ask to what extent the courts will recognize the power of one Parliament to bind future Parliaments.

Of course, the sudden rejection by the courts of the idea of the legislative supremacy of Parliament would itself be so fundamental that it could reasonably be characterized as revolutionary, and therefore it is unlikely to be undertaken lightly, if at all. However, the question of how far one Parliament can bind its successors has arisen in the very real context of the relationship between English law and Community law. This is examined in some detail in Chapter 5.

### 4.3.6 A modern example of the legislative supremacy of Parliament

In *Burmah Oil Ltd v Lord Advocate* [1964] 2 All ER 348, the House of Lords held that the Crown was liable to compensate the oil company for certain losses sustained during the Second World War. Parliament promptly passed the War Damage Act 1965, saying that the Crown was not, and never had been, under any such liability. In *British Railways Board v Pickin* [1974] 1 All ER 609, Pickin wished to advance a challenge to the validity of the British Railways Act 1968 on the basis that the Board had obtained the passing of the Act by misleading Parliament. The House of Lords held that the courts had no jurisdiction to entertain such challenges.

### 4.3.7 The nature and status of delegated legislation

Statutes, which are *primary* legislation, must be rigorously distinguished from *secondary* (more usually known as *delegated* or *subordinate*) legislation. Delegated legislation is made by people such as Ministers of the Crown, local authorities and others, under authority conferred by statute. In each case, the relevant statute will prescribe the procedure which must be followed when making the delegated legislation. The procedure may, or may not, require Parliamentary approval of each piece of delegated legislation, but, in any case, as a matter of Constitutional doctrine, delegated legislation may be quashed by the courts if its maker has acted unlawfully by either exceeding the relevant statutory power, or failing to follow the prescribed procedure. Common forms of delegated legislation include statutory instruments and byelaws.

For many years there was an academic controversy over the status of statutes passed under the provisions of the Parliament Acts 1911 and 1949 (in accordance with which they received the Royal Assent, having been passed by the House of Commons alone, rather than having been passed by both the House of Commons and the House of Lords). One view was that, for the purposes of the Parliament Acts procedure, Parliament had been *redefined* in such a way as to consist simply of the Commons and the Crown; and that, therefore, statutes passed under that procedure were fully fledged Acts *of Parliament*. However, the competing view was that the effect of the Parliament Acts was to *delegate* to the Commons and the Crown the power to make law; and that, therefore, the products of this process must be delegated legislation. The House of Lords resolved the dispute in *R (Jackson) v Attorney-General* [2005] UKHL 56, [2005] 4 All ER 1253, upholding the view that statutes passed under the Parliament Acts are Acts of Parliament and are, therefore, protected by the doctrine of the legislative supremacy of Parliament. (It is significant that the Appellate Committee which decided *Jackson* consisted of nine Law Lords. The standard number is five, with the standard exception – when it is thought that a larger bench is appropriate in order to give added weight to a decision – being seven. Nine is very unusual indeed.)

## 4.4 The separation of powers

It is commonplace to trace the doctrine of the separation of powers back to *L'Esprit des Lois*, in which the 18th-century French philosopher Montesquieu maintained that the doctrine played a vital part in ensuring the political stability of Britain. At its simplest, the doctrine states that political power is of three types (*legislative, executive* and *judicial*) and that these should be separated from each other so that no one person or institution exercises more than one type of power.

It must be said immediately that Montesquieu was wrong: the strict doctrine of the separation of powers does not characterize the British Constitution, nor has it ever done so. For example, the members of the executive form part of the legislature. Furthermore, as we shall see in Part 2 of this book, the courts have substantial practical power to develop the law through the doctrine of precedent. It is plain, therefore, that Montesquieu's view of the significance of the separation of powers in the British context involved substantial overstatement. Nevertheless, the doctrine is not without importance, and at various stages it will become apparent that the doctrine does exercise the minds of the judges when they are seeking to identify the constitutionally legitimate scope of the judicial role.

For example in *R v Cambridge Health Authority ex parte B* [1995] 2 All ER 129, the health authority had decided not to provide medical treatment for a child suffering from leukaemia. When the child's father applied for judicial review, the health authority sought to justify its decision on both medical and resource grounds. The first stage, which would cost about £15,000, was estimated to have a 10–20 per cent chance of success. If this stage was successful, the child would then progress to the second stage, which would cost about £60,000, and which would again have a 10–20 per cent chance of success. At best, therefore the overall chances of success were estimated at 20 per cent of 20 per cent, and at worst they were 10 per cent of 10 per cent. The High Court refused to order the health authority to proceed with the treatment, but did order it to reconsider the matter. The Court of Appeal felt that it was inappropriate even to order reconsideration. Sir Thomas Bingham MR dealt with the medical aspect of the case thus:

> 'Were we to express opinions as to the likelihood of the effectiveness of medical treatment, or as to the merits of medical judgment, then we would be straying far from the sphere which under our constitution is accorded to us.'

He was equally unwilling to interfere with the health authority's decision as to how it should allocate its resources:

> 'I have no doubt that in a perfect world any treatment which a patient, or a patient's family, sought would be provided if doctors were willing to give it, no matter how much it cost, particularly when a life was potentially at stake. It would however, in my view, be shutting one's eyes to the real world if the court were to proceed on the basis that we do live in such a world. It is common knowledge that health authorities of all kinds are constantly pressed to make ends meet ... Difficult and agonizing judgments have to be made as to how a limited budget is best allocated to the maximum advantage of the maximum number of patients. That is not a judgment which the court can make.'

## 4.5 Balancing the constitutional doctrines

It will be apparent at various stages throughout this book that the three constitutional doctrines may create conflicts which the courts must resolve. Although the doctrine of the legislative supremacy of Parliament will always receive at least lip service, it can scarcely be denied that the courts play a genuinely creative role. The practical difficulty is to identify in advance how far the courts will be willing to go. Two cases, decided within a few years of each other, will illustrate the problem. The particular context is that which arises where an Act has been passed but is not yet in force.

In *R v Walsall Justices ex parte W* [1989] 3 All ER 460, a juvenile was charged with assault occasioning grievous bodily harm to a 12-year-old boy. The defendant pleaded not guilty, whereupon the case was adjourned for a hearing. On the day fixed for the hearing the parties attended court but the prosecution informed the court that there was no independent evidence to corroborate the victim's allegation against the defendant. It followed that, if the magistrates took the view that the victim was of insufficient understanding to take the oath, the inevitable consequence in accordance with s. 38(1) of the Children and Young Persons Act 1933 would be that the prosecution would fail. The prosecution also pointed out that the following day, when s. 34 of the Criminal

Justice Act 1988 came into effect, the need for corroboration would be abolished. On this basis the prosecution applied for an adjournment, which the court granted on the basis of 'the interests of justice'.

The defence applied for judicial review of the decision. Granting the application, the High Court said that what the magistrates had done was to pass a qualitative judgment on the existing law. This approach was inconsistent with the principle that it is the function of the courts to apply the law, and amounted to taking an illegitimate consideration into account when deciding to grant the adjournment. In passing, it is interesting, and not a little curious, to note that the court indicated that the position might be different if the imminent change in the law had related only to procedural matters. This case is, therefore, an example of the fact that the courts sometimes approach substantive and procedural provisions differently. (The nature of the distinction between substantive and procedural provisions is discussed at page 33.)

An instructive comparison with the *Walsall* case may be found in *R v Parole Board and Another ex parte Wilson* (1992) 4 Admin LR 525, where the Parole Board had repeatedly refused to recommend the release of a prisoner. He claimed the right to see the reports on himself which had been considered by the Parole Board. The European Court of Human Rights had said that there should be such a right, and Parliament had responded obediently by including appropriate provisions in the Criminal Justice Act 1991. These provisions had not, however, been brought into force. The Court of Appeal felt able to extend the common law in such a way as to give the prisoner the right which he claimed, since it would have been unfair to have made him wait until the 1991 provisions came into force. (This case is considered further at pages 99 and 196.)

Cases such as these involve the judges in making decisions without any clear and explicit legal authority to guide them. However, it is worth noticing that in both these cases the decisions favoured the liberty of the subject over the interests of the authorities.

## Summary

▷ Legal method is an aspect of constitutional law.

▷ The doctrine of the rule of law requires that the subject is entitled to be ruled according to law, and that the law should be predictable.

▷ The doctrine of the legislative supremacy of Parliament means that Parliament can make or unmake any law, and that (subject to European Community law) nobody else may override or set aside the law which Parliament has made. However, the courts do have power to quash delegated legislation, either in whole or in part.

▷ The doctrine of the separation of powers states that political power is of three types (legislative, executive and judicial) and that these should be separated from each other so that no one person or institution should exercise more than one type of power.

▷ The three principal constitutional doctrines may create conflicts which the courts will have to resolve.

## Exercises

1 Explain what each of the following means: (a) the rule of law; (b) the legislative supremacy of parliament; (c) the separation of powers.

2 How did the revolution of 1688 clarify the relationship between the Crown and Parliament?

3 Give one example of a case involving a conflict between constitutional doctrines.

# Chapter 5

# European Community law and English law

Introduction

This chapter begins by identifying the two *European Communities*, namely the *European Atomic Energy Community* (commonly known simply as *Euratom*) and the *European Community*. (A third Community the *European Coal and Steel Community* or *ECSC* – which came into being in 1953 under the Treaty of Paris, 1951, was created for a fixed term of 50 years. Accordingly, this Community ceased to exist in 2003, when its functions were transferred to the *European Community*.) This chapter then proceeds to distinguish between the *European Union* and the *European Community*, before outlining the functions of the principal Community institutions and discussing the relationship between Community law and English law. Aspects of precedent in the *Court of Justice of the European Communities* (to give the full name of the body usually known simply as the *European Court of Justice* or the *ECJ*), and the interpretation of Community legislation, are dealt with in Chapters 15 and 21, respectively.

The two European communities

The *European Atomic Energy Community*, whose objectives are to develop nuclear energy, to distribute it throughout the Community and to sell the surplus to the outside world, was created by the Treaty of Rome 1957. Secondly, and for our purposes more importantly, the *European Economic Community* was established by another Treaty of Rome, also dated 1957, the purpose of which was, in the words of the preamble to the Treaty, to 'lay the foundations of an ever closer union among the peoples of Europe'.

In practice it became common to refer to the European Economic Community (or EEC) simply as the European Community (or EC). This usage was formalized by the Maastricht Treaty, which is more formally known as the Treaty on European Union 1992 (TEU). (In passing, it may be noted that the shortening effect of common usage continues, and the EC is now often known simply as the *Community*.) The potential for confusion caused by two Treaties of Rome being signed in the same year is resolved in practice by referring to either the *Euratom Treaty* or the *EC Treaty* (or, before the TEU 1992, the *EEC Treaty*), as appropriate.

The citation of articles in the EC Treaty was complicated by the Treaty of Amsterdam 1997 (ToA), which incorporated some new material, as a result of which the vast majority of the original articles in the EC Treaty had to be renumbered. Additionally, the opportunity has been taken to replace the original combinations of letters and numbers of the articles in the TEU with the more traditional and straightforward system of numerical numbering. The Community itself has adopted the practice of citing the new article number first, followed by its predecessor. For example, the article dealing with preliminary references to the European Court of Justice is now cited as 'art. 234 [ex 177] EC'.

Although the origins of each community were, and their continued existences are, distinct from each other, after the Merger Treaty 1965 all three communities shared the same institutions, and the remaining two continue to do so. Similarly, all three communities were, and the remaining two are, subject to the same general principles of law.

Finally, with the admission of Bulgaria and Romania at the beginning of 2007, membership of the Communities has expanded from the six original member states to 27.

## 5.3 The European *Union* and the European *Community*

Despite the renaming of the *Community* by the Treaty on European *Union*, the Union and the Community are *not* interchangeable concepts. In particular, the Union lacks legal personality, being essentially a composite of the three Communities, together with a Common Foreign and Security Policy (CFSP) and Police and Judicial Co-operation in Criminal Matters (PJCCM). These three elements are commonly known as the 'three pillars' of the Union. However, the fact that the CFSP and PJCCM operate only at the *political* level of intergovernmental co-operation means that the European Court of Justice has no jurisdiction in respect of them.

The essential difference, therefore, between the *Union* and the *Community* is that the former is a *political* entity while the latter is a *legal* entity. However, the interface between the two is by no means always as straightforward as this labelling exercise may suggest. For example, art. 17 [ex 8] EC, which was inserted by the TEU, provides that anyone holding the nationality of a member state is automatically also a citizen of the Union, and has certain rights under the Treaty. Furthermore, the range of content of each pillar may change, as evidenced by the fact that although the TEU constituted the third pillar as Co-operation in Justice and Home Affairs (CJHA), the ToA transferred visas, asylum, immigration and judicial co-operation in civil matters from CJHA to the Community itself, leaving PJCCM as the only content of the third pillar.

The nature of the distinction between the *Union* and the *Community* has one important consequence. Despite extremely widespread usage to the contrary, the fact that the Union is not a *legal* entity suggests that it is less than totally accurate to refer to *Union* law. Even the legal consequences which flow from the political status of citizenship of the *Union* are contained in the *Community* treaty. However, if the draft constitution of the *Union* ever comes into force, following ratification by all member states, the Union will become a legal entity, and it will then be correct, as well as common, to speak of *Union* law.

## 5.4 The principal Community institutions

### 5.4.1 Introduction

Under the EC Treaty, the principal Community institutions are the *European Commission*, the *Council of the European Union*, the *European Parliament*, the *Court of Justice of the European Communities* and the *Court of First Instance*. Additionally, a body known as the European Council may usefully be mentioned.

### 5.4.2 The European Commission (arts 211–219 [ex 155–163] EC)

Members of the European Commission are politicians, appointed by the common accord of the member states, on the grounds of their general competence. Despite the national and party-political character of the Commission's membership, it is a fundamental principle that Commissioners shall be completely independent in the performance of their duties, being guided only by the 'general interest of the Community' (art. 213(2) [ex 157(2)] EC). The Commission's main function is to formulate policies, which must, of course, be consistent with the framework of the Treaty. The President of the Commission is appointed from among the Commissioners, by the common accord of the member states acting with the consent of the European Parliament (art. 214(2) [ex 158(2)] EC). The President holds office for two years.

### 5.4.3 The Council of the European Union (art. 202 [ex 145])

Policies formulated by the Commission are submitted to the Council of the European Union, which is the Community's principal legislative body. (Before the TEU, the Council was technically known as the

*Council of Ministers*, but in practice it was and is commonly known simply as the *Council*.) Unlike the Commission, the Council's membership is constantly fluctuating, because the Council's composition at any particular meeting will depend entirely on the subject-matter under discussion. Thus, for example, if the business of the day involves agricultural policy, there will be a meeting of the 'Agricultural Council', attended by the Agriculture Minister from each member state. A meeting of the 'General Council', consisting of Foreign Ministers, has the widest remit.

The office of President of the Council rotates round the member states at six-monthly intervals.

At a purely practical level, the variable nature of the Council means that its members must rely on the support of Community officials to an even greater extent than organizations usually rely on their secretariats. The Council's secretariat is known as COREPER, which is an acronym based on the French title of the Committee of Permanent Representatives. COREPER derives its existence from art. 207 [ex 151] EC. It consists of officials having ambassadorial rank, and in practice it undertakes much of the routine work of the Council, with the Council itself then simply endorsing what has been done. Alan Clark, a former Conservative Cabinet Minister, describes the relationship between COREPER and the Council thus:

'Not, really, that it makes the slightest difference to the conclusions of a meeting [of the Council] what Ministers say at it. Everything is decided, horse-traded off, by officials at COREPER, the Council [sic] of Permanent Representatives. The Ministers arrive on the scene at the last minute, hot, tired, ill or drunk (sometimes all of these together) read out their piece, and depart.' (*Diaries*, 1994, p. 139.)

### 5.4.4    The European Parliament (arts 187–201 [ex 137–144] EC)

A body, which was originally known as the European Assembly, became known as the European Parliament in 1962, with the change of name being confirmed by the Single European Act 1986. Until 1979 its members were appointed by the Parliaments of member states, but they are now directly elected. Members of the European Parliament (MEPs) serve for five years.

The Parliament, which began as a discussion chamber, has a supervisory role, which includes approving the appointment of Commissioners and the President of the Commission (art. 214(2) [ex158(2)] EC), as well as receiving and debating an annual General Report from the Commission (art. 200 [ex 143] EC). It can pass a motion of censure on the Commission, and if such a motion were carried by a two-thirds majority, the Commission would be required to resign (art. 201 [ex 144] EC).

Additionally, the Parliament is slowly evolving towards becoming a fully-fledged part of the legislative process. More particularly, the Commission and the Council may consult the Parliament when formulating policy or framing legislation respectively, and in some cases it may even veto proposed legislation. Overall, however, its legislative function is still far less than the use of the word *Parliament* may suggest. The Parliament elects one of its members to be its President.

### 5.4.5   The Court of Justice of the European Communities (art. 220–244 [ex 188–245] EC)

The Court of Justice of the European Communities, which is commonly called the *European Court of Justice* (ECJ), or simply the *Court*, consists of one judge from each member state, together with eight Advocates-General. (A ninth was appointed for the period 1 January 1995 to 6 October 2000.) Both Judges and Advocates-General, who are appointed by common accord of the governments of the member states for six years, must be 'persons whose independence is beyond doubt and who possess the qualifications required for appointment to the highest judicial offices in their respective countries or who are jurisconsults of recognized competence'. The judges elect one of their number to be President of the Court, for a period of three years (art. 223 [ex 167] EC).

The office of Advocate-General is based on that of the French *Commissaire du Gouvernement* in the *Conseil d'Etat* (the French constitutional court), and is sometimes described as being the 'disembodied conscience of the court'. (This is a curious phrase. It would be more accurate to say that the Advocate-General is the 'embodiment of the conscience of the court'. But the existing usage is firmly established and there is no point in challenging it.) More particularly, art. 222 [ex 166] EC provides:

'It shall be the duty of the Advocate-General, acting with complete impartiality and independence, to make, in open court, reasoned submissions on cases brought before the Court of Justice, in order to assist the Court in the performance of the task assigned to it ...'

In accordance with continental legal tradition, the Court always delivers a *judgment of the Court*, with no possibility of dissenting judgments. However, when the Court disagrees with the Advocate-General's opinion, the latter may have persuasive authority in later cases and may therefore be regarded as something akin to a dissenting judgment.

For many years the Court of Justice was the Communities' only judicial body, but the Single European Act 1986 relieved the pressure on the Court by providing for the creation of the *Court of First Instance* (CFI) (see below). Article 225 [ex 168a] EC empowers the Council, from time to time and after consulting both the Commission and the Parliament, to allocate different classes of work to the Court of Justice and the Court of First Instance, subject to the exception that all preliminary references under art. 234 [ex 177] EC must be heard by the Court itself.

Preliminary references, which constitute the bulk of the Court's work, arise where a national court or tribunal considers it necessary to obtain the opinion of the Court before it can give judgment. Any court or tribunal *may* make such a reference, but a court or tribunal against whose decision there is no judicial remedy under national law *must* do so.

The Court hears appeals on points of law from the Court of First Instance, but is not itself subject to appeal.

### 5.4.6    The Court of First Instance (art. 225 [ex 168a] EC)

Judges of the Court of First Instance (CFI ) are, like judges of the Court of Justice, appointed by common accord of the governments of the member states for six years, but the criteria for appointment are less rigorous. More particularly, appointment is open to 'persons whose independence is beyond doubt and who possess the ability required for appointment to judicial office' (art. 225(3) [ex 168a(3)] EC). There are no Advocates-General in the Court of First Instance, but the judges may agree that one of their number shall perform that role in a particular case if they so wish.

### 5.4.7    The European Council

The European Council originated as an unofficial body consisting of the heads of government of the member states. However, the Single European Act 1986 formally recognized its existence, as well as requiring it to meet at least twice a year and giving it special responsibility for encouraging European political co-operation. It is further recognized by art. 4 [ex D TEU] EC, which provides:

> 'The European Council shall provide the Union with the necessary impetus for its development and shall define the general political guidelines thereof.
>
> 'The European Council shall bring together the Heads of State or of Government of the Member States and the President of the Commission.'

Additionally, art. 13 [ex J.13 TEU] EC provides that the European Council shall provide general guidelines within which the Council of the European Union shall decide whether a matter should be the subject of joint action, which will commit the member states, as part of the Common Foreign and Security Policy.

Finally, it is important not to confuse the *European Council* with either the *Council of the European Union* (see above) or the *Council of Europe*. More particularly, the Council of Europe is a totally distinct legal entity from the European Communities, although there is overlapping membership. Its responsibilities include the European Court of Human Rights, which sits in Strasbourg and must be rigorously distinguished from the European Court of Justice, which sits in Luxembourg.

## 5.5 The Enforceability of European Community Law in the United Kingdom

### 5.5.1 Introduction

This section of this chapter examines the extent to which Community law enters into the legal systems of member states and becomes enforceable in their courts. The English perspective will be taken as the primary focus, but the system of Community law is an integrated whole, and therefore some cases involving other member states will also be relevant. Since treaties are the basic sources of Community law, the status of treaties in English law provides a useful starting point.

### 5.5.2 The status of treaties in English law

Because treaties and other international agreements are entered into by the government, which is technically exercising the royal prerogative on behalf of the Crown (see page 64), one consequence of the legislative supremacy of Parliament (see page 61) is that they operate only at the international level, unless and until they are incorporated into English law by statute. In relation to the United Kingdom's accession to the EC Treaty, incorporation was effected by the European Communities Act 1972, s. 2(1) of which provides:

> 'All ... rights, powers, liabilities, obligations and restrictions from time to time created or arising by or under the Treaties, and all such remedies and procedures from time to time provided for by or under the Treaties, as in accordance with the Treaties are without further enactment to be given legal effect or used in the United Kingdom shall be recognized and available in law, and be enforced, allowed and followed accordingly; and the expression "enforceable Community right" and similar expressions shall be read as referring to one to which this subsection applies.'

This provision is reinforced by the interpretative obligation contained in s. 2(4) of the Act:

'Any enactment passed or to be passed ... shall be construed and have effect subject to the foregoing provisions of this section.'

Community obligations may generally be implemented by delegated legislation (see page 68 for the nature of delegated legislation), but the second schedule to the 1972 Act lists four types of provision where nothing short of primary legislation will suffice. These are provisions which impose or increase taxation, which give retrospective effect to any provision, which confer power to make delegated legislation (other than rules of procedure for courts and tribunals) and which create new criminal offences punishable beyond certain specified limits.

Discussion of the enforceability of Community law requires an analysis of the various forms of law, namely the Treaty provisions themselves, Regulations, Directives and Decisions. However, before the discussion can proceed further, we must consider the distinction between the concepts of the *direct applicability* and the *direct effect* of Community law within the legal systems of member states, together with the liability of member states under the *Francovich* doctrine.

### 5.5.3 Direct applicability and direct effect of Community law

*The distinction between direct applicability and direct effect*

The distinction between *direct applicability* and *direct effect* is essentially straightforward, although an element of confusion arises from time to time because some commentators – and even some courts, including the European Court of Justice itself – have been known to use both terms loosely, and even interchangeably.

The essence of the distinction is that a provision of Community law will be *directly applicable* if it becomes part of the law of a member state automatically. Thus, not only is there no need for member states to do anything to incorporate directly applicable provisions into their legal systems, but also there is no possibility of member states countermanding such provisions. On the other hand, a provision of Community law will be *directly effective* if, and only if, it creates rights which are enforceable by the courts of a member state at the instance of people who are aggrieved by breaches of the provision. In other words, the concept of *direct applicability* is concerned solely with the *reception* of Community law into the legal system of a member state, while the concept of *direct effect* deals with the more essentially practical question of the *enforceability* of Community law once reception has occurred.

At first sight, it may seem odd to say that something can be part of the law without being enforceable by the courts. In reality, however, the idea of law without enforceability is not uncommon. For example, in public law, a decision may be illegal, without anyone possessing the necessary standing (see page 33) to bring the matter before the court in order to seek an order establishing the illegality. Furthermore, and more commonly, some areas of law are *power-conferring* rather than *duty-imposing*, and therefore in their nature do not give rise to rights at all. For example, local authorities have a statutory power to adopt a scheme of licensing in respect of sex shops, but they are under no duty to do so. It follows, therefore, that a local authority that chooses not to adopt the scheme is not infringing anybody's legal rights. Similarly, anyone of full age and sound mind may make a will disposing of his property on his death, but nobody has the right to compel anyone else to make a will. Turning specifically to Community law for an example of direct applicability without direct effect, we need look no further than art. 234 [ex 177] EC (see page 78).

Returning to the main theme, however, while it would seem logical to say that *direct applicability* is a necessary precondition to *direct effect*, the cases on Directives and Decisions (see pages 83 and 85, respectively) show that the European Court of Justice will not withhold direct effect from these measures simply because the Treaty does not declare them to be directly applicable. Indeed, it can be said that the European Court of Justice has shown a marked tendency to regard direct effect as the norm rather than the exception. However, this proposition is subject to the purely practical consideration that a court cannot enforce something unless it knows precisely what it is being asked to enforce. Therefore a provision of Community law cannot be directly effective unless it is both clear and precise in its expression (so that national courts can know what it is they are being asked to enforce) and self-contained (in the sense that its implementation must not depend on the exercise of discretion by the public authorities of member states). For obvious reasons, these two qualities are known as the *criteria for direct effect*. However, one indication of the European Court of Justice's enthusiasm for promoting the effectiveness of Community law is that the whole of the provision in question does not need to satisfy the criteria for direct effect.

### 'Vertical' and 'horizontal' direct effect

Where a provision of Community law is enforceable against a member state in its own courts, the direct effect is said to be *vertical*, because a state is politically superior to its subjects. Where a provision of

Community law is enforceable by one person against another people in the courts of a member state, the direct effect is said to be *horizontal*, because, politically, all the subjects of a state are on the same level as each other.

### 5.5.4 Direct applicability and direct effect of different types of Community legislation and the *Francovich* doctrine

#### Treaty articles

The position in relation to treaty articles has been clear since the early days of the Community. In the leading case of *van Gend en Loos v Nederlandse Administratie der Belastingen* [1963] ECR 1, a Dutch company was aggrieved by a contravention of art. 12 of the EEC Treaty, which prohibited member states from 'introducing between themselves any new customs duties'. The question was whether the company could bring an action in the Dutch courts, in order to enforce art. 12 against the Dutch customs authorities. The European Court of Justice said:

> 'The wording of art. 12 contains a clear and unconditional prohibition which is not a positive but a negative obligation. This obligation, moreover, is not qualified by any reservation on the part of states which would make its implementation conditional upon a positive legislative measure enacted under national law. The very nature of this prohibition makes it ideally adapted to produce direct effects in the legal relationship between the member states and their subjects ...
>
> 'It follows ... that ... art. 12 must be interpreted as producing direct effects and creating individual rights which national courts must protect.'

In *van Gend en Loos* the direct effect was vertical, but the decision of the Court in *Defrenne v Sabena (No 2)* [1976] 2 CMLR 98 established that treaty provisions may also have horizontal direct effect.

*Defrenne* arose from the Belgian airline's practice of paying female flight attendants less than their male colleagues, despite the fact that both were doing identical jobs. Article 119 of the EEC Treaty required member states to ensure 'the application of the principle that men and women should receive equal pay for work of equal value'. Clearly, there could be cases where it would be very difficult to establish whether different types of work were nevertheless of equal value, and in these cases it may be that art. 119 would lack sufficient precision to enable national courts to enforce it. In *Defrenne*, however, it was obvious – and the airline did not dispute – that the work was identical and that the sex of the employees was the only reason for the differential rates of pay. Furthermore, the Court of Justice saw no reason why the inability of other employees to rely on the direct effect of art. 119 in more complicated cases should be used as a ground for denying Defrenne the right to do so.

## Regulations

Article 249 [ex 189] EC expressly provides that a Regulation 'shall have general application [and] ... shall be binding in its entirety and directly applicable in all member states'. In practice, subject to satisfying the criteria for direct effect (see page 81), Regulations will be both vertically and horizontally directly effective.

## Directives

Article 249 [ex 189] EC makes it plain that Directives are generically different from Regulations. A Directive is 'binding, as to the result to be achieved, upon each member state to which it is addressed, but shall leave to the national authorities the choice of form and methods'. It is clear, therefore, that the drafter of the Treaty envisaged Directives as being catalysts which would produce changes in the national legal systems of member states, rather than being themselves the vehicles of such changes. Two points arise from this.

First, the article does *not* make Directives *directly applicable*.

Secondly, as Directives are not directly applicable, it would appear that they lack the necessary precondition for direct effect. However, the European Court of Justice has approached this aspect of Directives in a singularly creative way.

The starting point is that it is obviously in the nature of Directives that a period of time must be allowed for implementation by the member states. The question then arises as to the consequences which should flow from a member state's failure to implement a Directive within the specified period of time. The answer to this question depends on the identity of the defendant.

In the German case of *Grad v Finanzamt Traustein* [1971] CMLR 1, the European Court of Justice said that, once the time for compliance had expired, a Directive which satisfied the criteria for direct effect could become directly effective against the member state which had failed to implement it. The Court took the view that any other result would amount to allowing member states to gain advantage from their own wrongdoing in failing to implement Directives. (For the presumption against deriving advantage from wrongdoing as a principle of English statutory interpretation, see page 322.) Furthermore, the Court took the view that this consideration outweighed the counter-argument that because the Treaty did not make Directives directly applicable, the necessary precondition to direct effect was lacking. Clearly, however, any argument based on preventing people from gaining advantage from their own wrongdoing cannot be used against defendants who have no power to introduce legislation to implement the Directive anyway, and who cannot therefore be regarded as being at fault. In other words, as the Court of Justice recognized in *Marshall v Southampton & South West Hampshire Area Health Authority* [1986] 1 CMLR 688, the direct effect of Directives can only ever be vertical, and never horizontal. Obviously, therefore, it becomes essential to know where Community law draws the line between defendants who count as being part of the member state for the present purposes, and those who are treated as being simply private individuals and organizations. The leading case of *Foster v British Gas plc* [1991] 2 WLR 258 established that the answer to this question lies in whether the member state has made the defendant responsible for providing a public service under the control of the state, as a result of which the defendant has acquired special powers beyond those resulting from the normal rules applicable in relationships between individuals. In *Foster* itself, British Gas plc was held to come within this category, as were health authorities in *Marshall* and local authorities in *R v London Boroughs Transport Committee ex parte Freight Transport Association Ltd and Others* [1991] 3 All ER 916. On the other hand, in *Doughty v Rolls-Royce plc* [1992] IRLR 126, a nationalized industry, which had not been made responsible for providing a public service under the control of the state, was held not to be within the category.

Despite the apparent attractiveness of the concept of vertical direct effect as a means of imposing liability on those member states who have defaulted on their Community obligations, the distinction between vertical and horizontal direct effect can create injustice in two ways. First, from the point of view of potential claimants, it is unfair that the availability of a remedy should depend upon the public or private status of the potential defendant. Secondly, from the point of view of potential defendants, the fundamental argument that vertical direct effect is necessary to prevent states from gaining advantage from their own wrongful inaction is not strictly relevant to other public bodies within the state, yet such bodies are clearly at risk from the vertical version of direct effect.

The Court of Justice has sought to eliminate this injustice by creating the principle of state liability, which is also known as the *Francovich* doctrine.

### The Francovich doctrine

In *Francovich v Italian State* [1991] IRLR 84, Italy had failed to implement a Directive which would have ensured that employees received any arrears of wages which were due if their employers became insolvent. In the absence of horizontal direct effect for Directives, and bearing in mind that the employers were insolvent anyway, the employees who were aggrieved in this case might appear to have had no effective remedy. However, the Court turned to the duty of member states, under art. 5 EC, to 'take all appropriate measures' to ensure compliance with their Community obligations. From this starting point, the Court took the view that it was inherent in the scheme of the Treaty that member states should pay compensation when they had failed to implement a Directive. However, this obligation was said to be subject to three conditions being satisfied: namely the Directive must confer rights on individuals, the content of those rights must be identifiable from the Directive, and there must be a causal link between the member state's failure and the claimant's loss.

The Court has subsequently developed the *Francovich* doctrine so that it applies to *any* breach of Community law, but has added the proviso that the breach must be 'sufficiently serious'. (See *Brasserie du Pêcheur v Germany* and *R v Secretary of State for Transport ex parte Factortame (No 4)* [1996] 2 WLR 506.) Total failure to implement a Directive is sufficiently serious (see *Dillenkofer v Germany* [1996] 3 CMLR 469), but faulty implementation, in good faith, of a Directive which is open to a variety of interpretations is not (see *R v.Her Majesty's Treasury ex parte British Telecommunications plc* [1996] 2 CMLR 217).

*Decisions*

For completeness, it is necessary to note that art. 249 [ex 189] EC provides that a Decision is 'binding in its entirety upon those to whom it is addressed, who may be either individuals or member states'. Although the article does not make Decisions directly applicable, the Court of Justice held in the *Grad* case (see page 83) that they were nevertheless capable of direct effect.

## 5.6  Indirect effect of Community law

Finally, it should be noted that, even where Community law lacks direct effect, it may still have an *indirect effect* through its impact on the interpretation of the laws of member states. The seminal case was *von Colson v Land Nordrhein-Westfalen* [1986] 2 CMLR 702, in which the European Court of Justice said that where national legislation has been enacted in order to implement a Directive, national courts must interpret that legislation, wherever it is possible to do so, 'in the light of the wording and the purpose of the Directive in order to achieve the result referred to in [the Treaty]'. Subsequently, in *Marleasing SA v La Comercial Internacional de Alimentación SA* [1992] 1 CMLR 305, the Court extended the *von Colson* principle, so that national courts must interpret *all* national law in accordance with Community law, wherever it is possible to do so, *even if the national legislation in question was not enacted specifically to comply with Community law.*

In practice, as we shall see in Part 3 of this book, the scope for interpretation will usually be so wide that conflicts between national law and Community law need seldom arise. However, the Court has recognized that the existence of the principle of state liability, deriving from the *Francovich* case (see page 84), may reduce the need to impose unduly strained interpretations on national law, without leaving claimants remediless. (See, for example, *Wagner Miret* [1995] 2 CMLR 469 and *Arcaro* [1997] 1 CMLR 179.)

## 5.7 European Community law and national sovereignty

### 5.7.1 Introduction

Our discussion of the nature of Community law, and its reception and enforcement within the courts of member states, has so far managed to avoid the crucial question of national sovereignty. At its simplest, the issue is: *does Community law prevail over inconsistent provisions of the national legal systems of member states?*

### 5.7.2 The Community Law view of national sovereignty

From the point of view of the Community, there can be no doubt that Community law does prevail over national law. In the seminal case of *van Gend en Loos* (see page 82), the Court said: 'The Community constitutes a new legal order ... for whose benefit the states have limited their sovereign rights'. Additionally, it is clear from *International Handelsgesellschaft mbH* [1974] 2 CMLR 540 that Community law prevails even in the face of the most fundamental constitutional doctrines of member states. The facts were that a German company challenged the validity of a Community Regulation on the basis that it infringed the principle of proportionality (see Chapter 15), which was a fundamental principle of the German Constitution. There was nothing in the Constitution to give primacy to Community law. On the merits of the case, the European Court of Justice decided that there had been no breach of the principle of proportionality, but the significance of the case lies in the force with which the Court of Justice stated that the validity of Community law cannot be judged by reference to national law:

'The law born from the Treaty [cannot] have the courts opposing to it rules of national law of *any nature whatsoever* ... the validity of a Community instrument or its effect within a member state cannot be affected by allegations that it strikes at either the fundamental rights as formulated in that state's constitution or the principles of a national constitutional structure.' (Emphasis added.)

### 5.7.3    The English view of sovereignty in the Community context

From the point of view of English law, the question can be very precisely stated. What is the impact of membership of the Community on the doctrine of the legislative supremacy of Parliament? Or, in other words, has the enactment of the European Communities Act 1972 disabled Parliament from passing subsequent statutes which would conflict with Community law? (For discussion of the problem of the self-bindingness of Parliament generally, see page 63.) The answer to this question lies in a series of cases which arose from a conflict between, on the one hand, certain provisions of the EC Treaty (which prohibited discrimination on the grounds of nationality) and, on the other hand, Part 2 of the Merchant Shipping Act 1998 (which provided that fishing boats which were registered in the United Kingdom, and which were fishing for quotas which the EC had allocated to the United Kingdom, must also be owned and managed by United Kingdom citizens).

When the matter reached the House of Lords (as *Factortame Ltd v Secretary of State for Transport (No 2)* [1991] 1 All ER 70), Lord Bridge dealt with the heart of the matter in a wholly pragmatic way:

'Some public comments on the decision of the Court of Justice, affirming the jurisdiction of the courts of member States to override national legislation if necessary to enable interim relief to be granted in protection of rights under Community law, have suggested that this was a novel and dangerous invasion by a Community institution of the sovereignty of the United Kingdom Parliament. But such comments are based on a misconception. If the supremacy within the European Community of Community law over the national law of member States was not always inherent in the EEC Treaty, it was certainly well established in the jurisprudence of the Court of Justice long before the United Kingdom joined the Community. Thus, whatever limitation of its sovereignty Parliament accepted when it enacted the European Communities Act 1972, it was entirely voluntary. Under the terms of the 1972 Act it has always been clear that it was the duty of a United Kingdom court, when delivering final judgment, to override any rule of national law found to be in conflict with any directly enforceable rule of Community law. Similarly, when decisions of the Court of Justice have exposed areas of United Kingdom law which failed to implement Council Directives, Parliament has always loyally accepted the obligation to make appropriate and prompt amendments. Thus there is nothing in any way novel in according supremacy to rules of Community law.'

Finally, it may be worth repeating the point (see page 62) that the doctrine of implied repeal cannot be invoked in order to argue that a subsequent, inconsistent, statute should prevail over the 1972 Act.

## Summary

- There are two European Communities, namely Euratom and the European Community (previously known as the European Economic Community). There is also the European Union. (The European Coal and Steel Community was dissolved in 2003, when its functions were transferred to the European Community.)

- The European *Community* is a legal entity. The European *Union* is a *political* entity, therefore it is more accurate to speak of *Community* law than *Union* law.

- The main function of the European Commission is to formulate policies.

- The main function of the Council of the European Union is to legislate.

- The European Parliament originated as a discussion chamber but it is developing a legislative role.

- The Communities' courts are the Court of Justice of the European Communities (commonly called the *European Court of Justice*, or *ECJ*), and the Court of First Instance (CFI).

- Community law was incorporated into English law by the European Communities Act 1972.

- To say that a provision of Community law is *directly applicable* means that it is automatically received into the legal systems of the member states.

- To say that a provision of Community law is *directly effective* means that it gives rise to rights which are enforceable by the courts of the member states.

- To say that a provision of Community law has *vertical* direct effect means that it is enforceable only against a member state. To say that a provision of European Community law has *horizontal* direct effect means that it is also enforceable by one person against another. The *Francovich* doctrine may impose liability on member states for breaches of their Community law obligations.

- Community law is said to be *indirectly effective* when it affects the interpretation of the law of member states.

- Where Community law conflicts with the law of member states, Community law prevails.

# Exercises

1   What are the two European Communities?

2   Identify the roles of the *Commission*, the *Council* and the *Parliament*.

3   Identify the leading cases on *direct applicability* and *direct effect*.

4   Why did the *Francovich* doctrine develop, and what does it provide?

5   What happens when Community law conflicts with the law of a member state?

# Chapter 6

# The protection of human rights and fundamental freedoms

## 6.1 Introduction

This chapter considers the ways in which English law seeks to deal with the protection of human rights and fundamental freedoms (a phrase which is usually abbreviated simply to 'human rights'). More particularly, it emphasizes the position under the Human Rights Act 1998, almost all of which came into force on 2 October 2000, although it had been possible to bring some provisions into force soon after the Act received the Royal Assent. (Delays in bringing statutes into force are common: see page 296.) However, by way of establishing the context within which the Act was passed, but without wishing to pre-empt Chapter 14's wider discussion of the suitability of the common law as a vehicle for law reform, it will be useful to begin by illustrating the less than wholly consistent way in which English law had previously protected human rights.

## 6.2 The English legal system and the protection of human rights before the Human Rights Act 1998

The common law is undoubtedly capable of protecting human rights. For example, in *R v Lord Chancellor ex parte Witham* [1997] 2 All ER 779, the Lord Chancellor, relying on powers conferred on him by the Supreme Court Act 1981 (and acting with the concurrence of the Lord Chief Justice, the Master of the Rolls, the Vice-Chancellor and the President of the Family Division), made certain rules which substantially increased court fees and removed an exemption for people on income support. Even though the new rules contained a power for the Lord Chancellor to reduce or remit the fees in individual cases of undue financial hardship, the High Court granted a declaration that he had exceeded his statutory powers, because the effect of the increases would be to exclude many people from access to the courts.

Unfortunately, the common law cannot always be relied upon to exercise its undoubted power to protect human rights. In *Malone v Metropolitan Police Commissioner (No 2)* [1979] 2 All ER 620, a man who had been convicted of handling stolen goods complained that the police had tapped his telephone during the investigation which led to his prosecution. Sir Robert Megarry V-C held that, in the absence of any lawful restriction on the activities of the police in this field, the telephone tap had been lawful, and was unwilling to find the existence of a right, merely in order to say that the police had infringed it:

'If the principles of English law, and not least analogies from the existing rules, together with the requirements of justice and commonsense, pointed firmly to such a right existing, then I think the court should not be deterred from recognizing the right.

'On the other hand, it is no function of the courts to legislate in a new field. The extension of the existing laws and principles is one thing, the creation of an altogether new right is another. At times judges must, and do, legislate; but as Holmes J once said, they do so only interstitially and with molecular rather than molar motions: see *Southern Pacific Co v Jensen* (1917) 244 US 205, in a dissenting judgment. Anything beyond that must be left for legislation. No new right in the law, fully-fledged with all the appropriate safeguards, can spring from the head of a judge deciding a particular case: only Parliament can create such a right ... Where there is some major gap in the law, no doubt a judge would be capable of framing what he considered to be a proper code to fill it; and sometimes he may be tempted. But he has to remember that his function is judicial, not legislative, and that he ought not to use his office to legislate in the guise of exercising his judicial powers.

'One of the factors that must be relevant in such a case is the degree of particularity in the right that is claimed. The wider and more indefinite the right claimed, the greater the undesirability of holding that such a right exists ... To create a right for one person, you have to impose a corresponding duty on another.'

Even within the factual context of a single case, the judges may disagree among themselves. In *R v Secretary of State for Social Security ex parte B and Another* [1996] 4 All ER 385, the Secretary of State had made certain regulations under the Social Security (Contributions and Benefits) Act 1992. The content of the regulations was such that some people, who would previously have been eligible for benefits while pursuing their claims to asylum under the Immigration and Asylum Appeals Act 1993, would be reduced, in the words of Simon Brown LJ, to 'a life so destitute that to my mind no civilized nation can tolerate it'. However, Neill LJ dissented, on the basis that the regulations had been aimed primarily at, and would impact principally upon, people who were not genuine asylum-seekers; and that although the regulations would 'also have a very serious effect on a considerable number of genuine asylum-seekers and those who might be hoping to obtain exceptional leave to remain', the Secretary of State had not crossed 'the threshold of illegality', bearing in mind both the 'objects to be achieved by the legislation and its results' and the need 'to strike a balance' in 'the allocation of the resources made available to him'.

Similarly, in *Fitzpatrick v Sterling Housing Association* [1997] 4 All ER 991 (CA); [1999] 4 All ER 705 (HL), which involved the right of the surviving partner of a homosexual relationship to inherit the tenancy of their home on the death of his partner, in whose name the tenancy had been held, both the Court of Appeal and the House of Lords were divided (by 2:1 and by 3:2 respectively) Subsequently, in the very similar case of *Ghaidan v Mendoza*, the House of Lords divided by 4:1. (These cases are discussed further at page 279, while the more specific issue raised in *Ghaidan*, namely the correct approach to interpretation in the light of s. 3 of the Human Rights Act 1998, is discussed at paragraph 20.7.)

Furthermore, even where the courts are prepared to countenance 'the extension of the existing laws and principles', there will commonly remain the linked problems of delay and uncertainty. In the words of Sedley J, when discussing the extent of the emerging common law duty to give reasons for decisions within the field of Public Law:

> 'No doubt the common law will develop, as the common law does, case by case. It is not entirely satisfactory that this should be so, not least because experience suggests that in the absence of a prior principle irreconcilable or inconsistent decisions will emerge. But from the tenor of the decisions principles will come, and if the common law's pragmatism has a virtue, it is that these principles are likely to be robust.' (*R v Higher Education Funding Council ex parte Institute of Dental Surgery* [1994] 1 All ER 651.)

An American commentator puts the matter thus:

> 'There are those who will wax quite eloquent on the byzantine beauty of what is sometimes called the common law method, one of reaching what instinctively seem the right results in a series of cases, and only later (if at all?) enunciating the principle that explains the pattern – a sort of connect-the-dots exercise.' (John Hart Ely, *Democracy and Distrust: A Theory of Judicial Review*, 1980, p. 54.)

Of course, the courts are not the only institutions which develop the law. More particularly, various statutes dealing with matters such as discrimination on the grounds of race, sex and disability demonstrate that Parliament can and does intervene in order to protect human rights. In practice, however, such statutory activity is also less than wholly consistent, often resulting from nothing more structured or principled than perceived political need.

Finally, the presumption of statutory interpretation that Parliament intends to legislate in accordance with the United Kingdom's international obligations, is capable of being used to protect human rights, but this topic is most appropriately considered under the next heading.

## 6.3 The European Convention for the Protection of Human Rights and Fundamental Freedoms

### 6.3.1 Introduction

The European Convention for the Protection of Human Rights and Fundamental Freedoms (the ECHR) was agreed in 1950 by the states of Western Europe, and came into force on 3 September 1953. (This date has symbolic significance as the anniversary of the outbreak of the Second World War.) Even though the United Kingdom was one of the first parties to ratify the ECHR, Parliament has never enacted any legislation to incorporate it into English law. (For the proposition that international agreements to which the United Kingdom is a party do not enter into domestic law in the absence of statute, see page 79; and for the relationship of the ECHR with English law after the Human Rights Act 1998, see most of the remainder of this chapter.)

Before considering the ECHR more closely, it is essential to note that it is a product of the *Council of Europe*, and *not* the *European Community*. More particularly, the judicial institution of the Council of Europe is the *European Court of Human Rights*, which sits at *Strasbourg*, and must not be confused with the *European Court of Justice*, which sits at *Luxembourg*. It cannot be emphasized too strongly, therefore, that the status of the European Community institutions and the supremacy of European Community law (see Chapter 5) are both irrelevant within the context of the ECHR (although Community law does recognize the protection of fundamental rights as one of the principles of Community law, and the ECHR is one of the bases of the European Union Charter of Fundamental Rights, which is discussed at page 230).

Judges of the Court are full-time, and are elected for periods of six years by the Parliamentary Assembly of the Council of Europe from lists of candidates submitted by the contracting parties, with the possibility of re-election (art. 23, ECHR). Candidates must be either eligible for 'appointment to high judicial office, or jurisconsults of recognized competence' (art. 24(1), ECHR). Judges sit as individuals, rather than as national representatives, and while in office 'shall not hold any position which is incompatible with their independence and impartiality as members of the Court' (art. 21(3), ECHR).

### 6.3.2 Interpretation

A well-established principle of international law, currently contained in art. 31 of the Vienna Convention on the Law of Treaties 1969, requires that a treaty 'shall be interpreted in good faith in accordance with the ordinary meaning to be given to the terms of the treaty in their context and in the light of its object and purpose'. The preamble to the ECHR not only makes it plain that its object and purpose are 'the maintenance and further realization of Human Rights and Fundamental Freedoms', but also recites the contracting states' 'profound belief ... [that] ... Fundamental Freedoms ... are ... best maintained on the one hand by an effective political democracy and on the other by a common understanding and observance of the human rights upon which they depend'. In accordance with art. 33(4) of the Vienna Convention, the authentic texts (which in the case of the ECHR are in English and French) must be construed in such a way as to 'reconcile them as far as possible', but where this is impossible, the decision in *Wemhoff v Federal Republic of Germany* (1979–80) 1 EHRR 55 shows that the 'object and purpose' will be decisive.

By way of illustration of this purposive (or teleological) approach to interpretation, in *Artico v Italy* (1980) 3 EHRR 1, the Court found a breach of the right to legal assistance under art. 6(3)(c) where a lawyer nominated to represent someone under a legal aid scheme never actually did so, because of ill-health and other professional commitments. The court held that the right could be satisfied only by *effective* legal assistance.

### 6.3.3 Precedent

In accordance with the civil law tradition of continental legal systems, the Court does not follow the doctrine of *binding* precedent. However, in practice 'it usually follows and applies its own precedents, such a course being in the interests of legal certainty and the orderly development of the Convention case-law', while being ready to depart where there are 'cogent reasons' for doing so, including the need to 'ensure that the interpretation of the Convention reflects societal changes and remains in line with present day conditions'. (See *Cossey v United Kingdom* (1990) 13 EHRR 622, in which the Court refused to depart from its decision in *Rees v United Kingdom* (1987) 9 EHRR 56, to the effect that the United Kingdom was entitled to refuse to allow transsexuals to have their birth certificates amended in order to show their acquired sex.)

Article 30 ECHR (see page 98) provides additional evidence of the Court's normal tendency to follow its own decisions.

Although the abolition of the Commission naturally means that there will be no more rulings from that body, its past rulings will continue to be an important part of case-law under the EHCR.

### 6.3.4    Some Convention case-law and some English responses

It is important to notice that, with the exception of the prohibition of torture or inhuman or degrading treatment or punishment by art. 3, the rights and freedoms are all subject to some kind of limitation or qualification. Of particular interest in this respect are arts 8 to 11, which may all be restricted by law to such extent as is 'necessary in a democratic society' for the reasons set out in each of the articles. It is useful to notice, therefore, that in *Dudgeon v United Kingdom* (1982) 4 EHRR 149, where homosexual relationships were said to fall within the category of private life (rather than family life), the court identified 'tolerance and broad-mindedness' as two of the 'hallmarks' of a democratic society. What may 'be necessary in a democratic society' will, of course, be a question for the court in each case, but some indication of its scope can nevertheless be given.

For example, in *Handyside v United Kingdom* (1979–80) 1 EHRR 737, while upholding the law relating to the forfeiture of obscene publications the Court said that 'while the adjective "necessary" … is not synonymous with "indispensable", neither has it the flexibility of such expressions as "admissible", "ordinary", "useful", "reasonable" or "desirable"'. More positively, in *Olsson v Sweden* (1988) 11 EHRR 259, while finding that there was no basis in the then current state of Swedish law for the practice of social workers of restricting parental access to children who were in the care of public authorities, the Court said:

> 'According to the court's established case-law, the notion of necessity implies that an interference corresponds with a *pressing social need* and, in particular, that it is *proportionate* to the legitimate aim pursued.' (Emphasis added.)

In practice, this test clearly requires the application of both the doctrine of *proportionality* (to which it explicitly refers) and the doctrine of the *margin of appreciation*.

Taking these in turn, the doctrine of proportionality is not only commonplace in the domestic legal systems of continental Europe, but is also one of the principles of *Community* law (see page 226), and therefore it is hardly surprising that it has been incorporated into *Convention* law as well. At its simplest, the doctrine merely requires that the means which are used must be proportionate to the ends which are to be achieved.

The problem which this approach poses for the English courts is that one of their traditional bases for determining whether executive decision-making is lawful has been the test of whether the decision is so unreasonable that no reasonable decision-maker could have made it. In other words, the courts allow decision-makers a considerable degree of latitude, which, in turn, excuses the courts from adjudicating on the correctness of the decision. Although it is clear that, in practice, the overall test of unreasonableness may be applied with varying degrees of intensity (so that, for example, decisions which adversely affect human rights are more difficult to justify than those which do not do so, as evidenced by *R v Ministry of Defence ex parte Smith* [1996] 1 All ER 257, where homosexuals had been discharged from the armed forces simply becasue of their sexual orientation), it is equally clear that the test of proportionality makes it practically impossible for the courts to avoid making explicit judgments about the appropriateness of executive decisions.

The difficulty which this causes was well captured in *Brind v Secretary of State for the Home Department* [1991] 1 All ER 720, where Lord Lowry said that 'there can be very little room for judges to operate an independent judicial review proportionality doctrine in the space which is left between the conventional judicial review doctrine and the admittedly forbidden appellate approach'. (The distinction between *appeal* and *review* is discussed at page 33.) However, in the light of the 1998 Act, it is clear that, in some cases at least, the judges will have no option but to become involved in this way. This means that, for the first time, they will have to work out the basis on which to do so. Two cases are particularly instructive.

In the Privy Council case of *de Freitas v Permanent Secretary of Ministry of Agriculture, Fisheries, Lands and Housing* [1999] 1 AC 69, Lord Clyde said that a court should ask itself:

> 'Whether: (i) the legislative objective is sufficiently important to justify limiting a fundamental right; (ii) the measures designed to meet the legislative objective are rationally connected to it; and (iii) the means used to impair the right or freedom are no more than is necessary to accomplish the objective.'

These observations were expressly approved by Lord Steyn in *R (Daly) v Secretary of State for the Home Department* [2001] 2 WLR 1622, who continued:

> 'The starting point is that there is an overlap between the traditional grounds of review and the approach of proportionality. Most cases would be decided in the same way whichever approach is adopted. But the intensity of review is somewhat greater under the proportionality approach.'

He proceeded to offer 'a few generalisations':

> 'First, the doctrine of proportionality may require the reviewing court to assess the balance which the decision maker has struck, not merely whether

it is within the range of rational or reasonable decisions. Secondly, the proportionality test may go further than the traditional grounds of review inasmuch as it may require attention to be directed to the relative weight accorded to interests and considerations. Thirdly, even the heightened scrutiny test developed in *R v Ministry of Defence ex parte Smith* ... is not necessarily appropriate to the protection of human rights ...'

More particularly:

'The intensity of review, in similar cases, is guaranteed by the twin requirements that the limitation of the right was necessary in a democratic society, in the sense of meeting a pressing social need, and the question whether the interference was really proportionate to the legitimate aim being pursued.'

Turning to the concept of the *margin of appreciation*, in *Handyside* the Court said:

'By reason of their direct and continuous contact with the vital forces of their countries, state authorities are in principle in a better position than the international judge to give an opinion on the ... "neccesity" of a "restriction" or "penalty" ... It is for the national authorities to make the initial assessment of the reality of the pressing social need ...

'Consequently art. 10(2) leaves to the contracting states a margin of appreciation. This margin is given both to the domestic legislator ("prescribed by law") and to the bodies, judicial amongst others, that are called upon to interpret and apply the laws in force.

'Nevertheless, [the Convention] does not give the contracting states an unlimited power of appreciation. The court, which ... is responsible for ensuring those states' engagements, is empowered to give the final ruling on whether a "restriction" or "penalty" is reconcilable with [a Convention right or freedom] ... The domestic margin of appreciation thus goes hand in hand with a European supervision. Such supervision concerns both the aim of the measure challenged and its "necessity"; it covers not only the basic legislation but also the decision applying it, even one given by an independent court.'

In other words, the European Court of Human Rights recognizes the existence of an area of discretion which it leaves entirely to national legal systems. Therefore the court may be said to be exercising a supervisory jurisdiction, similar to that exercised by the English courts in judicial review.

Finally, although the meaning of the rather odd phrase 'margin of appreciation' has become clear, the phrase itself is 'a solecism originating in the literal rendering in the English text of the decision in *Handyside v UK* ... of the French phrase 'marge d'appréciation', meaning margin of appraisal or judgment'. (See the joint judgment of Thorpe and Sedley LJJ in *Evans v Amicus Healthcare Ltd* [2004] EWCA 727, [2004] 3 All ER 1025.)

### 6.3.5　Procedure

Originally, there was an institution of the Council of Europe known as the European Commission on Human Rights. The Commission gave initial consideration to allegations of breaches of the ECHR, and in some cases referred the matter to the Court. However, the Eleventh Protocol to the ECHR, which came into force in November 1998, abolished the Commission and introduced a two-stage procedure, beginning with a preliminary scrutiny by a committee of three judges, whose function is to decide whether a complaint is admissible and whether a friendly settlement is possible (art. 27(1) ECHR). A case which survives this filtering process will then proceed to a Chamber of seven judges, who will normally, provided they themselves are satisfied as to admissibility, determine it (art. 27(2) ECHR). Exceptionally, however, and provided the parties agree, a seven-judge Chamber may refer a case to a Grand Chamber of seventeen judges, provided that either it raises a serious question affecting the interpretation of the Convention or its protocols, or there is the prospect of the decision deviating from a previous decision of the Court (art. 30, ECHR). Clearly, the second ground reinforces the proposition that the Court will normally follow its own decisions, even though it is never, strictly speaking, bound to do so. (For further comment on the Court's attitude to precedent, see the previous section.)

### 6.3.6　Remedies

The principal remedy is merely a declaratory judgment that a breach of the Convention has occurred, but the Court may also award compensation. Although by art. 46(1) ECHR the contracting parties have undertaken to abide by the judgments of the Court to which they are parties, there is no enforcement mechanism. The Human Rights Act 1998 does not give art. 46 any status in English law, and therefore compliance with the judgments of the Court will continue to be strictly voluntary, although there will almost always be good political reasons for complying promptly and with good grace.

### 6.3.7　The English presumption of compliance with international law

There is a presumption that Parliament intends to legislate in accordance with the United Kingdom's international obligations, and this clearly requires the courts to have regard to any relevant international conventions when seeking to resolve ambiguities of statutory wording (see page 320). However, this presumption has had only limited success in protecting human rights.

In *Brind v Secretary of State for the Home Department* [1991] 1 All ER 720, where the freedom of expression of television journalists was restricted by certain directives issued by the Secretary of State, the House of Lords refused to say that the presumption of statutory interpretation justified a finding that the Secretary of State had acted unlawfully in exercising an *administrative discretion* without having had regard to the ECHR. More particularly, Lord Bridge, having acknowledged the existence of the presumption, said:

> 'But where Parliament has conferred on the executive an administrative discretion without indicating the precise limits within which it must be exercised, to presume that it must be exercised within Convention limits would be to go far beyond the resolution of ambiguity. It would be to impute to Parliament an intention not only that the executive should exercise the discretion in conformity with the Convention, but also that the domestic courts should enforce that conformity by the importation into domestic administrative law of the text of the Convention and the jurispruduence of the European Court of Human Rights in the interpretation and application of it ... When Parliament has been content for so long to leave those who complain that their Convention rights have been infringed to seek their remedy in Strasbourg, it would be surprising suddenly to find that the judiciary had, without Parliament's aid, the means to incorporate the Convention into such an important area of domestic law and I cannot escape the conclusion that this would be a judicial usurpation of the legislative function.'

However, some judges have been able to identify circumstances which justify disregarding the restrictive approach exemplified by *Brind*. The classic example is *R v Secretary of State for the Home Department and Another ex parte Norney and Others* (1995) 7 Admin LR 861, where the administrative discretion in question had been conferred by a statute that had been passed to bring English law on prisoners' rights into line with the ECHR. Dyson J said that, despite the decision in *Brind*, in the present circumstances it would be perverse for the court to ignore the relevant Convention provision. (As we saw at page 71, a prisoner's application for judicial review was also successful in *R v Parole Board and Another ex parte Wilson* (1992) 4 Admin LR 525, but on a somewhat different basis.)

In *Derbyshire County Council v Times Newspapers Ltd* [1993] 1 All ER 1011, both the Court of Appeal and the House of Lords agreed that a local authority cannot sue for libel, but differed in their opinion of the relevance of the Convention. Emphasizing that the public interest in freedom of speech outweighed the local authority's interest in protecting its own reputation, Lord Keith, with whom the other Law Lords agreed, said:

'It is of the highest public importance that a democratically elected governmental body, or indeed any governmental body, should be open to uninhib-
ited public criticism. The threat of a civil action for defamation must
inevitably have an inhibiting effect on freedom of speech.

'The conclusion must be, in my opinion, that under the common law of
England a local authority does not have the right to maintain an action of
damages for defamation. That was the conclusion reached by the Court of
Appeal, which did so principally by reference to art.10 of the European
Convention on Human Rights ... My Lords, I have reached my conclusion
upon the common law of England without finding any need to rely upon the
European Convention.'

## 6.4  The Human Rights Act 1998

### 6.4.1  The aims of the Act

According to the White Paper which accompanied the Bill which became the Human Rights Act 1998, the aims of the Act are four-fold. First,
United Kingdom citizens should be able to have their rights under the
ECHR protected in United Kingdom courts by United Kingdom judges.
Secondly, by eliminating the need to go to Strasbourg, the protection of
rights under the ECHR should become both quicker and cheaper.
Thirdly, United Kingdom judges should be able (in the words of para.
1.14 of the White Paper) to 'make a distinctively British contribution to
the development of human rights in Europe'. Finally, there should be
closer scrutiny of the human rights implications of new legislation and
policies.

### 6.4.2  How the Act achieves its aims

#### Introduction

The first point which must be made is that, in the words of Lord Clyde,
'the Act did not incorporate the rights set out in the Convention into the
domestic laws of the United Kingdom'. (*R v Lambert* [2001] 3 WLR 206.)
Instead, it adopts a much more subtle and sophisticated approach, as a
result of which the content of the ECHR is very largely enforceable in
the English courts, while the constitutional principle of the legislative
supremacy of Parliament remains intact.

#### The concept of 'Convention rights'

The scheme of the Act depends on the core concept of 'Convention
rights', which s. 1(1) of the Act defines as meaning:

'the rights and fundamental freedoms set out in –

(a) articles 2 to 12 and 14 of the Convention, and
(b) articles 1 to 3 of the First Protocol, and
(c) articles 1 and 2 of the Sixth Protocol,

as read with articles 16 to 18 of the Convention.'

The relevant articles and protocols are set out in full, as Appendix 3 (at pages 351–6) but may be summarized as follows:

art. 2    the right to life;
art. 3    prohibition of torture or inhuman or degrading treatment or punishment;
art. 4    prohibition of slavery and forced labour;
art. 5    the right to liberty and security of the person;
art. 6    the right to a fair trial;
art. 7    freedom from the imposition of retrospective criminal liability and punishment;
art. 8    the right to respect for private and family life;
art. 9    freedom of religion;
art. 10   freedom of expression;
art. 11   freedom of assembly and association;
art. 12   the right to marry and found a family;
art. 14   prohibition of discrimination in enjoyment of rights under the Convention.

*First Protocol*
art. 1    the right to property;
art. 2    the right to education;
art. 3    the right to free elections.

*Sixth Protocol*
arts 1 & 2 prohibition of the death penalty.

Pausing only to notice that both art. 1 (which requires the contracting states to 'secure to everyone within their jurisdiction the [substantive] rights and freedoms' guaranteed by the Convention) and art. 13 (which requires the provision of 'an effective remedy before a national authority') were omitted on the ground that their inclusion would have been superfluous, it must be said that s. 1(2) makes the operation of these articles subject to derogations and reservations. More particularly, Schedule 3 to the Act contains derogations, notified to the Council of Europe in 1988 and 1989, and a reservation, notified in 1952. The derogations permit the United Kingdom to fail to comply in certain detailed respects with the Convention where non-compliance is considered to be justified by terrorist activity connected with the affairs of Northern Ireland, while the reservation is that the United Kingdom accepts the principle of respect for the right of parents to ensure that their children are educated 'in conformity with their own religious and philosophical convictions' (see page 356 ) 'only so far as it is compatible with the provision of efficient instruction and training, and the avoidance of unreasonable public expenditure'.

### The judicial duty to take case-law under the Convention into account

Section 2 of the Act provides that any court or tribunal which has to determine any question in relation to a Convention right 'must take into account' the case-law which has developed under the Convention. At first sight, the obligation merely to 'take into account' Convention case-law may seem less than whole-hearted, particularly when seen in the context of the judicial approach to an almost identical form of statutory words, which required local planning authorities to 'have regard to' their own planning policies when determining applications for planning permission. In *Simpson v Edinburgh Corporation* 1961 SLT 17, Lord Guest took these words at face value, expressly declining to say that they required the authorities to 'slavishly adhere' to those policies. However, it was always likely that, in the light of the context and purpose of the 1998 Act, the courts would take a stricter view of the obligation imposed by s. 2, and indeed in *R (Alconbury Developments Ltd) v Secretary of State for the Environment, Transport and the Regions* [2001] 2 WLR 1389, Lord Slynn, while acknowledging that decisions of the European Court of Human Rights were not binding on English courts, nevertheless said:

> 'In the absence of some special circumstances it seems to me that the court should follow any clear and constant jurisprudence of the European Court of Human Rights. If it does not do so, there is a least a possibility that the case will go to that court, which is likely in the ordinary case to follow its own constant jurisprudence.'

Similarly, in *R (Anderson) v Secretary of State for the Home Department* [2002] UKHL 46, [2002] 4 All ER 1089, Lord Bingham also emphasized that the House of Lords would require a 'good reason' to 'depart from the principles laid down in a carefully considered judgment of the [European] Court [of Human Rights] sitting as a Grand Chamber'. (A sitting of the Court as a Grand Chamber consists of 17 judges rather than the usual seven.)

However, while Lord Slynn's view clearly reflects the realities of precedent in the European Court of Human Rights (see page 94), and while Lord Bingham's view recognizes the additional weight to be given to a larger than usual bench, both are only statements of general principle. Accordingly, an English court may choose to remind itself that, with the exception of s. 6 (see page 104), the Act does not make Convention case-law binding within the English legal system. For

example, in *Gough and Another v Chief Constable of Derbyshire* [2001] 4 All
ER 289, although the court made a decision in accordance with Convention case-law, Laws LJ, with the concurrence of Poole J, went out of his
way to say that 'our duty is to take account of the Strasbourg jurisprudence, not necessarily to apply it'.

Furthermore, in *Myles v Director of Public Prosecutions* [2004] EWHC
594 (Admin), [2004] 2 All ER 902, the High Court emphasized that
where there was a conflict between decisions of the courts of other
Convention states on the one hand and the English courts on the other,
the English authorities were to be given decisive weight.

In *Kay v Lambeth London Borough Council* [2006] UKHL 10, [2006] 4 All
ER 128, the House of Lords held that, except in extreme circumstances,
other English courts should follow decisions of the House rather than
later, conflicting, decisions of the European Court of Human Rights.
The doctrine of the margin of appreciation (see page 97), enables this
approach to promote certainty in English law, while the possibility of an
appeal takes Convention case-law into account.

## Interpretation and validity of legislation

Section 3(1) imposes what has come to be known as 'the interpretative
obligation', namely that:

> 'so far as it is possible to do so, primary and subordinate legislation must be
> read and given effect in a way which is compatible with the Convention
> rights.'

Section 3(2) provides that s. 3(1) applies to all legislation enacted at any
time, and the provision is, therefore, retrospective to the extent that it
does not apply merely to post-Act legislation. Pausing only to comment
that the Act's retrospectivity in relation to matters of *fact* will be discussed below, it must be emphasized that s. 3(2) also provides that s. 3(1)
does not affect the *validity* of any *primary* legislation, nor of *delegated*
legislation made under a parent Act containing a provision to that
effect. (In practice, *primary legislation* almost always means Acts of
Parliament, although it may also mean certain exercises of the royal
prerogative. As we saw at page 68, *subordinate legislation* is simply
another form of words for *delegated legislation*.) On the assumption that
primary legislation made in exercise of the royal prerogative is unlikely
to be encountered, and that parent Acts containing exempting provisions will be extremely rare in practice, the practical effect of these
provisions is, therefore, to introduce a new principle of interpretation
while respecting constitutional orthodoxy in respect of both the legislative supremacy of Parliament and the quashability of delegated

legislation. (In passing, it may be useful to recall that experience in relation to Community law has shown that English courts are generally able to construe legislation in such a way as to be compatible with some other scheme of things when they are required to do so.)

The question of how far the courts can legitimately go when identifying 'possible' interpretations, in order to achieve compliance with Convention rights, is discussed at page 325, but assuming for the moment that compliance with the interpretative obligation is possible in a specific case, it may take one of two forms. First, it may amount simply to a compatible interpretation in that case. Secondly, it may amount to a general statement as to how the provision in question should be interpreted. However, the second alternative will be relatively rare, because, as Lord Hope said, in *R v A (No 2)*, 'it would only be if there was a material risk of incompatibility ... in *all* such cases that it would be appropriate to lay down a rule of *general* application as to how ... [the incompatible provision] ... ought to be read ...' (Original emphasis.)

Finally, in *Ghaidan v Mendoza* [2004] 3 All ER 411, the House of Lords emphasized that Parliament had intended the interpretative obligation to be the principal means of protecting Convention rights; and that declarations of incompatibility (see immediately below) were intended to be used only as a last resort.

### Declarations of incompatibility

Although the Act contains nothing to diminish the legislative supremacy of Parliament, s. 4 does give a court at (or above) the level of the High Court the power to make declarations of incompatibility where primary legislation conflicts with Convention rights.

Declarations of incompatibility have no effect on the cases in which they are made, nor on the continuing validity and operation of the statutes in respect of which they are made. However, under s. 10 of the Act, they may result in the provisions being amended or repealed by remedial orders. (Remedial orders will typically take the form of delegated legislation, in order to avoid the pressures on time which beset the government's legislative programme and which are discussed in Chapter 17. However, where the declaration of incompatibility relates to an Order in Council made in exercise of the royal prerogative, the remedial order may be in the form of a further Order in Council made in the same way.) The section also provides that remedial orders may be made where the incompatibility of English law is identified by the European Court of Human Rights.

Finally, it is worth repeating the point which was made when discussing the interpretative obligation under s. 3 of the Act (above), that declarations of incompatibility are intended to be used only as a last resort.

### The duty imposed on public authorities

Section 6 of the Act makes it unlawful for a public authority (which is defined as *excluding* both Houses of Parliament but as *including* courts and tribunals, as well as 'any person certain of whose functions are functions of a public nature') to act in a way which is incompatible with Convention rights. (The meaning of the phrase 'functions of a public nature' is being worked out on a case-by-case basis, in true common law fashion.) The effect of s. 7 of the Act is that a person who wishes to establish that there has been a breach of the duty under s. 6, may do so proactively by claiming judicial review, or reactively by way of defence to proceedings brought by, or at the instigation of, the public authority.

### Statements of compatibility

Under s. 19 of the Act, which came into force on 24 November 1999 (almost a year before the bulk of the Act came into force), Ministers who are in charge of Bills in either House of Parliament must, before the Second Reading of the Bill, state either that in their view there is no incompatiblity with Convention rights, or that they wish the House to proceed in the absence of such a statement. The latter alternative is unlikely to arise, although it may do so. (See, for example the Parliamentary proceedings which resulted in the passage of the Communications Act 2003.) While the courts may refer to a Ministerial statement of compatibility when interpreting a statute (see *Pepper v Hart* [1993] 1 All ER 42, discussed at pages 303–6), they will do so only with caution. As Lord Hope said, in *R v A (No 2)* (above), having commented approvingly on counsel's decision not to rely on a statement of compatibility:

> 'These statements may serve a useful purpose in Parliament. They may also be seen as part of the parliamentary history, indicating that it was not Parliament's intention to cut across a Convention right ... No doubt they are based on the best advice that is available. But they are no more than expressions of opinion by the Minister. They are not binding on the court, nor do they have any persuasive authority.'

### 6.4.3   Is the Act retrospective as to matters of fact?

Although, as we saw at page 103, s. 3(2) of the Act clearly provides that the interpretative obligation imposed by s. 3(1) applies to pre-Act statutes, the Act makes only one express provision relating to its own retrospectivity as to matters of fact. More particularly, the combined effect of s. 7(1)(b) and s. 22(4) is that where a public authority acted in breach of a Convention right before the Act came into force, and legal proceedings are subsequently brought by, or at the instigation of, that authority, the defence may rely on the breach of the Convention right even though the breach of the Convention right occurred before the 1998 Act came into force.

A particular problem in relation to retrospectivity arose in *R v Lambert* [2001] 3 WLR 206. A majority in the House of Lords held that where both the facts and the hearing of any case arising from those facts, occurred before the Act came into force, any subsequent appeal against that decision which is heard now the Act is in force, must be determined in accordance with the pre-Act position. Although this conclusion may be thought to be no more than an application of the presumption against retrospectivity in statutory interpretation (see page 308), Lord Steyn dissented on the basis that public authorities (including the courts) are under a duty to act compatibly with Convention rights, and therefore the appellate court must do so. On this basis, the fact that the previous court was not subject to the duty is nothing to the point. The sequel to *Lambert* came quickly in the form of *R v Kansal (No 2)* [2002] 1 All ER 257, where a majority of the House held that *Lambert* had indeed been wrongly decided, although they decided to follow it because it represented a possible view of the law and there were no compelling reasons to depart from it. (The proposition that the House of Lords may choose to follow a decision which it considers to be wrong is discussed at page 177.)

### 6.4.4 The *vertical* and *horizontal* effect of the Act

The fact that the Human Rights Act places a duty on public authorities to act in a way which is compatible with Convention rights, without imposing a similar duty on anyone else, might seem to make the Act enforceable only against the state and its emanations, or to use the terminology which has developed in relation to *Community* law (see page 81), *vertically* but *not horizontally*. Furthermore, this view might appear to be supported by a contribution which the Lord Chancellor made to the Committee stage in the House of Lords, when he said that 'the Convention had its origins in a desire to protect people from the misuse of power by the state, rather than from the actions of individuals' and therefore s. 6 of the Act 'does not impose a liability on organizations which have no public functions at all.' (HL Deb, November 13, 1997, cols 1231–1232.)

However, some eleven days later, he produced a more refined version:

> 'We ... believe that it is right as a matter of principle for the courts to have the
> duty of acting compatibly with the Convention not only in cases involving

other public authorities but also in developing the common law in deciding cases between individuals.' (HL Deb, November 24, 1997, col 783.)

Reading these two statements carefully, it is clear that the Lord Chancellor's view was that there is nothing in the Act to create any new causes of action against private individuals and organizations; and, therefore, borrowing the terminology of *Community* law again, the Act has no horizontal *direct* effect. On the other hand, the status of the courts as public authorities means that they have a duty to develop *existing* causes of action in the light of Convention rights. In other words, the intention was that in cases brought against private individuals and organizations, any relevant Convention rights would (borrowing the terminology of Community law yet again) have horizontal *indirect* effect. Furthermore, the courts have agreed that this was not only the intention of the Act but also its effect (see, for example, *Douglas v Hello Ltd (No 3)* [2005] EWCA Civ 596, [2005] 4 All ER 128).

It remains to be seen whether, as time goes by, some judges may acquire a taste for the kind of creativity which the Act already requires them to exercise, and may decide that their power to develop the common law does, after all, extend to the creation of new causes of action. In other words, the Act may still be held to have *horizontal* direct effect.

## Summary

▶ Historically, English law has shown itself capable of protecting human rights, but it has not always done so effectively.

▶ The Human Rights Act 1998 does not incorporate the European Convention on Human Rights into English law, but does, to a large extent, make most of the rights under the Convention enforceable in English courts, while fully respecting the legislative supremacy of Parliament.

## Exercise

How does the Human Rights Act 1998 seek to achieve the effective protection of human rights without affecting the legislative supremacy of Parliament?

# Chapter 7

# Finding, citing and using the sources of law

## 7.1 Introduction

When you are looking for the law you will usually use textbooks, periodicals, law reports and statutes, in either paper or electronic form. This chapter examines each of these in turn, as well as providing a brief overview of some of the more readily accessible sources of Community law and materials on the European Convention on Human Rights.

One point of general application may, however, usefully be made at the outset. Sometimes the date in a law report reference is in square brackets, and sometimes it is in round ones, as in [1973] 2 All ER 97 and (1989) 155 JP 494. The difference is vitally important. A date in square brackets is an essential part of the reference: there has been a volume 2 of the *All England Law Reports* every year since the series started in 1936, and each of those volumes has had a page 97. It follows that the bare reference 2 All ER 97 is useless. On the other hand, a date in round brackets is not an essential element of the reference. For example, the *Justice of the Peace Reports* first appeared in 1837 and have been numbered annually, on a serial basis, ever since. It follows that 155 JP 494 is a perfectly adequate reference to enable you to find the report. In practice, however, it is common to use the date as well, because it may be useful to know at a glance whether the case is old, middle-aged or recent, as well as being able to identify its chronological relationship with other decisions on the same subject matter.

As a rule of thumb, the square bracket style is the more modern, but occasionally new series start on a serially numbered basis (see, for example, *Administrative Law Reports*, which first appeared in 1989). Also as a rule of thumb, the square bracket style will apply if the volume number is 1, 2, 3 or 4. It will be obvious, however, that this principle is not infallible, because even the serially numbered volumes started somewhere, and therefore have volume numbers of 1 to 4.

The same distinction between square and round brackets applies to references to periodicals. For example, the annual volumes of the *Law Quarterly Review* are serially numbered, but those of *Public Law* are not.

## 7.2 Conventions in case names

The usual convention in case names is that the name of the party who is initiating the current stage of the proceedings will be placed first. So if Smith is suing Jones for breach of contract, the case will be *Smith v Jones*. If Smith loses and appeals, the case will still be *Smith v Jones* on appeal. However, if Jones loses and appeals, the case will become *Jones v Smith* on appeal. There are two principal exceptions to the usual convention.

First, the modern practice in the House of Lords is for the case name to revert to whatever form it had at first instance, irrespective of who is the appellant. Secondly, in criminal law case names are usually given in the form of *R v Smith*, whether at first instance or on appeal. (The *R* stands for either *Rex* or *Regina*, depending upon the sex of the monarch at the time of the case.)

Additionally, some proceedings give rise to case names in special forms. One of the most common examples is judicial review, where historically the application to the court was made by the Crown on behalf of the real applicant. Although this is now pure fiction, the case names still reflect the original practice. Thus, before the introduction of Part 54, Civil Procedure Rules, on 2 October 2000, judicial review case names took the form of (for example) *R v Secretary of State for Whatever ex parte Smith*. Since the introduction of Part 54, this form has changed to *R (on the application of Smith) v Secretary of State for Whatever*, which, in practice, often becomes *R (Smith) v Secretary of State for Whatever*. Other exceptional usages include cases involving ships, which are sometimes given the ship's name, as in *The Skylark*. Similarly, cases involving the estate of someone who has died are often given the name of the deceased, preceded by the word 'Re', which means 'in the matter of'. So if Smith has died, a case dealing with the estate may be reported as *Re Smith*. A similar form is often used when cases deal with the welfare of children, except that the convention there is to use only an initial, as, for example, in *Re J S (A Minor)* [1980] 1 All ER 1061 (see page 41), in order to preserve anonymity.

Despite the existence of broadly understood conventions, the naming of cases is neither a precise science nor a highly developed art. Accordingly, it is not uncommon to find the editors of different series of law reports giving different names to the same case. References to such a case may indicate what has happened by using the abbreviation *sub nom* (meaning *sub nomine*, or 'under the name of'). For example, you may encounter the following: *Ellerman Lines Ltd v Murray* [1930] All ER Rep 503, *sub nom The Croxteth Hall, The Celtic* 47 TLR 147. In this example, the editor of one series has used the names of the parties, while another has used the names of the ships involved in the case.

## 7.3 Textbooks and periodicals

The use of textbooks and periodicals raises the question of whether statements made by authors can be cited as authoritative pronouncements of what the law actually is. The traditional answer to this question falls fairly neatly into two parts, which may conveniently be labelled ancient and modern.

Starting with the ancient authors, there is a select band from Glanvill in the 12th century to Blackstone in the 18th century, and including Bracton, Fitzherbert, Littleton, Coke, Hale, Hawkins and Foster on the way. Historically, the courts were willing to treat these authors' statements of law as being authentic and therefore binding. Even in modern times, when the works of these authors are all very old, the courts may speak in terms which seem to indicate that the writings of certain authors are authoritative sources of law. For example, in the case of *Reid v Metropolitan Police Commissioner* [1973] 2 All ER 97, which raised a nice point of law concerning the ownership of stolen goods which had subsequently been sold to a third party, Lord Denning MR felt it necessary 'to go back to the works of Sir Edward Coke'.

Two points must be made here. First, the ancient authors did not always agree with each other, thus leaving the court with the task of choosing between them. To find an example of this in practice it is necessary to do no more than return to the decision in *Reid*, where Lord Denning MR concluded, for various reasons, that the court 'should follow the words of Sir Edward Coke rather than those of Sir William Blackstone'. Secondly, it will be very seldom that works which are anything from 200 to 800 years old will be found to contain statements of law which are relevant to modern conditions, and yet have escaped entering the more formally established canon of legal sources, namely case-law and statute.

The most balanced view of the status of the ancient authors, therefore, is that, although their works were originally treated as being authoritative, and may still be treated with considerable respect, they will certainly not be binding on a modern court. Nevertheless, a modern court may treat their works as being excellent evidence of what the law was at the time when they were writing, and the court may (or may not) choose to infer that the law is still the same today.

One significant factor in the decline in the importance of the ancient authors was that the reliability of law reports improved significantly during the 19th century, thus reducing the need to rely on the old works. Additionally, as the rate of social and economic change accelerated, those works became increasingly out of touch with the needs of contemporary society, and in any event statutes became the major source of law. Thus the formerly authoritative textbooks came to have no more than persuasive value in the task of identifying the law.

Turning to modern authors, the very fact that they are contemporary was initially held against them. In *Greenlands (Limited) v Wilmshurst and Others* (1913) 29 TLR 685, Vaughan Williams LJ said:

'No doubt Mr Odger's book [on the law of libel] is a most admirable work, which we all use, but I think we ought in this Court still to maintain the old idea that counsel are not entitled to quote living authors as authorities for a proposition they are putting forward, but they may adopt the author's statements as part of their argument.'

Two points may be made. First, the distinction between citing a statement as authority and merely incorporating it into an argument may be too fine to be discernible. Secondly, the view that simply being alive intrinsically disqualifies authors from being authoritative rests on the fact that living authors can change their minds as to what they think the law is, whereas dead ones clearly cannot do so. The transparently unconvincing nature of this argument becomes obvious if we compare authors with judges. Judicial pronouncements are clearly treated as being sources of law, despite the fact that individual judges can – and do – change their minds, as we shall shortly see in the context of *R v Shivpuri* [1986] 2 All ER 334 (see page 114). Perhaps Sir Robert Megarry, beneath his usual light turn of phrase, identifies the true reason for some judges' scepticism of some authors:

'The passage of years and the activities of those who edit the books of the departed tend to produce criticism and sometimes the elimination of frailties, and so give greater confidence in what remains. Further, many books by dead authors represent mature views after a lifetime of studying and, often, practising in the particular branch of the law concerned, whereas all too many books by the living are written by those who, laudably enough, have merely hoped to learn the rudiments of a subject by writing a book about it. Finally, it must be admitted that there are a number of living authors whose appearance and demeanour do something to sap any confidence in their omniscience which the printed page may have instilled; the dead, on the other hand, so often leave little clue to what manner of men they were save the majestic skill with which they have arrayed the learning of centuries and exposed the failings of the bench.' (*Miscellany-at-Law*, 1955, revised impression 1958, p. 328.)

Or, slightly more cynically, and admittedly from a non-legal context, there is Alexander Pope's comment:

'Authors, like coins, grow dear as they grow old;
It is the rust we value, not the gold.'

(*An Essay on Criticism*, 1711.)

A particular problem arises in connection with the works of authors who also happen to be judges. Even more particularly, what is a judge to do when an advocate cites the judge's own writings? Megarry, himself a distinguished author, dealt with this matter thus:

> 'The process of authorship is entirely different from that of judicial decision. The author ... has the benefit of a broad and comprehensive study of his chosen subject ... But he is exposed to the perils of yielding to preconceptions and he lacks the ... sharpening of focus which the detailed facts of a particular case bring to the judge. Above all, he has to form his ideas without the aid of the purifying ordeal of skilled argument on the specific facts of a contested case ... and I would, therefore, give credit to the words of any reputable author ... as expressing tenable and arguable ideas, as fertilizers of thought, and as conveniently expressing the fruits of research in print ... But I would expose those views to the testing and refining process of argument.' (*Cordell v Second Clanfield Properties* [1968] 3 All ER 746.)

On the other hand, academic detachment may be considered an advantage. As Denning J said, in a book review at (1947) 63 LQR 516:

> '[Textbooks] are not digests of cases but repositories of principles. They are written by men who have studied the law as a science with more detachment than is possible to men engaged in busy practice.'

In similarly sympathetic vein, in *Spiliada Maritime Corporation v Cansulex Ltd* [1987] AC 460, Lord Goff described academic authors as 'pilgrims with us on the endless road to unattainable perfection'. (In this case, however, it may not be wholly irrelevant that Lord Goff was writing as the co-author of a leading textbook on the law of restitution, and as a former Fellow of Lincoln College, Oxford.)

The true position, as any substantial reading of the law reports will show, is that the courts will use the views of modern authors, but will not be bound by them. Sir George Jessell MR explained the point thus: 'Although textbooks do not make law, they show more or less whether a principle has been generally accepted'. (*Henty v Wrey* (1882) 21 ChD 332.) Nevertheless, the courts are often concerned with the need for predictability in the law, which makes it important to emphasize the point made by Lord Goddard CJ in *Bastin v Davies* [1950] 1 All ER 1095, when speaking of *Bell's Sale of Food and Drugs*:

> '[A court] would never hesitate to disagree with a statement in a textbook ... if it thought fit ... [but] ... if a statement has appeared in a well-known textbook for a great number of years and has never been dissented from by a judicial decision, it would be most unfortunate to throw doubt on it after it had been acted on ... for so long.'

Some textbooks, such as the massively multi-volumed *Halsbury's Laws of England*, are encyclopaedic in nature, and some, such as the

*Encyclopaedia of Planning Law and Practice*, are even so by name. Useful though such works are, they are no more infallible than any other books. Examples of cases where the courts have commented adversely on individual textbooks include *Watson v Thomas S Witney & Co Ltd* [1966] 1 All ER 122, where the Court of Appeal refused to accept the accuracy of a clear statement in *Halsbury's Laws of England*. Similarly, in *R v Oxford Crown Court and Another ex parte Smith* (1990) 2 Admin LR 395, the High Court gave short shrift to one aspect of the case, with Simon Brown J explaining the matter thus:

'The reason why I can deal with this argument comparatively briefly is because it flies in the face of clear Court of Appeal authority directly and indistinguishably in point – *Britt v Buckinghamshire County Council* [1964] 1 QB 77. This case alas did not feature in [counsel for the applicant's] arguments save in reply. That, it emerged, was because he was unaware of it until [counsel for the respondent's] submissions... he candidly admitted to sitting transfixed when it came to be cited. One wonders whether any of this litigation would have occurred had it been earlier discovered by the applicant's advisers. It is certainly unfortunate that it finds no mention in the *Planning Encyclopaedia*.'

Another work which most lawyers habitually regard as authoritative was nevertheless found wanting in *Commission for the New Towns v Cooper (GB) Ltd* [1995] 2 All ER 929. The Court of Appeal pointed out that the fourth edition of *Halsbury's Statutes* cited an extract from the Law Commission's report which resulted in the Law of Property (Miscellaneous Provisions) Act 1989, even though the relevant section as enacted was significantly different from that which the Law Commission had proposed.

No doubt many authors have had cause to be relieved at the outcome of *Holmes and Bradbury v Bradford Metropolitan City Council* (1994) 158 LG Rev 561. The case brought to light an inaccurate statement of law in the *Encyclopaedia of Planning Law and Practice*. Perusal of that part of the transcript of the judgment which, in accordance with the usual practice, is not reported, shows that when the question of costs came to be discussed, Staughton LJ said: 'We cannot really make the editor [of the *Encyclopaedia*] pay the costs'. When counsel replied: 'Sadly, no', the judge replied: 'We would rather like to'. In fact, no order as to costs was made against anyone.

Although authors and editors, being only human, may make mistakes, there can be no doubt that the legal profession and the courts would both find life practically impossible if they were left only with the primary sources of law. Judges, in particular, not infrequently acknowledge their indebtedness to legal authors. In this context Lord

Bridge, in the case of *R v Shivpuri* [1986] 2 All ER 334, deserves full marks for judicial candour. The background to *Shivpuri* was that in *Anderton v Ryan* [1985] 2 All ER 355, the House of Lords had formulated a principle, the details of which need not be explored here, which had aroused the almost universal wrath of academic criminal lawyers. The House had the opportunity of returning to the point in *Shivpuri*, when it decided to overrule its previous decision. Lord Bridge, who was in the unenviable position of being a member of the House on both occasions, concluded the substance of his speech with the following words:

> 'I have had the advantage, since the conclusion of argument in this appeal, of reading an article by Professor Glanville Williams ... The language in which he criticizes the decision in *Anderton v Ryan* is not conspicuous for its moderation, but it would be foolish, on that account, not to recognize the force of the criticism and churlish not to acknowledge the assistance I have derived from it.'

(The cases of *Anderton v Ryan* and *R v Shivpuri* are discussed further, in the context of the doctrine of precedent, at pages 187–8.)

One potentially useful publication for anyone undertaking serious research is *The Digest* (formerly entitled *The English and Empire Digest*), which is literally a massive digest of case-law, arranged by subject matter. However, its scope goes far beyond the needs of most law students, and it has been somewhat eclipsed by the widespread availability of computerized databases.

## 7.4 Law reports

### 7.4.1 Introduction

Since the English legal system depends so heavily on the doctrine of precedent, there is an obvious need for accessible, accurate and reliable reports of what the courts have decided. It is not surprising, therefore, that there are many series of law reports, although it may be thought more surprising that there is no such thing as 'official' law reports. The closest to 'official' law reports are those published by the Incorporated Council of Law Reporting for England and Wales, which is a non-profit-making body, created and run by the legal profession.

### 7.4.2 The range of law reports

Although any series of reports of the decisions of the courts may be, and often are, referred to as 'law reports', the phrase is sometimes used in a somewhat stricter sense, in which case it refers to the principal products of the Incorporated Council. Using the phrase in this strict sense for the moment, the *Law Reports* currently contain sub-series entitled *Appeal Cases*, which abbreviates to AC, and which covers the House of Lords; *Chancery Division*, which abbreviates to Ch; *Family Division*, which abbreviates to Fam; and *Queen's Bench Division*, which abbreviates to QB. The Chancery, Family and Queen's Bench reports cover not only the decisions of the respective divisions of the High Court, but also the decisions of the Court of Appeal arising from them. Somewhat oddly, in view of their title, the *Law Reports* also contain an annual volume containing statutes, but the topic of the citation of statutes will be left until page 121.

The Incorporated Council also publishes the *Weekly Law Reports*, which abbreviates to WLR. As their title implies, these are published in weekly parts, although they are also available annually in three bound volumes. Each weekly part is divided into cases destined for volume one on the one hand or volumes two or three on the other. The cases appearing in volumes two and three also appear again, after some delay, in the appropriate volume of the *Law Reports*, while those published in volume one will not do so. The later version is more valuable when it appears because it contains summaries of the arguments which were presented to the court. The production of the *Weekly Law Reports* is nevertheless justified by their earlier publication.

Unlike the products of the Incorporated Council, however, the majority of series of law reports are published as purely commercial ventures.

The leading series of general law reports produced on a commercial basis is the *All England Law Reports* (All ER) which appears in weekly parts. The *All England Law Reports* themselves commenced publication in 1936, but a selection of previous cases appear as the *All England Law Reports Reprints* (All ER Rep) series. There are also two sub-series, one containing European Community cases originating from outside the United Kingdom (All ER (EC)) and one containing commercial law cases (All ER (Comm)).

Additionally, there are many specialized series, such as *Building Law Reports* (BLR), *Housing Law Reports* (HLR) and *Road Traffic Reports* (RTR), to name but three. The frequency of appearance of the specialist series varies, but their content is almost always self-evident from their titles. (A list of the most frequently encountered law reports and their abbreviations is provided in Appendix 1.)

Some newspapers publish law reports, as do many periodicals. In the case of the latter, the reports will, naturally, relate to the periodical's subject matter, which will generally be apparent from its title. (See, for example, the *Criminal Law Review* (Crim LR) and the *Journal of Planning and Environmental Law* (JPL or JPEL).)

The value of the specialized series of free-standing reports, and of the reports incorporated into periodicals, is that their editors may well include cases which lack sufficient general or lasting interest to justify inclusion in the more mainstream series, and yet are of topical or specialized interest. Such reports may also be accompanied by useful academic commentaries, as exemplified by the *Criminal Law Review* and the *Journal of Planning and Environmental Law*. However, it is important to remember that, unlike the free-standing series of reports, reports in newspapers and periodicals are shortened versions of the judgment, which means that they are merely the reporter's version of what the judge has said. Inevitably, therefore, there will always be a question mark over the accuracy and reliability of any short report. In *Export Credits Guarantee Department v Universal Oil Products Co* [1983] 2 All ER 205, Lord Roskill described a case reported only in the *Solicitors' Journal* as being 'virtually unreported'. Even more pointedly, in *Brentnall & Cleland Limited v London County Council* [1945] 1 KB 115, Humphreys J, speaking of a report of one of his own previous decisions, said:

> 'These short reports ... ought to be accepted with a good deal of care. If I am correctly reported in *The Law Times* ... I can only say, first that that was an *obiter dictum*, and secondly that I think it was wrong. I have no recollection of saying anything of the sort, and I cannot believe that I said it.'

(The meaning of *obiter dictum* is discussed in Chapter 9.)

The unreliability of short reports does not mean that the whole of a full-transcript report should be read uncritically. In particular it is important to distinguish between the headnote and the judgment itself. The headnote, which is the introductory summary of the decision, is written by the reporter rather than by the judge, and therefore it is not authoritative. Many headnotes are of a very high standard, but, to adopt the words of Megarry: 'The composition of a ... headnote to a law report is generally recognized as calling for a high degree of skill'. (*Miscellany-at-Law*, 1955, revised impression 1958, p. 289.) It is not altogether surprising, therefore, that headnotes vary in their clarity or accuracy, or both.

The proper utility of the headnote is limited to telling readers what the case is about, so that they can decide whether to invest further time and energy in reading the judgment itself.

### 7.4.3　Neutral citation of cases

Quite apart from the question of providing references to law reports, there is now an official system known as neutral citation.

The *Practice Direction (Judgments: Form and Citation (Supreme Court))* [2001] 1 WLR 194, introduced neutral citation into the Administrative Court and both divisions of the Court of Appeal. Each case is numbered sequentially, as exemplified by the following forms:

| | |
|---|---|
| High Court (Administrative Court) | [2000] EWHC Admin 1 (or 2 or 3, and so on); |
| Court of Appeal (Civil Division) | [2000] EWCA Civ 1 (or 2 or 3, and so on); |
| Court of Appeal (Criminal Division) | [2000] EWCA Crim 1 (or 2 or 3, and so on). |

The *Practice Direction (Judgments: Neutral Citation)* [2002] 1 WLR 346, extended the system to the remainder of the High Court, as exemplified by the following forms:

| | |
|---|---|
| High Court (Queen's Bench Division) | [2002] EWHC QB 1 (or 2 or 3, and so on); |
| High Court (Family Division) | [2002] EWHC Fam 1 (or 2 or 3, and so on); |
| High Court (Chancery Division) | [2002] EWHC Ch 1 (or 2 or 3, and so on). |

The House of Lords has also adopted the practice of neutral citation, in the following form:

[2002] UKHL 1 (or 2 or 3, and so on).

In cases falling within the system of neutral citation, the paragraphs of the judgments are numbered consecutively throughout. This facilitates reference to precise passages, rather than having to rely on the pagination of law reports, which, naturally, varies from one series to another.

### 7.4.4    The citability of law reports in court

Initially law reports are used by practitioners and others for guidance as to what the law is. In this context, reports may be very useful when giving advice to clients and in achieving negotiated settlements. However, many matters do go to court, so it will be apparent that the ultimate utility of a law report would be seriously diminished if the courts were not willing to look at it if occasion demanded. An important question, therefore, becomes: 'which law reports are citable in court?'

The traditional view is: 'A "law report" means any account of a case vouched for by a barrister who was present at the hearing'. (Dias, *Jurisprudence*, 5th edn, p. 134, relying on Pollock's *Essays in the Law*, p. 243.) The Court of Appeal reflected this view in *Birtwistle v Tweedale* [1953] 2 All ER 1598, where Somervell LJ, speaking of an *Estates Gazette* report, said that he did not wish to have cases cited if they were not reported by barristers, since such reports 'might mislead rather than assist the court'. Denning LJ said that there were sufficient cases that could be cited apart from those in the *Estates Gazette*. Romer LJ agreed with both his colleagues.

The proposition that reporters must not only be barristers but must also be present at the hearing appears to be deeply ingrained in the academic consciousness. For example, in *The Limits of Citation Determined* (1983), 80 LS Gaz, 1337, Roderick Munday said: 'Anyone today is entitled to publish law reports, *provided that the judgments are attested to by a member of the Bar present at the decision*'. (Emphasis added.) However, the fact that a proposition is deeply ingrained does not make it correct, or even defensible, and in the present context the lack of justification for the traditional view is apparent when the nature of a law report in analysed.

A full-transcript report consists of a copy of the judgment of the court (which is publicly available anyway), together with any apparatus by way of headnote, cross-references to textbooks and so on, which the reporter considers to be appropriate. Since headnotes are never authoritative anyway, there can be no basis for challenging the accuracy of a report merely because the headnote-writer is not a barrister and worked from a transcript of the judgment (which has almost always been approved by the judge anyway), rather than being present in court. Furthermore, the modern practice in many cases is for the court to announce its decision and then to hand down the judgment, without occupying court time by reading it out. In such cases, therefore, any reporter will have no option but to work from the transcript.

Since it is obviously in the best interests of the administration of justice that the courts should be able to refer to the widest possible range of legal sources, it is fortunate that current judicial practice does not reflect the traditional view of the citability of law reports. To take a single, but by no means unrepresentative, example, the *Justice of the Peace Reports* are, among many others, frequently cited. For example, in *Wellingborough Borough Council v Gordon* (1991) 155 JP 494, the High Court relied on the report of *Cooke v Adatia and Others* (1989) 153 JP 129, which was prepared by a solicitor who was not present at the hearing. This series of reports having been cited for well over a century, it is not surprising that the court made no comment whatsoever as to the provenance of the earlier report.

In passing, it is interesting to note that those instructing the drafter of s. 115 of the Courts and Legal Services Act 1990 appear to have shared the common misconception as to the citability of law reports. The section provides that a law report prepared by a solicitor, or anyone else who has acquired the right of advocacy in the higher courts, 'shall have the same authority as if it had been made by a barrister'. This provision is clearly superfluous.

In the final analysis, each court must be the master of its own practice in relation to the citation of reports. However, the fact that, as we have seen, all law reports may be cited, does not mean that courts have no preferences in the matter. In a *Practice Note* [1995] 3 All ER 256, Sir Thomas Bingham MR said:

> 'If a case is reported in the official Law Reports published by the Incorporated Council of Law Reporting for England and Wales, that report should be cited. These are the most authoritative reports; they contain a summary of the argument; and they are most readily available.
>
> 'If a case is not (or not yet) reported in the official Law Reports, but is reported in the Weekly Law Reports or the All England Law Reports, that report should be cited.
>
> 'If a case is not reported in any of these series of reports, a report in any of the authoritative specialist series of reports may be cited ...
>
> 'It is recognized that occasions arise when one report is fuller than another, or when there are discrepancies between reports. On such occasions, the practice outlined above need not be followed.'

The preference of the High Court and the Court of Appeal for the official *Law Reports* was repeated in *Practice Direction (Judgments: Form and Citation) (Supreme Court)* [2001] 1 WLR 194.

Whether the *Law Reports* are necessarily more accurate than any other series is open to question. In *Re C* [1937] 3 All ER 783, Luxmoore J is reported as having read two extracts from the Parliamentary proceedings which produced the Adoption of Children Act 1926. At that time, judicial references to Parliamentary proceedings were not allowed, although this rule has since been relaxed (see page 303). When the case came to be reported in the *Law Reports* (at [1938] Ch 131), the offending section of the judgment was omitted, presumably as a result of the judge's intervention, or at least to avoid causing him embarrassment.

## 7.4.5 Editorial discretion in law reporting

With the possible exception of a series of law reports dealing with a very small and specialized area of law, it would be impossible for any series to include all the cases falling within its scope. The question therefore arises as to how the editors of the various series of law reports decide which cases to include. The answer, which may seem less than satisfactory, is that it is simply a matter of editorial judgment.

If the series is a general one, such as the *All England Law Reports*, the editor will have regard to the perceived needs of the general practitioner. More particularly, according to the publishing director of Butterworths, the proprietors of the *All England Law Reports*, the editors of that series exercise their discretion according to the following criteria: does the case make new law or contain a modern restatement of an existing principle; does it clarify conflicting decisions of lower courts or interpret legislation which is likely to be of wide application; does it interpret a common clause in documents such as wills or contracts, or clarify an important point of practice or procedure? (Brown, *Law Reporting: the Inside Story* (1989) 20 *The Law Librarian*, 15.)

Naturally, in addition to any explicit statement of editorial policy, any commercial enterprise must always bear in mind that the level of subscription income will determine the upper limit on the number of pages which can be produced in each year, and even the Incorporated Council prefers to have paid its way at the end of the year. The editors of the more specialized series will use their judgment in a similar fashion. However, having regard to their perceptions of the needs of their subscribers, they can obviously justify the inclusion of cases which would not be appropriate in a general series. Particularly in the case of specialist series, subscribers themselves may sometimes draw the editors' attention to cases in which they have been involved, and which they believe may be of interest to other specialists.

### 7.4.6 The problem of delay in law reporting

The process of preparing, printing and distributing law reports clearly takes some time. In the case of a newspaper report this may only be a day or so, but in the case of the free-standing series it may often be several months, or even a year or more. This is simply one of the less happy facts of legal life, and in no way detracts from the validity of the proposition that the bindingness of precedent operates immediately, as illustrated by the cases of *Re Schweppes Ltd's Agreement* and *Re Automatic Telephone and Electric Co Ltd's Agreement*, which are discussed at page 134.

Some instances of late reporting are explicable on the basis that an elderly but unreported case has been cited in a more recent case which attracts an editor's attention. The case of *Scherer v Counting Instruments*

*Ltd* was decided in 1977, but not then reported. Subsequently it was cited in *Aden Refinery Co Ltd v Ugland Management Co*, which was reported at [1986] 3 All ER 737. The editor of the reports took the opportunity to report the earlier case, which appears at [1986] 2 All ER 529.

Sometimes there may be prompt reporting in one series and less prompt reporting in another, with the specialist series often gaining a substantial march on their more mainstream contemporaries. For example, the case of *City of London Corporation v Bovis* was reported at (1988) 153 LG Rev 166, but not until [1992] 3 All ER 697. Similarly, when the House of Lords decided *Cremin v Thomson* it was promptly reported at (1941) 71 Ll Rep 1. The *All England Law Reports* did not include the case until [1953] 2 All ER 1185, where it appears as *Thomson v Cremin*.

**7.4.7** Computer databases

No discussion of law reporting would be complete without mentioning the availability and use of computer databases, such as *Lexis Nexis* (commonly known simply as *Lexis*). In *Stanley v International Harvester Co Ltd* [1983] *The Times*, 7 February, the Court of Appeal urged counsel to practise 'proper discretion' in citing cases which have not appeared in any series of law reports. A few days later, in *Roberts Petroleum Ltd v Bernard Kenny Ltd* [1983] 1 All ER 564, the House of Lords rather more forthrightly said that it did not wish to receive unreported cases unless counsel stated that the case dealt with a principle which was not only binding on the Court of Appeal, but which additionally was not covered by a case contained in the recognized reports.

House of Lords judgments are available, usually within two hours of being delivered, at http://www.parliament.uk/.

**7.5** Statutes

The usual way of citing a statute is by its short title: for example, the Local Government Act 1972. The short title is usually found towards the end of the body of the text, but before the schedules (if any). To pursue the example of the Local Government Act 1972, the relevant provision is s. 274.

The convenience of being able to refer to a statute by its short title may seem to be obvious, but it becomes even clearer when the alternatives are considered. First, there is the long title, which is found at the beginning of the statute. To give an indication of the unwieldy nature of the long title, it is necessary to do no more than return to the example of the Local Government Act 1972:

'An Act to make provision with respect to local government and the functions of local authorities in England and Wales; to amend Part 2 of the Transport Act 1968; to confer rights of appeal in respect of decisions relating to licences under the Home Counties (Music and Dancing) Licensing Act 1926; to make further provision with respect to magistrates' courts committees; to abolish certain inferior courts of record; and for connected purposes.'

A technical way of referring to a statute, and one which is hardly ever encountered in practice, is by its year and chapter number – thus the Local Government Act 1972 may be cited as '1972, c.70', meaning that it was the seventieth statute to receive the Royal Assent in 1972. While this form of citation enables the statute to be identified, it has the clear drawback of conveying nothing of any real meaning on the face of the reference.

Finally, there is the question of what is the best source for finding the actual wording of a statute. The textbook answer must be that the most authoritative version which is readily available is the text of the Queen's Printer's copy as published by Her Majesty's Stationery Office. However, in this, as in so many other things, the textbook answer overlooks a whole dimension of pure practicality. The principal deficiencies of the Queen's Printer's version are that it contains no editorial matter by way of commentary, explanation or even cross-reference and – even more seriously – of necessity it represents the text of the Act as it was at the date of the Royal Assent, without the incorporation of subsequent amendments. As well as being published by the Stationery Office as individual statutes, and in bound volumes as Public and General Acts and Measures, the Queen's Printer's version of the text is also reproduced in the Statutes volume of the Incorporated Council's Law Reports.

The full text of all Public Acts from the beginning of 1996 onwards (and Private Acts from the beginning of 1997), together with the long titles and arrangements of sections of many earlier Acts may be found at http://www.hmso.gov.uk/acts.htm. Similarly, statutory instruments from the beginning of 1997, and draft statutory instruments from November of that year, may be found at http://www.hmso.gov.uk/stat.htm. Public Bills before Parliament, together with explanatory notes, are available at http://www.parliament.the-stationery-office.co.uk/pa/pabills.htm.

The commercially published series, *Current Law Statutes Annotated*, supplements the Queen's Printer's text with very full annotations, section by section. The format usually includes a useful introductory essay commenting on the background and purposes of the statute, but the editorial process inevitably involves some delay between the Royal

Assent and publication of the annotated version of the statute. Perhaps the most useful version overall, however, is *Halsbury's Statutes of England*, which is another commercial publication, with the advantage that the text is supported, not only by full annotations, but also by an updating service which makes it relatively easy to keep track of repeals and amendments as they take place. However, although editorial commentaries are useful, they are never as authoritative as judicial interpretations of the words of the statute itself, and may even be simply wrong. (See, for example, *Commission for the New Towns v Cooper (GB) Ltd* [1995] 2 All ER 929, which is discussed at page 113.)

## 7.6 European Community law

Since Community law is a whole legal order in itself, you will not be surprised to learn that it enjoys an enormous range of sources. Apart from the *European Court Reports* (ECR) the *Common Market Law Reports* (CMLR) and the treaties themselves, the most useful official sources are probably the *Official Journal* and the bulletin called the *Proceedings of the Court of Justice and the Court of First Instance of the European Communities*.

The *Official Journal* is published in several parts. The three most generally useful parts are the L series (containing the text of agreed legislation), the C series (containing draft legislation, official announcements and information on Community activities) and the Annexe (containing the full text of debates in the European Parliament).

The Court of Justice's *Bulletin* contains digested versions of recent decisions. Inevitably, these are not as authoritative as full reports, but they do become available a great deal more quickly.

The Community's website at http://europa.eu.int/ provides access to a large amount of information, including recent judgments of the Court of justice.

There are also various commercial publications, including a number of loose-leaf encyclopaedias. A particularly accessible text may be found in volumes 51 and 52 of *Halsbury's Laws of England*, which must, however, be read with the aid of the Current Service.

## 7.7 Reports of the European Court of Human Rights

The *European Human Rights Reports* (EHRR), published by Sweet & Maxwell, contain a selection of case-law. Additionally, the Council of Europe's own publications include *Series A*, which contains the judgments of the Court and may include the Commission's opinion; *Series B*, which contains the Reports of the Commission; *Decisions and Reports of the Commission* (D&R), which may be summaries; and the *Yearbook of the*

*European Convention on Human Rights.* Judgments and summaries of judgments of the European Court of Human Rights are available at http://www.dhcour.coe.fr/eng/Judgments.htm.

## 7.8 Miscellaneous sources

The Internet contains many useful sites, including that of the British and Irish Legal Information Institute (http://www.bailii.org/), access to which is free. Other free sites include the current day's issue of *The Times* newspaper (http://www.thetimes.co.uk/) and the Stationery Office (http://www.the-stationery-office.co.uk/), which contains a variety of official publications, including statutes and statutory instruments. Still dealing with free sites, http://www.parliament.uk/ publishes House of Lords judgments, usually within two hours of delivery. Access to the *Daily Law Notes* section of the Incorporated Council of Law Reporting for England and Wales' website (http://www.lawreports.co.uk/) (see page 114) is also free and particularly useful.

## 7.9 Keeping up-to-date

Keeping up-to-date is a life-long (not to say life-shortening) nightmare for many lawyers. Yet the courts are insistent that it must be done. In *Stokes v Sayers* [1987] *The Times*, 16 March, the High Court emphasized that even while an appeal is pending, the lawyers must keep the relevant case-law under constant review, because there may be developments which make the outcome of the appeal a foregone conclusion, in which case they should either withdraw the appeal or cease to resist it, as the case may be. Similarly, in *Copeland v Smith* [2000] 1 All ER 457, Buxton LJ expressed the Court of Appeal's displeasure at a situation in which relevant, recently reported Court of Appeal authority had not been cited in the County Court, saying that it is

> 'essential for advocates who hold themselves out as competent to practise in a particular field to bring and keep themselves up to date with recent authority in their field. By "recent authority" I am not necessarily referring to authority which is only to be found in specialist reports, but authority which has been reported in the general law reports. If a solicitors' firm or barristers' chambers only take one set of the general law reports, for instance the *Weekly Law Reports* as opposed to the *All England Law Reports*, or the *All England Law Reports* as opposed to the *Weekly Law Reports*, they should at any rate have systems in place which enable them to keep themselves up to date with cases which have been considered worthy of reporting in the other series.'

In addition to the online sources identified in the previous section, it is worth commenting that the monthly parts of *Current Law*, with their annual cumulation into the *Current Law Year Books*, provide a generally reliable guide to recent developments, including the publication of textbooks and articles.

The *Current Law* family of publications includes case and statute citators, which enable you to trace cases in which earlier cases and statutes have been cited, as well as delegated legislation and amendments to statutes.

*Halsbury's Laws of England* and *Halsbury's Statutes of England* both have loose-leaf current service volumes, and specialist encyclopaedias are also usually loose-leaf. Once you have enough basic knowledge of the law to be able to understand and assess recent developments, one of the best ways of keeping up-to-date in a broadly based way is to skim one or more of the generalist weekly journals (of which the *Law Society's Gazette*, the *Solicitors' Journal* and the *New Law Journal* are typical).

Specialists will, of course, probably read the relevant journals more closely. Experienced lawyers often find that they retain the knowledge that they have known something long after the content of that specific knowledge has gone. It is then simply a case of retracing the source.

## Summary

▷ When you are looking for the law you will usually use textbooks and journals, law reports and statutes. Where a reference contains a date in square brackets, the date is an essential part of the reference. Where a date is in round brackets it is not an essential element of the reference.

▷ Textbooks and journals are very useful, but they are not authoritative in the way that statutes and judicial decisions are.

▷ There are many series of law reports. The superior courts prefer to receive the Incorporated Council for Law Reporting's *Law Reports*, but any court may receive any report. The old rule, according to which no one other than a barrister present at the hearing can produce an authoritative law report, no longer exists.

▷ There are various ways of citing statutes, but the use of the short title is the most usual and convenient method.

▷ Keeping up-to-date with legal developments requires mastery of a law library, including the use of electronic sources.

## Exercises

1   What is the distinction between round brackets and square brackets in the citation of legal references?

2 Are textbooks and journals authoritative sources of English law?

3 Which law reports do the superior courts prefer to have cited to them? Why?

4 What is the most common and convenient way of citing a statute?

5 What does the *Official Journal* of the European Communities contain?

6 What does the citation *EHRR* mean?

# Part 2

# Case-law and precedent

Having read this Part you should understand the basic concepts of the English doctrine of binding precedent and appreciate how those concepts are applied in practice. More particularly, you should be able to understand how the doctrine attempts to balance the interests of flexibility and predictability. You will also gain a comparative insight from considering the practice of the European Court of Justice.

# Chapter 8

## An introduction to the doctrine of binding precedent

### 8.1 Introduction

Briefly, the doctrine of binding precedent states that all courts bind all lower courts, and some courts, at least to some extent, also bind themselves. The hierarchy of the courts, which was outlined in Chapter 3, clearly becomes relevant in the present context. In this Part we will examine the operation of the doctrine of precedent in some detail, both in conceptual terms and through each of the superior courts.

### 8.2 Bindingness, flexibility and the rule of law

First, and without wishing in any way to bypass the discussion which follows, it is worth commenting that a proper understanding of the doctrine of precedent will lead you to the conclusion that in many cases the bindingness, which is alleged to be the basis of the doctrine, is more apparent than real. In the words of Carleton Kemp Allen:

'Whatever merits precedent may possess (and they are many) certainty is the very last quality which can be attributed to it ... Nobody knows, until a case has come to trial, what will emerge from all the "authorities" ... Every lawyer is aware of points on which the authorities are conflicting and obscure, and as precedents multiply, so do the conflicts and obscurities.' (*Case Law: An Unwarrantable Intervention* (1935) 51 LQR 333.)

Secondly, it follows that a central task facing any discussion of the doctrine of binding precedent is to identify as precisely as possible the extent of the discretion available to the judges in cases. More particularly, it will be apparent that there is a constant tension between the separation of powers (see page 69), which allows judges sufficient independent discretion to interpret and apply the law on a case-by-case basis, and the rule of law (see page 61), which requires that people should be able to predict the legal consequences of their conduct with some degree of certainty. Although the attainment of both these objectives may be thought to be desirable, it is nevertheless obvious that there is a significant extent to which they are mutually inconsistent. In other words, a balance must be struck.

Thirdly, this Part will conclude by considering the practice of the European Court of Justice with regard to precedent. This material is useful not only as a necessary foundation on which to study Community law in its own right, but also because a comparative perspective may prompt lawyers in any jurisdiction to question their own system when they see how others tackle the same problems.

## 8.3 A wide view of precedent

The idea of precedent may be formulated in a relatively wide way, by simply saying that it is desirable that similar cases should be decided in a similar manner. This wide view of precedent is based partly on the proposition that consistency is an important element of justice; partly on the fact that the practice of following previous decisions results in improved efficiency, because points of law which have once been decided can simply be applied subsequently, without being subject to repeated re-argument; and partly on judicial comity. (Judicial comity simply means the mutual respect which judges have for their colleagues.)

It is not surprising, therefore, that the courts in any developed legal system are likely to follow precedent to a significant extent. Certainly there is nothing peculiarly English about such a practice. However, the idea of precedent may also develop in a rather narrower sense, with the result that courts may regard themselves as being actually bound to follow earlier decisions. The use of precedent in this narrow sense is largely peculiar to English law, although it is also evident to some extent in the other common law jurisdictions which derive from English law.

## 8.4 A narrow view of precedent: the doctrine of *stare decisis*

The Latin tag of *stare decisis* is sometimes attached to the doctrine of binding precedent as the doctrine *stare decisis*, but since this phrase translates as 'to stand by decisions', it adds nothing to an understanding of the concept.

Taking a more functional view, at its simplest the doctrine of binding precedent states that all courts bind all lower courts, and some courts may also bind themselves. The two halves of this proposition may respectively be labelled the *vertical* and *horizontal* dimensions of precedent. We will consider both these dimensions in due course, but before doing so it will be useful to draw a distinction between the doctrine of binding precedent and the doctrine of *res judicata*.

## 8.5 The distinction between binding precedent and *res judicata*

The practical administration of justice in any legal system plainly requires that once a case has been decided the parties should be bound by the decision, because endless reopening of cases is wasteful of resources, as well as creating injustice to those who have to defend themselves repeatedly in respect of the same matter. The point at which finality will be imposed will depend on the detail of any appeal system which may be available, but at some stage the appeals must run out and finality must be imposed. This requirement of finality is provided by the doctrine of *res judicata*. There is no convenient English equivalent for this phrase, but it may be translated as 'the matter has been decided'. The conceptual difference between binding precedent and *res judicata* is simply that the former deals with matters of law, which may (according to the principles discussed in this Part of this book) be binding in future cases, while the latter deals with disputes before the courts in individual cases, and the bindingness of the outcomes of those cases as between the parties.

The relationship between the two doctrines is well illustrated by a short series of cases decided during, and shortly after, the Second World War. In order to understand these cases, however, it is necessary to understand something of the law relating to the taxation of certain kinds of legacies.

It is common for testators, when drawing up their wills, to make provision for beneficiaries to receive annual incomes out of the estate. Furthermore, testators may decide that such annuities (to use the technical term) should be 'free of tax', thus ensuring that the beneficiaries will continue to receive the same income even if the rate of income tax changes. Of course, testators have no legal power to exempt people from income tax, so, in order to illustrate how these tax-free annuities actually work in practice, it will be useful to look at a hypothetical set of facts. Suppose:

- I leave an annuity of £5000 to $X$, payable for the rest of his life, and I state it to be free of tax;
- I leave all the other income from my estate to $Y$ for the rest of her life; and
- five years after my death, income tax is increased.

Because I stated $X$'s annuity to be free of tax, he will continue to receive the benefit of £5000 a year. Nevertheless, the tax has to be paid. In fact, therefore, the loss falls on $Y$ because the increased tax which must be paid on *X*'s £5000 means that the amount of income left for *Y* is reduced. Since this is what the testator intended, *Y* will have no legitimate grounds for complaint. Moreover, any decreases in the rate of tax will effectively increase *Y*'s income, so there is a swings-and-roundabouts argument.

However, if unforeseeable circumstances cause a very large increase in the rate of taxation, you could argue that the testator might not have wished the arrangement to continue. This is exactly what happened during the Second World War, when income tax rose from 5s 6d in the £ to 10s in the £ (that is, from 27.5p to 50p in the £). As a result, Parliament included a provision in the Finance Act 1941 to the effect that where this type of 'provision ... was made before 3 September 1939' the beneficiary would get the annuity free from the first 5s 6d of tax, but would have to bear the burden of the increase.

The statutory provision may seem clear enough, but careful consideration of it reveals a problem. What would be the position where the will was made before 3 September 1939, but the death occurred after that date? In other words, when was the provision made in a case such as this? On the one hand, it can be argued that a testator who makes a will would probably regard himself as having made provision for the beneficiaries. On the other hand, if a testator wishes to change his will for any reason, he may do so at any time before his death; and therefore it is not until the death that anyone can say with certainty what provision has been made and for whom.

This problem came before the courts on a number of occasions. In *Re Waring, Westminster Bank v Awdrey and Others* [1942] 1 Ch 425, the will had been made before 3 September 1939, but the death did not occur until after that date. There were two annuitants, but only one of them was able to be a party to the case, the other one being in German-occupied Belgium. The Court of Appeal held that the 1941 Act applied, and that therefore the annuities were subject to the top slice of income tax. Another case, involving the same point of law but arising out of a totally separate set of facts, came before the courts in *Berkeley v Berkeley* [1946] AC 555. The House of Lords held that the 1941 Act did not apply, on the basis that provision was not made until the death occurred. In other words the annuitant was protected and the rest of the estate had to bear the whole of the income tax liability.

This decision led to the case of *Re Waring, Westminster Bank v Burton-Butler* [1948] 1 Ch 221, which involved the same will as the previous *Re Waring* case, but this time, the war having ended, both the annuitants were parties. The court held that the annuitant who had been a party to the earlier case was not entitled to the benefit of the House of L decision in *Berkeley*, because the matter was *res judicata* as a result of the earlier case. However, the position of the other annuitant was different because she had not been involved in the earlier case. As far as she was concerned, therefore, the doctrine of binding precedent operated in the ordinary way, so she was entitled to the benefit of the decision in *Berkeley*. Accordingly she received the annuity completely free of tax.

## 8.6  Retrospectivity and prospectivity in the operation of binding precedent

### 8.6.1  Introduction

Whenever the law is changed, an issue arises as to the date on which the change takes effect.

Statutes which change the law may, of course, contain express provision as to the effective date of the changes which they introduce; and they commonly do so. However, in the absence of such express provision, the courts will begin with a very strong presumption that Parliament intends the changes to apply only to future transactions and events – or in other words, that the changes shall only be *prospective* and not *retrospective*. (This presumption, which may be seen as one consequence of the constitutional doctrine of the rule of law – see page 61 – is discussed and illustrated at p. 308.)

On the other hand, where the courts change the law through the doctrine of binding precedent, they have no such constitutional qualms, and *retrospectivity* is the order of the day. Thus, in the *Waring–Berkeley–Waring* saga (see above), the *Berkeley* decision affected the outcome of the second *Waring* case – at least as far as one of the beneficiaries was concerned – even though all the facts of that case had occurred before the *Berkeley* decision was made. Therefore, when the courts declare what the law *is*, they are also declaring what it *was* at the time of the transactions or events giving rise to the litigation in question. It follows that the law, as it is now declared to be, will affect all previous fact-situations, including those which have no connection whatsoever with the case in which the overruling occurs. In practice, of course, the doctrine of *res judicata* (as illustrated by the *Waring–Berkeley–Waring* sequence of cases) may make it impossible to enforce the new law, as may the application of the time limits within which proceedings must be commenced and appeals must be brought. However, the basic proposition as to the retrospective operation of the doctrine of binding precedent remains valid, and may be illustrated by the following pair of cases.

Three judges of the Court of Appeal heard the cases of *Re Schweppes Ltd's Agreement* [1965] 1 All ER 195, and *Re Automatic Telephone and Electric Co Ltd's Agreement* [1965] 1 All ER 206, on the same day. The cases involved different sets of facts, but the point of law was the same in each case. In the first case Willmer LJ dissented, but in the second case he accepted that, under the doctrine of binding precedent, he was bound by the decision in the first case. In other words, the doctrine of binding precedent operates in such a way that the outcome of a case may depend on a statement of the law, which had not been made when the facts occurred and the decision to embark on legal proceedings was made.

A further illustration of the retrospective operation of precedent is provided by *Kleinwort Benson Ltd v Lincoln City Council* [1998] 4 All ER 513, where the parties had entered into a financial transaction known as an interest rate swap agreement. Although the general understanding at the time of the agreement had been that such transactions were lawful, in *Hazell v Hammersmith & Fulham London Borough Council* [1991] 1 All ER 545, the House of Lords subsequently held that, when entered into by local authorities, they were not. In *Kleinwort Benson*, the issue was whether what was now seen to be a mistake of law was a good ground for allowing recovery of the money which had previously changed hands. The House of Lords held, by a majority, that it was. Lord Goff, who regarded the retrospectivity of precedent as being 'inevitable', said that he could not 'imagine how a common law system, or indeed any legal system, can operate otherwise if the law is to be applied equally to all and yet be capable of organic change'. He specifically rejected the idea that what was happening was 'an aberration of the common law', regarding it instead as 'an inevitable attribute of judicial decision-making ... [which] ... must ... [also] ... be applied in civil law countries'.

In *R v Governor of Her Majesty's Prison Brockhill ex parte Evans (No 2)* [1998] 4 All ER 993, the duration of a prisoner's detention had been calculated on a basis which was then understood to be lawful, but which a court subsequently held to be unlawful. If the law as subsequently stated had been available when Evans' discharge date was calculated, she would have been freed almost two months earlier than she actually was. The Court of Appeal held, by a majority, that she had been unlawfully detained for the excess period, in respect of which she was, therefore, entitled to damages for false imprisonment. Lord Woolf MR acknowledged that this was an 'undoubtedly highly artificial result' which involved 'a fairytale' but took the view that it was 'not open to this court to abandon the fairytale'. In due course, the

House of Lords (see [2000] 4 All ER 15) upheld the Court of Appeal. (We shall return to this case shortly in the context of prospective overruling.)

It is, of course, possible to argue that in *Evans* the individual *benefited* from the retrospectivity of precedent and that therefore there was no unfairness. While this is, of course, true, there was at least notional unfairness to the other party, which is not diminished in principle (although its impact was doubtless diminished in practice) by the fact that the party suffering the unfairness was the state, with its practically limitless resources.

Exceptionally, the courts may impose some limits on the retrospective operation of precedent. For example, in *Percy v Hall* [1996] QB 924, the Court of Appeal said a decision that a byelaw is invalid will operate retrospectively to the extent that it will justify setting aside convictions which have been imposed in respect of offences under the byelaw, but will not justify imposing liability for false imprisonment on police officers who arrested people in respect of such offences. (The possibility of delegated legislation, such as byelaws, being held to be unlawful is discussed at page 63.)

Although the Master of the Rolls in *Evans* accepted that the court's view in *Percy* was correct in the context of byelaws, it is difficult, if not impossible, to reconcile the two decisions at the level of principle, and the courts clearly have more work to do in clarifying the retrospective operation of precedent. (Admittedly, at a formal level, the conflict between *Evans* and *Percy* may be resolved by simply noting that the relevant statements in the former were *ratio*, while those in the latter were merely an *obiter dictum*, because, in all the circumstances of the case, the byelaw in question was held to be lawful anyway. (The concepts of *ratio* and *dictum* are discussed in Chapter 9.) However, relying on the distinction between *ratio* and *dictum* in the context of these particular cases is unattractive because it overlooks the careful treatment which the court gave the issue in *Percy*, as a result of which the *dicta* in that case may be seen as being practically as authoritative as *ratio*: see page 161.)

Perhaps surprisingly, the retrospectivity of precedent operates even in criminal cases, as illustrated by the cases of *R v R (Rape: Marital Exemption)* [1991] 4 All ER 481, and *R v W* (Crown Court, 1991, unreported).

In the first case, R had been charged with attempting to rape his wife. He had argued that English law did not recognize the possibility of a man raping his wife; and, therefore, it could not be an offence to attempt to rape her. The basis of his argument was Sir Matthew Hale's statement, dating from 1736, that

> 'the husband cannot be guilty of rape committed by himself upon his lawful wife, for by their mutual matrimonial consent and contract the wife hath given herself up in this kind unto her husband which she cannot retract.' (*History of the Pleas of the Crown*, vol. 1, p. 629.)

Furthermore, s. 1 of the Sexual Offences (Amendment) Act 1976 provided: 'A man commits rape if (a) he has *unlawful* sexual intercourse with a woman who at the time of the intercourse does not consent to it'. (Emphasis added). Could it be argued that the statutory use of the word 'unlawful' indicated the need for an additional element over and above the lack of consent; and if so, was that additional element the unmarried status of the parties?

When the trial judge ruled against him, the defendant pleaded guilty and was convicted (in July 1990). On appeal, both the Court of Appeal (in March 1991) and the House of Lords (in October 1991) held that the husband could be convicted. The House noted that there were already several exceptions to the rule, and concluded that the modern view of the nature of marriage, and of equality within marriage, meant that the old rule had become offensive to the point where it could no longer be sustained. According to Lord Keith, with whom all the other Law Lords agreed, the word 'unlawful' in the 1976 Act is mere surplusage: 'The fact is that it is clearly unlawful to have sexual intercourse with any woman without her consent, and that the use of the word in the subsection adds nothing'. He went on to quote, and endorse, the words of Lord Lane CJ at the Court of Appeal stage of the case:

> 'The remaining and no less difficult question is whether ... this is an area where the court should step aside to leave the matter to the parliamentary process. This is not the creation of a new offence, it is the removal of a common law fiction which has become anachronistic and offensive and we consider that it is our duty having reached that conclusion to act upon it.'

The difficulty with this comment is that, while the outcome of the case may represent a wholly welcome development of the law, from the point of view of the defendant there can surely be no difference between the removal of a pre-existing defence and the imposition of substantive liability. Additionally, of course, the decision affected other cases, notably *R v W*, where the facts alleged to constitute the offence had occurred in February 1989. As in *R v R*, following a ruling by the trial judge that the traditional doctrine no longer applied, the defendant had (in April 1991, which was one month after the Court of Appeal's decision in *R v R*) pleaded guilty to attempted rape of his wife. The defendant then lodged an appeal against conviction, but withdrew his appeal when the House of Lords decided *R v R*.

On the face of it, the retrospectivity contained within this sequence of events appears to contravene art. 7 of the European Convention on the Protection of Human Rights and Fundamental Freedoms, which provides that 'no one shall be held guilty of any criminal offence on account of any act or omission which did not constitute a criminal offence ... when it was committed'. (For the full text of art. 7, see page 353.) However, when the European Court of Human Rights considered the case, it found no breach of the Convention, on the basis that, if the defendants had taken legal advice, they could reasonably have foreseen that the law would be changed. Moreover, the

'debasing character of rape was so manifest that ... [the decisions of the English courts] ... could not be said to be at variance with the object and purpose of art. 7, namely to ensure that no one should be subjected to arbitrary prosecution, conviction or punishment'

and additionally the rejection of the former doctrine

'was in conformity not only with a civilized concept of marriage, but also, and above all, with the fundamental objectives of the Convention, the very essence of which was respect for human dignity and human freedom.' (*S W v United Kingdom* and *C R v United Kingdom* (1995) 21 EHRR 363.)

In *R v C* [2004] 3 All ER 3, an appeal against conviction in respect of an offence of marital rape committed in 1970 was argued on the basis that pursuing a prosecution after such a lapse of time had been an abuse of the process of the court. More particularly, the appellant argued that even if it had been reasonably foreseeable, in 1989, that the courts would change the law, the same could not have been said in 1970. The Court of Appeal rejected this argument, saying that, on a proper analysis of the development of the law since Sir Matthew Hale's day, such development of the law had been reasonably foreseeable even in 1970. (Without wishing to detract from the persuasiveness of the court's detailed reasoning, it may not be entirely fanciful to recall Oliver Wendell Holmes' concept of the *inarticulate major premise*: see page 9. The indictment in this case contained 17 counts of sexual and violent offences, against four different women, over the period from 1967–87, the seriousness of which may be gauged from the fact that the appellant was sentenced to a total of 12 years' imprisonment. It may well be that the appellant was unlikely to have engaged the sympathy of the court.)

Sometimes, however, the retrospective operation of the doctrine of precedent will inhibit the courts from making what would otherwise be highly desirable decisions. In *Prudential Assurance Co Ltd v London Residuary Body* [1992] 3 All ER 504, the House of Lords followed a body of case-law concerning a technical aspect of the law relating to leases. One aspect of Lord Browne-Wilkinson's speech, which both Lord Griffiths and Lord Mustill endorsed, is significant for the present purposes:

> 'If, by overruling the existing authorities, this House were able to change only the law for the future I would have urged your Lordships to do so. But for this House to depart from a rule relating to land law which has been established for many centuries might upset long-established titles [to land]. I must therefore confine myself to expressing the hope that the Law Commission might look at the subject ...'

While the case-law, therefore, makes it clear that the retrospective operation of the doctrine of binding precedent may or may not inhibit the courts from changing the law, it offers little in the way of practical guidance as to when the courts will feel so inhibited that they will decide that making no change is the preferable option. As Lord Russell once said, a party may have 'all the law on his side, but [be] (in effect) facing the prophets'. (*Sudbrook v Eggleston* [1982] 3 All ER 1.)

Briefly, therefore, the retrospective operation of the doctrine of binding precedent, involving as it does the application of new law to past transactions and events, is open to criticism on a number of grounds.

Perhaps most importantly, it sits very uneasily with the constitutional doctrine of the rule of law (see page 61).

At a more practical level, it may also produce results which offend many people's instinctive ideas of justice (see, for example, the marital rape cases which are discussed at p. 135).

Thirdly, it may inhibit the courts from undertaking law reform which would otherwise be desirable (see, for example, the *Prudential Assurance* case which is discussed at page 137).

It is against this background that the courts have slowly come round to accepting that, in some cases, it may be appropriate to restrict the retrospective operation of the doctrine of binding precedent. The doctrine which would achieve this result is usually called *prospective overruling*; but this is a little misleading because all overruling operates prospectively. What the phrase *prospective overruling* is intended to convey is more accurately described as *non-retrospective overruling*, but the terminology is so firmly established that any attempt to change it would be likely to cause more confusion than it would avoid. Accordingly, we must now consider the idea of prospective overruling.

### 8.6.2 The idea of prospective overruling

The first point to make – and it is one which cannot be emphasized too strongly – is that (with the exception of certain cases arising from the devolution legislation affecting Scotland, Wales and Northern Ireland, to which we shall return very shortly), no kind of prospective law-making by judicial decision forms any part of the practice of any courts within the United Kingdom. The discussion which follows, therefore, does no more than consider the leading judicial comments on the possibility of its future adoption.

The idea that changes in the law should apply only to the future is deceptively simple. There still remains the question of the precise point at which such changes should become effective. Statutes answer this question either by making express provisions in commencement sections or by relying on s. 4 of the Interpretation Act 1978 (both of which are discussed at page 296). In the case of prospective overruling, however, it is up to the courts to formulate their own answers.

One possibility is that the court which overrules a decision may apply the old law to the instant case, while going on to say that the new law shall be applied in all future cases arising from transactions and events occurring after the date of the instant case. Alternatively, the court may take this approach to the prospective operation of the new law, while following the retrospective tradition to the extent of applying the new law to the instant case.

Another possibility is that the court which overrules a decision may apply the old law to the instant case, while specifying a future date on which the new law will come into effect. The purpose of this delay is to give the government an opportunity to make remedial delegated legislation, or secure the passing of remedial primary legislation (as the case may be), which will, in either case, replace the new law which the court has just formulated. (Whether the government will wish to nullify the effect of the new law will, of course, depend on all the circumstances.)

A variation on this possibility is the only form of purely prospective judicial law-making which is practised in any of the legal systems of the United Kingdom. However, this variation, which is limited to certain devolution cases, is not, strictly speaking, a form of prospective *overruling*, since it does not depend on the existence of a previous, erroneous decision. The relevant provisions are typified by s. 102 of the Scotland Act 1998, under which a court which decides that the Scottish Parliament has exceeded its legislative competence may make an order removing or restricting the retrospective effect of its decision or suspending the effect of its decision, so as to enable the defect to be corrected. Corresponding provisions appear in s. 110 of the Government of Wales Act 1998 and s. 81 of the Northern Ireland Act 1998.

### 8.6.3    Judicial attitudes to prospective overruling

As we shall see, the English common law has only recently reached the point where it is prepared to regard the adoption of prospective overruling as a realistic possibility. Even this tentative position is ahead of most other common law jurisdictions, with the principal exceptions being the United States of America and India. In the former, the idea has had a somewhat varied history. In the latter it has been limited to constitutional cases (although, as with the devolution provisions in the United Kingdom – see above – this power of prospective law-making is available where there is no existing decision, as well as where there is an erroneous one). Occasional exceptions have also arisen in the Republic of Ireland and Canada. (Lord Nicholls' speech in *Re Spectrum Plus Ltd, National Westminster Bank plc v Spectrum Plus Ltd* [2005] UKHL 41, [2005] 4 All ER 209 – which is now the leading case on the subject and to which we shall shortly return – contains a useful overview of the position in a variety of common law countries.)

Returning to the English common law, the standard objection to the introduction of prospective overruling is based on the constitutional doctrine of the separation of powers (see page 69). This objection has a number of aspects, which may be summarized as follows.

First, those versions of the doctrine of binding precedent which allow the court to formulate new law which is to to be applied in future cases only (that is to say, without affecting the outcome of the instant case), must necessarily breach the separation of powers, because this practice means that the courts are plainly exercising a legislative function. However, it is equally true that this objection can credibly be made of any version of the doctrine of binding precedent. The only difference is that the retrospective version benefits from at least a fig leaf of respectability, because the new version of the law is a necessary part of the decision in the instant case. Moreover, and perhaps more importantly, the power of the courts to make new law has been established for centuries. (Additionally, and looking further afield – albeit to courts which do not follow the doctrine of *binding* precedent – judgments of the European Court of Human Rights operate only with prospective effect, while the European Court of Justice may limit the retrospective effect of its own judgments, where it considers there is good reason to do so. See pages 94 and 227, respectively.)

Secondly (and this objection is really no more than a practical consequence of the previous one), if the formulation of the new law is not a necessary part of the decision in the instant case, it can be no more than an *obiter dictum*, and cannot, therefore, be binding on later courts. This objection, however, is overly technical and ignores the fluid nature of the distinction between *ratio* and *dictum* (see Chapter 9 generally; and, more particularly, *Anderson (WB) & Sons Ltd v Rhodes* [1967] 2 All ER 850, which is discussed at page 161).

Thirdly (and again this objection is really no more than a practical consequence of the first one), if the new law is not applied in the instant case, why should aggrieved parties bother to take their grievances to the courts, thus triggering the possibility of any kind of overruling? At least a partial answer to this objection is that some litigants (for example, large organizations involved in much litigation of a repetitive nature) may find it worth pursuing a point in one case because of the future value of a reforming judgment. In other words, there would be a long-term benefit to that litigant, irrespective of the actual outcome of the instant case. Leaving such litigants aside, however, the existence of prospective overruling could make unrealistic demands on the altruism of ordinary individuals, who are never likely to bring another case involving the same point of law.

Moving on to the leading cases in which the English courts have considered the introduction of prospective overruling, Lord Simon was an early advocate in both *Jones v Secretary of State for Social Services* [1972] 1 All ER 145 and *Miliangos v George Frank (Textiles) Ltd* [1975] 3 All ER 801 (which are discussed in their respective contexts at pages 177 and 165). He was supported, in principle, by Lord Diplock in *Jones*. However, in *Kleinwort Benson Ltd v Lincoln City Council* [1998] 4 All ER 513 (which we have previously encountered at page 134) Lord Goff specifically rejected prospective overruling, which 'although it has occasionally been adopted elsewhere with, as I understand, somewhat controversial results, has no place in our legal system'.

The idea enjoyed a somewhat better reception at the Court of Appeal stage of *R v Governor of Her Majesty's Prison, Brockhill ex parte Evans (No 2)* [1998] 4 All ER 993, where the skeleton argument of one advocate was prefaced by a note explaining the American case-law on prospective overruling. (For the nature of skeleton arguments, see page 216.) This prompted Lord Woolf MR to comment that the practice 'results in a much more flexible position than that which exists within this jurisdiction ... [and] ... has much to commend it'. When the case reached the House of Lords (see [2000] 4 All ER 15), the idea of prospective overruling was raised again, although it met a mixed reception. Lord Slynn's speech was the most favourable:

> 'I consider that there may be situations in which it would be desirable, and in no way unjust, that the effect of judicial rulings should be prospective or limited to certain claimants ...'

At the other end of scale, Lord Hobhouse, while saying that decisions on procedural matters and on remedies constituted exceptions to the general rule of exclusively retrospective effect, was singularly unenthusiastic about prospective overruling generally:

'It is a denial of the constitutional role of the courts for courts to say that the party challenging the *status quo* is right, that the previous decision is overruled, but that the decision will not affect the parties and only apply subsequently. They would be declining to exercise their constitutional role and adopting a legislative role deciding what the law shall be for others in the future ...'

Occupying the middle ground between the two extremes, Lord Browne-Wilkinson, Lord Steyn and Lord Hope were all more or less neutral, although Lord Hope did acknowledge that 'the issue of retrospectivity is likely to assume added importance [under the Human Rights Act 1998].'

In *Arthur JS Hall & Co (a firm) v Simons, Barratt v Ansell (t/a Woolf Seddon (a firm)), Harris v Scholfield Roberts & Hill (a firm)* [2000] 3 All ER 673, Lord Hope gave further support to the adoption of prospective overruling.

In *Re Spectrum Plus Ltd, National Westminster Bank plc v Spectrum Plus Ltd* [2005] UKHL 41, [2005] 4 All ER 209, the House of Lords unanimously accepted that prospective overruling could be used in appropriate cases, while also being unanimously of the opinion that the instant case was not one of them. Before looking more closely at this case, it is interesting to note that, at the invitation of the House of Lords, the Attorney-General instructed an advocate to appear as counsel to the court, in order to provide information on the use of prospective overruling in other common law jurisdictions.

The issue was whether the decision of the High Court in *Siebe Gorman & Co Ltd v Barclays Bank Ltd* [1979] 2 Lloyd's Rep 142 (which related to fixed and floating charges in company law), was wrong and should be overruled. The House answered both these questions in the affirmative; but, for the purposes of legal method, the interest of the case lies entirely in its discussion of prospective overruling.

Lord Nicholls, delivering the leading speech on this aspect of the case, recognized that there were 'compelling pointers' that prospective overruling should not be within 'the normal reach of the judicial process', but that these pointers 'do not lead to the conclusion that prospective overruling can never be justified as a proper exercise of judicial power'. He continued:

'[40] ... In this country the established practice of judicial precedent derives from the common law. Constitutionally the judges have power to modify this practice. Instances where this power has been used in courts elsewhere suggest there could be circumstances in this country where prospective over-ruling would be necessary to serve the underlying objective of the courts of this country: to administer justice fairly and in accordance with the law. There could be cases where a decision on an issue of law, whether common law or statute law, was unavoidable but the decision would have such gravely unfair and disruptive consequences for past transactions or happenings that this House would be compelled to depart from the normal principles relating to the retrospective and prospective effect of court decisions.

'[41] If, altogether exceptionally, the House as the country's supreme court were to follow this course I would not regard it as trespassing outside the functions properly to be discharged by the judiciary under this country's constitution. Rigidity in the operation of a legal system is a sign of weakness, not strength. It deprives a legal system of necessary elasticity. Far from achieving a constitutionally exemplary result, it can produce a legal system unable to function effectively in changing times. "Never say never" is a wise judicial precept, in the interest of all citizens of the country.'

There can be very little doubt that a suitably constituted House of Lords will not only hold itself to have, but will also exercise, the power of prospective overruling when an appropriate case arises. Of course, appropriate cases may be few and far between, and it will be necessary to develop criteria which will help lawyers to predict with some confidence (and without recourse to crystal balls) which they are. However, on the strength of *Re Spectrum* alone it is possible to make one prediction and identify one area of doubt.

The prediction concerns cases involving Convention rights under the Human Rights Act 1998 (see page 100) and arises from Lord Nicholls' reference to the relevance of the practice of the European Court of Human Rights:

'[42] ... in one particular context the courts' ability to give a ruling having only prospective effect seems irresistible ... at times the Strasbourg court interprets and applies the Convention with prospective effect only. It would be odd if in interpreting and applying Convention rights the House was not able to give rulings having a comparable limited temporal effect (see Lord Rodger of Earlsferry, *A Time for Everything under the Law: Some Reflections on Retrospectivity* (2005) 121 LQR 57, p. 77).'

The area of doubt concerns cases which turn on points of statutory interpretation. More particularly, Lord Scott, with whom Lord Steyn agreed, took the view that a court which identified the meaning of a statute and declined to give retrospective effect to that meaning would be contravening the spirit of the prohibition (contained in the Bill of Rights 1689 – see page 66) on suspending legislation. Admittedly, Lord Nicholls, Lord Hope, Lord Walker, Lord Brown and Baroness Hale, in the majority, did not share this view. Nevertheless, it may be straw in the wind for the development of a restriction on prospective overruling.

## 8.7 Are the decisions of the courts actually the law or merely evidence of the law?

At one level it seems to be obvious that the decisions of the courts do actually make the law, and there is no shortage of judicial comment to this effect. For example, in *Attorney-General v Butterworth* [1962] 3 All ER 326, Lord Denning MR said:

> 'It may be that there is no authority to be found in the books, but, if this be so, all I can say is that the sooner we make one the better ... I have no hesitation in declaring that the victimization of a witness is a contempt of court, whether done while the proceedings are still pending or after they have finished.'

Similarly, although in an extra-judicial context, Lord Edmund-Davies said:

> 'But, like it or not, the fact remains that judges will continue to make law as long as our present system of determining disputes remains ... The simple and certain fact is that judges inevitably act as legislators.' (*Judicial Activism* in *Current Legal Problems*, 1975, p. 1.)

Inevitability and desirability are, of course, not the same thing, but we will adjourn discussion of the desirability of judicial legislation until Chapter 14. At this stage we will simply ask: if it is abundantly clear that the judges make law, how can anybody raise any doubt in the matter?

The problem is that judicial law-making offends some people's constitutional sensibilities, since the judges lack any apparent legitimacy as legislators, in addition to which judicial decisions will generally have almost unlimited retrospective effect (see page 133), whereas it is only exceptionally that statutes will do so (see page 308). Furthermore, if the decisions of the courts are law, why are only some other courts (namely those in the appropriate hierarchical relationship to the deciding courts) bound by those decisions, since this effectively means that those courts which are not bound are being placed above the law?

Historically, the arguments against the judges making law were generally accepted, and the so-called *declaratory theory* held sway. For example, in his *History of the Common Law*, originally published in 1713, Sir Matthew Hale said:

> '[The decisions of the courts cannot] make a law properly so-called, for that only the King and Parliament can do; yet they have great weight and authority in expounding, declaring and publishing what the law of this Kingdom is, especially when such decisions hold a consonancy and congruity with resolutions and decisions of former times, and though several such decisions are less than a law, yet they are a greater evidence thereof than the opinion of any private persons.' (6th edn, p. 90.)

Subsequently, some commentators began to doubt the validity of the declaratory theory. Probably the most famous dissenting comment came from John Austin, a Victorian legal theorist, who spoke of:

> 'The childish fiction employed by our judges that judiciary or common law is not made by them, but is a miraculous something, made by nobody, existing, I suppose, from eternity, and merely declared from time to time by the judges.' (*Jurisprudence*, 5th edn, ii, p. 655.)

Nevertheless, even at the end of the 19th century, Lord Esher MR said:

> 'There is in fact no such thing as judge-made law, for the judges do not make the law though they frequently have to apply existing law to circumstances as to which it has not previously been authoritatively laid down that such law is applicable.' (*Willis v Baddeley* [1892] 2 QB 324.)

The argument that the decisions of the courts do not actually make law, but are merely evidence of the law, proceeds by way of an analogy with evidence as to matters of fact, where several witnesses to a factual occurrence may find that their evidence differs depending on their perceptions of what happened.

According to this argument, if the decisions of the courts are actually the law, the judges should have no difficulty in identifying the law and applying it. Yet dissenting judgments, and judgments which are reversed on appeal, are both commonly encountered. Are these judgments simply wrong, because they are inconsistent with the majority judgments and the appellate judgments respectively? If so, the incidence of incompetence among the judges is remarkably high, especially in the context of a group of people who have reached the pinnacle of their profession.

One attempt to avoid this problem lies in equating the relationship between the judges and the law with that between witnesses and the facts. Just as different witnesses who all see the same incident may nevertheless give different versions of what happened, so different judges who all use the same legal sources, and who all hear the same arguments, may nevertheless give different versions of what the law is.

Unfortunately, although this argument is attractive in turning differences between judges into matters of perception rather than of competence, it is not without its difficulties.

First, at a purely practical level, there is no doubt that an earlier decision may effectively dictate a later one. On this basis, therefore, the statements of the judges certainly appear to be law.

Secondly, witnesses observe facts which would exist even if there were no witnesses present to observe them, so if the parallel between witnesses and judges is to be maintained, it is necessary to show that the rules of common law possess a separate existence, independently of their being identified by the judges. Additionally, it is necessary to show how the law, in whatever separate existence it may have, is capable of changing to meet the changing needs of society.

The argument that the decisions of the courts are merely evidence of the law, rather than actually being the law, is, therefore, difficult if not impossible to sustain. Perhaps those who are troubled by the legitimacy of judicial law-making may console themselves with the thought that judicial decisions may be, and not infrequently are, reversed by statute (see page 208), and therefore it is only decisions which Parliament is willing to tolerate that will have any long-term existence.

## Summary

- The doctrine of binding precedent states that all courts bind all lower courts, and some courts also bind themselves.

- However, in many cases the bindingness is more apparent than real. It follows that we must identify as precisely as possible the extent of the discretion available to the judges in each case.

- The idea of precedent may be formulated in a relatively wide way, by simply saying that it is desirable that similar cases should be decided in a similar manner.

- The idea of precedent may also be formulated more narrowly, by saying that similar cases must be decided in a similar way.

- The practical administration of justice in any legal system plainly requires that once a case has been decided the parties should be bound by the decision. This is achieved by the doctrine of *res judicata*.

- Binding precedent, as currently practised, operates immediately a decision is made. This means that binding precedent is effectively retrospective because it applies to facts occurring before the date of the decision.

- The introduction of prospective overruling appears to be a realistic possibility. If it is introduced, it could remove the problem of retrospectivity.

- It can be argued that the decisions of the courts are merely evidence of the law, rather than actually being the law. However, this argument is not without difficulty, and in any event, there is no doubt that effectively the courts do make law.

## Exercises

1 What is meant by 'precedent' in (a) a wide sense; (b) a narrow sense?

2 Distinguish between binding precedent and *res judicata*.

3 What is meant by saying that (a) the doctrine of binding precedent operates retrospectively; and (b) prospective overruling could solve this problem? Why do some people wish to argue that the courts do not make law? What difficulties does their argument generate?

# Chapter 9

# *Ratio decidendi* and *obiter dictum*

## 9.1 Introduction

Although the doctrine of binding precedent states that all courts bind all lower courts and some courts, at least to some extent, also bind themselves, it would be wrong to conclude that everything contained in a decision is of equal weight. More particularly, the traditional view holds that there is a crucial distinction between the *ratio decidendi* (commonly reduced to *ratio*) of a judgment, which will be the binding part, and the *obiter dicta* (commonly reduced to *dicta*, or, in the singular, *dictum*) which will be the non-binding part.

This chapter discusses the traditional view and reveals its limitations in explaining the nature of bindingness.

## 9.2 The concept of *ratio decidendi*

### 9.2.1 Introduction

The phrase *ratio decidendi* may be translated as *the reason for the decision*. Obviously, however, merely attaching a label to a concept is of little practical utility: what matters is, how are we to identify the *ratio* of a case? Before pursuing this question in definitional terms, however, it will be useful to understand the essentially dynamic nature of the concept of *ratio*.

When speaking of the *ratio decidendi* of a case it is tempting to think in terms of a fixed and single entity with an objective and continuing existence, which merely needs to be located and identified, just as a treasure hunter may seek to locate and identify a sunken wreck within a given area of the seabed. As we shall see in the remainder of this chapter, however, this model is seriously misleading. 'If we think of the rule of law as a line on a graph, then the case itself is like a point through which that line is drawn.' (*Salmond on Jurisprudence*, 12th edn, 1966, p. 170.) More prosaically, formulating the *ratio* of a case is a creative enterprise, and one which will often involve choosing between various possibilities.

### 9.2.2 Goodhart's view

One of the most influential commentators on the concept of *ratio* was Goodhart, whose essay *The Ratio Decidendi of a Case* first appeared in

(1930) 40 Yale LJ 161, and was reprinted in 1931 in *Essays in Jurisprudence and the Common Law*, p. 1.

The essence of Goodhart's argument is that the *ratio* can be discovered by taking into account the material facts and the decision based on those facts. Furthermore, facts as to person, time, place, kind and amount are all presumed to be not material unless there is good reason to the contrary. Identifying the *ratio* by reference to the material facts is explicable on the basis that it is reasonable to suppose that both the judge and the advocates were concentrating on the law as it related to those facts, and therefore the quality of those parts of the judgment which relate to the material facts is likely to be higher than the quality of anything else which the judge says. Two consequences flow from this.

First, a judgment given in proceedings to determine a preliminary point of law (when, by definition, the facts will not yet have been decided) may carry reduced weight in terms of precedent. In *Murphy v Brentwood District Council* [1990] 2 All ER 908, the House of Lords decided that its own previous decision in *Anns v Merton London Borough Council* [1977] 2 All ER 492 had been wrongly decided and should no longer be followed. Lord Mackay LC pointed out that, even though the earlier decision 'was taken after very full consideration by a committee consisting of most eminent members of this House', it was nevertheless

> 'taken as a preliminary issue of law and accordingly the facts had not at that stage been examined in detail and the House proceeded upon the basis of the facts stated in the pleadings supplemented by such further facts and documents as had been agreed between the parties.... When one attempts to apply the proposition established by the decision to detailed factual situations, difficulties arise.'

Secondly, if there is no argument on a point of law, the ensuing judgment may lack any weight whatsoever. In *Re Hetherington* [1989] 2 All ER 129, Sir Nicolas Browne-Wilkinson V-C had to consider whether the High Court was bound by a particular aspect of the decision of the House of Lords in *Bourne v Keane* [1919] AC 815, where the House had simply assumed the point in question to be the law without the benefit of hearing argument. Having surveyed the case-law generally, the Vice-Chancellor said:

> 'In my judgment the authorities ... clearly establish that, even where a decision of a point of law in a particular sense was essential to an earlier decision of a superior court, but that superior court merely assumed the correctness of the law on a particular issue, a judge in a later case is not bound to hold that the law is decided in that sense.'

The importance of the materiality of the facts may, therefore, be thought to be clear enough, but one crucial question remains: who decides which facts are material – the earlier judge or the later one? No satisfactory answer to this question can be given without recognizing that the phrase *ratio decidendi* is capable of being used in two distinct ways: *descriptively* and *prescriptively*.

9.2.3 Descriptive and prescriptive *ratios*

In its *descriptive* sense, the phrase *ratio decidendi* is used to *describe the way in which the earlier judge reached the decision*. Clearly, therefore, in this context a later judge must acknowledge the materiality of the facts which the earlier judge treated as being material. However, the crucial question arising from the doctrine of binding precedent in practice is the extent to which later courts are bound by earlier ones. The essential question, therefore, is not *how did the earlier judge come to the decision?* but *what is it in the earlier case which is binding on the later judge?*

The answer to this question lies in identifying the *prescriptive ratio* of the earlier case or, in other words, the statement of law derived from the earlier case which that case *prescribes as being the law for later courts to follow*. Julius Stone's version of the distinction is as succinct as any:

> 'Should we not ... try scrupulously to respect the distinction between that use of the term *ratio decidendi* which describes the process of reasoning by which a decision was reached (the "descriptive" *ratio decidendi*), and that which identifies and delimits the reasoning which a later court is bound to follow (the "prescriptive" or "binding" *ratio decidendi*)?' (*The Ratio of the Ratio Decidendi* (1959) 22 MLR 597.)

This is not to say that the idea of material facts has become unimportant. As Lord Halsbury LC said in *Quinn v Leathem* [1901] AC 495: 'The generality of the expressions which may be found ... are not intended to be expositions of the whole law, but govern and are qualified by the particular facts of the case'. But it is to say that the later judge has a vital role in interpreting earlier cases in order to formulate the rule which will then become binding in the present case:

> 'The truth of the matter is a truth so obvious and trite that it is somewhat regularly overlooked by students. *That no case can have a meaning by itself!* Standing alone it gives you no guidance. It can give you no guidance as to how far it carries, as to how much of its language will hold water later. What counts, what gives you leads, what gives you sureness, *that is the background of the other cases* in relation to which you must read this one. They colour the language, the technical terms used in the opinion. But above all they give you the wherewithal to find which of the facts are significant, and in what aspect they are significant, and how far the rules laid down are to be

trusted.' (Original emphasis, Karl Llewellyn, *The Bramble Bush*, 1950, pp. 48–9.)

Similarly, in *Osborne to Rowlett* (1880) 13 ChD 774, Lord Jessel MR said:

'Now, I have often said, and I repeat it, that the only thing in a judge's decision binding as an authority upon a subsequent judge is the principle upon which the case was decided: but it is not sufficient that the case should have been decided on a principle if that principle is not itself a right principle, or one not applicable to the case; *and it is for a subsequent judge to say whether or not it is a right principle, and, if not, he may himself lay down the true principle*. In that case the prior decision ceases to be a binding authority or guide for any subsequent judge.' (Emphasis added.)

However, in *Elliott v C (A Minor)* [1983] 2 All ER 1005, Robert Goff LJ, while acknowledging the legitimacy of subsequent judicial interpretation, emphasized that the process nevertheless has its limits:

'I feel ... that I would be lacking in candour if I were to conceal my unhappiness about the conclusion which I feel compelled to reach. In my opinion, although of course the courts of this country are bound by the doctrine of precedent, sensibly interpreted, nevertheless it would be irresponsible for judges to act as automata, rigidly applying authorities without regard to consequences. Where, therefore, it appears at first sight that authority compels a judge to reach a conclusion which he senses to be unjust or inappropriate, he is, I consider, under a positive duty to examine the relevant authorities with scrupulous care to ascertain whether he can, within the limits imposed by the doctrine of precedent (always sensibly interpreted), *legitimately interpret or qualify the principle expressed in the authorities to achieve the result which he perceives to be just or appropriate in the particular case*. I do not disguise the fact that I have sought to perform this function in the present case.' (Emphasis added.)

### 9.2.4 Identifying the appropriate level of generality of the facts

Part and parcel of the process of identifying the material facts of a case is the identification of the appropriate level of *generality*, or *abstraction*. Returning to Llewellyn:

'Each concrete fact of the case arranges itself, I say, as a representative of a much wider abstract category of facts and it is not in itself but as a member of the category that you attribute significance to it. But what is to tell you whether to make your category "Buicks" or "motor cars" or "vehicles"? What is there to make your category "road" or "public highway"? The court may tell you. But the precise point that you have up for study is how far it is safe to trust what the court says. The precise issue which you are attempting to solve is whether the court's language can be taken as it stands, or must be amplified, or whittled down.' (*Op. cit.*, p. 48.)

The more *general*, or *abstract*, the statement of the facts is, the greater the number of subsequent cases which will fall within the principle which is being formulated, and therefore the *wider* the *ratio* will be.

For example, in *Donoghue v Stevenson* [1932] AC 562, the House of Lords held that a manufacturer of ginger beer could be liable to the ultimate consumer if the ginger beer became contaminated during the manufacturing/bottling process by the presence of a dead snail and the consumer became ill as a result of drinking the ginger beer. At one extreme, this could be approached on a very specific basis, so that the case would be binding only in relation to precisely similar facts. On this basis the earlier case would not be binding in a later case where the drink was lemonade. However, it is impossible to see why, as a matter of law, there should be any distinction between ginger beer and lemonade, and therefore any degree of sensitivity to the concerns of the legal process will make it apparent that it would be hopelessly unrealistic to seek to rely on such a distinction. At the very least, the principle of the case must be capable of applying to all items of food and drink.

Putting it another way, formulating the principle in terms of *ginger beer* will produce a very narrow *ratio*, whereas formulating it in terms of *food and drink* will produce a relatively wide *ratio*. Going one stage further and formulating the principle in terms of *manufactured goods* will produce a still wider *ratio*.

In fact, shortly after the decision in *Donoghue v Stevenson*, the *manufactured goods* approach was applied by the Privy Council in *Grant v Australian Knitting Mills* [1936] AC 85, so that a manufacturer of woollen underwear was held liable when the garments contained chemicals which caused dermatitis. A yet further extension, beyond the realm of both manufactured goods and physical illness, can be seen in the case of *Hedley Byrne & Co Ltd v Heller & Partners Ltd* [1963] 2 All ER 575, which is discussed more fully at page 160.

It is difficult to overstate the importance of identifying the appropriate level of generality when seeking to identify the material facts, since the outcome of a case may well depend on the level of generality which the court can be persuaded to accept as being appropriate. In *Scruttons Ltd v Midland Silicones Ltd* [1962] 1 All ER 1, Lord Reid, while attempting to identify the *ratio* of an earlier case, said: 'If I had to try, the result might depend on whether or not I was striving to obtain a narrow *ratio* ...'.

Sometimes the comments of subsequent judges may result in the *ratio* of a case becoming so narrow that the decision is effectively confined to its own facts, which is a way of saying that unless absolutely identical facts were to recur – and this, of course, is unlikely to the point of impossibility – the case should never be binding at all. (The process of confining a decision to its own facts is also discussed at page 157.)

The possibility of multiple *ratios*

So far we have been assuming that a case has a single *ratio*, but in practice multiple *ratios* may occur. There are two possibilities.

First, a judge may base the decision on more than one line of reasoning. In this situation it is clear from the judgment of Devlin J in *Behrens v Bertram Mills Circus Ltd* [1957] 1 All ER 583 that both *ratios* will be binding, and that a later court cannot simply pick and choose between them.

Secondly, it is common for there to be more than one judge in an appellate court, and each judge may deliver a fully reasoned judgment. Even if each judgment contains only one *ratio*, therefore, the case as a whole will appear to contain more than one *ratio* – unless, of course, all the judges agree fully with each other, which is unlikely if they have all taken the trouble to prepare full judgments. Logically, you might well think that the *Behrens* principle should apply equally in cases of disagreement, and that such a case should simply be treated as having multiple *ratios*. The reality, however, is that in this situation a later court will take the view that wherever possible one or more of the judgments must be identified as containing the *ratio* of the case, with the *Behrens* principle being used only as a last resort.

There are two principal possibilities, namely that there will be disagreement on the reasoning, but there will nevertheless be agreement on the result; or there will be disagreement on both the reasoning and the result. Taking these in turn, where there is agreement on the result and a majority agreement as to the reasoning, it is clear that this reasoning should be the *ratio* of the case as a whole. If there is agreement as to the result, but no majority agreement as to the reasoning, and the individual *ratios* vary in their width, the decision of the Court of Appeal in *Gold v Essex County Council* [1942] 1 KB 293 establishes that the *ratio* of the whole case will be the *narrowest* of the individual *ratios*. If there is agreement as to the result, and the various *ratios* are simply different – rather than some being wider and some being narrower – logic requires that the case should be treated as having more than one *ratio*, and the *Behrens* principle reasserts itself.

In the situations mentioned above, it is immaterial which court is involved. However, where there is equal division as to the result, the identity of the court does become relevant, although unfortunately the matter remains less than clear-cut.

Where the House of Lords is equally divided, *Beamish v Beamish* (1861) 11 ER 735 established that the decision which is the subject of the appeal is confirmed, and then becomes binding on a subsequent House of Lords. (In practice, of course, an equal division is unlikely to occur, because the Appellate Committee usually consists of an odd number of Law Lords, but death or illness may occur at any time during a hearing.)

Where the Court of Appeal is equally divided, *The Vera Cruz* (1880) 9 PD 96 established that, although the appeal fails, the decision does not then become binding on a subsequent Court of Appeal. The difference between the Court of Appeal and the House of Lords in this respect was said to turn on the greater need for certainty in the latter, because it was the court of last resort. On the other hand, in *Hart v Riversdale Mill Ltd* [1928] 1 KB 176, the Court of Appeal came to the conclusion that the House of Lords' practice in *Beamish* also applied to itself. Unfortunately, however, the authority of *Hart* is open to question, because *The Vera Cruz* was not cited to the court. In *Galloway v Galloway* [1954] P 312, the court resumed its original position, holding that the later court could choose between the *ratios* of the earlier, equally divided, court. Once again, however, the status of this authority is open to question, since neither *The Vera Cruz* nor *Hart* was cited. Admittedly, as with the House of Lords, it will be rare for the Court of Appeal to be equally divided, since it is usual for an odd number of judges to sit (although s. 54 of the Supreme Court Act 1981 makes provision for appeals against sentence in the Criminal Division of the Court of Appeal to be heard by two judges rather than three). However, the section specifically provides that, in the event of an equal division, the appeal shall be re-heard before an odd number of judges, which in practice is usually three. Appeals against sentence are usually the shortest kind of appeals; therefore the time which s. 54 could potentially waste is kept to a minimum.

In the context of the Divisional Court, *Grocock v Grocock* [1920] 1 KB 1, establishes that the later court is free to choose between the *ratios* of an equally divided, earlier one.

In view of the confusing situation revealed in the previous paragraphs, it is tempting to argue that, even where a court has a number of judges, there should be only one judgment. Indeed, this is sometimes effectively the position where there is one leading judgment, with the others being simply short statements of concurrence. In some cases even the short statements of concurrence are omitted, with the leading judgment stated to be 'the judgment of the court'.

Some judges may have a temperamental reluctance to dissent. As the American judge R H Jackson J said:

'Each dissenting opinion is a confession of failure to convince the writer's colleagues, and the true test of a judge is his influence in leading, not in opposing, his court.' (*The Supreme Court in the American System of Government*, p18, quoted by Megarry, *A Second Miscellany-at-Law*, 1973, p. 149.)

However, judges from the Common Law tradition do not generally welcome the idea of single judgments on a compulsory basis. (The continental tradition is different, with single judgments being standard. Not surprisingly, this practice has been adopted by the European Court of Justice and the Court of First Instance; although, surprisingly, not the European Court of Human Rights.) The common law tradition stems partly from the judges' fear that single judgments would often be compromises, and may therefore be lacking in the desired clarity; and partly from the feeling that dissenting judgments can usefully sow the seeds of future legal developments. In the law, as in other subjects, it is not unknown for yesterday's heterodoxy to become tomorrow's orthodoxy. Moreover, Lord Reid saw a particular advantage in multiple judgments:

> 'I think that it is desirable to try to extract from the authorities the principles on which most of them are based. When we are trying to do so, my experience has been that there are dangers in there being only one speech in this House. The statements in it have often tended to be treated as definitions and it is not the function of a court or of this House to frame definitions: some latitude should be left for future developments. The true *ratio* of a decision generally appears more clearly from a comparison of two or more statements in different words which are intended to supplement each other.' (*Saunders v Anglia Building Society* [1970] 3 All ER 961.)

### 9.2.6   Does every case have a *ratio*?

In view of the difficulties that can arise in identifying the *ratio* of a case, it is sometimes tempting to give up, and to simply conclude that a particular case has no *ratio*. Although such a conclusion will be strictly exceptional, there is some authority to suggest that it is possible. In *The Mostyn* [1928] AC 57, Lord Dunedin said: 'If it is not clear, then I do not think it is part of a tribunal's duty to spell out with great difficulty a *ratio decidendi* in order to be bound by it'. On the other hand, Lord Reid took a more conventional view in *Nash v Tamplin & Sons Brewery (Brighton) Ltd* [1951] 2 All ER 869: 'It matters not how difficult it is to find the *ratio decidendi* of a previous case, that *ratio* must be found'. Given the enormous flexibility of precedent, this particular difference of opinion is of little practical significance.

## 9.3   Techniques used in handling *ratios*

### 9.3.1   Introduction

A number of terms have acquired relatively well-defined meanings in the context of describing the way courts handle *ratios*.

### 9.3.2    Following, approving and applying

An earlier decision is said to be *followed* in a later case where the facts of the two cases are sufficiently similar for the judge in the later case to be persuaded that the same principle of law should be used. Any court may follow a decision of any other court, but where the later court is higher than the earlier one, the principle may be said not simply to have been *followed* but to have been *approved*. If a later court finds an earlier decision attractive, and the facts of the cases fall short of being substantially the same but can be said to be not dissimilar, the later court may *apply* the earlier decision.

### 9.3.3    Not following, doubting, disapproving and overruling

An earlier case may not seem attractive to a later court, even though the facts of both cases are substantially the same. Where this happens, and the hierarchical relationship of the courts concerned is such that the later court is not bound by the earlier decision, the later court may *not follow* it. *Not following* may result in the earlier case being said to have been *doubted* or even *disapproved*. If the later court is hierarchically superior to the earlier one, and is satisfied not only that the earlier decision is wrong, but also that it should no longer be followed, the later court may *overrule* the earlier decision, thus depriving it of any power to bind any court in the future.

### 9.3.4    Distinguishing

In practical terms, however, perhaps the most significant technique of all is *distinguishing*. This takes us back to the idea of material facts. If the material facts of the earlier case, having been formulated at the appropriate level of generality, are not the same as the material facts of the later one, the later court may simply distinguish the earlier one. For example, in *Bridges v Hawkesworth* (1851) LJ 21 QB 75, a customer was held to be entitled to keep money which he had found on the floor of a shop. By way of contrast, in *South Staffordshire Water Company v Sharwood* [1896] 2 QB 44, the finder of two gold rings in the mud at the bottom of a reservoir was held to be not entitled to retain them, because the site of the finding had not been open to the public.

Distinguishing an earlier case is simply a way of saying that it is irrelevant to the later case. Therefore distinguishing does not usually imply any criticism of the correctness of the earlier decision in relation to its own facts, nor does it undermine that decision's bindingness in other cases. However, it is worth noticing that there is one special form of distinguishing which may be taken as implying doubt as to the correctness of the earlier decision. This arises where the later court expresses the view that the earlier decision should be *confined to its own facts*. For example, in *Jobling v Associated Dairies Ltd* [1981] 2 All ER 752, the House of Lords chose not to follow its own earlier decision in *Baker v Willoughby* [1970] AC 467, on a point concerning damages for personal injuries. The House expressed some doubts as to whether the earlier case had been justified by the state of the authorities at the time of that decision, and could therefore have chosen to depart from the decision in exercise of the power conferred upon it by the *Practice Statement (Judicial Precedent)* [1966] 3 All ER 77. However, the decision actually proceeded on the basis that the earlier case should be confined to the status of a decision on its own facts.

Confining cases to the status of being decisions on their own facts is rare and, cases such as *Jobling* notwithstanding, it is likely to occur only where the later court would otherwise be bound to follow a decision which it really cannot tolerate, but from which it can see no other way of escaping within the generally recognized limits of the doctrine of precedent. Such cases may perhaps be most accurately regarded as involving the formulation of a prescriptive *ratio* in particularly narrow terms. Whether a judge will confine an earlier decision to its own facts, or follow it with great reluctance, is a matter which does not lend itself to easy and accurate prediction.

In addition to the basic terminology which is explained in the preceding paragraphs, two rather more substantial matters must be mentioned, namely the *per incuriam* rule and the *changed circumstances* rule. Both of these rules – or it may be better to think of them as being *doctrines* to avoid implying a degree of rigidity which they do not possess – can be used to justify a decision to ignore a previous, and apparently binding, precedent. We will consider each of them in turn.

### 9.3.5 The *per incuriam* doctrine

A literal translation of *per incuriam* is simply 'through lack of care' but the way the doctrine works shows that rather more than mere carelessness is required.

Unfortunately, the courts have not always agreed with each other as to the precise content of the doctrine. In *Duke v Reliance Systems Ltd* [1987] 2 All ER 858, Sir John Donaldson MR stated what may be called the strong version of the doctrine:

'I have always understood that the doctrine of *per incuriam* only applies where [a court] has reached a decision in the absence of knowledge of a decision binding on it or a statute, and that in either case it has to be shown that, had the court had this material, it must have reached a contrary decision ... I do not understand the doctrine to extend to a case where, if different arguments had been placed before it, it might have reached a different conclusion.'

More recently, however, in *R v Simpson* [2003] EWCA Crim 1499, [2003] 3 All ER 531, Lord Woolf CJ, presiding over a five (rather than the usual three) member Court of Appeal, stated a weaker version, saying that the court agreed with Bennion that

'the basis of the *per incuriam* doctrine is that a decision given in the absence of relevant information cannot safely be relied upon. This applies whenever it is at least probable that if the information had been known the decision would have been affected by it'. (*Statutory Interpretation*, 4th ed, 2002.)

Clearly, therefore, there is agreement that it is not generally open to a later court to escape from the binding authority of an earlier case simply because the court in the earlier case did not refer to a still earlier authority which appears to have been binding upon it. The explanation for this is that the later court must generally assume that the earlier court was aware of, and able to distinguish, the still earlier authority, even though the judgment does not state that this was so. The disagreement between the two views is this: does the later court think that the earlier court would inevitably have reached a different conclusion from that which it did, in fact, reach if it had been aware of the still earlier authority, or is the mere probability of a different result sufficient? In *Miliangos v George Frank (Textiles) Ltd* [1975] 3 All ER 801, which is discussed more fully at pages 165 and 175, Lord Simon emphasized that the *per incuriam* doctrine should be 'modestly invoked', thus providing some support for Lord Donaldson MR's strong version of the doctrine, but it remains to be seen whether *R v Simpson* will be generally accepted as correct, or whether the existence of both views will continue.

One thing, however, is clear. Neither version of the doctrine allows a decision to be labelled *per incuriam* simply because the case which was treated as being binding had not been fully argued.

One complication which can arise in connection with the *per incuriam* doctrine is illustrated by the background to the Court of Appeal's decision in *Rakhit v Carty* [1990] 2 All ER 202. The background was that in 1988 the Court of Appeal had reluctantly accepted the authority of one of its own decisions given in 1982. At the Court of Appeal stage of *Rakhit v Carty*, however, it emerged that the 1982 decision had been *per incuriam*, and therefore had not actually been binding on the court in 1988. Clearly the court was not bound by the 1982 decision, but what about the 1988 one? Lord Donaldson MR said:

'The decision in [the 1982 case] was indeed given *per incuriam* ... However, the same cannot be said of [the 1988 decision]. If, therefore, that court having had all the relevant authorities before it, had concluded that [the 1982 case] was rightly decided, I would have felt bound to follow it, leaving it to the House of Lords to rectify the error. However, I do not think that this court is bound in all cases to follow a previous decision which is based solely on the authority of an earlier decision which was itself given *per incuriam*. In this case we are concerned not only with the rights of the immediate parties, but, indirectly, with those of thousands of landlords and tenants throughout the country. In these exceptional circumstances I think that we are entitled, and should, decline to follow [the 1988 decision].'

### 9.3.6 The changed circumstances doctrine

A useful starting point when considering the *changed circumstances* doctrine is that it is sometimes identified by the Latin tag *cessante ratione, cessat ipsa lex*. This may be translated as *with the ceasing of the reason for the existence of a legal rule, the legal rule itself ceases to exist*.

This doctrine has acquired particular significance in relation to the practice of the House of Lords when deciding whether to follow or depart from one of its own previous decisions (see Chapter 11). Although it is not limited to this context, it was in such a case that Lord Simon gave the best modern explanation of the rule:

'(1) The maxim in the form *cessante ratione cessat ipsa lex* reflects one of the considerations which your Lordships will weigh in deciding whether to overrule, by virtue of the 1966 declaration, a previous decision of your Lordships' House; (2) in relation to courts bound by the rule of precedent the maxim... in its literal and widest sense is misleading and erroneous; (3) specifically, courts which are bound by the rule of precedent are not free to disregard an otherwise binding precedent on the ground that the reason which led to the formulation of the rule embodied in such precedent seems to the court to have lost cogency; (4) the maxim in reality reflects the process of legal reasoning whereby a previous authority is judicially distinguished or an exception is made to a principal legal rule; (5) an otherwise binding precedent or rule may, on proper analysis, be held to have been impliedly overruled by a subsequent decision of a higher court or impliedly abrogated by an Act of Parliament; but this doctrine is not accurately reflected by the citation of the maxim *cessante ratione cessat ipsa lex*.' (*Miliangos v George Frank (Textiles) Ltd* [1975] 3 All ER 801.)

In reality, therefore, it is best to regard the changed circumstances doctrine as a special form of distinguishing. However, unlike ordinary distinguishing, which is available to any court, the doctrine does not itself confer a power to depart from a previous decision. All it does is to justify the exercise of the power to depart, provided that the hierarchical aspects of the case are such that that power already exists.

Having considered at some length what is meant by *ratio decidendi*, and how *ratios* are identified and handled by the courts, we must now move on to a corresponding consideration of the complementary concept of *obiter dictum* which is often referred to simply as *dictum* (or *dicta* in the plural).

## 9.4 The concept of *obiter dictum*

The starting point is that the concept of *obiter dictum* is defined negatively, in the sense that it embraces all those parts of a judgment which are capable of being statements of law but which do not fall within the definition of *ratio decidendi*. The functional distinction, as opposed to the definitional one, is that *obiter dicta* are not binding. This is explicable on the bases not only that the court may not have heard full argument on the points covered by the *dicta*, but also that, even where full argument has been received, it is likely that the court will have delivered the *dicta* without giving them the same careful consideration which would be appropriate to the more central aspects of the case.

Although *dicta* are not binding, it does not follow that they are worthless in terms of the doctrine of precedent. Indeed, it is quite clear that *dicta* may be persuasive, and that their degree of persuasiveness will vary from virtually nothing to something which in practice is indistinguishable from *ratio*.

One form of terminology which some commentators employ in an attempt to convey the possible variations in the weight of dicta is *gratis dicta* and *judicial dicta*, although it must be said immediately that this terminology is seldom if ever encountered in the judgments of the courts themselves. *Gratis dicta* are mere throwaways (sayings which are given away, as it were, free) and so of very little, if any, value or persuasive force. It is likely, therefore, that *gratis dicta* will not have been the product of much thought by the judge. *Judicial dicta*, on the other hand, will have been preceded, not only by a great deal of careful thought, but also by extensive argument on the point in question. In reality, therefore, judicial dicta may be so strongly persuasive as to be practically indistinguishable from *ratio*. An example will make the matter clear.

In *Hedley Byrne & Co Ltd v Heller & Partners Ltd* [1963] 2 All ER 575, the facts were that A gave B a banker's reference about C. The reference was stated to have been given 'without responsibility', but B nevertheless relied on it and extended credit to C. The reference was inaccurate and B suffered financial loss as a result. The House of Lords decided that, in principle, there could be liability in negligence for a misstatement resulting in financial loss. However, on the present facts, all the House of Lords needed to do was to say that, even if liability existed in principle, the disclaimer would be effective to prevent B from succeeding against *A*. Therefore, on the material facts of the case, there was no need to decide whether the liability did actually exist in principle, and it follows that the statement to this effect could be regarded as an *obiter dictum*.

Nevertheless, the House of Lords actually examined the issue of principle in great detail, even though on the present facts the disclaimer operated to negate any liability there may have been. It follows that it would be wholly artificial to discount the statement that such liability exists in principle simply because that statement was not strictly necessary to the actual outcome of the case. As Cairns J said, in *Anderson (W B) & Sons Ltd v Rhodes* [1967] 2 All ER 850:

> 'When five members of the House of Lords have all said after close examination of the authorities that a certain type of tort exists, I think that a judge of first instance should proceed on the basis that it does exist, without pausing to embark on an investigation whether what was said was necessary to the ultimate decision.'

Further support for the artificiality of any strict dichotomy between *ratio* and *dictum* may be derived from the Attorney-General's reference procedure under s. 36 of the Criminal Justice Act, 1972 (see page 53). In the present context, the difficulty arising from the s. 36 reference procedure is that juries simply give a verdict, without identifying their findings of fact or their reasoning based on those facts. Therefore it may well be almost impossible for the Court of Appeal to identify the jury's view of the facts with any degree of precision or certainty.

According to a strict application of the definition of *ratio* which depends on material facts, therefore, it would seem possible to mount a credible argument to the effect that decisions in s. 36 cases cannot have any *ratios*. On the other hand, however, the creation of the procedure in the first place was clearly based on the assumption that it would produce authoritative rulings, and there is no doubt that in practice the main thrust of a judgment resulting from a s. 36 reference is accorded equal status with any other decision of the Court of Appeal.

## Summary

- Any judgment can be analysed into *ratio decidendi*, which may be said to be the binding part, and *obiter dicta*, which are not binding.

- More particularly, the *ratio decidendi* is found in the central legal issue of the case. There is a *descriptive ratio*, which is a description of the reasoning adopted by the judge in reaching his conclusion. There is also a *prescriptive ratio*, which is the interpretation which a later judge places on an earlier judgment when deciding whether or not it is binding. It is the *prescriptive ratio* which is *binding*. When formulating the *prescriptive ratio* of a case, the judge must identify the *appropriate level of generality* (or *abstraction*) at which the facts of the earlier case should be viewed.

▷ There are various techniques which may be used when handling *ratios*. The ability to *distinguish on the facts* is particularly useful.

▷ An otherwise binding authority will cease to be binding if it was *per incuriam* but there are two views of what this means.

▷ *Obiter dicta* are those parts of a judgment which are capable of being statements of law but which are not *ratio*. Although, strictly speaking, *obiter dicta* are never actually binding, they may be so strongly persuasive that they are practically binding.

## Exercises

1 Distinguish between *ratio decidendi* and *obiter dictum*. Discuss the bindingness of each.

2 Distinguish between *descriptive ratios* and *prescriptive ratios*. Why may they differ? Which one is binding on the later court? Who identifies the *prescriptive ratio*?

3 What is meant by *distinguishing on the facts*?

4 What does *per incuriam* mean? What is meant by saying that there is a strong version and a weak version of the doctrine of *per incuriam*?

5 What is the *changed circumstances* rule? How is the rule misleading if it is taken literally?

# Chapter 10

# Vertical and horizontal dimensions of precedent

## 10.1 Introduction

Chapter 3 contains a diagram showing the hierarchy of the courts (see page 44), and Chapter 8 contains the general proposition that all courts bind all lower courts, and that some courts, at least to some extent, also bind themselves (see page 129). The first half of this proposition can conveniently be described as the *vertical* dimension of precedent, and the second half as the *horizontal* dimension.

The next three chapters are devoted to exploring the horizontal dimension in some detail on a court-by-court basis. However, the vertical dimension, although much more straightforward, is not wholly without interest, as the bulk of the remainder of this chapter demonstrates. This chapter concludes with some brief comments on the anomalous position of decisions of the Judicial Committee of the Privy Council, which does not warrant a chapter of its own but which must nevertheless be mentioned somewhere.

## 10.2 The vertical dimension of precedent

### 10.2.1 The House of Lords and the Court of Appeal

In practical terms, there is seldom any doubt that the Court of Appeal will hold itself bound by decisions of the House of Lords. Occasionally, however, some challenges to this proposition have emerged, as the following cases show.

In *Conway v Rimmer* [1967] 2 All ER 1260, the issue was whether the Crown could refuse to produce certain evidence which would have been useful to the plaintiff. According to the decision of the House of Lords in *Duncan v Cammell Laird & Co Ltd* [1942] 1 All ER 587, the Crown had an absolute right to withhold the evidence. However, when *Conway v Rimmer* reached the Court of Appeal, Lord Denning MR, albeit in a dissenting judgment, indicated that he thought *Duncan v Cammell Laird & Co Ltd* should not be followed. He was particularly influenced by the fact that the Supreme Courts of many other Commonwealth countries had considered, and rejected, the law contained in that decision, and also by the House of Lords' *Practice Statement (Judicial Precedent)* of 1966 (see page 173), which at that time had only recently been issued. According to Lord Denning MR: 'The doctrine of precedent has been transformed by the recent statement of Lord Gardiner LC. This is the very case in which to throw off the fetters'.

In fact, as we shall see when we consider the House of Lords' *Practice Statement* in the next chapter, this comment was entirely illegitimate, and was not surprisingly rejected by the House of Lords when *Conway v Rimmer* reached the end of the appellate process. Nevertheless, as an example of an attempt to loosen the formal constraints of the doctrine of binding precedent, the comment is worth noticing.

Another example of wayward decision-making in the Court of Appeal, although on this occasion all three judges concurred, arose in *Broome v Cassell & Co Ltd* [1971] 2 All ER 187. The problem arose out of the court's application of the *per incuriam* doctrine (which is discussed at page 157) in relation to the House of Lords' decision in *Rookes v Barnard* [1964] 1 All ER 367. The substantive issue involved the availability of exemplary or punitive damages (which are discussed at page 27), but for the present purposes the point is simply that the Court of Appeal unanimously concluded that the decision of the House of Lords in *Rookes v Barnard* was *per incuriam* because the House had not taken account of two of its own previous decisions. Since a decision which has been validly characterized as being *per incuriam* need not be followed by any subsequent court, it follows that, if this statement by the Court of Appeal was legitimate, the somewhat startling result would be that the lower court had deprived the House of Lords' decision of its authority. When the case went to the House of Lords, as *Cassell & Co Ltd v Broome* [1972] 1 All ER 801, all the Law Lords agreed that it was not open to the Court of Appeal to say that a decision of the House of Lords was *per incuriam*. Approaching the matter on the basis that the discipline inherent in the doctrine of binding precedent is a necessary consequence of a hierarchical system of courts, Lord Hailsham said:

> 'It is not open to the Court of Appeal to give gratuitous advice to judges of first instance to ignore decisions of the House of Lords ... The fact is, and I hope it will never be necessary to say so again, that, in the hierarchical system of courts which exists in this country, it is necessary for each lower tier, including the Court of Appeal, to accept loyally the decisions of the higher tiers.'

(For further examples of decisions which, on the basis Lord Hailsham's approach might be labelled 'undisciplined', see para. 10.4.) The Court of Appeal again found itself in difficulty with the House of Lords in relation to the form in which judgment should be given in a dispute arising from a contract which was expressed in foreign currency. In *Re United Railways of Havana and Regla Warehouses Ltd* [1960] 2 All ER 332, the House of Lords had held that an English court giving judgment in damages must express the amount in sterling, and not in the foreign currency which the parties had specified as the means of payment.

The point arose in the Court of Appeal in *Schorsh Meier GmbH v Henning* [1975] 1 All ER 152, where Lord Denning MR and Foster LJ relied on the changed circumstances doctrine (which is discussed at page 159), to justify holding that judgments expressed in foreign currency had become permissible. The crucial arguments justifying this conclusion were that sterling was no longer a stable currency; that British membership of the European Economic Community, and more particularly the terms of art. 106 of the Treaty of Rome, required the change; and that changes in the standard wording of English judgments meant that the change would not be objectionable on technical grounds. Lawton LJ, however, refused to join his colleagues, preferring to say: 'I stand in awe of the House of Lords ... It is my duty to apply the law, not to reform it'.

The *Schorsh Meier* case did not go to the House of Lords, but precisely the same point arose very shortly afterwards in *Miliangos v George Frank (Textiles) Ltd* [1975] 3 All ER 801. At first instance, Bristow J, faced with choosing between the House of Lords in *Havana Railways* and the Court of Appeal in *Schorsh Meier*, chose to follow the House of Lords. When the case reached the Court of Appeal, the court, which included Lord Denning MR, unanimously held itself bound by its own decision in *Schorsh Meier*. (When you have considered Lord Denning's record in relation to the self-bindingness of the Court of Appeal, which is discussed in Chapter 12, you may find something odd in his enthusiasm to be bound in this case.) In due course, the House of Lords, with Lord Simon dissenting, upheld the decision of the Court of Appeal as to the result. In other words, the House departed from its earlier decision. However, for the present purposes the main interest of the case lies in some of Lord Simon's observations on the precedent aspects of the case. (The fact that he was dissenting on the merits of the case in relation to the foreign currency point need not detract from the weight of those observations in relation to the precedent point.)

In the first place, Lord Simon criticized the trial judge for following the House of Lords, saying that this meant the trial judge was passing judgment on, and finding fault with, the Court of Appeal:

'It is the duty of a subordinate court to give credence to the decision of the immediately higher court, notwithstanding that it may appear to conflict with the decision of a still higher court. The decision of the still higher court must be assumed to have been correctly distinguished (or otherwise inter-preted) in the decision of the immediately higher court.'

Secondly, however, Lord Simon did say that, once the Court of Appeal had erred in *Schorsh Meier*, it had been right to follow that decision in the present case because the pursuit of self-bindingness in this context would give at least some measure of certainty. Lord Cross agreed with Lord Simon in part, saying that 'it is not for any inferior court ... to review decisions of this House ...', but he went on to say that 'it was wrong for the Court of Appeal in this case to follow the *Schorsh Meier* decision'.

In passing, it is worth noticing that the *Miliangos* case is also impor-tant as the source of Lord Simon's explanation of the operation of the maxim *cessante ratione cessat ipsa lex*. (This aspect of the case is discussed at page 159.)

Before leaving the relationship between the Court of Appeal and the House of Lords, it is worth noticing *Pittalis v Grant* [1989] 2 All ER 622. The background to the case was that originally the only right of appeal from the County Court to the Court of Appeal was on a point of law. Furthermore, in *Smith v Baker & Sons* [1891–94] All ER Rep 69, the House of Lords had held that a point of law could not be raised on appeal unless it had already been raised at the trial, although a more relaxed view was taken in the case of appeals on points of law from other courts. Section 77(1) of the County Courts Act 1984 amended the law, so that issues of fact could also form the basis of appeals from the County Court to the Court of Appeal. Quite apart from the 1984 reform, however, the common law had itself developed a number of exceptions to the orig-inal rule, up to and including the decision of the Court of Appeal in *Jones v Department of Employment* [1988] 1 All ER 725, where Glidewell LJ, while limiting himself to the creation of another exception, indicated that, in the light of the 1984 reform, the basic rule 'may be open to future consideration'. In *Pittalis v Grant* the Court of Appeal took the bull by the horns when Nourse LJ, giving the judgment of the court, said:

> 'The rule in *Smith v Baker & Sons* ought no longer to be applied. We are conscious that it may seem a strong thing for this court to hold thus of a rule established by the House of Lords, albeit one enfeebled by exceptions, the statutory support which gave it life at last turned off. *But, where it can see that the decision of the higher court has become obsolete, the lower court, if it is not to deny justice to the parties in the suit, is bound to say so and to act accordingly.'* (Emphasis added.)

At a technical level, it must be noted that *Miliangos* was not cited in *Pittalis*, and therefore it is possible to argue that the latter is *per incuriam*. However, it may also be that the decision in *Pittalis*, irrespective of the manner in which it was reached, represents an element of flexibility which is inherent – if strictly exceptional – within the doctrine of precedent.

Additional evidence that such flexibility exists may be found in the High Court's decision in *Derby & Co Ltd v Weldon (No 3)* [1989] 3 All ER 118. This case involved a defendant's application to strike out a claim, on the basis that the facts which were alleged (and which of course at that stage must have been hypothetical in the sense that they had not yet been proved) did not disclose a cause of action. Vinelott J held that, where such an application is made on the basis of a recent decision of the Court of Appeal which might be reversed by the House of Lords, the High Court's decision need not be governed by the decision of the Court of Appeal, but may take into account the possibility of that decision's future reversal.

### 10.2.2  The Court of Appeal and Divisional Courts

There are some ways in which Divisional Courts and the Court of Appeal appear to enjoy approximately equal status. For example, criminal appeals from Divisional Courts go directly to the House of Lords, and there is a substantial overlap of judges who sit in both courts. Nevertheless, it is clear that decisions of the Court of Appeal bind Divisional Courts in both criminal and civil cases (see *Ruse v Read* [1949] 1 KB 370 and *Read v Joannon* (1890) 25 QBD 300 respectively).

### 10.2.3  Divisional Courts and the Crown Court

The starting point is that the Crown Court is clearly part of the Supreme Court (the current authority being s. 1 of the Supreme Court Act 1981). Moreover, in *R v Colyer* [1974] Crim LR 243, the Crown Court held that this gives it equal status with the High Court, which in turn means that it is not bound by a Divisional Court decision. This decision is problematic.

First, the premise is suspect. Section 1 of the 1981 Act provides that 'the Supreme Court of England and Wales shall consist of the Court of Appeal, the High Court of Justice and the Crown Court...'. Since the Court of Appeal and the High Court are clearly not co-equals, it is less than self-evident that the statute is conferring equal status on the High Court and the Crown Court. Secondly, it is difficult to see why a single judge, whether in the High Court or the Crown Court, should be free to depart from a decision which, in accordance with *Police Authority for Huddersfield v Watson* (see page 205), would be binding on a three-judge

High Court. Thirdly, the application of *R v Colyer* could produce the following less than logical situation.

Suppose a magistrates' court, which is clearly bound by an appellate decision of the Divisional Court, convicts a defendant, who then appeals to the Crown Court. Such an appeal would be essentially on the facts (see page 46) but the Crown Court would obviously need to have regard to the law as well, and, according to *Colyer*, it would be free to make a decision at odds with that of the Divisional Court in a previous case. However, if it did so, and the prosecution made the point of law the basis of an appeal to the Divisional Court, the Divisional Court would have to treat its own earlier decision as being binding, thus making the Crown Court stage a waste of time and money. If this genuinely is the way in which the doctrine of precedent operates, it would be reasonable to expect a leapfrog procedure, similar to that contained in s. 12 of the Administration of Justice Act 1969 (see page 203), enabling appeals from the Crown Court to go straight to the Court of Appeal in civil cases and to the House of Lords in criminal cases. There is no such procedure. The only sensible conclusion seems to be that *R v Colyer* was wrongly decided and that the Crown Court is hierarchically subordinate to the Divisional Court.

## 10.3 The horizontal dimension of precedent

If a legal system is going to have a doctrine of binding precedent at all it may seem to be reasonably obvious that higher courts will bind lower ones. Furthermore, as we have seen, this vertical dimension of precedent raises relatively few difficulties in practice. Unfortunately, the question of whether courts also bind themselves, and if so which courts and to what extent – which we have labelled the horizontal dimension of precedent – produces answers which are both less obvious and less straightforward, as the next three chapters will show. However, before progressing to a detailed consideration of the horizontal dimension, it will be convenient to comment on the position of the Judicial Committee of the Privy Council in relation to precedent.

## 10.4 Precedent in relation to the Judicial Committee of the Privy Council

Beginning with the vertical dimension of the doctrine of binding precedent, the Judicial Committee of the Privy Council does not bind any English court. Admittedly, the fact that the Judicial Committee consists almost entirely of Law Lords means that its decisions are, in the absence of any other binding authority, usually treated as being very strongly persuasive. Nevertheless, strictly speaking, they are never binding.

However, three recent cases have dealt with conflicts between decisions of the Privy Council and those of the English courts, and these must now be discussed.

First, in *Daraydan Holdings Ltd v Solland International Ltd* [2004] EWHC 622 (Ch), [2005] Ch 119, Lawrence Collins J said that even if he had been unable to distinguish the instant case from the Court of Appeal's decision in *Lister & Co v Stubbs* (1890) 45 ChD 1, he would still have chosen to follow the Privy Council's decision in *Attorney-General for Hong Kong v Reid* [1994] 1 AC 324. More particularly, he said:

> '[85] The system of precedent would be shown in a most unfavourable light if a litigant in such a case were forced by the doctrine of binding precedent to go to the House of Lords ... in order to have the decision of the Privy Council affirmed. That would be particularly so where the decision of the Privy Council is recent, where it was a decision on the English common law, where the Board [i.e. the Judicial Committee as constituted for the case in question] consisted mainly of serving Law Lords, and where the decision had been made after full argument on the correctness of the earlier decision.'

Secondly, in *Re Spectrum Plus Ltd, National Westminster Bank plc v Spectrum Plus Ltd* [2005] UKHL 41, [2005] 4 All ER 209, the High Court followed the Privy Council decision in the New Zealand case of *Agnew v Commissioners of Inland Revenue* [2001] UKPC 28; [2001] 2 AC 710, rather than its own previous decision in *Siebe Gorman v Barclays Bank* [1979] 2 Lloyd's Rep 142 and the Court of Appeal's decision in *Re New Bullas Trading* [1994] 1 BCLC 485. The Court of Appeal, taking a more conventional approach to the doctrine of binding precedent, regarded itself as being bound by *Re New Bullas Trading*, and accordingly it reversed the decision of the High Court. The House of Lords, which was, of course, bound by neither *Siebe Gorman* nor *New Bullas*, overruled them both and then followed *Agnew* (on the basis that that decision was correct). In short, therefore, only the High Court had departed from conventional wisdom in relation to binding precedent.

However, for the present purposes, the real interest of the Law Lords' decision in *Re Spectrum* lies in their views as to how courts which are bound by English authority (according to the conventional view of precedent) should deal with conflicting authority emanating from the Privy Council. Three of the four Law Lords who expressed an opinion on the point (Lord Scott, Lord Walker, Lord Steyn and Baroness Hale), supported the conventional view that the English authority should prevail. (On this basis, the High Court had acted wrongly and the Court of Appeal had acted correctly.) Only Baroness Hale was willing to give the lower courts the freedom which the High Court had in fact asserted. As we shall see (at page 202), it is possible to argue that any observations made in the House of Lords as to the way in which the doctrine of binding precedent should operate in other courts, can never be part of the *ratio* in the House of Lords. The consequence of this argument is, of course, that such observations cannot, strictly speaking, be binding on those other courts. However, as we saw (at page 161), this argument is overly formalistic and ignores the realities of how the doctrine of binding precedent actually works.

The attitude of the House of Lords in *Re Spectrum* to the possible introduction of prospective overruling is irrelevant for the present purposes, even though – as we saw at page 142 – the case is probably destined to be regarded as a turning point in this aspect of the law.

Thirdly, in *R v James* [2006] EWCA Crim 16, [2006] 1 All ER 759, a five-member Court of Appeal preferred the Privy Council's decision (by a majority of 6:3) in *Attorney-General for Jersey v Holley* [2005] UKPC 23, [2005] 3 All ER 371, to the House of Lords' decision (by a majority of 3:2) in *R v Smith (Morgan)* [2004] 4 All ER 289. (In passing, it may be noted that nine-member sittings of the Judicial Committee of the Privy Council are very rare. The usual number is five.) Lord Phillips CJ justified the court's unconventional approach to the force of the previous authorities on three grounds. First, 'all nine of the Lords of Appeal sitting in *Holley* agreed in the course of their judgments that the result reached by the majority clarified definitively English law on the issue in question'. Secondly, the majority in *Holley* consisted of half the full complement of Law Lords. Thirdly, if the Court of Appeal in the instant case were to follow *Smith (Morgan)*, as the conventional notion of precedent required it to do, the outcome of an appeal to the House of Lords against that decision would be 'a foregone conclusion'.

In short, therefore, the prevailing view is that the Court of Appeal may, in exceptional circumstances, depart from a decision of the House of Lords in favour of a conflicting decision of the Privy Council. What those exceptional circumstances may be (in addition, of course, to those identified by Lord Phillips in *James*) remains to be explored in subsequent cases. Once it is accepted that this is the position in the Court of Appeal, it will be difficult to withhold the same (albeit strictly limited) freedom from the High Court. (By way of comment, it may be noted that this conclusion undermines Lord Hailsham's view (see page 164) that the doctrine of binding precedent is a practical consequence of the hierarchical structure of the courts.)

Turning to the horizontal dimension of precedent, the Privy Council does not bind itself (see *Bakhshuwen v Bakhshuwen* [1952] AC 1), nor is it bound by the House of Lords (see *Australian Consolidated Press Ltd v Uren* [1967] 3 All ER 523). In practice, however, it will normally follow both its own decisions and those of the House of Lords, with decisions such as *Holley* being unusual in the extreme.

## Summary

- The proposition that all courts bind all lower courts can be described as the *vertical dimension* of precedent.

- The proposition that some courts bind themselves can be described as the *horizontal dimension* of precedent.

- The Court of Appeal almost always accepts that it is bound by the House of Lords, but in wholly exceptional cases it may refuse to follow the House of Lords if it thinks that the interests of justice require it do so.

- The Court of Appeal binds Divisional Courts.

- There is authority to the effect that Divisional Courts do not bind the Crown Court, but this authority is suspect.

- The Judicial Committee of the Privy Council binds neither itself nor any other court. However, in practice, its decisions are usually treated as being very strongly persuasive, and, in exceptional circumstances, may even be followed by lower courts in preference to decisions of the House of Lords. It is not bound by decisions of the House of Lords but it will usually follow them.

## Exercises

1  What is meant by (a) the *vertical* and (b) the *horizontal* dimension of precedent?

2  Why may it be said that the authority which holds that Divisional Courts do not bind the Crown Court is suspect?

3  In what circumstances may an English court follow a decision of the Judicial Committee of the Privy Council rather than a decision of the House of Lords?

# Chapter 11

# Does the House of Lords bind itself?

## 11.1 Introduction

This chapter discusses the extent to which the House of Lords is bound to follow its own previous decisions, and the extent to which it ought to be bound to do so, together with the extent to which there is, and ought to be, any difference between civil and criminal cases for the present purposes. However, it is useful to begin with a brief consideration of the historical perspective.

## 11.2 The historical perspective

Until the mid-19th century the House of Lords took the view that it was not bound by its own previous decisions (*Bright v Hutton* (1852) 3 HLC 341). However, shortly after that decision, in *Beamish v Beamish* (1861) 11 ER 735, the House changed its mind, although the definitive statement of the position at that stage of its evolution is usually taken from the speech of Lord Halsbury LC, nearly 50 years later, in *London Street Tramways Ltd v London County Council* [1898] AC 375:

> 'Of course I do not deny that cases of individual hardship may arise, and that there may be a current of opinion in the profession that such and such a judgment was erroneous; but what is that occasional interference with what is perhaps abstract justice as compared with the inconvenience – the disastrous inconvenience – of having each question subject to being re-argued and the dealings of mankind rendered doubtful by reason of different decisions, so that in truth and in fact there would be no real final court of appeal? My Lords, *interest rei publicae* [i.e. it is in the public interest] that there should be *finis litium* [i.e. an end to litigation] at some time, and there could be no *finis litium* if it were possible to suggest in each case that it might be re-argued, because it is not "an ordinary case", whatever that may mean. Under these circumstances I am of the opinion that we ought not to allow this question to be re-argued.'

There seems to have been an element of confusion in Lord Halsbury's thinking, since it is the doctrine of *res judicata*, and not the doctrine of precedent, which provides *finis litium*. (The distinction between the two doctrines is explained at pages 131–3.) However, the matter is of no real consequence since it is abundantly clear that Lord Halsbury's view no longer represents the current position of the House of Lords in relation to its own self-bindingness.

## 11.3 The current position

### 11.3.1 The Practice Statement of 1966

*The content and status of the Practice Statement*

In 1966, Lord Gardiner LC, with the concurrence of all the other Law Lords, issued a practice statement to the effect that the House was changing its practice in relation to the self-bindingness of its own decisions. The full text of the statement, which is reported under the heading *Practice Statement (Judicial Precedent)* [1966] 3 All ER 77, is as follows:

> 'Their Lordships regard the use of precedent as an indispensable foundation upon which to decide what the law is and its application to individual cases. It provides at least some degree of certainty upon which individuals can rely in the conduct of their affairs, as well as a basis for orderly development of legal rules.
>
> 'Their Lordships nevertheless recognize that too rigid adherence to precedent may lead to injustice in a particular case and also unduly restrict proper development of the law. They propose therefore to modify their present practice and, while treating former decisions of this House as normally binding, to depart from a previous decision when it appears right to do so.
>
> 'In this connection they will bear in mind the danger of disturbing retrospectively the basis on which contracts, settlements of property and fiscal arrangements have been entered into, and also the especial need for certainty as to the criminal law.
>
> 'This announcement is not intended to affect the use of precedent elsewhere than in this House.'

A Press Release issued in connection with the Practice Statement said that the new power to depart would be exercised only rarely. By way of an example, it was said that the House might wish to depart where there were changed conditions. The Press Release also pointed out that one of the advantages of the new power was that it would enable the House to take account of the decisions of other superior courts elsewhere in the Commonwealth.

Perhaps the most startling aspect of the contrast between the attitude which the House of Lords developed in the 19th century and the 1966 revision of that attitude is that a single factor – the position of the House of Lords as the highest court of appeal – is used to justify diametrically opposed conclusions, namely that it should not, or conversely should, have power to depart from its own previous decisions.

Before turning to the operation of the Practice Statement, there is at least an academic point to be taken in relation to its status and effect. The problem is that, by their very nature, Practice Statements deal with matters of practice rather than law. The use of a Practice Statement to amend the doctrine would seem, therefore, to assume that no more than practice is involved, although, as we shall see (at pages 201–2) when we consider the self-bindingness of the Court of Appeal, the House of Lords sometimes prefers to regard the content of the doctrine of precedent as being a matter of law.

### The Practice Statement in operation

Turning to the way in which the Practice Statement has been put into operation, there is the purely practical point that the *Practice Direction (House of Lords: Preparation of Case)* [1971] 2 All ER 159 requires a party who intends to invite the House to depart from one of its own previous decisions to draw attention to this intention in the appeal documents. The normal practice will then be for a seven-member court to be convened, although five-member courts are not unknown even for this purpose, as evidenced by the decisions in *The Johanna Oldendorff* and *R v C* (which are discussed at pages 181 and 137, respectively) and *Horton v Sadler* [2006] UKHL 27, [2006] 2 WLR 1346, in which the House of Lords departed from *Walkley v Precision Forgings Ltd* [1979] 2 All ER 548, in order to establish the power of a court of first instance to extend the time limit for commencement of certain legal proceedings.

Two other preliminary points of a more conceptual nature also arise.

First, the Practice Statement itself makes no mention of *overruling*, but merely of *departing from*, earlier decisions. This may simply have been natural timidity arising from the constitutional context of what the House was doing, but from the academic perspective, at least, the distinction between *overruling* and *departing from* earlier decisions is not without significance. If a decision is *overruled*, its *ratio* ceases to have any binding effect whereas, if it is merely *departed from*, the result is that thereafter there are two mutually inconsistent decisions. In this situation, therefore, theoretically at least, a future court may choose between the two decisions. Admittedly, a subsequent court would normally be very reluctant to follow a decision from which the House of Lords had expressly departed. However, this would not necessarily be so if the departure has been on the grounds of changed circumstances, and the circumstances had subsequently changed back to those which had prevailed at the date of the first decision. It is arguable that, if this situation were to arise, *any* court could choose to follow the earlier decision.

The point appears never to have arisen in practice, but the potential difficulty may be illustrated by speculating on the case of *Yorke Motors v Edwards* [1982] 1 All ER 1024, where the House of Lords departed from its own decision in *Jacobs v Booth's Distillery Co* (1901) 85 LT 262. The cases involved the exercise of judicial discretion on a point of High Court procedure, and the House of Lords said that changed circumstances, namely high inflation and high interest rates, which made it more attractive to a creditor to pay late rather than on time, justified departing from the earlier case. The House made it clear that this was not a matter of overruling the earlier decision. It would follow that, if the national economy were to return to a situation in which low inflation and low interest rates prevailed, the earlier decision could in turn be resurrected without overruling the later one.

Although departing from decisions rather than overruling them may, therefore, be an identifiable and legitimate technique, in *Miliangos v George Frank (Textiles) Ltd* [1975] 3 All ER 801, Lord Simon criticized his colleagues' reluctance to speak of overruling their own decisions: 'I say "overrule" expressly. It is better to avoid euphemisms like "depart from". A wise decision is more likely to be achieved if the reality is faced'. It should also be noted that law reporters have not generally shared whatever qualms the House may have experienced, with the result that headnotes often speak of earlier decisions being *overruled* where the speeches themselves refer only to *departure from* them.

The second preliminary point involves the well-known logical fallacy of *post hoc ergo propter hoc*, which may be translated as 'after this, therefore because of this'. Although it is obvious that one thing which happens *after* another does not necessarily happen *because of* the other, it is surprisingly easy to lose sight of the fallacy when it is submerged within a complex context. For example, although it is tempting to think that the Practice Statement must have been the direct causal factor in every subsequent House of Lords decision which has departed from an earlier one, it may well be that, in some cases at least, the departures would have resulted from the established techniques of handling precedents, and especially the technique of *distinguishing* earlier cases (see page 156).

Nevertheless, it is probably true to say that the Practice Statement created a new atmosphere in which the House of Lords was prepared to be more critical of some of its earlier decisions. This explains the apparent discrepancy between the research findings of Paterson and those of Harris. Paterson, in his book *The Law Lords*, published in 1982, concluded that by 1980 there were eight cases in which the House had used the Practice Statement. Harris, in an article entitled *Towards Principles of Overruling – When Should a Final Court of Appeal Second Guess?* (1990) 10 OJLS 135, found only seven instances, despite the fact that his work was undertaken significantly later than Paterson's. Harris explains the discrepancy thus:

'[Paterson] includes cases in which, although in their opinions Law Lords did not indicate that they were overruling, they have, after the event, told him in personal interviews that they consider that that was what they were really doing. Such anecdotal information is of value to the role-analysis in which Paterson is engaged, since it throws light on the psychological significance of the Practice Statement. It cannot be used in the present enquiry, since we are concerned with principles which underlie the reasons actually given in announced instances of the exercise of the power.' (*Op. cit.*, p. 140, n. 27.)

Since the Practice Statement itself spoke of the 'especial need for certainty as to the criminal law', it may be useful to consider civil and criminal cases separately.

### 11.3.2    The leading civil cases

The first case to consider is *Conway v Rimmer* [1967] 2 All ER 1260, where the House of Lords departed from its decision in *Duncan v Cammel Laird & Co Ltd* [1942] 1 All ER 587. In the earlier case the company built a submarine, the *Thetis*, which foundered while undergoing sea trials, with the loss of 99 lives. In the ensuing litigation, the widow of one of the men wanted to have access to the plans and technical specifications of the submarine. The First Lord of the Admiralty objected to their production on the grounds of Crown Privilege (a concept which has since been redefined as Public Interest Immunity). The House of Lords held that in a case like this the relevant Minister should see the documents himself and form a personal opinion. If he did this, the opinion could relate either to a specific document, on the basis that disclosure would injure national defence or good diplomatic relations, or to a class of documents, on the basis that all documents of that class should be protected from disclosure in the interests of the proper functioning of the public service. The mere fact that the Minister did not wish the documents to be disclosed was not sufficient, but, provided he made a decision on the correct basis, the court would not entertain any challenge.

In *Conway v Rimmer*, Conway was a probationary police constable in Cheshire, and Rimmer was a Superintendent. Conway was charged with the theft of a torch and was acquitted. Nevertheless, he was dismissed, whereupon he sued Rimmer for malicious prosecution. Various reports had been prepared on Conway during his time with the police force, and he wanted them to be produced in evidence. The Home Secretary objected to their production on the ground that they were within a class of documents which should be withheld in the interests of the proper functioning of the public service. The House of Lords held that the Home Secretary's claim would be conclusive only if the documents were such that it would obviously be in the public interest that they should be withheld, and on the present facts this was not so. Therefore the court itself should look at the documents and decide whether or not they should be withheld.

Clearly viewing the case as involving departure from the earlier decision, Lord Morris echoed the text of the Practice Statement itself when he said:

> 'Though precedent is an indispensable foundation upon which to decide what is the law, there may be times when a departure from precedent is in the interests of justice and the proper development of the law.'

However, it is quite clear that, even without the Practice Statement, the House of Lords could have distinguished on the facts between a warship in time of war and a probationary police constable in time of peace, had it wished to do so.

*Jones v Secretary of State for Social Services* [1972] 1 All ER 145 is of greater significance than *Conway v Rimmer* in terms of the principles of precedent. Under the industrial injuries legislation in force at the time, claims for long-term benefit were determined in two stages, by two different tribunals. In the first place, the question was whether an injury had been caused by an accident arising out of employment. If this question were answered in the affirmative, the second stage was to decide the extent of the disablement, and therefore the amount of benefit payable. The legislation stated that the answer to the first question was to be 'final'. In *Re Dowling* [1967] AC 725, the House of Lords had held that the tribunal determining the second question could not reopen consideration of the first question.

In *Jones*, on legislation which was substantially the same as that which was before the court in Dowling, the majority of a seven-member House of Lords decided to follow *Dowling*. On the face of it, this decision may appear to be unexceptionable. However, the fact that four Law Lords thought that *Dowling* was wrongly decided, but only three were willing to depart, seems rather odd, and therefore the case requires some closer analysis. Four significant points emerge. First, the House made it clear that the power to depart from earlier decisions should be exercised very sparingly. In other words, the advantage of finality should not be thrown away lightly. Secondly, it had not been shown that the rule in *Dowling* was causing administrative inconvenience. The other two points are neatly encapsulated in a short passage from Lord Reid's speech:

> 'I would not seek to categorize cases in which [the Practice Statement] should or cases in which it should not be used. As time passes experience will

provide some guide. But I would venture the opinion that the typical case for reconsidering an old decision is where some broad issue is involved, and that it should only be in rare cases that we should reconsider questions of construction of statute or other documents ... Holding these views, I am firmly of opinion that *Dowling's* case ought not to be reconsidered. No broad issue of justice or public policy is involved nor is any question of legal principle. The issue is simply the proper construction of complicated provisions in a statute. There must be a large number of decisions of this House of this character.'

However, Lord Reid did acknowledge that overruling could actually promote certainty rather than undermining it:

'It is notorious that where an existing decision is disapproved but cannot be overruled courts tend to distinguish it on inadequate grounds. I do not think that they act wrongly in so doing: they are adopting the less bad of the only alternatives open to them. But this is bound to lead to uncertainty for no one can say in advance whether in a particular case the court will or will not feel bound to follow the old unsatisfactory decision. On balance it seems to me that overruling such a decision will promote and not impair the certainty of the law.'

Returning to the actual decision in *Jones*, it may seem odd that the House of Lords was prepared to follow an earlier decision which it thought was wrong, but a moment's thought indicates the consequences which would flow from the opposite conclusion. As Lord Pearson put it in that case:

'If a tenable view taken ... in the first appeal could be overruled by ... another tenable view in a second appeal, then the original tenable view could be restored by ... a third appeal. *Finality of decision would be utterly lost.*' (Emphasis added.)

Of course, you may wish to argue that, in reality, the degree of uncertainty which is present within the legal system is such that 'finality of decision' has already been lost to a large extent, if not quite 'utterly'. However, even if you do wish to argue this, you may still be willing to concede that there is a distinction between, on the one hand, uncertainty arising from factors such as the varying skills of the lawyers who prepare and present cases, coupled with inevitable variations of judicial psychology on the part of those who decide those cases, and on the other hand, the institutionalization of such uncertainty by the explicit adoption of principles of precedent which justify decision-making on the basis of purely subjective criteria.

In *R v Kansal (No 2)* [2002] 1 All ER 257, the House of Lords once again decided to follow one of its own previous decisions, even though a majority of the House thought it had been wrongly decided. (See page 106.)

*Fitzleet Estates Ltd v Cherry* [1977] 3 All ER 996 is another case involving statutory interpretation. The case involved some complex aspects of liability to income tax. The House of Lords declined to depart from its earlier decision in *Chancery Lane Safe Deposit Co Ltd v IRC* [1966] 1 All ER 1. More particularly, Lord Wilberforce said:

> 'There is therefore nothing left to the appellant but to contend – as he frankly does – that the 1965 decision is wrong. This contention means, when interpreted, that three or more of your Lordships ought to take the view which appealed then to the minority. My Lords, in my firm opinion, the Practice Statement of 1966 was never intended to allow and should not be considered to allow such a course. Nothing could be more undesirable, in fact, than to permit litigants, after a decision has been given by this House with all appearance of finality, to return to this House in the hope that a differently constituted committee might be persuaded to take the view which its predecessors rejected. True that the earlier decision was by a majority: I say nothing as to its correctness or as to the validity of the reasoning by which it was supported. That there were two eminently possible views is shown by the support for each by at least two members of the House. But doubtful issues have to be resolved and the law knows no better way of resolving them than by the considered majority opinion of the ultimate tribunal. It requires much more than doubts as to the correctness of such opinion to justify departing from it.'

Emphasizing that mere wrongness is not enough, Viscount Dilhorne said:

> 'If the decision in the *Chancery Lane* case was wrong, it certainly was *not so clearly wrong and productive of injustice* as to make it right for the House to depart from it'. (Emphasis added.)

Although Lord Wilberforce regarded the smallness of the majority in the earlier decision as being irrelevant, it can in fact be argued that this is a factor against overruling or departing from the decision. As Harris says, 'where dissenting speeches have been delivered, it is more likely that all pertinent reasons were considered than where unanimity prevailed'. (*Op. cit.*, p. 135.)

The fact that *Jones* and *Fitzleet Estates* both involved statutory interpretation must not be taken to indicate that there is always an absolute prohibition on overruling, or departing from, all earlier decisions in such cases. Thus, in another income tax case, *Vestey v IRC (Nos 1 & 2)* [1979] 3 All ER 976, the House of Lords overruled its own decision in *Congreve v IRC* [1948] 1 All ER 948, on the basis that the earlier court had not envisaged a set of facts such as the present, with the result that the law established by the earlier case gave rise to what Lord Edmund-Davies described as 'startling and unacceptable consequences'. He was also deeply concerned that the only way to achieve justice within the law as established in the earlier case was to allow the Inland Revenue to exercise an unappealable discretion to an extent which he characterized as being 'unconstitutional'. The final point worth noticing in relation to *Vestey* is that Lord Edmund-Davies also said: 'There can be no absolute veto against overruling decisions turning on the construction of statutes or other documents – or indeed any other type of decision'.

The first case in which the House of Lords appears to have relied unequivocally on the Practice Statement is *British Railways Board v Herrington* [1972] 1 All ER 749. The Board knew not only that there was a defective fence alongside one of its electrified railway lines, but also that people habitually took a short-cut across the line and that children frequently played on it. Using the line for the purposes of a short-cut and as a playground were both activities which, in law, amounted to trespass. The question of the Board's liability to trespassers arose when Herrington, a six-year-old boy, was burnt while playing on the live rail. The difficulty facing Herrington's claim for damages was the decision of the House of Lords in *Addie (Robert) & Sons (Collieries) Ltd v Dumbreck* [1929] AC 358, where a four-year-old boy, who was trespassing at the time, was killed by being crushed in the terminal wheel of a haulage system belonging to the company. The company knew that the equipment was attractive to children. The company's officials had warned the children from time to time, but their warnings were ignored. The accident happened when the machinery was started without taking any precautions to protect any trespassers who might be present. The House of Lords held that the company was not liable because there was no general duty of care to trespassers. The only duty which an occupier of land owed to trespassers was to avoid inflicting harm on them wilfully.

In *Herrington*, the House of Lords was undeterred by *Addie*, and held the Board liable because the presence of a child trespasser on the line was reasonably foreseeable. Nevertheless, the Law Lords showed some equivocation. Lord Wilberforce said: 'The law as stated in *Addie's Case* is developed but not denied: not, I venture to think, developed beyond what is permissible and indeed required of this House in its judicial capacity'. Lord Pearson was more forthright, saying that the rule in *Addie* had been rendered obsolete by changed physical and social conditions. As the proportion of the population living in towns increased, so there was a tendency for children to become short of playing space, with a correspondingly increased temptation to trespass. At the same time, technological developments made it ever more likely that trespassing children would encounter dangerous articles. Similarly, Lord Diplock accepted that the present decision meant rejecting the earlier case, but insisted: 'It takes account, as this House as the final expositor of the Common Law should always do, of changes in social attitudes, circumstances and general public sentiment'.

In *The Johanna Oldendorff* [1974] AC 479, the House, by a majority of four to one, overruled its own previous decision in *The Aello* [1960 ] 2 All ER 578. Both cases turned on the question of when a ship which is let on a charterparty (or, in other words, a sort of lease of a ship) is to be considered to have arrived at a given port, and thus to have become 'an arrived ship'. The earlier case had decided that a ship had not arrived until it was at a place where it could be loaded or unloaded, but in the later case the House preferred to substitute the view that merely being in a position where ships customarily lie while awaiting an available berth is sufficient. This change was thought to create additional certainty which would make it easier for members of the shipping community to know where they stood in individual cases. The dissenting voice was that of Lord Morris, who had been one of the majority in *The Aello*.

One aspect of *The Johanna Oldendorff* which is worthy of comment is that the House took the view that, once it was decided that the earlier case had been wrongly decided, a decision to overrule it would promote certainty rather than undermining it. This was based on the proposition, in Lord Reid's dissenting speech in *Jones* (see page 178), that allowing a case to stand when it is acknowledged to be wrong may result in subsequent courts yielding to the temptation to distinguish it, even if only on artificial grounds (as indeed Lord Denning MR had done at the Court of Appeal stage of the present case).

In *The Hannah Blumenthal* [1983] 1 All ER 34, the House of Lords refused to depart from its own decision in *The Bremer Vulkan* [1981] AC 909, which had decided that an arbitration agreement could not be treated as having been repudiated even though one of the parties was guilty of inordinate and inexcusable delay. As far as the principles of precedent are concerned, Lord Brandon said:

> 'It was contended ... that this was a case in which it would be right ... to exercise the freedom conferred ... by the Practice Statement ... to depart from ... *Bremer Vulkan* ... In support of this contention four main points were put forward. The first point was the obvious regret of the two lower courts at the decision, and the consequent efforts of the trial judge and the majority of the Court of Appeal in the present case to find a way round it if they could possibly do so. The second point concerned the observations of Griffiths LJ in his judgment ... He ... said that, if he had not had the advantage of reading Lord Diplock's speech in *Bremer Vulkan*, he would have fallen into the same error as the judge of first instance, the Court of Appeal, and the two of their Lordships who dissented in this House in that case ... The third point was that the decision, if carried to its logical conclusion, would lead to situations

arising in which, although a satisfactory trial of a reference was no longer possible, that reference must nevertheless still proceed to trial. The fourth point was that, since actions and arbitrations were alike adversarial in character the same principles with regard to inordinate and inexcusable delay were expected by commercial men to apply, and should as a matter of justice and common sense apply, equally to both.'

Having cited with approval the view which Lord Wilberforce expressed in *Fitzleet Estates* (see page 179), Lord Brandon continued:

'I express no opinion one way or another as to the conclusion which I might have reached if I had been a member of the Committee which decided the *Bremer Vulkan* case. It is sufficient to say that that decision was reached by what Lord Wilberforce described as the best way of resolving doubtful issues known to the law, and that no special or unusual circumstances have been put forward as justifying a departure from it.

'Dealing specifically with the four points put forward ... above, I would say this. With regard to the first point, the fact that a decision of your Lordships' House is so unpopular with members of courts below that they are led to seek a way to get round it if they can, reflects greater credit on their independence of mind than on their loyalty to the established and indispensable principle of judicial precedent. With regard to the second point, it is not difficult to understand the reaction of Griffiths LJ, and of solicitors and others engaged in arbitrations, that it seems hard on a party against whom a claim is being made, to oblige himself to ensure that his opponent proceeds with it with proper dispatch. Against that, it is to be remembered that the primary object sought to be achieved by parties who have agreed to refer a dispute between them to arbitration, is that the dispute should be decided on its merits by the arbitral process which they have chosen with reasonable speed, and not that it shall end up, after inordinate and inexcusable delay, by not being decided on its merits by that process at all. With regard to the third point, I do not consider that the consequence flows from the premise. If a claimant is guilty of inordinate and inexcusable delay in the prosecution of a reference to arbitration, the respondent can and should apply to the arbitrator to give peremptory directions to the claimant to end the delay ... With regard to the fourth point, that illustrates very well the situation described by Lord Wilberforce ... in *Fitzleet Estates* ... where two eminently possible views of a question may be taken; where a decision between them has to be made by the best method known to the law; and where, once such a decision has been made, it must for the future be followed and acted upon without the risk of its being later held to have been wrong and departed from on that account. In this connection I would lay stress on what is generally accepted to be the special need for certainty, consistency and continuity in the field of commercial law.'

The case of *Miliangos v George Frank (Textiles) Ltd* [1975] 3 All ER 801, dealing with the earlier case of *Re United Railways of Havana and Regla Warehouses Ltd* [1960] 2 All ER 332, which is discussed at page 165, becomes relevant again. In the later case the House of Lords decided that an English court can give judgment expressed in terms of foreign currency, notwithstanding the decision to the contrary in the earlier case.

The facts were that the defendant, an English company, agreed to buy a quantity of yarn from the plaintiff, a Swiss national. The contract price was expressed in Swiss francs. The defendant did not pay in accordance with the terms of the contract and the plaintiff sued, claiming the sterling equivalent of the contract price at the date when payment should have been made in accordance with the contract. Before the date of the hearing, however, the value of sterling fell against the Swiss franc, so that conversion of the contract price into sterling would leave the plaintiff significantly worse off in terms of Swiss francs. The question therefore was whether, at the hearing, the plaintiff should be allowed to amend his claim so that it was expressed in Swiss francs.

The crucial argument advanced on behalf of the plaintiff was that sterling was no longer a stable currency, and that therefore justice required that compensation for loss should be expressed in the terms of the currency in which the loss had been incurred. The plaintiff also argued that a technical objection which had previously prevented judgment being expressed in foreign currency and which had been based on the standard wording of the form of English judgments, was no longer valid because the form of judgment had recently been changed. The House of Lords agreed that, as a result of the changed circumstances, judgment could be expressed in foreign currency.

In *R v Secretary of State for the Home Department ex parte Zamir* [1980] 2 All ER 768, the House of Lords held that when an immigration officer has decided that a person is an illegal immigrant, a court which is dealing with a challenge to this decision is limited to considering whether there was evidence on which the immigration officer could reasonably have come to his decision, and could not decide whether the decision was actually correct. However, in *R v Secretary of State for the Home Department ex parte Khawaja* [1983] 1 All ER 765, the House – including two members who had decided the earlier case – decided that it had erred in *Zamir*, and that the courts should approach such cases by asking themselves whether the person concerned actually was an illegal immigrant. Lord Scarman said:

'My Lords, in most cases I would defer to a recent decision of your Lordships' House on a question of construction, even if I thought it wrong. I do not do so in this context because ... I am convinced that the *Zamir* reasoning gave insufficient weight to the important – I would say fundamental – consideration that we are here concerned with the scope of judicial review of a power which inevitably infringes the liberty of those subjected to it. This consideration, if it be good, outweighs, in my judgment, any difficulties in the administration of immigration control to which the application of the principle might give rise.'

At a general level, Lord Scarman also considered the effect of that part of the Practice Statement which states that former decisions are 'normally binding', but that there is scope for departing from them 'when it appears right to do so', saying:

'This formula indicates that the House must be satisfied not only that adherence to the precedent would involve the risk of injustice and obstruct the proper development of the law, but also that a judicial departure by the House from the precedent is the safe and appropriate way of remedying the injustice and developing the law. The possibility that legislation may be the better course is one which, though not mentioned in the Practice Statement, the House will not overlook.'

The possibility that legislation may be the better course can be illustrated by *Pirelli General Cable Works Ltd v Oscar Faber and Partners* [1983] 1 All ER 65, which concerned the length of limitation periods after which action in the courts will be time-barred. The general principle is that limitation periods run from the date when the cause of action accrues. The question in the present case was whether an action in tort accrues at the date when damage is done, even though at that date the damage is not discoverable, or only at the subsequent date when the damage was, or could reasonably have been, discovered. The problem is particularly acute in cases involving building works, where defects in construction may not manifest themselves for several years. In following its own previous decision in *Cartledge v Jopling and Sons Ltd* [1963] 1 All ER 341, the House opted for the first alternative, even though it acknowledged that this produced a result which was unreasonable and contrary to principle, because a plaintiff could be time-barred even before any defects became apparent. Despite the fact that the House had not been invited to exercise its powers under the Practice Statement anyway, Lord Fraser, delivering the leading speech, made it plain that this was a situation in which Parliamentary action was more appropriate than judicial law reform. Any change in the law would have to recognize that fairness does not operate only one way, and that potential defendants should be entitled to the benefit of a long-stop provision to provide an absolute cut-off date after which no action could be brought even if the defect had not manifested itself by then.

In *Woolwich Equitable Building Society v IRC* [1992] 3 All ER 737, the building society had paid money by way of tax. When the court subsequently held that the demand for the tax was unlawful, the building society received a refund, together with interest from the date of the judgment establishing the unlawfulness. Not unnaturally, the building society wished to receive interest for the whole of the time it had been out of its money, and not simply for the period following the judgment. The pre-existing law was against the building society, but the majority of the House of Lords agreed to overturn that law on the basis that common justice required the payment of interest in full, unless the facts of a particular case revealed some overriding issue of policy which justified a contrary result. Any other conclusion would mean that a public authority would have had the benefit of an interest-free loan as the fruit of its unlawful action. On the other hand, the minority view was that reform should be left to Parliament, on the grounds that the matter should be governed by a detailed scheme of a sort which the courts cannot devise and implement.

The point may be further illustrated by *President of India v La Pintada Compania Navigacion SA* [1984] 2 All ER 773, where the House refused to depart from its own decision in *London, Chatham and Dover Railway Co v South Eastern Railway Co* [1893] AC 429, to the effect that a creditor who receives late payment is not entitled to recover interest by way of general damages, even though it felt that the earlier decision was unjust. The basis of the refusal to interfere with the earlier decision was that Parliament had created a statutory regime dealing with the whole topic of interest on damages, and an alteration of the common law would not be coherent with this regime.

The decision in *Murphy v Brentwood District Council* [1990] 2 All ER 908 suggests that the House may be more easily persuaded to depart if the earlier decision was made on a preliminary point of law. The House decided that *Anns v Merton London Borough Council* [1977] 2 All ER 492 was wrongly decided and should be departed from. Lord Mackay LC pointed out:

> '[*Anns*] had been taken as a preliminary issue of law and the facts had not been examined in detail. When one attempted to apply the proposition established by the decision to detailed factual situations, difficulties arose.'

This is, of course, wholly consistent with the explanation of the distinction between *ratio* and *dictum* which was given at page 160. The proposition, which we first encountered in Chapter 1, that the courts will not allow themselves to become involved in disputes which are academic, in the sense that there is no real issue between the parties, becomes relevant again in the context of the Practice Statement.

In the arbitration case of *Food Corporation of India v Anticlizo Shipping Corporation* [1988] 2 All ER 513, the House refused to overrule *The Bremer Vulkan*, even though it accepted that the reasoning in the earlier decision was defective, and had led to harmful consequences. The basis of the refusal was that, on the findings of fact which had already been made, the case had only one possible outcome. Lord Goff, having referred *inter alia* to their Lordships' refusal to consider academic points in cases such as *Sun Life Assurance Co of Canada v Jervis* [1944] 1 All ER 469 (see page 19), went on: '*A fortiori* they should not do so where the inquiry involves a review of a previous decision of your Lordships' House, because it cannot be right to hold, *obiter*, that such a previous decision was wrong'.

### 11.3.3   The leading criminal cases

At this stage it is appropriate to recall that the Practice Statement itself spoke of the 'especial need for certainty as to the criminal law'. Common sense is sufficient to indicate that the underlying reasoning here is that it is unfair to create criminal liability on a retrospective basis. Unfortunately, however, the House has not always recognized this point, and has even on some occasions argued that, where the law has been incorrectly stated by the House, with the result that some people have been 'wrongly' convicted, the interests of certainty require that such convictions should continue in the future.

In *Shaw v Director of Public Prosecutions* [1961] 2 All ER 446, Shaw had published a booklet which he called *The Ladies' Directory*. This consisted of advertisements which prostitutes inserted and paid for, giving details of the services which were available and the relevant charges. Shaw was convicted of conspiracy to corrupt public morals and the House of Lords upheld the conviction. There was a great deal of academic argument over whether this offence actually existed or whether it had been invented for the occasion, and many people felt that, if given the opportunity to do so, the House would overrule the decision. This opportunity arose in *R v Knuller* [1972] 3 WLR 143, where a journal entitled *International Times* carried advertisements which were intended to bring homosexual men together. In the event, a seven-member House decided to follow *Shaw*.

Four Law Lords said that the 'especial need for certainty' in the criminal law meant that the House must be satisfied that there is a very good reason for departing from an earlier decision, with three of the four also saying that the need for certainty overrides any consideration of how wrong in principle the previous decision may have been. Incredible though it may seem, three Law Lords also said it would be wrong to upset the earlier decision if many convictions have resulted from it. The House gave effect to the principle of comity with Parliament when three of its members said that it is not for the House to abolish a common law offence through the use of the Practice Statement when

Parliament has recognized the existence of the offence through a subsequent statute, even if this recognition is only oblique (the reference here being to the Theatres Act 1968, which recognizes the offence of conspiracy to corrupt public morals). It was also relevant that there was controversy over whether the conduct which constituted the offence should be criminal at all. Nevertheless, the House did acknowledge that it would be right to reconsider a decision which has created real uncertainty as to whether an offence exists, but this situation has to be carefully distinguished from the situation where the offence clearly exists and the uncertainty arises merely on the evidence in each case as to whether a particular defendant is guilty.

One of the most unsatisfactory elements of *Knuller* was taken to an extreme by Lord Hailsham LC in *R v Cunningham* [1981] 2 All ER 863. The facts involved the elements of murder. As it happens, the Lord Chancellor accepted the correctness of the earlier relevant decisions and therefore did not have to consider the operation of the Practice Statement, but he did nevertheless speculate on what he might have thought if he had reached a different conclusion on the merits. Having said he was impressed by the 'wrong conviction' argument in *Knuller*, he went on to say:

> 'Nor can I disregard the fact that had I reached a different conclusion I should have been saying that between 1957 [the date of a relevant earlier decision] and the abolition of capital punishment for murder, a number of persons ... would have been executed when they ought only to have been convicted at common law of manslaughter had the trial judge anticipated my putative decision.'

This sounds suspiciously close to saying that once people have been wrongly hanged it is better to continue hanging people wrongly than to admit the error and change the law. If this is so, it would be taking the idea of certainty in the criminal law to depths of inanity which cannot have been in the minds of the framers of the Practice Statement.

In *Anderton v Ryan* [1985] 2 All ER 355, Ryan dishonestly handled a video recorder, genuinely but mistakenly believing it to be stolen. Obviously she could not be convicted of handling stolen goods, because the goods were not stolen, but could she be convicted of attempting to do so? Answering this question in the negative, the House held that, if the goods were not stolen, there could be no offence of handling them, and therefore there could be no attempt to do so. It was, however, widely believed that this decision resulted from the House's failure properly to understand s. 1 of the Criminal Attempts Act 1981.

In *R v Shivpuri* [1986] 2 All ER 334, Shivpuri genuinely believed that a certain substance with which he was concerned was a controlled drug, although in fact it was harmless. The question arose as to whether he could be convicted of attempting to be knowingly concerned in dealing with and harbouring a controlled drug. The House of Lords unanimously decided that *Anderton v Ryan* had been wrongly decided. Lord Bridge said: 'If a serious error embodied in a decision of this House has distorted the law, the sooner it is corrected the better'. One of the factors which the House felt to be relevant in justifying the overruling of *Anderton v Ryan* was that

> 'in the very nature of the case, [no one] could have acted in reliance on ... *Anderton v Ryan* in the belief that he was acting innocently and now find that, after all, he is to be held to have committed a criminal offence.' (Lord Bridge.)

In *R v Howe* [1987] 1 All ER 771, the House held that duress is never available as a defence to a charge of murder. This involved overruling the case of *Lynch v Director of Public Prosecutions for Northern Ireland* [1975] 1 All ER 913, and even Lord Hailsham LC agreed that this was appropriate. The main basis of the decision was that *Lynch* had not been justified by authority in the first place, but Lord Mackay LC also said that the reasoning which prevailed in *Shivpuri* should be applied equally in the instant case.

In *R v G* [2003] 4 All ER 765, the House of Lords concluded that *R v Caldwell* [1981] 1 All ER 961, the leading decision of the House (by a bare majority of 3:2) on the law relating to recklessness in the context of criminal damage under s. 1 of the Criminal Damage Act 1971, was wrong and should not be followed. At a purely technical level, it is interesting to note that Lord Bingham and Lord Steyn spoke of *departing from* the earlier case, while Lord Rodger spoke of *overruling* it. Lord Browne-Wilkinson and Lord Hutton both made short, formal speeches, in which the former agreed with the reasons given by Lord Bingham, and the latter agreed with the reasons given by both Lord Bingham and Lord Steyn. Lord Steyn also agreed with the reasons given by Lord Bingham. (For the distinction between *departing from* and *overruling*, see page 174.)

The facts were that a blaze, which had been started by two boys aged 11 and 12 setting fire to some paper under a wheelie bin, caused damage to adjoining premises to the tune of approximately £1,000,000. The legal issue was whether the fact that the boys had created a risk which would have been obvious to a reasonable, adult, bystander but which they themselves did not appreciate, meant that they had been reckless for the purposes of s. 1 of the 1971 Act.

Lord Bingham, delivering the speech which, in accordance with the agreements noted above must be the *ratio* of the case in relation to the question of the bindingness (or otherwise) of the earlier decision, made four points.

First, 'it is a salutary principle that conviction of serious crime should depend on proof ... [that the defendant's] ... state of mind ... was culpable'. Secondly, 'it is neither moral nor just to convict a defendant (least of all a child) on the strength of what someone else would have apprehended if the defendant had no such apprehension' and therefore the earlier decision was 'clearly ... capable of leading to obvious unfairness'. Moreover, not only was it clear that both the trial judge and the jury saw the instant case as an example of that unfairness, but also 'a law which runs counter to ... the sense of fairness [of juries and magistrates] ... must cause concern'. Thirdly, the extent and quality of criticism directed at the earlier decision by academics, judges and practitioners, while not determinative of its correctness, should not be ignored. Fourthly, the decision in the earlier case had been based on a 'misinterpretation' of the relevant section.

While there will be very few, if any, cases where all four of these points will arise together, there may well be cases in which one or more of them will provide useful ammunition for a party who is seeking to persuade the House of Lords to depart from (or overrule) one of its own previous, criminal, decisions.

## 11.4 Is the use of the Practice Statement predictable?

Even when the House of Lords was still proclaiming self-bindingness was the established orthodoxy, A P Herbert suggested that the decisions of the House of Lords were so unpredictable that they should be regarded as being Acts of God (*Uncommon Law*, 1935, p. 414). Nevertheless, some 20 years later Megarry felt that matters could still get worse. He began by pointing out that within a period of six years the United States' Supreme Court had 'fourteen times reversed one or more earlier decisions of its own, many of them recent' and proceeded to quote the view of the American judge, Roberts J, that such decisions tended 'to bring adjudications of this tribunal into the same class as a restricted railroad ticket, good for this day and train only', before concluding that if the House of Lords were free from the doctrine of precedent 'the variations in the composition of the House when hearing appeals (unlike the fixed composition of the United States' Supreme Court) would doubtless make uncertainty more unsure'. (*Miscellany-at-Law*, 1955, revised impression 1958, pp. 321–32.)

In fact, as we have seen, more than a quarter of a century's experience of the Practice Statement in operation indicates that the House of

Lords exercises its power to depart from its own decisions with an abundance of caution. Nevertheless, the question remains whether we can predict when departure will occur. Two matters seem to be clear.

First, the House will require the presence of some factor over and above mere wrongness before it will depart from its own previous decisions. Typical examples of such factors are changed circumstances and the recognition of errors of constitutional principle.

Secondly, among the factors militating against, but not absolutely preventing, departure, the Practice Statement's own emphasis on 'the especial need for certainty as to the criminal law' is now less important than it once was, and may be no more than a specific variant of the general principle that the House will be particularly reluctant to innovate in situations where it thinks many people may have relied on the law as previously understood. However, *Khawaja* (see page 183) seems to indicate that even this general principle applies only where the reliance has been on the part of the subject, and does not operate where it is the state which has relied on the earlier statement of the law.

## 11.5 Departure from previous decisions without relying on the Practice Statement

It is obvious that the principles contained in the Practice Statement, as subsequently developed, are usually central to any argument as to whether the House of Lords should depart from one of its own previous decisions. Nevertheless, the House occasionally departs from its own previous decisions on other bases.

First, in *Moodie v IRC* [1993] 2 All ER 49, the House of Lords departed from its own previous decision in *IRC v Plummer* [1979] 3 All ER 775, where the House had upheld the effectiveness of a particular tax avoidance scheme. Subsequently, in *Ramsay (W T) Ltd v IRC* [1981] 1 All ER 865, the House had taken a stricter line, to the effect that schemes of the type in question, where a series of transactions cancelled each other out, so that they simply generated tax-deductible losses on paper without having any substantial effect in the real world, were not effective for tax avoidance purposes. Expressly renouncing reliance on the Practice Statement, Lord Templeman, in the only substantial speech, expressed the position thus:

'If *Plummer's* case had been decided after *Ramsay*, the Crown would have succeeded, though not on any of the grounds advanced in *Plummer*. The present appeals are heard after *Ramsay* and this House is bound to give effect to the principle of *Ramsay*. I do not consider that it is necessary to invoke the 1966 Practice Statement which allows the House "to depart from a previous decision when it appears right to do so" ... The result in *Plummer's* case (which is a decision of this House) is inconsistent with the later decision in *Ramsay* (which is also a decision of this House). Faced with conflicting decisions, the courts are entitled and bound to follow *Ramsay* because in *Plummer's* case this House was never asked to consider the effect of a self-cancelling scheme and because the *Ramsay* principle restores justice between individual taxpayers and the general body of taxpayers.'

Secondly, in *R v Bow Street Metropolitan Stipendiary Magistrate ex parte Pinochet Ugarte (No 2)* [1999] 1 All ER 577 arose from a case in which the House of Lords had held, by a majority of three to two, that a former Head of State was not immune from extradition proceedings which had been brought to enable him to be tried for a variety of offences involving abuses of human rights for which he was alleged to have been responsible during his period of office. Almost immediately after this decision, it emerged that Lord Hoffmann (who had been a member of the majority but who had merely delivered a formal speech of concurrence) had certain links with Amnesty International, who had been allowed to intervene in the proceedings in order to support the application for extradition. The matter was brought back before the House, which held itself to have inherent jurisdiction to entertain proceedings such as those in the present case, in order to correct injustices to parties who, through no fault of their own, had been the victims of procedural unfairness. However, the House clearly emphasized that no proceedings could be brought simply because an earlier order was thought to be wrong.

## Summary

▷ Consideration of the historical perspective is a useful introduction to a discussion of the self-bindingness of the House of Lords.

▷ From the mid-19th century until 1966 the House regarded itself as being bound by its own decisions. The Practice Statement of 1966 reaffirmed the importance of the doctrine of binding precedent generally, but indicated that the House would nevertheless be willing to depart from its own decision where it appeared to be right to do so.

▷ The House has been restrained in its use of the Practice Statement. In civil cases it is clear that mere wrongness is not enough, and that some additional factor, such as changed circumstances or an issue of principle, is also necessary. In criminal cases the House began by being particularly reluctant to use the Practice Statement, but subsequently it relaxed this attitude to some extent.

▷ Experience has shown that the House uses the Practice Statement relatively infrequently, and with a reasonably high degree of predictability.

▶ The House may depart from one of its own previous decisions, without relying on the Practice Statement, where it has to choose between earlier, inconsistent decisions of its own.

## Exercises

1 What is the gist of the 1966 Practice Statement? Which types of case did it identify as requiring special consideration? Which other types of case (if any) have since been added to the list?

2 Why is mere wrongness not sufficient to justify departure from a previous decision?

3 What, if anything, is the difference between the House of Lords' approach to departing from its own decisions in civil and criminal cases?

# Chapter 12

# Does the Court of Appeal bind itself?

Introduction

This chapter discusses the way the doctrine of precedent operates in the Court of Appeal. The primary concern is to identify the extent to which the court binds itself, but some cases also raise the question of how, if at all, the principles governing this question at this level in the judicial hierarchy differ from those which operate in the House of Lords, and whether they should do so. As with the House of Lords, the distinction between civil and criminal cases is sometimes said to be relevant, so this chapter proceeds on the basis of that classification.

## 12.2 The position in civil cases

The leading statement of principle in relation to the self-bindingness of the Court of Appeal in civil cases is found in *Young v Bristol Aeroplane Co Ltd* [1944] 2 All ER 293, where the Court of Appeal held that the court is generally bound by its own previous decisions in civil cases, but went on to say that this proposition is subject to three exceptions, with the possibility of further exceptions being added from time to time.

The first exception arises where the court encounters two conflicting decisions of its own. In this situation the court clearly cannot follow both decisions, and therefore it must choose to follow one and not the other.

The second exception arises where the House of Lords makes a subsequent decision which does not expressly overrule a decision of the Court of Appeal but which the Court of Appeal nevertheless feels is of such a nature that the two cases cannot stand alongside each other. In such cases the Court of Appeal will decline to follow its own decision. The position is less clear where the inconsistent House of Lords decision precedes the Court of Appeal decision. In this situation it may be possible simply to conclude that the Court of Appeal decision is *per incuriam*. (The *per incuriam* doctrine is discussed at page 157, and forms the basis of the third exception, which is discussed in the next paragraph.) Certainly, in *R v Terry* [1983] RTR 321, the *Criminal Division* of the Court of Appeal held that in these circumstances it should follow its own decision. (The position in criminal cases generally is discussed at page 196.)

The third exception is that the court is not bound to follow one of its own decisions if it is satisfied that that decision was given *per incuriam*. It is significant that in *Young* the court felt that for these purposes the doctrine of *per incuriam* should be interpreted liberally, and this was accepted by Lord Evershed MR in *Morelle v Wakeling* [1955] 1 All ER 708, but both cases also expressed the view that liberal interpretations of the doctrine would nevertheless be extremely unusual in practice. (In other words, it seems that the strong version of the doctrine, formulated by Sir John Donaldson MR and quoted at page 158, will not always be applicable in this context.)

For example, in *Williams v Fawcett* [1985] 1 All ER 787, Sir John Donaldson MR indicated that, where the court has made a 'manifest slip or error', the resulting decision may be treated as being *per incuriam* provided that the growth of the error can be clearly detected in earlier cases; the subject matter involves the liberty of the subject; and the cases are such that they are unlikely to progress to the House of Lords which will, therefore, be denied the opportunity to correct the error.

In *Rickards v Rickards* [1989] 3 All ER 193, the facts were that an ex-husband was aggrieved by a County Court Registrar's order for financial provision in favour of his ex-wife. Having allowed time for an appeal to expire, the ex-husband applied unsuccessfully to a County Court judge for an extension of time. He then appealed to the Court of Appeal, although there were two previous decisions of that court which indicated that the court had no jurisdiction to hear an appeal in the present circumstances. The first case was *Podbery v Peake* [1981] 1 All ER 699, which had been reluctantly treated as being binding in *Bokhari v Mahmood* (unreported). The court held that, despite the earlier decisions, it did have jurisdiction to hear the appeal. The court said that *Podbery v Peake* had taken the well-established principle that the grant or refusal of leave to appeal is itself unappealable, and wrongly applied it to the refusal of an extension of time for appealing. All the judges pointed out that even *Young* itself envisaged further rare exceptions based on unusual applications of the *per incuriam* principle, and Lord Donaldson MR and Balcombe LJ went on to say that *Podbery v Peake* was such a case.

Nicholls LJ, who had been a party to the *Bokhari* decision, said that in that case the court had felt bound by *Podbery*, but had granted leave to appeal to the House of Lords in the hope that their Lordships would correct the error. In the event, the appeal did not proceed, apparently on financial grounds. He went on, forthrightly, to ask:

'[Is] the Court of Appeal ... bound to go on indefinitely refusing to entertain a particular class of appeals, even though in practice the House of Lords is unlikely to have the opportunity to consider the decision in *Podbery v Peake*? I am so oppressed by the injustice which this might well cause that I cannot think that this is the law today. This would indeed bring the law into disrepute. For the reasons given by Lord Donaldson MR, I think that this case is in a very special category. Both Lord Greene MR (in *Young v Bristol Aeroplane Co Ltd* ... and Evershed MR (in *Morelle v Wakeling* ...) envisaged that there might be rare and exceptional cases where the Court of Appeal could properly consider itself entitled not to follow an earlier decision of its own even though the earlier decision did not fall strictly within the normal definition of a decision reached *per incuriam*. This is such a case. In the instant case there are the two features that (a) the point concerns the jurisdiction of the court and (b) the remedy which the system of judicial precedent assumes will be available to review the earlier decision is, for practical reasons, not so available.'

Although the practical reasons for not proceeding with an appeal to the House of Lords will often be financial, there may be other reasons. In *Rickards*, the Court of Appeal dismissed the ex-husband's appeal on the merits, on the basis that the County Court judge had made a proper decision to refuse an extension of time in view of the lack of merit in the appeal itself. This led Lord Donaldson MR to say: 'In the light of our decision on the merits of the husband's appeal, he has no incentive to appeal; and the wife, having succeeded, cannot do so'.

The court in *Young* acknowledged that the list of exceptions was capable of extension, and some extensions have undoubtedly occurred.

In *Boys v Chaplin* [1968] 1 All ER 283, the court held that a two-judge court dealing with an interlocutory matter does not bind a three-judge court. The precise status of this proposition is open to question as a result of *Langley v North West Water Authority* [1991] 3 All ER 610, where there are dicta to the effect that it is the interlocutory nature of the proceedings rather than the number of judges which is significant. (This is, of course, consistent with the view discussed at page 149 that judicial observations which are made before the facts have been established are worth less than those made in the light of the facts.)

In *R v Secretary of State for the Home Department ex parte Al-Mehdawi* [1989] 1 All ER 777, the Court of Appeal held that, where a case progresses from the Court of Appeal to the House of Lords, and the House of Lords decision proceeds on a basis which renders it unnecessary to decide an issue on which the Court of Appeal made a decision, but without expressing an opinion on the correctness or otherwise of the Court of Appeal's decision on that issue, a subsequent Court of Appeal is not bound by the earlier one in relation to that issue. Assessing the status of this exception is complicated by the fact that, in due course, this case went to the House of Lords, where it is reported at [1989] 3 All ER 843. The House decided the appeal on its merits in such a way that it was unnecessary to comment on the precedent issue which had been before the Court of Appeal, and indeed the House specifically declined to do so. Nevertheless, it is at least arguable that where the House of Lords could have endorsed a statement made in the Court of Appeal but declined to do so, there is a degree of implicit criticism of that statement. On the other hand, this situation may simply provide additional support for the proposition that the principles of precedent are matters of practice, and it is for each court to determine its own practice in this as in other matters. (The question of whether precedent is a matter of law or practice is discussed at pages 201–3.)

Further evidence of increasing flexibility on the civil side may be found in *R v Parole Board ex parte Wilson* (1992) 4 Admin LR 525, where the question was whether a prisoner who was serving a discretionary life sentence (i.e. a sentence which the court had chosen to impose, rather than one which was dictated by law) was entitled to see the reports on him which the Parole Board had considered when deciding not to recommend that he should be released on licence. The background was that *R v Secretary of State for the Home Department ex parte Gunnell* (1984, unreported) had established that the common law was against the prisoner, but the European Court of Human Rights had found in favour of Gunnell, and accordingly provisions had been inserted into the Criminal Justice Act 1991 to bring English law into line with the European Convention on Human Rights. Unfortunately for Wilson, however, these provisions were not yet in force. Taking a robust attitude, Taylor LJ, giving the only substantial judgment in the Court of Appeal, held that although the present case could not be distinguished from *Gunnell*, the liberty of the subject and the requirements of natural justice entitled the court not to follow the earlier case, because it would be unjust to the prisoner to make him wait until the relevant provisions of the 1991 Act were brought into force.

*Wilson* is, of course, a relatively rare example of a civil case in which the liberty of the subject was at stake, although many cases concerning prisoners and immigrants also fall into that category. On the criminal side, however, the liberty of the subject is often said to be the factor which governs the operation of precedent. It is appropriate, therefore, to turn our attention to criminal cases.

## 12.3 The position in criminal cases

The operation of the doctrine of binding precedent in the Criminal Division of the Court of Appeal is clearly based on the principles which apply in the Civil Division under *Young v Bristol Aeroplane Co Ltd* [1944] 2

All ER 293. However, there are two lines of authority which hold that the transition to the criminal context makes it appropriate to graft on to those principles a somewhat greater degree of flexibility. The difficulty (as much of the remainder of this chapter will show) lies in identifying the extent of this additional flexibility.

The older line of authority indicates that greater flexibility is available only in those cases where it would protect the liberty of the subject. This line of authority begins with *R v Taylor* [1950] 2 All ER 170, in which Lord Goddard CJ, contrasting the position of the civil and criminal sides of the Court of Appeal, said:

> 'This court, however, has to deal with ... the liberty of the subject, and if it finds, on reconsideration, that in the opinion of a full court assembled for that purpose, the law has either been misapplied or misunderstood in a decision which it had previously given, *and that on the strength of that decision, an accused person has been sentenced and imprisoned*, it is the bounden duty of the court to reconsider the earlier decision with a view to seeing whether that person has been properly convicted. The exceptions which apply in civil cases ought not to be the only ones applied in such a case as the present, and in this particular instance the full court of seven judges is unanimously of the opinion that [the earlier decision] was wrong.' (Emphasis added.)

(In passing, it is interesting to note that the convening of a seven-judge court in this case – rather than the usual bench of three judges – appears to reflect the same thinking as that manifested in the *Practice Direction (House of Lords: Preparation of Case)* [1971] 2 All ER 159, which is discussed at page 174.)

In *R v Gould* [1968] 1 All ER 849, Diplock LJ said that it was proper to overrule where the law had been 'either misapplied or misunderstood in an earlier decision' even though none of the exceptions in *Young* was applicable. He returned to the theme in *Director of Public Prosecutions v Merriman* [1972] 3 All ER 42, saying

> ' ... although the Criminal Division of the Court of Appeal is not so strictly bound by its own previous decisions as is the Civil Division, its liberty to depart from a precedent which it is convinced was erroneous is restricted to cases *where the departure is in favour of the accused*.' (Emphasis added.)

Similarly, in *R v Spencer* [1985] 1 All ER 673, May LJ said:

> 'As a matter of principle we respectfully find it difficult to see why there should in general be any difference in the application of the principle of *stare decisis* between the Civil and Criminal Divisions of this court, save that we must remember that in the latter we may be dealing with the liberty of the subject and *if a departure from authority is necessary in the interests of justice to an appellant*, then this court should not shrink from so acting. In our opinion, *R v Gould* must be read in this sense and subject to this the principles laid down in *Young v Bristol Aeroplane Co Ltd* should apply.' (Emphasis added.)

The other, and slightly more recent, line of authority does not restrict the greater flexibility of precedent in criminal cases to those situations in which it would protect the liberty of the subject.

For example, in *R v Leaney* [1995] Crim LR 669, the question was whether an appeal lay against a judge's recommendation as to the minimum period which a convicted murderer should spend in prison. The answer depended on whether the recommendation was technically part of the sentence. Lord Taylor CJ, giving the judgment of the court, pointed out that there were three authorities, delivered by three successive Lord Chief Justices from 1966 onwards, all of which were to the effect that the recommendation was not part of the sentence. Additionally Parliament had amended the relevant statutory provision four times, without having created a right of appeal against such a recommendation. Unmoved by *R v Spencer*, the Lord Chief Justice, who acknowledged that the minimum recommendation in the instant case was excessive, said:

> 'We do not think we should depart from the authorities in the present case having regard not only to the strength and consistency of judicial decisions on the issue over an extended period of time but also to the attitude of the legislature towards those decisions.'

While it is not necessarily wrong in principle to go against the liberty of the subject since (as we saw, at page 17) the doing of justice to individuals is only one of the considerations with which the law concerns itself, the decision in *Leaney* falls short of supporting the line of authority with which we began.

The cases of *R v Cook* (1995, unreported), and *R v Shoult* [1996] RTR 298, are also worth noticing. In *Cook*, which was an appeal against sentence by a defendant who had driven with 140 micrograms of alcohol per 100 millilitres of blood (as against the legal limit of 35 micrograms per 100 millilitres), the Court of Appeal substituted a fine of £500 for the sentence of two months' imprisonment which the Crown Court had imposed. More particularly, Sachs J, giving the judgment of the Court of Appeal, had said:

> 'It can never be appropriate to send a man for this criminality, at the lower end of the scale as it is, to prison. There are other perfectly appropriate ways of dealing with people who drive with excess alcohol.'

In *Shoult*, however, the Court of Appeal expressly repudiated this comment, with the Lord Chief Justice saying that, having consulted the judges who decided *Cook*, 'we are clear that there was a misunderstanding about the effect of the figure as to the alcohol content of the breath sample', and that whatever may have been the appropriate sentence in the light of the strong mitigation which had been present in that case, the offence had not in reality been at the lower end of the scale. (In fact, the alcohol level was off the top of the Magistrates' Association's *Suggestions for Road Traffic Offence Penalties*.) Dealing with the case before it, the court declined to interfere with a sentence of three-and-a-half years for causing death by careless driving when analysis showed 147 micrograms per 100 millilitres of blood some two hours after the accident. Admittedly, the court in *Shoult* purported to justify its repudiation of the offending observation in the earlier case by classifying it as *obiter*, rather than on any intrinsic flexibility, but analysing Court of Appeal decisions on sentencing into *ratio decidendi* and *obiter dictum* is unusual. Furthermore, it is clear from the tone of the judgment in *Shoult* that the court regarded *Cook* as being simply wrong.

Similarly, in *R v Simpson* [2003] EWCA Crim 1499, [2003] 3 All ER 531 (which is discussed at page 158 in the context of the doctrine of *per incuriam*), Lord Woolf CJ, having acknowledged that there may be an argument for applying the doctrine of precedent in such a way as to avoid retrospective criminalization, continued:

> 'However, we do not understand why that should apply to a situation where a defendant … wishes to rely upon a wrongly decided case to provide a technical defence. While justice for a defendant is extremely important, justice for the public at large is also important. So is the maintenance of confidence in the criminal justice system. If the result in [an earlier case] had to be applied to other cases even though the Court of Appeal had acted in ignorance of the appropriate approach this would, indeed, reveal a most unattractive picture of our criminal justice system's ability to protect the public.'

By way of a limitation on the power of the court to depart from one of its own previous decisions, he also said that it was 'not wholly without significance' that the instant case was being heard by a five-member bench.

Finally, in *R v Newsome* and *R v Browne* [1970] 3 All ER 455, the court again refused to be bound by a previous decision, even though this resulted in the loss of liberty on the part of the defendant. More particularly, in the earlier case the trial judge had intended to pass an immediate custodial sentence of six months. However, within seconds of passing sentence, it was drawn to his attention that, under statute, the sentence he had just passed could only be suspended. He then increased the sentence from six months to seven months in order to escape the statutory restriction. The earlier Court of Appeal had held that, on these facts, the trial judge had exercised his discretion as to sentence wrongly, and that accordingly the six month sentence (suspended as it had to be) should be reinstated. In the instant case, a five-judge court unanimously rejected this decision, saying that

> 'if the court of five is duly constituted to consider an issue of discretion and the principles on which discretion should be exercised, then that court ought to have the right to depart from an earlier view expressed by the court of three, especially where that earlier view is very recent and especially where it was a matter in which the court did not take the opportunity of argument on both sides. Accordingly, within that restricted sphere, which is the only sphere on which we have to pronounce today, we take the view that a court of five can, and indeed should, depart from an earlier direction on the exercise of a judge's discretion if satisfied that the earlier direction was wrong.'

Overall, therefore, the older cases of *Taylor*, *Merriman* and *Spencer* restrict the Criminal Division of the Court of Appeal's greater flexibility to depart from its own previous decisions to situations where departure will protect the liberty of the subject, with *Gould* being expressed in neutral terms. On the other hand, the more recent cases of *Leaney*, *Shoult* and *Simpson* all support the view that this greater flexibility also exists in situations where departure from previous decisions will be harmful to the liberty of the subject. The later line of authority must, presumably, be taken to represent the current state of the law, even though it sits uneasily with the underlying tendency of the common law to favour defendants in criminal cases. (For evidence in support of this tendency, see pages 32 and 312 for discussion of, respectively, standards of proof and the presumption of strict interpretation of penal statutes.)

## 12.4 Should the Court of Appeal and the House of Lords apply the same principles?

Although the House of Lords' Practice Statement of 1966, which is discussed at length in Chapter 11, clearly stated that 'this announcement is not intended to affect the use of precedent elsewhere than in this House', Lord Denning MR was quick to argue that the freedom which the House of Lords had assumed for itself was also appropriate for the Court of Appeal. Although, as we have seen, this view has not taken root, it is nevertheless instructive to consider three cases in which the Court of Appeal considered the question of revising the principles of precedent in the Court of Appeal in the light of the Practice Statement.

At the Court of Appeal stage of *Conway v Rimmer* (also see page 163), Lord Denning MR said:

> 'My brethren today feel that we are still bound by the observations of the House of Lords in *Duncan v Cammell, Laird & Co Ltd* ... I do not agree. The

doctrine of precedent has been transformed by the recent statement of Lord Gardiner LC. This is the very case in which to throw off the fetters.'

In *Gallie v Lee* [1969] 1 All ER 1062, Lord Denning MR, speaking of the Court of Appeal's self-bindingness, said: 'It was a self-imposed limitation: and we who imposed it can also remove it'. But Salmon LJ, albeit with a clearly detectable lack of enthusiasm, took the more traditional view:

'I must accept the *law* as stated in the authorities ... in spite of the fact that it results too often in inconsistency, injustice and an affront to commonsense. The dicta ... that this court is absolutely bound by its own decisions are very strong ... It is ... only by a pronouncement of the whole court that we could effectively alter a *practice* which is so deeply rooted.' (Emphasis added.)

In passing, it is interesting to note that Salmon LJ seems to be confused as to whether the principles of precedent are matters of law or matters of practice.

In *Davis v Johnson* [1978] 1 All ER 1132, Lord Denning MR was more successful in persuading some of his colleagues in the Court of Appeal that precedent should be relaxed. The issue was whether an injunction could be granted under the Domestic Violence and Matrimonial Proceedings Act 1976, where the effect would be to exclude someone from property in which they have a proprietary interest. In two earlier cases the court had said that injunctions were not available in such cases, but in the instant case a majority refused to follow those cases. Lord Denning MR said:

'On principle, it seems to me that, while this court should regard itself as normally bound by a previous decision of the court, nevertheless it should be at liberty to depart from it if it is convinced that the previous decision was wrong. What is the argument to the contrary? It is said that, if an error has been made, this court has no option but to continue the error and leave it to be corrected by the House of Lords. The answer is this: the House of Lords may never have an opportunity to correct the error; and thus it may be perpetuated indefinitely, perhaps for ever.'

He went on to say:

'To my mind, this court should apply similar guidelines to those adopted by the House of Lords in 1966. Whenever it appears to this court that a previous decision was wrong, we should be at liberty to depart from it if we think it right to do so ... Alternatively, in my opinion, we should extend the principles in *Young v Bristol Aeroplane Co Ltd* when it appears to be a proper case to do so.'

Sir George Baker P agreed that the court should not be bound, but expressed the principle rather more restrictively:

'The court is not bound to follow a previous decision of its own if satisfied that the decision was clearly wrong and cannot stand in the face of the will and intention of Parliament expressed in simple language in a recent Act passed to remedy a serious mischief or abuse, and further adherence to the previous decision must lead to injustice in the particular case and unduly restrict proper development of the law with injustice to others.'

Shaw LJ formulated an even more restrictive principle:

'The principle of *stare decisis* should be relaxed where its application would have the effect of depriving actual and potential victims of violence of a vital protection which an Act of Parliament was plainly designed to afford them, especially where, as in the context of domestic violence, that deprivation must inevitably give rise to an irremediable detriment to such victims and create in regard to them an injustice irreversible by a later decision of the House of Lords.'

Even if we assume that statements such as these are matters of law rather than practice, and are therefore capable of forming part of the *ratio* of the case (and Salmon LJ's use of the term *dicta* in *Gallie v Lee* supports this assumption), the principles governing the identification of the *ratio* of a case in which different judges articulate different *ratios* (see page 153) make it plain that the very narrow comments of Shaw LJ would be the *ratio* of this case.

The House of Lords agreed with the Court of Appeal that an injunction could be granted, but disagreed emphatically on the precedent point, saying that the Court of Appeal had been wrong to deviate from the exceptions laid down in *Young*. Lord Diplock accepted that there was a need to balance certainty against undue restriction on development of the law, but he thought that the Court of Appeal should look after certainty, leaving the House of Lords to deal with development. Viscount Dilhorne also thought the two courts were essentially different, and spoke of 'the unique character of the House of Lords sitting judicially'. Lord Salmon offered perhaps the most perceptive comments:

'In the nature of things ... the point [that is, whether the Court of Appeal is bound by *Young*] could never come before your Lordships' House for decision or form part of its ratio decidendi ... I sympathize with the views expressed ... by Lord Denning MR, but until such time, if ever, as all his colleagues in the Court of Appeal agree with those views, *stare decisis* must still hold the field. I think this may be no bad thing.'

The reason that Lord Salmon said the issue could never form part of the *ratio* in the House of Lords is, of course, quite simply that it can never be strictly necessary for a decision of the House of Lords to deal with the precedent position in the Court of Appeal. However, as we saw in Chapter 8, the reality of the distinction between those parts of a judgment which are binding and those which are not is rather more sophisticated than Lord Salmon seems to imply. (In passing, it is interesting to note that Lord Salmon appears to be assuming here, contrary to his judgment in *Gallie v Lee*, that the principles of precedent are matters of law rather than practice.)

On balance, therefore, it seems that, apart from the decision in *Davis v Johnson*, which is of very limited application anyway, the Practice Statement of 1966 did nothing *directly* to change the way in which precedent operates in the Court of Appeal. However, several cases support the proposition that there is a trend towards increased flexibility on the civil side. Furthermore, the decision in *R v Spencer* (see page 197) notwithstanding, the pre-existing preference for flexibility on the criminal side has remained undiminished. Whether the Practice Statement has contributed *indirectly* to the current climate of opinion in the Court of Appeal, or whether that climate is simply the product of more fundamental changes in the way the judiciary perceives its role, must remain a matter for speculation.

## 12.5 The relevance of the leapfrog procedure

Section 12 of the Administration of Justice Act 1969 introduced a procedure, commonly known as 'the leapfrog', enabling certain appeals from the High Court to go directly to the House of Lords, thus bypassing the Court of Appeal altogether. The purpose of the leapfrog is to save time and money.

A leapfrog appeal will be available only where the trial judge certifies that a point of law of general public importance is involved, and either that it arises out of a point of statutory interpretation which was dealt with fully at the trial, or that the point is one on which the trial judge was bound by a decision of the Court of Appeal or the House of Lords, and that the point was dealt with fully in the report of the decision in the Court of Appeal or House of Lords. The certificate of the trial judge is only a preliminary: it is still necessary for either the trial judge or the House of Lords to grant leave to appeal.

The only justification for applying the leapfrog procedure to cases where the trial judge is bound by a decision of the Court of Appeal is that in these cases the Court of Appeal would also be bound by the same decision, and therefore an appeal to that court would be pointless. It is clear, therefore, that Parliament thinks that the Court of Appeal is bound by its own decisions.

Since appeals in criminal cases go straight from the High Court to the House of Lords anyway (see page 56), the leapfrog procedure is clearly irrelevant in that context.

# Summary

▶ When discussing the principles governing the self-bindingness of the Court of Appeal it is interesting not only to examine the principles themselves but also the way in which they differ from those governing the House of Lords.

▶ In civil cases the Court of Appeal usually considers itself to be bound by its own decisions, in accordance with the principles contained in *Young v Bristol Aeroplane Co Ltd*.

▶ Although the House of Lords' Practice Statement does not apply to the Court of Appeal, it may have created a change of atmosphere generally, and there is some evidence of increasing flexibility in the Court of Appeal, although overall *Young* remains the leading authority.

▶ There are two lines of authority in relation to flexibility on the criminal side, but the more recent line holds that the flexibility can be used even against the liberty of the subject.

▶ The existence of the leapfrog procedure, which enables some cases to go straight from the High Court to the House of Lords, supports the suggestion that the Court of Appeal binds itself.

## Exercise

Identify the extent to which the Court of Appeal binds itself in (a) civil cases; and (b) criminal cases.

# Chapter 13

# Does the High Court bind itself?

## 13.1 Introduction

As we saw in Chapter 3, the High Court has three types of jurisdiction, namely first instance, appellate and supervisory. This classification becomes relevant again in the context of the doctrine of precedent because the High Court's attitude to its own decisions will depend to some extent on the jurisdiction which is being exercised. The various jurisdictions will now be considered in turn.

## 13.2 The first instance jurisdiction

There is a tendency for the High Court, when exercising its jurisdiction at first instance, to follow its own previous decisions. For example, in *Poole Borough Council v B&Q (Retail) Ltd* [1983] *The Times*, 29 January, Goulding J said that, as a matter of judicial comity, he would follow another High Court decision, even though he was not bound to do so, and even though he seriously doubted its correctness. However, judicial comity is likely to be a less rigid constraint than bindingness, and therefore it is not surprising that conflicting decisions arise from time to time. Obviously, the existence of conflicting decisions will complicate the task of later judges, who will have to choose which one to follow. When this situation arose in *Colchester Estates (Cardiff) Ltd v Carlton Industries plc* [1984] 2 All ER 601, Nourse J took the view that the interests of certainty required that the second decision should normally be regarded as being correct, provided that it had been made after full consideration of the first. At the hearing of the third case, therefore, the judge should refuse to hear argument as to which case should be preferred, and should simply give judgment in accordance with the second decision. The parties would then be left to argue the point fully on appeal. The only exception to this, and it would be rare, would be where the third judge was convinced that the second judge had been wrong in not following the first: for example, where some binding or persuasive authority had not been cited in either of the first two cases.

## 13.3 The appellate jurisdiction

The leading case on the self-bindingness of the High Court when exercising its appellate jurisdiction is *Police Authority for Huddersfield v*

*Watson* [1947] 1 KB 842, where it was said that the principles articulated by the Court of Appeal in *Young v Bristol Aeroplane Co Ltd* [1944] 2 All ER 293, which are discussed at page 193, are equally applicable in the High Court. However, the most basic principle of precedent is that any case must be read in the context within which it was decided, and in *Young* that context was a court whose sole jurisdiction is appellate. Accordingly, the decision in *Watson* leaves open the question of whether the same principles apply when the High Court is exercising its supervisory jurisdiction. (Although the appellate and supervisory jurisdictions may superficially seem to be the same, as we saw at page 33 there is, in fact, a clear conceptual distinction between them.)

The question of the High Court's self-bindingness in the context of its supervisory jurisdiction must, therefore, be considered.

## 13.4 The supervisory jurisdiction

The leading case of *R v Greater Manchester Coroner ex parte Tal* [1984] 3 All ER 240 established that the principles formulated in *Young v Bristol Aeroplane Co Ltd* do not apply to a Divisional Court when it is exercising its supervisory jurisdiction, or to put it another way, when it is dealing with an application for judicial review. It follows, therefore, with even greater force, that those principles do not apply to a single judge exercising that jurisdiction. (The concept of a Divisional Court, and the possibility of a single judge exercising the High Court's supervisory jurisdiction are both discussed at page 51.) The basis of the decision in *Tal* is that the supervisory jurisdiction is effectively at first instance, because it is the legality of the decision-making process which is before the court, rather than the correctness of the decision itself, and it will be the first time that this issue has been considered.

However, in *Hornigold v Chief Constable of Lancashire* [1985] Crim LR 792, the court said that *Tal* had been intended to provide a sensible basis on which the High Court should approach its own previous decisions, rather than to provide a charter under which parties were free to take points which had previously been argued before another court and then re-argue them, simply in the hope that the second court might be persuaded to reach a different conclusion. The court was concerned that allowing such arguments to be advanced would undermine the legal stability which the doctrine of precedent was said to be designed to maintain. The court went on to say that departure from one of its own previous decisions could be justified only if that decision was plainly wrong, and that advocates seeking to persuade the court to undertake such departures must be able, at the outset of their arguments, to indicate how they intend to persuade the court of the wrongness of the earlier decision.

It must be noted that the tendency of the High Court to follow its own previous decisions in judicial review is a matter of judicial comity (with perhaps a dash of pragmatism) rather than of self-bindingness, and it will not, therefore, necessarily manifest itself in all cases. For example, in *R v Newcastle-upon-Tyne City Council ex parte Dixon* [1994] COD 217, Auld J dismissed an application for judicial review, holding that disputes between local authorities and care home proprietors as to the terms on which the former would place elderly residents in establishments run by the latter, were essentially contractual and were therefore matters of private law which were not susceptible to judicial review. However, in the substantially similar case of *R v Cleveland County Council ex parte Cleveland Care Homes Association* [1994] COD 221, Potts J came to the opposite conclusion, although he did acknowledge that the arguments in the two cases had been presented on different bases.

## Summary

▷ The High Court's attitude to self-bindingness depends on the type of jurisdiction which is involved.

▷ When exercising its first instance jurisdiction, the High Court is not bound by its own decisions but will usually follow them out of judicial comity.

▷ When exercising its appellate jurisdiction, the High Court follows the principles laid down by the Court of Appeal in *Young v Bristol Aeroplane Co Ltd*.

▷ The High Court's supervisory jurisdiction is at first instance.

### Exercise

Identify the factors which determine whether the High Court binds itself.

# Chapter 14

# Arguments for and against judicial law-making

14.1 Introduction

The previous chapters in this Part have all contained material describing and assessing the basic concepts which operate within the doctrine of precedent and the ways in which the courts use, or refuse to use, the doctrine to develop the law. At this stage, however, it will be useful to discuss the practice of judicial law-making as a whole. It is convenient to do so by surveying, in turn, a number of its perceived strengths and weaknesses, before concluding with a consideration of its constitutional limitations.

14.2 Perceived strengths of judicial law-making

14.2.1 Speed

The first, and most obvious, argument for the doctrine of binding precedent is speed. Subject to the technical and hierarchical aspects of the doctrine, and provided that a suitable case arises, a court may undertake development of the law as soon as the need to do so is identified. As Lord Wilberforce said, in *Miliangos v George Frank (Textiles) Ltd* [1975] 3 All ER 801: 'I am led to doubt whether legislative reform, at least prompt and comprehensive legislative reform ... is practicable'. Obvious though this argument for the doctrine of binding precedent is, it must not be thought that Parliamentary action is always and necessarily tardy.

In *Prescott v Birmingham Corporation* [1954] 3 All ER 698, the Court of Appeal held that a local authority had no power to give free bus travel to state retirement pensioners. Parliament promptly passed the Public Service Vehicles (Travel Concessions) Act 1955 legalizing such schemes.

Similarly, in *R v Preddy* [1996] 3 All ER 481, the House of Lords held that the offence of dishonestly obtaining property by deception, under the Theft Act 1968, was not committed where a defendant arranged for a sum of money to be debited from someone else's bank account and credited to his own. The reasoning was that a bank account which is in credit is really a debt owed by the bank to a customer (and, of course, a bank account which is overdrawn is really a debt owed by the customer to the bank). On this basis, any transfer between bank accounts merely adjusts the levels of indebtedness appropriately, rather than involving the transfer of property from one account to the other. It followed, therefore, that the defendant had not obtained any property belonging to the victim. While this analysis may be convincing as a matter of pure law, it flies in the face of both commonsense and commercial reality, so it is hardly surprising that Parliament swiftly passed the Theft (Amendment) Act 1996, which created a new offence of dishonestly obtaining a money transfer by deception.

The speedy introduction of amending legislation is nothing new. The Acts of Parliament (Commencement) Act 1793 abolished the pre-existing rule that all the Acts passed in one Parliamentary session were deemed to have come into force at the beginning of that session unless they contained specific provisions to the contrary, and introduced the current presumption that, in the absence of specific provision to the contrary, an Act comes into force at the beginning of the day on which it receives the Royal Assent (see page 296). The passage of the Act of 1793 was prompted by the decision in *Latless v Holmes* (1792) 100 ER 1230, where a statute which made annuities void if they were not registered within 28 days of being granted, was held to apply to an annuity granted earlier in the Parliamentary session, even though the 28-day period had expired before the Act was passed.

The fact remains, however, despite the examples which have just been given and a number of other similar cases which could have been mentioned, that law reform undertaken through the judicial process will often be swifter than Parliamentary action would be.

### 14.2.2 Judicial decisions deal with real situations

As the discussion of the concepts of *ratio* and *dictum* in Chapter 9 shows, the facts which give rise to a case also provide the basis for the legal essence of the decision. In the present context, this fact-based aspect of precedent is sometimes advanced as an argument for judicial law-making. For example, in *Miliangos v George Frank (Textiles) Ltd* [1975] 3 All ER 801, Lord Wilberforce said: 'Questions as to the recovery of debts or of damages depend so much on individual mixtures of facts and merits as to make them more suitable for progressive solutions in the courts'.

Here again, however, the argument is not quite as clear-cut as it may seem, since its corollary is that the courts may decide that the judicial process is not an appropriate vehicle for certain types of law-making. The differences of judicial opinion which emerged from the *Pirelli* and

*Woolwich* cases (see page 184) are particularly instructive in this context. Furthermore, the pitfalls which may await the courts when they make decisions other than on the basis of established facts have already been illustrated by *Murphy v Brentwood District Council* [1990] 2 All ER 908 (see page 185).

### 14.2.3 Precedent operates outside the party-political arena

The fact that the doctrine of precedent undoubtedly operates outside the party-political arena is sometimes advanced as an argument in support of the doctrine, since it means that the law can be changed without the need to find either the party-political will or the Parliamentary time which would otherwise be necessary. However, this argument is less clearly in favour of the doctrine of binding precedent than might at first sight appear to be the case, since it is, in effect, the other side of the coin of the constitutional constraints on judicial law-making, which are discussed at page 218.

## 14.3 Perceived weaknesses of judicial law-making

### 14.3.1 The process is haphazard

Whatever strengths the doctrine of precedent may possess, there can be no doubt that one of its weaknesses is that it is haphazard in its operation. There are three main elements in this, namely the need for cases to arise; the way in which cases are argued and decided; and the fact that one party may 'buy off' another. We will now consider these elements in turn.

#### The need for cases to arise

Law-making through precedent requires not only that an appropriate set of facts must arise, but also that the parties must be willing and able to litigate to a sufficiently elevated point in the hierarchy of the courts to ensure that any existing, and unsatisfactory, authorities can be either overruled or at least departed from. As Lord Diplock said, in *Gouriet v Union of Post Office Workers* [1977] 3 All ER 70, 'courts of justice do not act of their own motion. In our legal system it is their function to stand idly by until their aid is invoked ...'.

Unlike the need to find both the party-political will and the time for statutory reform, which can, of course, result in a kind of haphazardness, this aspect of judicial reform is not under any form of governmental supervision or control, which may be regarded as one of its strengths.

*The way in which cases are argued and decided*

One of the limitations of the adversarial system is that the quality of the decision is to a large extent dependent upon the quality of the argument which is presented to the court. At this point it is worth returning to *Air Canada v Secretary of State for Trade (No 2)* [1983] 1 All ER 910, in order to repeat the words of Lord Wilberforce (which we first encountered in Chapter 1):

> 'In a contest purely between one litigant and another... the task of the court is to do... justice between the parties.... There is no higher or additional duty to ascertain some independent truth. It often happens, from the imperfection of evidence, or the withholding of it, sometimes by the party in whose favour it would tell if presented, that an adjudication has to be made which is not and is known not to be, the whole truth of the matter; yet if the decision has been in accordance with the available evidence, and with the law, justice will have been fairly done.'

The point may be illustrated by *Aswan Engineering Establishment Co v Lupdine Ltd (Thurgar Bolle Ltd, Third Party)* [1987] 1 All ER 135, which raised the question of the extent to which the court can consult extrinsic material when seeking to identify the meaning of a statute. This is considered in more detail at page 288, but for the present purposes it is sufficient to note that Lloyd LJ said:

> 'We invited [counsel for Thurgar Bolle] to refer us to the Law Commission Report on Exemption Clauses in Contracts ... which preceded [the Act in question] and also to the Law Commission Working Paper on the Sale and Supply of Goods ... But [counsel for the appellants] objected. I can see no conceivable reason why we should not have been referred to the Law Commission papers, and good reason why we should ... In my judgment it is not only legitimate but also highly desirable to refer to Law Commission reports on which legislation has been based. But since [counsel for Thurgar Bolle] concurred in [counsel for the appellants'] objection, I can say no more about it.'

Bennion gives this view short shrift:

> 'To find out what the law is, the court is not merely entitled but under a duty to have recourse to all legitimate sources. If it hands down a judgment based on anything but what it believes is truly the law, a court denies its function. Moreover the judge or judges involved contravene the judicial oath or affirmation requiring them to apply in their judgments "the law and usages of this realm".' (*Statutory Interpretation*, 4th edn, 2002, p. 371.)

Unfortunately, this comment assumes that pre-Parliamentary reports are 'legitimate sources', which was, of course, precisely the point at issue.

Despite Bennion's adverse comment, it is clear that Lloyd LJ was merely reflecting judicial orthodoxy. Speaking of the House of Lords, although there is no reason in principle why the position should be different in other courts, Paterson says: '[There is] a shared expectation that a Law Lord in giving his reasons for deciding for or against the appeal ought to confine his propositions of law to matters covered by the arguments of counsel'. (*The Law Lords*, 1982, p. 38.) However, two further points arise.

First, Paterson's 'shared expectation' falls somewhat short of total unanimity. For example, Lord Simon was prepared to countenance a court undertaking its own researches, but felt that, having done so, it should 'proceed with special caution' (Paterson, *The Law Lords*, 1982, p. 40). More particularly, it seems that, in an exceptional case where a judge does undertake his own researches, he must then inform the advocates of the opinion which he has formed in consequence. In *Hadmor Productions Ltd v Hamilton* [1982] 1 All ER 1042, Lord Denning MR consulted *Hansard* (the official record of proceedings in Parliament) without telling the advocates that he had done so. In due course, Lord Diplock, giving the judgment of the House of Lords, rebuked Lord Denning on the basis that he had breached a fundamental principle of natural justice, namely 'the right of each party to be informed of any point adverse to him that is going to be relied on by the judge, and to be given an opportunity of stating what his answer to it is'. Since the decision in *Hadmor*, the House of Lords has reconsidered the use of *Hansard* (see page 303), but this does not affect the validity of Lord Diplock's comment in principle.

Admittedly, the court's powers of case management, under the Civil Procedure Rules, go some way (but not very far) to reducing the autonomy of the parties over the conduct of their case. More particularly, under CPR 3.1, the court may exclude an issue from consideration and may take other steps and make other orders in order to further the overriding objective, stated in CPR 1.1(1), of 'enabling the court to deal with cases justly'. Essentially, however, the way in which cases are argued remains a factor which may make judicial law-making less than wholly satisfactory.

Secondly, a court hearing a criminal case has a residual power to ensure that there is an argument. (The position is different in civil cases, where public policy is said to be best served by disputes being settled rather than proceeding to court: see page 13.) The issue in *R v McFarlane* [1994] 2 WLR 494, which involved a charge of living on the earnings of prostitution, was whether the term 'prostitute' is appropriate to describe a woman who gets money by purporting to offer sexual services for payment, when in fact she neither intends to fulfil her side of the bargain nor does in fact do so. The defendant argued that such a woman is a clipper rather than a prostitute, and that therefore he was not living on the earnings of prostitution. Counsel for the prosecution in the Crown Court agreed with this submission, but the judge did not and a trial ensued. In his summing up to the jury, the trial judge said:

> 'There are not two categories – a clipper and a prostitute. There are prostitutes who are honest and prostitutes who are dishonest.'

When an appeal against conviction came before the Court of Appeal, once again counsel on both sides agreed that the defendant's argument was correct, but once again the court disagreed, saying that there was a 'substantial argument' in favour of the trial judge's view. Accordingly, the case was adjourned to be argued by different counsel for the Crown, and eventually the Court of Appeal upheld the conviction.

Quite apart from the way in which cases are argued, their potential as vehicles for law reform may be restricted by the way in which they are decided. More particularly, all the issues raised by a case may not need to be decided, and those which are left undecided may nevertheless involve important issues of principle.

*R v Kuxhaus and Others* [1988] 2 All ER 75 involved ss. 87 and 88 of the Town and Country Planning Act 1971, which dealt with the powers of local planning authorities to enforce planning control. The basic mechanism was the issue of an enforcement notice, failure to comply with which was an offence. However, under s. 88 of the Act there was a right of appeal against an enforcement notice to the Secretary of State for the Environment, and under s. 246 of the Act there was the further possibility of an appeal against the Secretary of State's decision, on a point of law, to the High Court.

Section 88(10) of the Act provided that, 'where an appeal is brought under this section, the enforcement notice shall be of no effect pending the final determination or the withdrawal of the appeal'. In other words, the offence of non-compliance could not be committed until determination or withdrawal of the appeal.

On the facts of the case, two issues arose. First, did s. 88(10) refer only to the determination or withdrawal of the s. 88 appeal, or did it include the s. 246 appeal? Secondly, was the offence of non-compliance one of strict liability, or was *mens rea* required? (The concept of strict liability offences is discussed at page 313.) Having decided that the provision applied to the s. 246 appeal, it followed that the court did not have to decide – and indeed expressly declined to decide – the strict liability point, which therefore remained open to doubt.

The *Kuxhaus* problem is not, however, inevitable. As we saw at page 160, in the context of *Hedley Byrne & Co Ltd v Heller & Partners Ltd* [1963]

2 All ER 575, the courts may, and sometimes do, deal at length with matters which do not actually require to be decided. While this practice can give rise to statements that are, strictly speaking, merely *obiter*, they may nevertheless be so strongly persuasive as to be practically indistinguishable from *ratio*.

### One party may 'buy off' another

The rather cryptic comment that one party may 'buy off' another requires explanation. Briefly, it may well be that the facts of a case involve a small amount of money to one party, but the principle of the case may involve a much larger amount of money to the other party. Suppose, for example, that the holder of an insurance policy is in dispute with the insurance company as to whether a claim for £50 is covered by the policy. The most the policyholder stands to lose, leaving aside the question of costs, is £50. But multiplied out across all the similar policies which the company has issued, the potential cost to the company in terms of other, similar claims may be very considerable indeed.

Against this background, suppose that the policyholder with the £50 claim wins in the County Court but loses in the Court of Appeal. While he is contemplating an appeal to the House of Lords, the company comes to him and says: 'As a gesture of goodwill, and without accepting any legal liability, we will now pay you the £50 you are claiming – on condition that you do not go to the Lords'. The temptation for the policyholder to accept this is obvious, since £50 is all he will get anyway, even assuming he wins in the Lords. But if he does accept, the company has had to lay out only £50, and in return it has ensured that the development of the law is arrested at a stage which suits its commercial interests. In reality, the company may also agree to pay the policyholder's legal costs, and it will also have its own legal costs, so the deal may not be quite so attractive to it as the summary given above might indicate. Nevertheless, even when all things are considered, the principle of 'buying off' may be very attractive to one party, and the prospect of being 'bought off' may not be unattractive to the other.

It is difficult to know how widespread the practice is, because in the nature of things there is no official record of the reasons why people decide not to appeal. An additional obstacle to full public knowledge becoming available is that settlements may not only deal with compensation and costs, but may also contain confidence clauses to the effect that the party accepting the settlement must not disclose its terms to third parties. Despite lack of knowledge as to the extent of the practice, however, there is no doubt that it exists, or that it can result in the proper development of the law being stultified in order to serve the best interests of large organizations.

### Judicial law-making causes injustice in individual cases

There are two ways in which judicial law-making causes injustice in individual cases.

First, it puts the cost of law-making onto individual litigants, with the added twist that it will usually be the loser who pays for having had the law changed in favour of the winner. The principles of costs generally were outlined at page 27. In the present context the cost point may be self-evident, but it is nevertheless worth identifying explicitly. For example, even if the reform of the law in favour of child trespassers, as introduced by the House of Lords in *British Railways Board v Herrington* [1972] 1 All ER 749 (see page 180), was a thoroughly good idea, why should the individual landowner be liable not only for damages but also for the legal costs involved in securing this reform?

The solution to this problem is simple enough in principle. The courts could be given power to order that costs should be paid out of public funds in cases involving the development of the law in the general public interest. As it is, however, no such power exists in civil cases, although criminal courts, even down to the level of the magistrates' courts, do have power to award costs out of public funds, and this is not limited to cases involving development of the law. Indeed, leaving aside the possibility of disposing of a case after a preliminary reference to the European Court of Justice (see page 78), it is difficult to see how a magistrates' court could conceivably be involved in developing the law.

Where one party is effectively the state, in one guise or another, an *ad hoc* solution to the problem could be achieved by that party giving an undertaking to pay all the legal costs of both sides, irrespective of the outcome of the case. This practice has already been adopted by Her Majesty's Revenue and Customs in some cases, but even here there is no entitlement to such an undertaking.

The second element of unfairness is that any change in the law which the court makes is retrospective in the sense that new law is being applied to an old situation. This unfairness could be – but currently is not – remedied by the use of *prospective overruling*, which is discussed at page 138.

---

**14.3.2**     Judges are ill-equipped for the work of law-making

There are at least two reasons why judges are ill-equipped for the work of law-making, namely lack of training and lack of information.

## Lack of training

Judges are almost always (but see page 223) promoted from the ranks of practising lawyers who have spent their working lives advising clients and arguing cases. It is not surprising that a lifetime of strictly limited horizons tends to produce a similarly limited outlook. As Lord Simon said, in *Miliangos v George Frank (Textiles) Ltd* [1975] 3 All ER 801:

'The training and qualification of a judge is to elucidate the problem immediately before him, so that its features stand out in stereoscopic clarity. But the beam of light which so illuminates the immediate scene seems to throw surrounding areas into greater obscurity; the whole landscape is distorted to the view ... The very qualifications for the judicial process thus impose limitations on its use. This is why judicial advance should be gradual. "I am not trained to see the distant scene: one step enough for me" should be the motto on the wall opposite the judge's desk. It is, I concede, a less spectacular method of progression than somersaults and cartwheels; but it is the one best suited to the capacity and resources of a judge.'

## Lack of information

In *Morgans v Launchbury* [1972] 2 All ER 606, the House of Lords was invited to hold that the owner of a car, which was being driven by someone else at the request of the owner's husband, was liable to passengers injured as a result of the driver's negligence. Lord Wilberforce said:

'Liability and insurance are so intermixed that judicially to alter the basis of liability without adequate knowledge (*which we have not the means to obtain*) as to the impact which this might make on the insurance system would be dangerous and ... irresponsible.' (Emphasis added.)

By way of contrast, in the American legal system the appellate courts commonly receive arguments in the form of long, written documents known as *briefs*. These may contain a great deal of argument based on social and economic factors, rather than on propositions of law. In one case early in the 20th century, concerning statutory restrictions on the hours which women could work, an attorney called Brandeis delivered a lengthy brief of this nature. The Supreme Court commented favourably on its utility, and such documents have come to be known as *Brandeis briefs*.

The English courts' traditional commitment to reliance on oral argument may be illustrated by *Yorke Motors v Edwards* [1982] 1 All ER 1024, where the House of Lords expressly and firmly rejected the idea of the submission of written argument, saying that the only acceptable form of written submission is a written skeleton, containing the outline of the argument, together with case names, references and short quotations from the key judgments. 'The purpose of a skeleton argument is to identify and summarize the points, not to argue them fully on paper'. (*Practice Direction (Court of Appeal: Procedure)* [1995] 3 All ER 850, para. 37.) The importance of skeleton arguments was reinforced by *Practice Note* [1997] 4 All ER 830, which requires an advocate who is unable to deliver a skeleton argument in accordance with a prescribed timescale, to give a personal explanation to a Presiding Lord Justice of why this is so.

More recently, however, there has been some movement in relation to the reception of written argument.

In *Chief Adjudication Officer v Foster* [1993] 1 All ER 705, the House had heard oral argument and was considering its judgment when the decision in *Pepper v Hart* [1993] 1 All ER 42 was given. (*Pepper v Hart*, which is discussed at page 303, permits the courts to refer to *Hansard* provided certain conditions are satisfied.) The respondent invited the House to receive written representations from both parties on the relevance of *Hansard* to the point at issue in the case, and those representations were in fact received and considered before judgment was given.

In *Bolton Metropolitan District Council v Secretary of State for the Environment* [1995] 1 WLR 1176, the question of costs raised issues of general importance, quite apart from the substantive issue in the appeal. At the conclusion of oral argument on the substantive issue, the House of Lords invited the parties to make written submissions in relation to costs.

Even people who are not directly involved in the specific case before the court may be allowed to submit written representations. For example, in *R v Khan* [1997] AC 558, the House of Lords accepted written argument from Liberty (a public interest group) dealing with the wider implications of the case which was before the House. Similarly, in *Ridgeway Motors (Isleworth) Ltd v ALTS Ltd* [2005] EWCA Civ 92, [2005] 2 All ER 304, having refused to allow the Commissioners of Inland Revenue to be joined as a party to the proceedings, the court did allow them to make written submissions, on which the parties were then allowed to comment at the hearing.

While all the examples given above arose in somewhat unusual circumstances, they may turn out to be straws in the wind.

In passing, it is interesting to note that cases before the European Court of Human Rights proceed almost entirely on the basis of written submissions, with the entire oral hearing typically occupying no more than half a day.

## 14.4    Constitutional constraints on judicial law-making

### 14.4.1    Introduction

It is not surprising that judges who work under a constitution which is largely dominated by the doctrine of the legislative supremacy of Parliament and in which the separation of powers is only partial (see page 69), should be aware that their own lack of electoral accountability imposes constraints on their activities in the field of law-making. Admittedly, there is room for some debate as to exactly where the line should be drawn, beyond which only Parliament should reform the law, and the line itself may be rather fuzzy, but there would be general acceptance that, in any particular case, a line of some sort does exist somewhere. It will be useful to consider the main areas in which the judges may feel particularly inhibited.

### 14.4.2    The party-political context

There is general agreement that the judges should not take sides in matters of party politics. As Lord Scarman said, in *Duport Steels Ltd v Sirs* [1980] 1 All ER 529, when the House of Lords was dealing with the interpretation of politically contentious trades' union legislation:

> 'Within ... limits ... judges ... have a genuine creative role ... But the constitution's separation of powers, or more accurately functions, must be observed if judicial independence is not to be put at risk. For if people and Parliament come to think that the judicial power is to be confined by nothing other than the judge's sense of what is right ... confidence in the judicial system will be replaced by fear of it becoming uncertain and arbitrary in its application. Society will then be ready for Parliament to cut the power of the judges. Their power to do justice will become more restricted by law than it need be, or is today.'

### 14.4.3    Public policy

There are many judicial observations to the effect that the formulation of public policy is a matter for Parliament rather than the courts. For example, in *R v Cunningham* (see page 187), Lord Hailsham LC said:

> '"Public policy" [and] "concepts of what is right and what is wrong that command general acceptance in contemporary society" are difficult horses for the judiciary to ride, and, where possible, are arguably best left to the legislature to decide.'

Similarly, in *C (A Minor) v DPP* [1995] 2 All ER 43, a unanimous House of Lords was distinctly unhappy with the presumption of English criminal law that a child between the ages of 10 and 14 lacks the capacity to commit a criminal offence unless the prosecution proves that the child in question knows the difference between right and wrong. Nevertheless, the House reversed a decision of the High Court, which had held that the rule was no longer part of the law. Lord Lowry, delivering the only substantial speech, said:

> 'The distinction between the treatment and the punishment of child "offenders" has popular and political overtones, a fact which shows that we have been discussing not so much a legal as a social problem, with a dash of politics thrown in, and emphasizes that it should be within the exclusive remit of Parliament.'

(In due course, Parliament did take action, in the form of s. 34 of the Crime and Disorder Act 1998, by abolishing the presumption that children between the ages of 10 and 14 lack criminal capacity.)

The House of Lords was again conscious of its limited law-making role in *R v Clegg* [1995] 1 All ER 334, where a soldier on duty in Northern Ireland had been convicted of murder. The legal issue was whether someone who caused death by using excessive force, either in self-defence or while trying to prevent the commission of an offence by another person, could be convicted of the lesser offence of manslaughter rather than murder, and whether it was relevant that the defendant was a police officer or a member of the armed forces. The practical consequence of the distinction between conviction for murder and manslaughter was that life imprisonment was mandatory for the former, but discretionary for the latter.

Although clearly unhappy with the existing state of the law, the House of Lords chose to uphold it. In the only substantial speech, Lord Lloyd acknowledged that the power of the House to change the law was not necessarily excluded simply because the facts raise an issue of social policy, but nevertheless concluded:

> 'In the present case I am in no doubt that your Lordships should abstain from law-making. The reduction of what would otherwise be murder to manslaughter in a particular class of case seems to me essentially a matter for decision by the legislature, and not by this House in its judicial capacity. For the point in issue is, in truth, part of the wider issue whether the mandatory life sentence for murder should still be maintained. That wider issue can only be decided by Parliament. I would say the same for the point at issue in this case.'

### 14.4.4 Moral issues

Moral issues present the courts with a particularly acute problem in terms of public policy, and may therefore be worth considering separately.

The question in *R v Brown* [1993] 2 All ER 75 was whether homosexual sado-masochists who inflicted harm on others, with their consent, could properly be convicted of assault occasioning actual (or grievous) bodily harm, contrary to the Offences Against the Person Act 1861.

Answering this question in the affirmative, the majority of the House of Lords (Lords Templeman, Jauncey and Lowry) held that the common law does not recognize the general defence of consent to the infliction of bodily harm, and that it is only in special circumstances, such as lawful sports, and surgery, that consent is effective. Lord Templeman summarized the majority view thus:

'Society is entitled and bound to protect itself against a cult of violence. Pleasure derived from the infliction of pain is an evil thing. Cruelty is uncivilised.'

On the other hand, Lord Slynn, as part of the dissenting minority, endorsed the written submission of the Director of Public Prosecutions that:

'in the end it is a matter of policy. Is/are the state/courts right to adopt a paternalistic attitude as to what is bad or good for subjects, in particular as to deliberate injury?'

He dealt with the problem of who should make such decisions thus:

'It is a matter of policy in an area where social and moral factors are extremely important and where attitudes can change. In my opinion, it is a matter of policy for the legislature to decide. If society takes the view that this kind of behaviour, even though sought after and done in private, is either so new or so extensive or so undesirable that it should be brought now for the first time within the criminal law, then it is for the legislature to decide. It is not for the courts in the interests of "paternalism" ... or in order to protect people from themselves, to introduce into existing statutory crimes relating to offences *against* the person, concepts which do not properly fit there. If Parliament considers that the behaviour revealed here should be made specifically criminal, then the Offences Against the Person Act 1861 or, perhaps more appropriate, the Sexual Offences Act 1967 [which de-criminalized homosexual acts between consenting male adults in private] can be amended specifically to define it.'

Similarly, in *Re W (A Minor) (Adoption: Homosexual Adopter)* [1997] 3 All ER 620, Singer J declined to say that it was contrary to public policy for a lesbian to adopt a child. More particularly, he was conscious of 'how unruly is the horse of public policy which I am asked to mount, and upon what shifting sands I would be riding if I did so ... public policy considerations should not fall within the province of judges to define within this sphere'.

Further illustrations of judicial perceptions of the courts' proper role on moral issues may be found in the cases dealing with security of tenure for the surviving partners of non-marital relationships. (See pages 278 and 328 for cases involving homosexuals and heterosexuals, respectively.)

**14.4.5** The relevance of Parliamentary action and inaction

Both Parliamentary action and inaction may be relevant when a court is deciding whether it should reform the law. More particularly, judicial reluctance to intervene may be particularly noticeable in cases arising from areas of law in which Parliament has been active on a selective basis, since there may be a natural assumption that Parliament has impliedly approved those aspects of the law which it has not changed. The case of *Re Brightlife* [1986] 3 All ER 673 involved floating charges, which originated at common law, but have been subject to some statutory provisions. Floating charges are a type of secured loan and are widely used in commercial circles. In the event of insolvency, secured creditors are, of course, in a better position than unsecured creditors, but the question of how the balance should be struck between the two groups is ultimately a matter of public policy. The commercial community needs to be able to raise capital, but investors need some degree of protection. Against this background, Hoffmann J said:

> 'The limited and pragmatic interventions by the legislature make it, in my judgment, wholly inappropriate for the courts to impose additional restrictive rules on grounds of public policy. It is certainly not for a judge of first instance to proclaim a new head of public policy which no appellate court has even hinted at before.'

Similarly, the courts may decline to intervene where Parliament has, quite self-consciously, been totally inactive. As Lord Bridge said in *Brind v Secretary of State for the Home Department* [1991] 1 All ER 720, when upholding the pre-Human Rights Act 1998 position of the European Convention for the Protection of Human Rights and Fundamental Freedoms under English law:

> 'When Parliament has been content for so long to leave those who complain that their Convention rights have been infringed to seek their remedy in Strasbourg [i.e. in the European Court of Human Rights], it would be surprising suddenly to find that the judiciary had, without Parliament's aid, the means to incorporate the Convention into such an important area of domestic law and I cannot escape the conclusion that this would be a judicial usurpation of the legislative function.'

(The subsequent treatment of the Convention under the Human Rights Act 1998 is discussed in Chapter 6.)

## 14.5 Conclusion

It is clear that there are both advantages and disadvantages to the common law tradition of developing the law on case-by-case basis. However, what is clear, not only from this chapter but from the whole of this Part of this book, is that although it is conventional to speak of a doctrine of *binding* precedent, a substantial degree of flexibility is available to the courts in practice. It is now appropriate, in the next chapter, to consider how the civil law tradition operates, as evidenced by the workings of the European Court of Justice.

## Summary

- Having considered how precedent works in different courts, it is appropriate to consider some of the doctrine's perceived strengths and weaknesses as a vehicle for law reform, as well as the constitutional limitations on the role of the judges.

- The perceived strengths are that it is speedy; it is based on real facts situations; and it is outside the party-political arena.

- The perceived weaknesses are that it is haphazard in operation; it causes injustice in individual cases; and the judges are ill-equipped for the task of law reform.

- Judges are conscious that, because they operate outside the field of electoral accountability, there are limits to the kind of law reform they should undertake.

## Exercise

Assess the adequacy of the doctrine of binding precedent as a vehicle for law reform.

# Chapter 15

# Precedent and principle in the European Court of Justice

## 15.1 Introduction

Although most legal systems have no doctrine of *binding* precedent, there are nevertheless good reasons why the courts of any legal system should generally follow their own decisions. (See page 130.)

This chapter discusses the non-binding version of precedent which is followed by the European Court of Justice, and explains the principles of law which are an important part of the foundations of the Community's legal order. (Since there is no distinction between the European Court of Justice and the Court of First Instance for the present purposes, this chapter will adopt the expedient of referring to both courts by the name of the former.)

However, it is useful to begin by considering some of the formal ways in which its judgments differ from the English model.

## 15.2 Reading European Court of Justice reports

Anyone who is used to reading reports of cases decided by the English courts is likely to find the style of the European Court of Justice's decisions more than a little unfamiliar. There are three main reasons for this.

First, although the judges of the court will, of course, always be lawyers, there is no requirement that they must have been practitioners: academic lawyers are perfectly acceptable (see page 77). Historically, this has been, and largely remains, in marked contrast to the English practice. However, the careers of Brenda Hale (the first female member of the House of Lords in its judicial capacity) and Jack Beatson (a High Court judge) show that a more relaxed view may be taken. (Dame Brenda and Sir Jack came from Manchester and Cambridge universities respectively.) Secondly, the working language of the court is French. Thirdly, there are never any dissenting judgments.

In other words, an English-speaking reader will be reading a translation of a judgment which was written by a committee, not all of whose members are necessarily used to solving practical problems.

## 15.3 Precedent in the European Court of Justice

In *van Gend en Loos v Nederlandse Administratie der Belastung* [1963] ECR 1, which (as we saw at page 86) established the supremacy of Community law over national law, the Court held that where there was a progressive scheme of duties on different products, and one product was reclassified so that it attracted a higher rate of duty, there was an increase in duty, contrary to what was then art. 12 [now art. 25] EC. When precisely the same point of principle, although in relation to a different product, came before the Court in *Da Costa* [1963] ECR 31, the Court gave the same answer. More particularly, the Court said:

> 'The questions of interpretation posed in this case are identical with those settled ... [in *van Gend en Loos*] ... and no new factor has been presented to the Court.
>
> 'In these circumstances the [national court] must be referred to the previous judgment.'

The Court referred to *Da Costa* in *CILFIT v Minister of Health* [1982] ECR 3415, where it accepted that even national courts which appear to be under a duty to refer questions to the Court, under what was then art. 177 [now 234] EC, need not do so where 'previous decisions of the Court have already dealt with the point of law in question ... even though the questions at issue are not strictly identical'. Since it is difficult to see any basis for this statement other than that the Court would simply follow its own previous decision (and therefore a preliminary reference would be wasteful in terms of time and money for all concerned), it constitutes further evidence that the Court assumes that it will follow its own decisions.

The 'questions at issue' need not be 'strictly identical'. In other words, adopting the common law terminology (see page 151), it is necessary to identify the appropriate *level of generality* before a decision can be made as to whether precedent will be followed. Similarly, however, the Court's comment in *Da Costa* that 'no new factor has been presented to the Court' suggests that a court or tribunal *may* properly make a preliminary reference, even in the face of a relevant decision of the Court, if, adopting the common law usage again (see page 159), there are changed circumstances. Thus, for example, in *Keck* [1993] ECR I-6097 the Court noted 'the increasing tendency of traders to invoke art. 30 of the Treaty [which deals with quantitative restrictions on imports] as a means of challenging any rules whose effect is to limit their commercial freedom, even where those rules are not aimed at products of other member states', as a result of which the Court considered it 'necessary to re-examine and clarify its case-law on this matter'.

Similarly, and again adopting the common law usage, it might even be possible to argue something akin to the *per incuriam* doctrine (see page 157), although in the absence of a doctrine of bindingness in relation to previous decisions of the Court this would have to be limited to failures to consider relevant legislative texts, and perhaps, relevant principles of law. (The principles of Community law are discussed in the remainder of this chapter.) However, it is important not to lose sight of the fact that following decisions is much more common than departing from them.

One consequence of the Court's assumption that it will follow its own decisions is that it feels obliged to explain itself in those cases where it decides not to do so. Thus in *Parliament v Council (Comitology)* [1988] ECR 5615, the Court held that Parliament had no standing to bring an action for annulment in respect of a Decision of the Council. The fact that the Treaties did not confer such a power was 'a procedural gap' but this did not 'prevail over the fundamental interest in the maintenance and observance of the institutional balance laid down in the Treaties'. Subsequently, however, in *Parliament v Council (Chernobyl)* [1990] ECR I-2041, where a breach of a fundamental procedural requirement had adversely affected Parliament's participation in the legislative process, the Court held that Parliament did have standing to pursue the matter, because observance of the institutional balance within the Community means that each of 'the institutions must exercise its powers with due regard for the powers of the other institutions. It also requires that it should be possible to penalize any breach of that rule which may occur'. (The *Chernobyl* decision was subsequently endorsed by the TEU's amendment of art. 173 [now 230] EC, giving Parliament standing to proceed before the Court 'for the purpose of protecting [its] prerogatives'.)

Using the terminology adopted at page 151 in relation to the common law concept of *ratio decidendi*, therefore, the Court in *Chernobyl* may be said to have held that the *Comitology* decision was based on too high a level of generality, thus justifying the Court in creating a new right, albeit one limited to the protection of Parliament's prerogatives.

Of course, where the Court is asked to depart from one of its own decisions, it may well decide, after careful reconsideration, that the earlier decision should be reaffirmed. For example, in *Faccini Dori v Recreb srl* [1994] ECR I-3325, the Court refused to extend the direct effect of Directives horizontally, pointing out that the existence of the *Francovich* doctrine and the doctrine of indirect effect (see pages 84 and 85, respectively) made it unnecessary to do so.

The Court's view of precedent discussed here is not, of course, expressed in the same terms as the common law's binding version of the doctrine. However, as we have seen throughout the preceding chapters of this Part of this book, in reality even the common law's version allows a good deal more flexibility than the word 'binding' might suggest. It may be concluded, therefore, that in reality the difference between precedent in the Court of Justice and the English courts is more a matter of terminology than of substance.

Nevertheless, a new legal order has to obtain its content from somewhere; and, at least in its early stages, this can clearly not be from the previous decisions of its own Court. It is now appropriate, therefore, to turn to a consideration of the origins and content of the principles of Community law.

## 15.4 Principles of Community law

### 15.4.1 Introduction

Perhaps not surprisingly, in formulating the principles which apply across the spectrum of Community law, the Court has drawn on material from the legal systems of individual member states. In the words of the Advocate-General in *Internationale Handelsgesellschaft mbH* [1974] 2 CMLR 540:

> 'The fundamental principles of national legal systems ... contribute to forming that philosophical, political and legal substratum common to the member states from which, through the case-law, an unwritten Community law emerges.'

It is appropriate, therefore, to examine some of the more important of these principles, namely *proportionality*, *legal certainty* and the closely related concept of *legitimate expectation*, *equality*, *fundamental rights* and *procedural propriety*. We will consider these in turn, before commenting on the principle of *subsidiarity*, and concluding with a discussion of the extent to which the practice of the European Court of Justice differs from that of the English courts.

### 15.4.2 Proportionality

The idea of proportionality is simply an aspect of fairness, with things which are disproportionate being regarded as unfair. For example, in the case of *Atalanta* [1979] ECR 2137, people who agreed to buy produce from an intervention agency were required to give security to ensure that they performed their obligation. In the event of non-performance, a Regulation required forfeiture of the whole of the security irrespective of whether the non-performance was major or minor. The Court of

Justice held that the lack of any relationship between the extent of the non-performance on the one hand, and the amount of the penalty on the other, amounted to a breach of the principle of proportionality.

### 15.4.3 Legal certainty and legitimate expectation

The principles of legal certainty and legitimate expectation are very closely related to each other. Taking them in turn, the principle of legal certainty simply requires that people who are subject to the law should be able to ascertain their rights and obligations. Thus, for example, in *Goudrand Frères* [1981] ECR 1931, the Court of Justice said that in the field of financial liability, the principle of legal certainty requires that 'rules imposing charges on the taxpayer must be clear and precise so that he may know without ambiguity what are his rights and obligations and may take steps accordingly'. Where this principle is breached, any ambiguity should be resolved in favour of the individual.

The principle of legitimate expectation may be illustrated by the case of *Deuka* [1975] 2 CMLR 28. The essence of the case was that the Commission, faced with a surplus of wheat, adopted a policy of making payments in order to encourage the processing of wheat in such a way as to render it unfit for human consumption, provided that the processors obtained authorization before they embarked on the process. The amount of the payment varied from time to time. Deuka bought some wheat before 1 June 1970 with a view to processing it, and obtained the appropriate authorization. However, the processing itself did not actually occur until June and July, by which time a new Regulation reducing the amount of the payment had been introduced, with effect from 1 June. The Court of Justice held that the new Regulation was valid, but that it must be interpreted in such a way as not to disentitle Deuka to the higher payment which had been envisaged when the authorization had been obtained, because Deuka had clearly had a legitimate expectation of receiving payment at the higher rate.

Before leaving the principles of legal certainty and legitimate expectation, it is worth noticing that, as a matter of first impression, both principles may appear to require that judgments of the Court of Justice should have only prospective effect, in the sense that they should not affect existing rights and obligations. However, the case-law shows the position to be a little more complicated than this.

The Court stated the general principle in *Amministratzione delle Finanze dello Stato* [1981] ECR 2735:

> 'Although procedural rules are generally held to apply to all proceedings pending at the time when they enter into force, this is not the case with

substantive rules. On the contrary, the latter are usually interpreted as applying to situations existing before their entry into force *only in so far as it clearly follows from their terms, objectives or general scheme that such an effect must be given to them.*

'This interpretation ensures respect for the principles of legal certainty and the protection of legitimate expectation, by virtue of which the effect of Community legislation must be clear and predictable for those who are subject to it.' (Emphasis added.)

Pausing only to comment that the distinction between the retrospectivity of procedural and substantive rules reflects the position in English law before the decision in *Secretary of State for Social Services v Tunnicliffe* [1991] 2 All ER 712 (see page 309), it must be said that in practice the Court will generally require good reason to be shown before it will say that its judgment in any particular case should not operate retrospectively. Thus, for example, the decisions in both *Marshall v Southampton & South West Hampshire Area Health Authority (No 2)* [1993] 3 CMLR 293 and *Francovich* [1991] IRLR 84 (for the latter, see page 84) operate retrospectively, even though they both give rise to potentially massive financial liabilities. However, where good reason is shown why a decision should not be totally retrospective, the Court may nevertheless make it partially so. For example, in *Defrenne v Sabena (No 2)* [1976] 2 CMLR 98 (which is discussed at page 82), the Court said that its decision that art. 119 [now 139] EC was directly effective would apply retrospectively to cases where proceedings had already been instituted at the date of that judgment, but otherwise would be purely prospective in its effect. The reason for withholding full retrospective effect was said to be the large number of claims which would otherwise arise, and which could not have been foreseen, with the consequent risk of serious financial consequences, and perhaps even insolvency, for employers.

### 15.4.4 Equality

The principle of equality requires that any discrimination should be objectively justified. Two contrasting cases illustrate the point.

First, in *Royal Scholten-Honig Holdings Ltd* [1979] 1 CMLR 675 the facts were that glucose producers were in competition with sugar producers. Regulations were then made, introducing a system of subsidies whereby the production of sugar was, in part, financed by levies on glucose producers. The Court of Justice held that the Regulations were invalid because they breached the principle of equality.

Secondly, however, and by way of contrast, in *Walter Rau* [1987] ECR 2289, margarine producers challenged the legality of a Community policy which aimed to reduce surplus stocks of butter by selling it cheaply to certain categories of the population. Although it may seem to be obvious that the producers of butter and margarine were competing with each other, and that therefore this case was on all fours with *Royal Scholten-Honig Holdings Ltd*, the Court decided that there were differences between the general objectives of the organization of the Community butter market on the one hand and the oil and fats market on the other hand, and that, when viewed objectively, these differences justified the discrimination.

It will be apparent that Community lawyers are just as adept as those skilled in the common law when it comes to drawing fine distinctions between cases.

### 15.4.5 Fundamental rights

*Introduction*

In *Nold v Commission* [1974] 2 CMLR 338, the Court emphasized that 'fundamental rights form an integral part of the general principles of law, the observance of which it ensures'.

*Stauder v City of Ulm* [1969] ECR 419 arose from the Community's plan to reduce surplus stocks of butter by selling it cheaply to certain groups within the population. One individual objected to the way in which the German authorities implemented the scheme, because he was required to disclose his name to the retailer of the butter, as a result of which the retailer would know that he was receiving certain welfare benefits.

The Court of Justice acknowledged that this infringed the principle of equality, and was therefore a breach of the individual's fundamental rights. (In the event, however, the Court of Justice avoided the problem by saying that the Commission's decision, which formed the basis of the scheme, should be interpreted so that such disclosure by individuals was not a precondition to their obtaining cheap butter.)

*The Treaty on European Union and the Treaty of Amsterdam*
Article F.2 of the TEU provided that

> 'the Union shall respect fundamental rights, as guaranteed by the European Convention for the Protection of Human Rights and Fundamental Freedoms ... and as they result from the constitutional traditions common to the member states, as general principles of Community Law.'

Furthermore, when the ToA came into effect, art. F became art. 7 EC, and was substantially amended to enable the Community to suspend certain rights (including voting rights) of a member state which is found to be in 'serious and persistent breach' of the principles of 'liberty, democracy, respect for human rights and fundamental freedoms, and the rule of law'.

### The European Union Charter of Fundamental Rights

Finally, the European Union Charter of Fundamental Rights, was published at the Nice Conference in December 2000, but not incorporated into the subsequent Treaty. The Charter merely brings together and declares the rights which already exist and is unenforceable. However, the Charter now forms part of the draft constitution of the European Union. Therefore, when the constitution comes into force, following ratification by all member states, the Charter will acquire *legal* status and will, therefore, become enforceable. (Curiously, and perhaps objectionably, the Charter applies only to citizens of the European Union, rather than to everyone within the member states.)

### 15.4.6 Procedural propriety

The principle of procedural propriety may be illustrated by two cases.

First, in *Transocean Marine Paint Association v Commission* [1979] 2 CMLR 459, the Court of Justice held that people whose interests would be significantly affected by a decision of a public authority must be given an opportunity to make their views known.

Secondly, the court has held several times that a person who is subject to an adverse decision is entitled to be given the reasons for the decision. (See, for example, *UNECTEF v Heylens* [1987] ECR 4097.)

## 15.5 Subsidiarity

The principle of subsidiarity requires that action should be taken at the most local level at which it will be effective. Although essentially a political principle rather than a legal one, in the Community context it has acquired legal status through art. 5 [ex 3(b)] EC, which originated in the TEU:

> 'The Community shall act within the limits of the powers conferred upon it by the Treaty and of the objectives assigned to it therein.
>
> 'In areas which do not fall within its exclusive competence, the Community shall take action, in accordance with the principle of subsidiarity, only if and insofar as the objectives of the proposed action cannot be sufficiently achieved by the member states and can therefore, by reason of the scale or effects of the proposed action, be better achieved by the Community.
>
> 'Any action by the Community shall not go beyond what is necessary to achieve the objectives of the Community.'

Whatever this is held to mean in practice, it is clear that when determining whether subsidiarity has been observed as a matter of law, the courts will be unable to avoid having to make political judgments.

**15.6** To what extent does the Court of Justice differ in practical terms from the English courts with regard to precedent?

As we have seen throughout this Part, the English doctrine of precedent is a great deal less binding and a great deal more flexible than it might at first appear to be. Similarly, despite the lack of any formal doctrine of bindingness, the Court of Justice's insistence on the development and maintenance of legal principles means that its decisions exhibit a very substantial degree of coherence.

Perhaps the major difference between the Court of Justice and the English courts, at a purely practical level, is that it is impossible to conceive of the Court of Justice treating itself as being compelled to reach a particular decision, against its better judgment, simply because there was a single prior decision of its own supporting that decision. On the other hand, it may very plausibly be argued that even this is scarcely a point of distinction between the two systems, because, as we have seen throughout the earlier chapters of this Part, most modern English judges would be willing to use the recognized techniques of the doctrine of binding precedent in order to avoid being bound by a decision where they felt it right to do so.

## Summary

- The Court of Justice spent its formative years without being exposed to the common law tradition and the doctrine of binding precedent.

- Judgments in the Court of Justice are presented in a style which is different from those in the English courts.

- The Court of Justice proceeds by applying generally accepted principles of law rather than by following decisions in individual cases.

- The principle of proportionality requires that consequences should be in proportion to their causes.

- The principles of legal certainty and legitimate expectation require that people who are subject to the law should be able to ascertain their rights and obligations; and that, where a public authority creates a legitimate expectation on the part of an individual, that expectation should be fulfilled.

▷ Despite the requirements of the principle of legal certainty, in practice the Court of Justice will require good reason to be shown before it will say that a particular judgment should not be given retrospective effect.

▷ The principle of equality requires that discriminatory actions must be objectively justified.

▷ The Community attaches great importance to the protection of fundamental rights.

▷ The principle of procedural propriety requires that procedural fairness should be observed.

▷ The principle of subsidiarity requires that the Community should take action only where the desired objective cannot be achieved by the member states.

▷ Given both the tendency of the European Court of Justice to apply accepted principles of law, and the degree of flexibility inherent in the English doctrine of binding precedent, there is little difference in practice between Community law and English law in terms of their approaches to their own previous decisions.

## Exercises

1  How does the European Court of Justice seek to achieve a reasonable degree of consistency in its decisions?

2  Identify and explain any two principles of Community law.

3  What is the Court of Justice's attitude towards the retrospectivity of its own decisions?

4  In practical terms, to what extent does the European Court of Justice differ from the English courts with regard to following previous decisions?

# Part 3

# Legislation and legislative interpretation

Having read this Part you should understand both the ways in which English legislation is drafted and interpreted, and the way in which European Community law is interpreted. (The interpretation of the European Convention on Human Rights has already been discussed at page 93.) More particularly, you should understand how legislative drafting and interpretation give rise to some problems which are common to the process of communication generally, and to others which turn more specifically on the nature, and constitutional context, of legislation.

Throughout this Part, except where the context otherwise requires, the terms *statute* and *statutory* refer specifically to the context of the English legal system, while the terms *legislation* and *legislative* are used more generally, so as to include, for example, Community treaties, regulations, directives and decisions, and the European Convention on Human Rights.

# Chapter 16

# An introduction to statute law and statutory interpretation

## 16.1 Introduction

This chapter deals with a variety of matters by way of introduction to the study of English statute law and statutory interpretation. It will also help to put the doctrine of the legislative supremacy of Parliament into a practical context.

## 16.2 Drafting, interpretation and communication

### 16.2.1 Introduction

At one level the complementary processes of statutory drafting and interpretation can be seen simply as the two constituent parts of an exercise in communication, and we should never lose sight of the fact that many of the so-called 'principles of statutory interpretation' are no more than the ordinary principles of linguistic communication. However, it is also important to appreciate that the constitutional context of statutory drafting and interpretation creates additional complications.

As far as the English legal system is concerned, the doctrine of the legislative supremacy of Parliament, as currently understood, was created by the courts (see page 62) and both its scope and continued existence are largely in their hands, as the outcome of the *Factortame* litigation so clearly shows (see page 87). More particularly, just as different judges have different perceptions of the judicial role in relation to precedent (see Part 2 generally and Chapter 14 in particular), so there are various views as to the proper role of the judiciary when interpreting statutes.

### 16.2.2 *Interpretation* and *construction*

It is impossible to identify any difference in principle between the way in which the terms *interpretation* and *construction* are used in relation to statutes. However, neither term brings out one of the most crucial points, namely that the meaning of an ordinary word of the English language is a question of fact, while the legal consequence of that meaning is, by definition, a matter of law.

In *Brutus v Cozens* [1972] 2 All ER 1297, the facts were that anti-apartheid activists disrupted the Wimbledon tennis tournament with a political demonstration. The magistrates acquitted them of 'insulting behaviour whereby a breach of the peace was likely to be occasioned'. The House of Lords took the view that the question of whether specific conduct was 'insulting' was a matter of fact to be determined by the tribunal of fact, and was not a question of law to be taken on appeal. Lord Reid said: 'The meaning of an ordinary word of the English language is not a question of law. The proper construction of a statute is a question of law'. In the patents case of *Energy Conversion Devices Incorporated's Applications* [1982] FSR 544, Lord Diplock emphasized the second part of Lord Reid's statement when he expressed the following opinion on behalf of a unanimous House of Lords:

> 'Your Lordships should, however, in my view take this opportunity of stating once again the important constitutional principle that questions of construction of all legislation, primary or secondary, are questions of law to be determined authoritatively by courts of law ... [and that] ... no tribunal and no court of law has any discretion to vary the meaning of the words of primary or secondary legislation from case to case in order to meet what the tribunal or court happens to think is the justice of the particular case. Tempting though it might sound, to do so is the negation of the rule of law. If there are cases in which the application of the Patents Rules leads to injustice, the cure is for the Secretary of State to amend the Rules. If what is thought to be the injustice results from the terms of the Act itself, the remedy is for Parliament to amend the Act.'

## 16.3 The classification of Acts of Parliament

Acts of Parliament may be classified as either *public* on the one hand or *private and personal* on the other. Public Acts, which are sometimes known as *public and general Acts*, are intended to change the general law, and they constitute the vast bulk of Parliament's legislative output. Private and personal Acts relate either to particular places or to particular people. Examples of personal Acts include those which authorize the marriage of people who would otherwise be within the prohibited degrees, and examples of private Acts include those promoted by local authorities who wish to acquire powers which they would not have under the general law.

The doctrine of the supremacy of Parliament, which was discussed at page 61, applies equally to all Acts (*British Railways Board v Pickin* [1974] 1 All ER 609), but it does not necessarily follow that the same principles of interpretation apply equally in all cases. More particularly, the courts have sometimes argued that the promoters of private Acts have gained for themselves some additional legal advantage which is denied to other people, and that therefore private Acts should be construed strictly.

In *South Staffordshire Waterworks Co v Barrow* (1896–97) 13 TLR 549, two waterworks companies had been operating in adjoining areas. The basis on which they calculated their charges varied, with the result that consumers in one of the areas paid more than consumers in the other. Under the authority of a private Act of Parliament, the two companies merged and extended the area of their operation. Clearly the question then arose as to the basis of charging for those consumers who were in the area which had previously been served by neither company. The court held that they should be charged on the lower basis.

It seems, however, that there may be scope for an exception where the private Act is intended to operate for the public good rather than for commercial advantage. *Pyx Granite Co Ltd v Ministry of Housing and Local Government* [1959] 3 All ER 1 involved the interpretation of the Malvern Hills Act 1924, a private Act giving certain powers to the Malvern Hills Conservators, to enable them to conserve the Malvern Hills for the benefit of the public at large. A question arose as to the meaning of the phrase 'all lands common or waste'. Does it mean 'all common and waste lands' (thereby excluding all other categories of land) or does it mean 'all lands, all commons and all wastes' with commons and wastes being specified merely by way of emphasis and to forestall any possible argument that they were excluded? Opting for the second alternative, Viscount Simonds said:

> 'The meaning of the expression "all lands common or waste" has been debated, and it has been urged that ... the expression must be read as if it were "common or waste lands". The result of this would be to exclude from the conservators' jurisdiction any land in which they might have or acquire any right or interest other than common or waste land. So strange a consequence must be avoided if any other interpretation is possible. I think that it is, for I do not regard it as extravagant to suppose that the draftsman ... if only *ex majore cautela*, thought it proper to add "common or waste" in case it should be supposed that they were not "lands". It is legitimate to add that, if common or waste lands only were intended, the transposition to "lands common or waste" is one that requires explanation, which is not forthcoming.'

This interpretation clearly gave the statute a wider meaning rather than a narrower one, in the sense that it applied to all land within the conservators' jurisdiction, rather than merely to some of it.

**16.4** Precedent in relation to decisions on statutory interpretation

When considering the doctrine of precedent in cases involving statutory interpretation, we must return to the distinction which Lord Reid made in *Brutus v Cozens* [1972] 2 All ER 1297, between matters of fact and matters of law (see page 236). The distinction between law and fact is discussed more generally at pages 34–9, but for the present purposes two closely related consequences flow from it.

First, decisions on the meanings of ordinary words are not subject to the doctrine of binding precedent, because it is the nature of that doctrine to deal with issues of law as distinct from issues of fact. Secondly, although decisions on the construction of statutes, being matters of law, *may* constitute binding precedents, it does not necessarily follow that they *must* do so in every case. This cautionary note flows logically from the most elementary principle of statutory interpretation, namely that the essential task is to find the meaning of the words *for the purposes of the Act in which those words are used.*

In *Quillotex Co Ltd v Minister of Housing and Local Government* [1965] 2 All ER 913, stating the proposition at the level of general principle, Salmon LJ said:

> 'No real help can be gained as to the meaning of a word in statute A by reference to its meaning in statutes B, C, or D. *All one can derive from the cases are the relevant principles of construction to be applied.*' (Emphasis added.)

Putting this another way, decisions on the interpretation of one statute are no more than *persuasive* authorities in relation to other statutes, or as Lord Diplock said, in *Carter v Bradbeer* [1975] 3 All ER 158:

> 'a question of statutory construction is one in which the strict doctrine of precedent can only be of narrow application. The *ratio decidendi* of a judgment as to the meaning of particular words or combinations of words used in a particular statutory provision can have no more than a persuasive influence on a court which is called upon to interpret the same word or combination of words appearing in some other statutory provision.'

The cases of *Newman v Lipman* [1950] 2 All ER 832 and *Burgess v McCracken* (1986) 150 JP 529 provide good examples of the significance of the precise statutory context, and therefore of the need for extreme caution when dealing with precedent in relation to statutory interpretation. In *Newman v Lipman*, the High Court held that a professional photographer, who wandered round taking photographs of tourists against the backdrop of famous landmarks, in the hope that the tourists would buy the photographs, was not trading, and therefore was not contravening a prohibition on trading in the street. In *Burgess v McCracken*, a photographer was conducting his business in a precisely similar way, except that he was operating in a public park rather than in the street.

The High Court held that the prohibition on trading in the street was distinguishable from the prohibition on trading in public parks, because the purpose of the former is to prevent obstruction of the highway, whereas the purpose of the latter is wider, and includes protecting people, who are using the park for relaxation, from being annoyed by traders. Therefore, in a borderline case on the meaning of 'trading', an activity which is lawful on the highway may be prohibited in a park, because annoyance can occur without obstruction.

It would appear, at this stage, therefore, that a case which decides the meaning of a specific form of statutory words cannot bind a subsequent court unless it is considering the same form of words *in the same statute*. However, there is one, strictly limited, exception. A decision in relation to one statute may be binding in relation to another, provided that both statutes deal with the same subject matter or, to use the Latin tag, they are *in pari materia* with each other. The classic statement of the principle is from *R v Palmer* (1785) 168 ER 279: 'If there are several Acts *upon the same subject*, they are to be taken together as forming one system and as interpreting and enforcing each other'. (Emphasis added).

The courts take a strict approach to the question of whether statutes are *in pari materia* with each other. In *Crosley v Arkwright* (1788) 100 ER 325, statutes relating to stamp duties were held to be *in pari materia* with each other, but in *Powell v Cleland* [1947] 2 All ER 672 the Rent and Mortgage Interest Restrictions (Amendment) Act 1933 was held to be not *in pari materia* with the 1925 property legislation.

On the other hand, the courts are less strict when it comes to identifying the type of instrument to which the *pari materia* principle can apply. *R v Newcastle-upon-Tyne Justices ex parte Skinner* [1987] 1 All ER 349 indicates that the principle is not limited to statutes, but can be extended to enable statutory instruments to be used when interpreting earlier statutes, even where the statutory instrument was not made under the statute in question. The facts of the case were that s. 114 of the Magistrates' Courts Act 1980 provided that magistrates need not state a case for the High Court unless the appellant entered into a recognizance to proceed with the appeal. The Act said nothing as to how the amount of the recognizance was to be fixed, but r. 26 of the Crown Court Rules 1982 provided that, in appeals by way of case stated from the Crown Court, a recognizance was to be 'such sum as the Crown Court thinks proper, having regard to the means of the applicant'. In the Divisional Court, Glidewell LJ said: 'In our view, although the same phrase is not to be found in s. 114 of the 1980 Act, the same principle must necessarily apply to magistrates'.

Finally, just as the interpretation of one statute will not be binding in relation to another (unless they are *in pari materia*), so the court may easily distinguish a statutory formulation from a common law one.

Thus, in *Jones v Tower Boot Co Ltd* [1997] 2 All ER 406, the Court of Appeal held that for the purposes of s. 32(1) of the Race Relations Act 1976, an employer is liable for racially discriminatory conduct on the part of its employees, even though the conduct would not fall within the course of the employees' employment for the purposes of vicarious liability in the law of tort. As Waite LJ pointed out, upholding the employer's argument that the employees' discriminatory conduct was not part of what they were employed to do, this would mean that the more objectionable the employees' conduct, the less likelihood there was that the employer would be held liable; and this would be contrary to the whole policy of the Act.

## Summary

- A detailed consideration of statute law and statutory interpretation shows the doctrine of the legislative supremacy of Parliament in its practical context.

- The processes of statutory drafting and interpretation share many of the problems which are raised by communication generally, but their specifically legal context also raises special problems of a constitutional nature.

- The doctrine of the legislative supremacy of Parliament applies equally to all statutes, but for the purposes of interpretation it may be possible to distinguish between *public and general* statutes on the one hand and *private and personal* statutes on the other.

- Decisions on the meaning of statutory words are always made in the context of the statute in question, and therefore they do not constitute binding precedents where the same wording is used in other statutes.

## Exercises

1 In the present context, what (if anything) is the significance of the distinction between *public and general* statutes and *private and personal* statutes?

2 How does the doctrine of binding precedent apply to cases involving statutory interpretation?

# Chapter 17

## Statutory drafting

17.1 Introduction

17.1.1 The origins of Parliament

According to Radcliffe and Cross, 'few matters in English history are more controverted than the origins of Parliament', although it seems to be reasonably clear that it was initially 'some sort of special and formal gathering about the King ... an occasion ... rather than a body or an institution'. (*The English Legal System*, 6th edn, 1977, p. 53.) Additionally, at least two further things are reasonably clear. First, Parliament dates from very shortly after Magna Carta. Secondly, as the French origins of the term itself clearly denote, Parliament began life as a talking-shop.

In the early stages of Parliament's development, the business of legislating, or enacting statutes, was still in the hands of the King, who acted with the advice of the *Curia Regis*, which was the forerunner of the modern Privy Council. Originally statutes were drafted in either Latin or Norman French. The first Commons Bill in English appeared in 1414, which was, of course, only 14 years after the death of Geoffrey Chaucer, whose poetry had established the status of the English language as a proper medium for serious writing. The process by which the legislative function was transferred to Parliament may be traced in any of the standard works on legal history. However, one natural result of this transfer was that statutes – a term which basically means simply decrees which have been set up or established – became known as Acts of Parliament.

Securing the enactment of legislation by the King in Council involved the submission of a petition or Bill asking for a particular legal remedy to be made available, in response to which a committee of judges, royal advisers and other officials would draft a statute. The 15th century saw the origin of the modern practice of drafting Bills in the form of the statute which was itself the desired result of the legislative process.

Although very few of these early statutes are likely to be encountered by the modern lawyer, it is interesting to note that the history of statutory draftsmanship shows that there is nothing new in the complaint that statutes are unnecessarily obscure:

'From the laconic and often obscure terseness of our earliest statutes, especially when in Latin, we swung in the sixteenth, seventeenth and eighteenth centuries to a verbosity which succeeded only in concealing the real matter of the law under a welter of superfluous synonyms.' (Allen, *Law in the Making*, 7th edn, 1964, p. 482.)

Commentators on the law are not, of course, alone in noting the potential conflict between a multiplicity of words and clarity of meaning. As Alexander Pope said, albeit in another context:

'Words are like leaves, and where they most abound
Much fruit of sense beneath is seldom found.'

*(An Essay on Criticism,* 1711.)

Jonathan Swift noted one possible solution, albeit from a fictitious legal system:

'No law [in Brobdingnag] must exceed in words the number of letters in their alphabet, which consists only in two and twenty. But indeed few of them extend even to that length. They are expressed in the most plain and simple terms, wherein those people are not mercurial enough to discover above one interpretation; and to write a comment upon any law is a capital crime.' *(Gulliver's Travels: A Voyage to Brobdingnag,* 1726, ch. 7.)

Many students, faced with the vast literature on English law and the expectation that they will write essays and examination answers on it, might sympathize with the view that writing about the law should be a capital crime. On the other hand, no one could pretend that the Brobdingnagian restriction on the length of laws would be practical in a modern legal system, unless it had the obvious result of causing an immediate extension of the alphabet by several thousand characters, which would in turn produce its own difficulties.

### 17.1.2　The origins of the Office of the Parliamentary Counsel

The modern English orthodoxy that legislative drafting is a highly specialized skill is not shared by all other legal systems. For example, the American practice is for legislation to be prepared not only by the Offices of Legislative Counsel of the House of Representatives and the Senate, but also by the legal staffs of committees of Congress and individual government departments. According to Reed Dickerson, a distinguished American commentator who gave evidence to the *Committee on the Preparation of Legislation,* under the chairmanship of Sir David Renton:

'Most legislation in the United States is drafted by people who, however good they may be in their substantive specialities, have only fleeting acquaintance with the expertise required for good drafting. This is perhaps the main reason why so much of American legislation is inadequate ... [the British] are light years ahead of us in this respect.' (Para. 8.18 of the Committee's Report, 1975, Cmnd 6053.)

Even in England, the practice of specialized legislative drafting has been established for less than 150 years. In the early 19th century, the drafting of government Bills was still allocated either to drafters attached to individual government departments or to lawyers in private practice. The latter undertook the work of legislative drafting for the government just as they would undertake any other work for any other client.

## 17.2 The modern Office of the Parliamentary Counsel

### 17.2.1 Introduction

In 1869 Henry Thring was appointed to the newly created office of Parliamentary Counsel to the Treasury. The last three words are no longer part of the title, and the office is now part of the Cabinet Office. Although parliamentary counsel have a close working relationship with the Law Officers, they are not responsible to them in a departmental sense. Thring's appointment was probably one of the most important individual events in the history of English legislative drafting, introducing as it did the idea that it was desirable for legislative drafters to be full-time specialists.

While dissenting views are heard from time to time, there is no doubt that the currently prevailing – indeed entrenched – view is that such specialization in drafting is not merely desirable but practically essential. For example, in 1985 a very distinguished group of academic lawyers presented a report to the Law Commission, concerning the codification of the general principles of criminal liability. The group drafted a proposed code, but acknowledged that their code 'would require the expert attention of Parliamentary Counsel'. (Law Com 143, para. 0.5.)

In short, therefore, the orthodox English view of legislative drafting supports Alexander Pope's more general assertion:

'True ease in writing comes from art not chance,
As those move easiest who have learn'd to dance.'

*(An Essay on Criticism, 1711.)*

The Office of the Parliamentary Counsel has developed from its tiny origins with Thring and a single assistant into a group of approximately 65 lawyers, with both solicitors and barristers being eligible for appointment. The head of the Office has the style of First Parliamentary Counsel.

The functioning of the Office of the Parliamentary Counsel

The principal task of Parliamentary Counsel is the drafting of all government legislation, except that relating exclusively to Scotland and Northern Ireland, each of which has its own legislative drafters. Additionally, Parliamentary Counsel may draft delegated legislation if asked to do so by the responsible department, but usually each department's own lawyers will undertake such work themselves. In addition, where delegated legislation drafted by departmental lawyers amends primary legislation (which is particularly likely to be the case where English law is being amended in response to a Community obligation), the practice is for Parliamentary Counsel to settle the draft of the proposals. An increasing part of their workload consists of scrutinizing statutory instruments made under the Regulatory Reform Act 2001. The working methods of the Parliamentary Counsel Office were described by Sir George Engle, the then First Parliamentary Counsel, in a paper presented to a Franco-British Round Table on Legislative Drafting in 1986, the transactions of which were published by London University's Institute of Advanced Legal Studies as *British and French Statutory Drafting* (1987). Engle's account is worth considering at some length, in view of both the authoritative nature of its source and the central importance of the subject matter:

'Every Government Bill is drafted by Parliamentary Counsel upon the instructions of the Government Department concerned. These drafting instructions are normally in writing – I say "normally" because there can be some form of instant legislation required in which case it may be necessary for somebody to rush around and speak – and are prepared by one of the Department's legal advisers in consultation with its administrators ... Before they are sent to Parliamentary Counsel, drafting instructions are usually cleared with any other Government Department likely to be affected by the proposed legislation.

'Drafting instructions are expected to give, in plain language, a full explanation of the purpose and background of the Bill, and to state what existing legislation affects the subject ... [They] do not take the form of a draft of a Bill ... though they sometimes ask for provisions similar to those which appear in an existing Act ...

'On receipt of drafting instructions for a Bill, the First Parliamentary Counsel allocates the Bill to one of the senior Counsel, who from then on has full responsibility for it. Counsel usually work in pairs, so the senior Counsel (whom I will refer to as "the draftsman") will normally be assisted by a less experienced junior Counsel ... The draftsman is responsible for the actual wording of the Bill; and his functions include, to a greater or lesser extent, the clarification and detailed working out, in concert with the lawyers and administrators in the Department, of the policy to be given effect to by the Bill and of the conceptual and legislative structure appropriate for the purpose.

'When ... the draftsman fully understands the instructions and has cleared up any difficulties which they present, he produces a first draft of the Bill and sends it to the Department concerned, where it is examined both by the legal advisers and by the administrators ... Copies are also sent to other interested departments for comment. On the basis of the comments received, the draftsman produces a revised draft – and this process continues until the Bill is considered ready for presentation to Parliament ... A large Bill may take nine months or more to draft... and could go through ten or more drafts ... When a draft Bill is ready, it is circulated to all Government Departments, and its presentation to Parliament is finally authorized by a small committee of Ministers whose members include the Lord Chancellor [now, of course the Secretary of State for Constitutional Affairs] and the Law Officers ...

'... a Bill can be amended at various stages during its passage through each House of Parliament. Amendments propose the insertion, omission or substitution of words in the text of the Bill under consideration ... All amendments therefore need to be drafted with as much skill as the Bill itself. All amendments proposed by the Government are drafted by the draftsman of the Bill on instructions from the Department. Other proposed amendments are drafted by the Member proposing them or are supplied to him by organizations or pressure groups outside Parliament. Their drafting is nearly always unsatisfactory; so if the Government is willing to accept a badly drafted amendment in principle, the Minister will ask the proposer to withdraw it ... in return for an undertaking by the Government to propose a properly drafted Government amendment at the next stage of the Bill ... Similarly if, as sometimes happens, an unsatisfactorily drafted amendment is passed against the wishes of the Government, then unless this defeat can be reversed at a later stage, the draftsman will be instructed to prepare whatever further amendments are needed to remedy the defective drafting.' (*Op. cit.*, pp. 19–22.)

In passing, it is worth noticing that the practice of every government Bill being drafted by Parliamentary Counsel was subjected to an experiment in relation to the Bill which became the Finance Act 1996, part of which was drafted by private sector drafters, who were chosen following open competition. However, as Sir George Engle pointed out in a letter to *The Times* (27 February 1996), an answer to a question in the House of Commons had revealed that the cost of drafting 33.5 pages of the Act (including one page not included in the Bill for policy reasons), had been £130,000. Having said that this sum was

'more than the combined annual salaries (at the bottom of their respective pay scales) of one full and one deputy Parliamentary counsel, who between them could be expected to produce in the course of a year Bills totalling 200 pages, as well as working on regulations to give effect to European Community directives,'

Engle concluded that

> 'unless private sector drafting is immeasurably better than that of Parliamentary counsel – which it isn't – this experiment in privatization seems a reckless waste of public money. Or could it be that Parliamentary counsel – whose 200 pages at the private sector rate would cost all of £776,000 – are grossly underpaid.'

While Engle's calculation takes no account of the element of business overheads which the private sector drafters would have had to include in their fees, his point remains convincing. The experiment was not repeated.

The Office is expected to act on instructions, just as any other professional advisers are expected to act on behalf of their clients. Kent, a former Parliamentary Counsel, considered that the Office was governed by two rules:

> 'The first was that nothing was undraftable, if the conception was clear. The second was that whenever the Government demanded a Bill by a certain time, which might be twenty four hours later, that Bill would be delivered. It might be wrong, indeed it was bound to be wrong, but it would be there.' (*In on the Act: Memoirs of a Law Maker*, 1979, p. 19.)

One beneficial consequence of having a specialist Office is that it contributes to the integrity of the legislative process. The point can be made by way of contrast with the American practice whereby departmental lawyers draft many Bills. Commenting on this, Dickerson said:

> 'Some Bill drafters in the executive branch intentionally use fuzzy or misleading language to get the legislature unwittingly to enact policies that come to light only when the agency sponsoring the legislation is given a chance to administer it.' (*Legislative Drafting in London and Washington* [1959] CLJ 49.)

The calculated use of 'fuzzy or misleading language' by the drafter, as distinct from the politicians who are responsible for the formulation of the legislative policy, contrasts strongly with the British tradition. When one administrator commented that a particular provision in a draft Bill was 'nice and vague', Kent's response was that this was 'a dubious compliment'. (*Op. cit.*, p. 45.)

It is important to maintain a sense of perspective. The drafter must bear in mind the fact that the authority of those instructing him – or at any rate the authority of their political masters – ultimately derives its legitimacy from the electoral process: 'He operates only as a technician, but the democratic process requires that he does so as an ardent democrat. He needs to be fired by a sense of the public importance of his function'. (Bennion, *Statute Law*, 3rd edn, 1990, p. 21.) Similarly, insight may be derived from the following comment of the Renton Committee:

'Between the taking of policy decisions and the start of the drafting process, and shading into that process, is what a First Parliamentary Counsel has called "the grey area"'. (*The Preparation of Legislation*, 1975, para. 8.5.)

It is easy to discern here an echo of the inevitability, if not the despair, which T S Eliot noted in *The Hollow Men*:

'Between the idea
And the reality
...
Falls the Shadow.'

Two relatively recent innovations in the work of the Office of the Parliamentary Counsel are worth noticing.

First, it is now the practice to publish some Bills in draft so that consultation as to their detailed content becomes possible. While there are no exhaustive criteria for identifying which Bills are suitable for this treatment, positive indicators include lack of acute urgency, potential benefit from consultation and the legislative proposals being sufficiently advanced in terms of policy decisions. The publication of the draft Coroners Bill in 2006 introduced a further innovation, with the Explanatory Notes being incorporated into the Bill itself, rather than being published as a separate document. (Although this Bill was widely publicised as a breakthrough in plain language drafting, it was, in fact no such thing, being drafted entirely in the same style as any other Bill would currently be drafted. Those who took it as an example of plain language drafting were confusing the text of the Explanatory Notes with the text of the Bill itself.)

Secondly, a major project, known as the Tax Law Rewrite, is under way. As the title indicates, the idea underlying this project is to rewrite, and re-enact, existing taxing statutes. The point of the exercise is to take material which is necessarily dense and difficult in its nature, and present it in ways which are more accessible to its users.

## 17.3 The drafting process

According to Kent:

'There are two main objects that the draftsman aims at, and they are not easy to reconcile. First and foremost, to get the Bill right. The test is that when it is passed, and a trained lawyer or judge has mastered its intricacies, the meaning is clear (in the sense of unambiguous) and the intention carried out. Subject to this, the second object is to make the Bill as intelligible as possible to Parliament and the general public.' (*Op. cit.*, p. 97.)

Leaving aside the presumably unintentional implication that judges are not trained lawyers, the most interesting aspect of this comment is the use of the phrase 'clear (in the sense of unambiguous)'. This concept of clarity is further illuminated by an examination of, and a comment on, the provision that eventually became s. 89(8) of the Civil Defence Act 1939:

> 'For the purposes of this Act, the number of persons who work in or about a mine shall be deemed to be a number ascertained as follows, that is to say –
>
> (a) by having regard to all the people employed in or about the mine and ascertaining how many of them are from time to time simultaneously present in or about the mine otherwise than below the surface, and
> (b) if the numbers so ascertained fluctuate, by ascertaining the highest figure below which throughout any consecutive period of fifteen minutes the numbers do not fall.'

When told that the drafter was trying to simplify the provision, the responsible Minister, Sir John Anderson, replied that there was no need to change the wording because 'it's perfectly clear, when you understand it'. Kent acknowledged that 'this seemed to draw the proper distinction between clarity (intelligibility) and clarity (unambiguity)'. (*Op. cit.*, p. 118). This distinction between the two kinds of clarity, although easily overlooked, is also useful in perceiving the real meaning of a famous comment of another eminent Parliamentary Counsel, Sir John Rowlatt: 'The intelligibility of a Bill is in inverse proportion to its chance of being right'. (Quoted by Kent, *op. cit.*, p. 97.)

The problem is that, no matter how successful the drafter may appear to have been in achieving clarity in the sense of unambiguity, there will always be lawyers who wish to dispute the meaning of whatever words are used. There is perhaps more than a grain of truth in Jonathan Swift's description of lawyers as

> 'a society of men ... bred up from their youth in the art of proving by words multiplied for the purpose, that white is black, and black is white, according as they are paid'. (*Gulliver's Travels: A Voyage to the Country of the Houyhnhnms*, 1726, ch. 5.)

One consequence of this argumentative propensity on the part of the legal profession, is that, in the words of Stephen J,

> 'it is not enough [for the drafter] to attain to a degree of precision which a person reading in good faith can understand, but it is necessary to attain if possible to a degree of precision which a person reading in bad faith cannot misunderstand. It is all the better if he cannot pretend to misunderstand it.' (*In re Castioni* [1891] 1 QB 149.)

The next question to be considered, therefore, is: how does the drafter set about achieving this degree of precision?

The drafter's task is complicated by the fact that Bills are political instruments which suddenly (on receiving the Royal Assent) become legal ones. The Renton Committee addressed this problem thus:

> 'In principle the interests of the ultimate users should always have priority over those of the legislators: a Bill, which serves a merely temporary purpose, should always be regarded primarily as a future Act, and should be drafted and arranged with this object in view.' (*The Preparation of Legislation*, 1975, para. 10.3.)

Engle illustrated the nature of a Bill in an article entitled *Bills Are Made To Pass As Razors Are Made To Sell* [1983] Stat LR 7. This curious title, which is a much-quoted aphorism of Thring, first published in 1875 in a pamphlet on *Simplification of the Law*, is an allusion to an 18th century poem by the pseudonymous Peter Pindar. The poem concerns a street trader who sells razors very cheaply. When a disgruntled customer called Hodge returns to complain that the razors are useless for shaving, the poet reports the following conversation:

> '"Friend", quoth the razor-man, "I am no knave:
> As for the razors you have bought,
> Upon my soul, I never thought
> That they would *shave*".
> "Not think they'd shave!" quoth Hodge with wondering eyes
> And voice not much unlike an Indian yell;
> "What were they made for then, you dog?" he cries -
> "Made!" quoth the fellow with a smile, – "to sell".'
>
> (*Op. cit.*, p. 9.)

While conceding that Thring's aphorism was intended lightheartedly, Engle observed: 'Just as ... razors must indeed sell before they get a chance to shave, so ... Bills must pass before they can become law and do their work'.

In the same article, Engle identifies and comments on three constraints on Parliamentary drafting. The first constraint is that statutes are legal documents; the second is that time is always short; and the third is that it is impracticable continuously to redesign the fundamental structure of a Bill even when repeated amendments have distorted the original conception.

Taking these in turn, Engle cited Sir Bruce Fraser's 1973 revision of Sir Ernest Gowers' *The Complete Plain Words*, in order to illuminate the significance of the status of legal documents (and with more than the hint of an echo of Stephens J in *In re Castioni*):

> 'The legal draftsman ... has to ensure to the best of his ability that what he says will be found to mean precisely what he intended, even after it has been

subjected to detailed and possibly hostile scrutiny by acute legal minds ... What matters most to him is that no one will succeed in persuading a court of law that his words bear a meaning which he did not intend, and, if possible, that no one will think it worthwhile to try.'

In relation to constraints of time, almost anyone who writes anything which is to be taken seriously will usually wish for more time that is, in fact, available. However, as Sir Noel Hutton, another former First Parliamentary Counsel, pointed out, constraints of time may benefit Parliamentary Counsel in one way, because 'they are always striving after the perfection which ... is usually in fact unattainable; and the last bell, even if it comes too soon, does at least release them from that vain endeavour'. (*The Mechanics of Law Reform* (1961) 24 MLR 18.) There can be few Parliamentary Counsel who, whether with relief or frustration (or a mixture of the two) have never concluded that Bills, like poems, are never finished but merely abandoned.

Finally, the impossibility of continuously redesigning the structure of a Bill as it progresses through Parliament stems from the fact that such redesign would necessitate abandoning clauses which had already been debated and starting again with debates on their successors.

## 17.4 Consolidation and statute law revision

So far we have been considering what might be called 'new' law. It is appropriate to conclude, however, by mentioning the concepts of consolidation and statute law revision. Taking these concepts in turn:

'A consolidation statute ... is an expedient of convenience to assemble and re-enact a number of antecedent statutory provisions. It often happens that a long course of legislation on a particular subject, involving many repeals, amendments, and supplements, is scattered in unwieldy fashion over the so-called statute book, until the time comes when it is necessary to "tidy it up".' (Allen, *Law in the Making*, 7th edn, 1964, p. 477.)

It follows that, basically, consolidation does not change the law, but merely reorganizes it so as to improve its accessibility. Such Bills are usually called 'pure' consolidation. However, since the Consolidation of Enactments (Procedure) Act 1949, it has been possible to consolidate with the addition of 'corrections and minor improvements'. This phrase is defined by s. 2 of the Act as:

'Amendments of which the effect is confined to resolving ambiguities, removing doubts, bringing obsolete provisions into conformity with modern practice, or removing unnecessary provisions or anomalies which are not of substantial importance, and amendments designed to facilitate improvements in the form or manner in which the law is stated, and includes any transitional provisions which may be necessary in consequence of such amendments.'

Since the creation of the Law Commissions, however, this procedure has largely fallen into disuse, having been replaced by the practice of drafting consolidating Bills which incorporate amendments reflecting Law Commission recommendations. The two Law Commissions – one for Scotland and one for England and Wales – were created by the Law Commissions Act 1965. By s. 3(1) of the Act, the task of each Commission is:

'To take and keep under review all the law with which [it is] concerned with a view to its systematic development and reform, including in particular ... the elimination of anomalies, the repeal of obsolete and unnecessary enactments, the reduction of the number of separate enactments and generally the simplification and modernisation of the law.'

*Statute law revision* is the name often given to the process whereby a statute is enacted to repeal earlier statutes, or parts of statutes, which have become obsolete for one reason or another. Unlike Scots Law, which has a limited doctrine of desuetude extending to Acts of the Scots Parliament which existed before the Act of Union 1707, English Law has no doctrine, even of a limited nature, which could reduce the need for such revision.

The significance of the concepts of consolidation and statute law revision is that Bills of both kinds qualify for a specially expedited Parliamentary procedure, at the heart of which is the Joint Committee on Consolidation etc. Bills, composed of members from both the Commons and the Lords. The expedited Parliamentary procedure consists of the Bills being automatically referred to the Joint Committee after a formal Second Reading in the House into which they are first introduced, which in practice is the House of Lords. The procedure therefore is intended to provide sufficient Parliamentary scrutiny to satisfy constitutional propriety, while ensuring that the Bills entrusted to it occupy a bare minimum of time on the floor of each House.

The drafting of consolidation and statute law revision Bills is undertaken principally by Parliamentary Counsel on secondment to the Law Commission, although there has been some limited use of external expertise – for example, retired members of the Office. (*The Preparation of Legislation*, 1975, para. 14.16.) Although the drafting of consolidation Bills may sound a simple and straightforward process, the reality is rather different:

'Consolidation ... is really a matter very often of extreme difficulty ... There is very great difficulty in getting it done; it is a task requiring exceedingly skilled and rare labour, and the labour of months ... skilled labour of a character which I cannot always get; it is not altogether a question of money.' (Lord Thring, quoted in *The Preparation of Legislation*, 1975, para. 14.15, where the view was accepted as having continuing validity.)

## 17.5 *Tilling's Rules* for the drafting of legislation

The identity of Mr Tilling is a matter of some uncertainty, but he was clearly a civil service administrator. Although he obviously wrote his 'Rules' in lighthearted vein, they may not be wholly without a grain of truth, and they will at least provide a measure of light relief. *Tilling's Rules* reflect a tripartite relationship between an administrator from the instructing department (to whom the Rules are addressed), a solicitor from the instructing department and Parliamentary Counsel. This still represents the normal practice in most contexts, except that it is usual for administrators in the Inland Revenue to instruct Parliamentary Counsel directly, rather than through solicitors.

### Tilling's Rules

'1. Your first step in drafting your Bill consists in disclosing to the public the day on which the Bill will come into force.

'2. Immediately after that, your solicitor will tell you exactly what to do next. Insofar as the consent of any other adult is needed, he will have obtained it.

'3. You will then instruct your solicitor – i.e. you will disclose in writing that you do not know what the law is now or how you would like it altered.

'4. Your solicitor will then instruct your counsel – i.e. disclose to him in writing that he (the solicitor) does not know what the law is now or what it will be if his proposals for altering it are implemented.

'5. You will then be invited to take part in a discussion with your solicitor and your counsel. Remember that, before and during the event, the discussion is called "a conference". Not until afterwards may you call it "a shambles".

'6. Your solicitor will then send you drafts of sections which, to confuse you, he will call "clauses".

'7. Read them carefully. If in your opinion they accurately and intelligibly reflect your intentions, they will need correcting.

'8. Beware of the common error of telling your counsel how to draft. You must tell your solicitor why the results of the drafting will be disastrous. He will not agree with you but will explain that, for reasons which you have failed to see, the results will be disastrous in a way you will not comprehend.

'9. Action will follow as in 4 and 5 above. Do not be distressed if your solicitor hesitates to tell your counsel to "belt up and get on with it". Solicitors do not address counsel in this way, as both are descended from a common stock, known in English folklore as "the fiddlers three". You yourself may tell counsel to "belt up": but see 15 below.

'10. If your Bill is a hybrid Bill – i.e. bad only in parts – the third fiddler, called "an agent", will join the party. He will explain that it is now too late. Nobody else will believe this, so you must keep on with it.

'11. Eventually you will have either a General Election, a change of policy, a coronary, or a Bill. The last two may occur simultaneously.

'12. From now on it is vital that you consistently misinterpret the Bill. Your solicitor will claim to understand it, and – as the only available man who does – he will have to write the Clause Notes himself.

'13. You will then explain the Bill to your Minister. Do not waste too much time on this: it is unlikely that he will pay attention.

'14. Your Bill will then have two Readings, during which nobody will read it.

'15. After that it will go into Committee. At this stage people will put down amendments. There will be so many that only some can be selected for discussion. Nobody knows how amendments are selected, but if you have needled your counsel hitherto, Heaven help you now.

'16. Your Bill will then have a third Reading, which will resemble the Committee stage, but the accommodation provided for you will be even more uncomfortable.

'17. Your Bill may need "resolutions" and even "Queen's Consent". Do not ask about these complications. Tell your solicitor and your counsel what you have decided: they will enjoy putting you right.

'18. Your Bill will then go to the Lords, if they are still there. Do not worry about this: they are unlikely to commit suicide for your sake.

'19. You will then get the Royal Assent.

'20. All that remains is to disclose to the public the day on which will come into force the Bill putting right what you have just finished doing.'

# Summary

▶ For several centuries the English legal system had no specialist statutory drafters. However, from 1869 onwards, there has been an office of the Parliamentary Counsel.

The drafting process is complicated by a number of factors, including pressure of time and the possibility of *ad hoc* amendments which may distort the original conception of the Bill as a whole.

 Special legislative procedures are available for measures embodying consolidation and statute law revision.

 *Tilling's Rules* provide a lighthearted view of the drafting process as seen from the perspective of a civil service administrator.

## Exercises

1 What *two* meanings did Kent ascribe to *clarity*?

2 What did Engle identify as the constraints on statutory drafting?

# Chapter 18

# Plain meanings, mischiefs and purposes

## Introduction

It is tempting to assume that the process of statutory interpretation simply requires the identification and application of the *literal* (or *plain*) meaning of the enacted words. In fact, however, such simple literalism is fundamentally defective, because it proceeds on the false assumption that a word, or a group of words, will always have a plain meaning. The truth of the matter is that many words have a variety of meanings, and the only way of identifying their meaning on a particular occasion is by reference to the context within which they are used. This proposition is not limited to statutory interpretation, as the examples at page 7 illustrate. However, a useful judicial statement of the proposition may be found in the case of *Bourne v Norwich Crematorium Ltd* [1967] 1 All ER 576, the facts of which are discussed at page 4. Stamp J said:

> 'English words derive colour from those which surround them. Sentences are not mere collections of words to be taken out of the sentence, defined separately by reference to the dictionary or decided cases, and then put back again into the sentence with the meaning which one has assigned to them as separate words so as to give the sentence or phrase a meaning which as a sentence or phrase it cannot bear without distortion of the English language. That one must construe a word or phrase in a section of an Act of Parliament with all the assistance one can from decided cases and, if you will, from the dictionary, is not in doubt; but having obtained all that assistance, one must not at the end of the day distort that which has to be construed and give it a meaning which in its context one would not think it can possibly bear.'

Similarly, in *Attorney-General v Prince Ernest Augustus of Hanover* [1957] 1 All ER 49, Viscount Simonds said: 'Words, and particularly general words, cannot be read in isolation, their colour and content are derived from their context'. It follows that the principal task in any exercise in interpretation is to identify the correct context, and much of this Part of this book will be devoted to an examination of the way this is done in practice. Nevertheless, there are two reasons why we cannot totally disregard simple literalism.

First, since it is the inadequacy of simple literalism which gave rise to the modern approach to interpretation, it follows that our understanding of what happens now will be enhanced by an appreciation of the older technique.

Secondly, some judges may, albeit rarely, still make decisions on the basis of simple literalism, and therefore we need to be able to understand what is happening on those occasions. Pausing only to emphasize that, until we come to *The Purposive Approach to Interpretation* (page 263), the following discussion does not represent the mainstream of modern judicial technique, we must therefore consider the workings of simple literalism.

## 18.2 Simple literalism in practice

One classic statement of the so-called literal rule is in the *Sussex Peerage Case* (1884) 8 ER 1034, where Lord Tindal CJ said:

> 'If the words of the statute are in themselves precise and unambiguous, then no more can be necessary than to expound those words in their natural and ordinary sense. The words themselves alone do, in such a case, best declare the intention of the lawgiver.'

The case of *Whiteley v Chappell* (1868–69) LR 4 QB 147 is commonly cited in the context of the literal rule. It was a statutory offence to impersonate 'any person entitled to vote' at an election. The defendant, who had impersonated someone who had been entitled to vote but who had died before the date of the election, was convicted. The defendant's appeal was allowed on the basis that dead men are not 'entitled to vote', and therefore he was not guilty. Although the court came to this decision reluctantly, and the result of the case is commonly regarded as being contrary to common sense, the decision is, in fact, capable of being supported on grounds other than simple literalism. As with all questions of statutory interpretation, the first question is, or should be: why was the provision enacted? In this case there seem to be two possibilities.

First, if A does not vote on his own account but does vote in B's name, B will not subsequently be allowed to vote because the records will show that B has already voted. Therefore the purpose of the enactment may be to prevent A from 'stealing' B's vote. However, a voter who has died can no longer suffer this kind of loss, and therefore, arguably, A should not be convicted of an offence.

Alternatively, and assuming B to be dead, A may vote twice. This would clearly undermine the integrity of the democratic process, and therefore A should be guilty of an offence. However, if the purpose of the enactment is the prevention of such double voting, it is difficult to see why Parliament did not say so more directly.

The fact that *Whiteley v Chappell* is not as self-evidently absurd as it may appear to be at first sight does not detract from the fact that simple literalism can produce results which are plainly unsustainable. It is not surprising, therefore, that even some 19th century judges tried to provide themselves with an escape route by introducing a qualification which was often described as 'the golden rule'. In *River Wear Commissioners v Adamson* (1877) 2 App Cas 743, Lord Blackburn said:

> 'The golden rule is ... that we are to take the whole of the statute together, and construe it all together, giving the words their ordinary signification, unless when so applied they produce an *inconsistency*, or an *absurdity* or *inconvenience* so great as to convince the court that the intention could not have been to use them in their ordinary signification, and to justify the court in putting on them some other signification, which, though less proper, is one which the court thinks the words will bear.' (Emphasis added.)

*Ruther v Harris* (1876) 1 ExD 97 shows how the golden rule worked in practice. The Salmon Fishery Act 1861 prohibited net fishing for salmon at certain times, and also provided that contravention of the Act could result in forfeiture of 'all fish taken ... and any net ... used ... in taking the same'. The question which arose was whether the nets could be forfeited even though the poachers had been caught before they had taken any fish. Grove J, holding that the nets could be forfeited under these circumstances, said:

> 'It is no doubt a rule of interpretation that the grammatical construction of a sentence must be followed, but this is not to be adopted when it leads to *difficulty*. I think it is plain that the language of the section is not strictly accurate and grammatical; and it is my opinion that it was intended that the net should be forfeited ... whenever persons were unlawfully using it in fishing, although no salmon might be caught.' (Emphasis added.)

Although the operation of the golden rule did temper the rigour of the literal rule somewhat, the extent to which it did so was uncertain. This was partly due to the fact that the meanings of the terms which were used in order to justify the application of the rule (*inconsistency, absurdity, inconvenience, difficulty*) are all intrinsically vague, but also partly due to the fact that the very existence of the rule was denied by some judges.

For example, in *R v Judge of the City of London Court* [1892] 1 QB 273, Lord Esher MR said:

> 'If the words of an Act are clear, you must follow them, even though they lead to a manifest absurdity. The court has nothing to do with the question whether the legislature has committed an absurdity.'

Similarly, in *Hill v East & West India Dock Co* (1884) 9 App Cas 448, Lord Bramwell said:

'I should like to have a good definition of what is such an absurdity that you are to disregard the plain words of an Act of Parliament. It is to be remembered that what seems absurd to one man does not seem absurd to another.'

Although the history of statutory interpretation in the English courts during the second half of the 20th century may be summarized as having been the replacement of simple literalism by purposivism, the fact remains that the idea of simple literalism did spring from the basic constitutional doctrines of the legislative supremacy of Parliament, the separation of powers and the rule of law (all of which are discussed in Chapter 4). This emphasis on the constitutional nature of statutory interpretation is useful because it underlines the fact that we are concerned with the allocation of power within the state, rather than simply engaging in a sophisticated form of wordplay. However, as we saw in Part 2, the judges are by no means unanimous as to the scope of their proper role in developing the law through the doctrine of precedent, and therefore it is not surprising that they should be similarly inconsistent when considering the nature and extent of their power to manipulate the words which the supreme legislature has enacted.

One of the most famous differences of judicial opinion arose between Denning LJ and the House of Lords in *Magor & St Mellons Rural District Council v Newport Corporation* [1951] 2 All ER 839. This case cannot be fully understood without some background knowledge of local government finance. Briefly, a large part of any local authority's income came from a sort of local taxation known as the rates. Generally, rates were paid by the occupiers of all land, but it had long been a matter of national policy that, in the interests of a policy of cheap food, agricultural land was not rated. This meant that local authorities serving densely populated urban areas generated more rate income in relation to their geographical area than those serving sparsely populated agricultural areas. Therefore, in the common situation where a rural area included a dormitory village which functioned as a satellite to an adjoining urban authority, the rate income from the village would be very welcome to the rural authority. Equally naturally, the adjoining urban authority would prefer to see its boundaries redrawn so that the village became part of its area.

Where boundary disputes between local authorities result in the redrawing of boundaries, with a consequent increase in the burden on one authority, the other authority can be liable to pay compensation to its neighbour. In the instant case such a redrawing of boundaries occurred, in a situation where there had been one urban authority and two adjoining rural authorities. However, there was the added complication that, at the same time, the two rural authorities were merged into one new rural authority.

The urban authority argued, on a literal basis, that it had no liability to compensate either the old rural authorities (because they no longer existed), or the new rural authority (because it had just come into existence and therefore it could not be said to have lost anything). Both the Court of Appeal and the House of Lords accepted this argument, but for the present purposes the real interest of the case centres on the dissenting judgment of Denning LJ in the Court of Appeal:

> 'We sit here to find out the intention of Parliament and of Ministers and carry it out, and we do this better by filling in the gaps and making sense of the enactment than by opening it up to destructive analysis.'

However, this was roundly rejected by Lord Simonds in the House of Lords:

> 'The general proposition that it is the duty of the court to find out the intention of Parliament – and not only of Parliament but of Ministers also – cannot by any means be supported. The duty of the court is to interpret the words that the legislature has used. Those words may be ambiguous, but, even if they are, the power and duty of the court to travel outside them on a voyage of discovery are strictly limited.'

He went on to describe the approach which Denning LJ had adopted as 'a naked usurpation of the legislative function under the thin disguise of interpretation'.

On the other hand, Lord Radcliffe was able to reach the same conclusion as Denning LJ, but by more conventional means. Lord Radcliffe's argument had two stages. First, if the amount of compensation had been quantified before the reorganization had taken place, there could be no doubt that both the burden of paying it and the benefit of receiving it would have passed to the successor local authorities, in common with all the other liabilities and assets of the former authorities. Secondly, there could be no significance in the fact that the sum had not yet been quantified. (Before leaving this case, it is worth noting that the question of the relevance of Ministerial intention will arise again at page 303, in the context of the use of *Hansard* as an aid to interpretation.)

Another case which is often cited as a classic illustration of the inadequacy of simple literalism is *Inland Revenue Commissioners v Hinchy* [1960] 1 All ER 505, which turned on the interpretation of s. 25 of the Income Tax Act 1952. The section provided:

> 'A person who neglects or refuses to deliver ... or wilfully makes delay in delivering, a true and correct ... return ... shall ... forfeit the sum of £20 and *treble the tax which ought to have been charged under this Act* ...' (Emphasis added.)

The taxpayer under-declared interest on a savings account by about £33, thereby evading about £14 in tax. The Inland Revenue claimed the fixed sum of £20 plus treble the taxpayer's total tax bill for the year, which produced a total penalty of over £400. The Court of Appeal held that this was wrong, and that the true liability was the fixed sum of £20, plus treble the tax which had been evaded. This calculation produced a total of about £62.

However, the House of Lords held that the Inland Revenue had been right in the first place, on the basis that 'treble the tax which ought to have been charged' meant what it said, namely treble the total tax liability for the year. One line of reasoning which influenced the House of Lords was that the provision in the 1952 Act could be traced back about 150 years, to a time when methods of collection of taxes were much less efficient. It followed that, in those days, tax evasion was much easier, and therefore it made sense to have draconian penalties by way of deterrence. The trouble with this is that in other cases the courts have held that the meaning of a statutory provision can change over the years (see page 327) and that the bindingness of previous precedents may evaporate when the circumstances which gave rise to them no longer exist (see page 159), so the argument is not as self-evidently valid as it may appear to be.

On the other hand, there is a perfectly good argument in favour of the House of Lords' conclusion. Careful reading of the section shows that there was a single penalty (that is, a flat rate of £20 plus treble another figure), which could arise in a variety of ways (that is, *neglecting* or *refusing* to deliver a full and accurate return, or *delaying* in so doing). In a case where there was merely *delay*, the penalty would have to be calculated on the basis of the total tax liability, because there would be no other figure which could be trebled. Therefore, if the Court of Appeal was right, a taxpayer who dishonestly concealed part of his income would be liable to a smaller penalty than a taxpayer with the same total income who was merely late in making his return. However, most people's sense of justice suggests that if there is to be any disparity in the penalties, the dishonest should be dealt with more severely than the tardy.

## 18.3　The mischief rule

### 18.3.1　The mischief rule itself

The House of Lords' argument in *Inland Revenue Commisioners v Hinchy*, which was based on examining the original purpose of the provision, is an example of the rule of interpretation known variously as the mischief rule, and the rule in *Heydon's Case* (1584) 76 ER 637. The facts of that case concerned the intricacies of land law and are irrelevant for our purposes. What matters is the following statement of principle:

> 'For the sure and true interpretation of all statutes ... four things are to be discerned and considered:
>
> 1st  What was the Common Law before the making of the Act?
> 2nd  What was the mischief and defect for which the Common Law did not provide?
> 3rd  What remedy the Parliament hath resolved and appointed to cure the disease of the Commonwealth.
> 4th  The true reason of the remedy; and then the office of all the judges is always to make such construction as shall suppress the mischief and advance the remedy, and to suppress continuance of the mischief ... according to the true intent of the makers of the Act.'

### 18.3.2 How the mischief rule is applied

There was sometimes an element of doubt as to whether the rule in *Heydon's Case* should be regarded as the basic rule, to be applied before seeking a literal meaning, or whether it was a subsidiary rule which became relevant only where literalism had failed to provide a solution. To a large extent, the fact that we are rejecting the notion of simple literalism may seem to indicate that this question is scarcely worth either asking or answering. In fact, however, the question is worth some consideration, because the mischief-based approach to interpretation has developed into the modern basis of statutory interpretation, namely the purposive approach, and anything which enhances our understanding of that approach will be useful.

The leading case is *Maunsell v Olins* [1975] 1 All ER 16, where Lord Simon said:

> 'The first task of a court of construction is to put itself in the shoes of the draftsman – to consider what knowledge he had and, importantly, what statutory objective he had – if only as a guide to the linguistic register. Here is the first consideration of the "mischief". Being thus placed in the shoes of the draftsman, the court proceeds to ascertain the meaning of the statutory language. In this task "the first and most elementary rule of construction" is to consider the plain and primary meaning, in their appropriate register, of the words used. If there is no such plain meaning (i.e. if there is an ambiguity), a number of secondary canons are available to resolve it. Of these, one of the most important is the rule in *Heydon's Case*. Here, then, may be a second consideration of the "mischief".'

In passing, it is worth noticing that, when Lord Simon speaks of 'linguistic register', he is referring to one specific aspect of the general proposition that meaning depends on context, namely the fact that words may have different meanings when used in ordinary as opposed to technical ways, or in formal as opposed to vernacular ways. For example, the phrase 'black tie' may simply indicate an ordinary tie which is black, and which might therefore be worn at a funeral by a male mourner. On the other hand, in the context of certain types of social events, the phrase 'black tie' is commonly understood to mean that men who are attending should wear dinner jackets, and that women should dress with a corresponding degree of formality.

One practical difficulty with the mischief-based approach to interpretation is that the mischief is only one consideration which the court will take into account, and therefore it may not always be treated as being determinative of the issue. For example, in *Smith v Hughes* [1960] 1 WLR 830, it was an offence under s. 1 of the Street Offences Act 1959, for a prostitute 'to solicit in a street ... for the purpose of prostitution'. The facts were that prostitutes, who were either behind the windows or on the balconies of buildings overlooking the street, were soliciting men who were in the street. The section can, of course, be read in two ways. If the court takes the view that the section should be interpreted strictly in favour of the defendant, it would conclude that a prostitute cannot commit the offence of soliciting in a street unless she is in a street. Alternatively, the court may interpret the Act as meaning simply that it is an offence to solicit men who are in the street, in which case the precise location of the prostitute is irrelevant. The High Court upheld the second contention, with Lord Parker CJ saying:

> 'Everybody knows that this was an Act intended to clean up the streets, to enable people to walk along the streets without being molested or solicited by common prostitutes ... For my part, I am content to base my decision on that ground and that ground alone.'

A useful contrast to *Smith v Hughes* may be found in *Fisher v Bell* [1960] 3 All ER 731. It was an offence under the Restriction of Offensive Weapons Act 1959 to 'sell, hire, offer for sale or hire, or lend or give to any person' a flick knife. The High Court held that a defendant who displayed a flick knife in a shop window should be acquitted of offering it for sale, because technically, according to the law of contract, a shopkeeper does not make an offer to sell his goods: the customer makes an offer to buy, which the shopkeeper then accepts. Although this may be regarded as a perfectly legitimate application of the principle of strict interpretation of penal statutes (see page 312), the fact remains that it frustrates, rather than promotes, the suppression of the mischief at which the Act was clearly aimed. Incidentally, it is interesting to note that this case prompted the enactment of s. 1 of the Restriction of

Offensive Weapons Act 1961, which extended the offence under the 1959 Act to include anyone who 'exposes or has in his possession for the purpose of sale or hire' an offensive weapon.

Although it is impossible to reconcile *Smith v Hughes* with *Fisher v Bell* as exercises in statutory interpretation, it may not be altogether fanciful to discern the operation of differing inarticulate major premises in terms of the judges' attitudes towards shopkeepers and prostitutes. (See pages 4 and 9 for an explanation of the concept of the inarticulate major premise.)

## 18.4 The purposive approach to interpretation

### 18.4.1 Introduction

General recognition of the inadequacies of simple literalism has led modern judges to look elsewhere for a guiding principle. More particularly, the judges have been increasingly willing to accept that the purpose underlying the words which they are considering is an important part of the context within which those words are used. This has led them to adapt the idea of the mischief rule into what is now commonly called the purposive approach. As Lord Diplock said in *Carter v Bradbeer* [1975] 3 All ER 158:

> 'If one looks back to the actual decisions of this House ... over the last thirty years one cannot fail to be struck by the evidence of a trend away from the purely literal towards the purposive construction of statutory provisions.'

The closeness of the link between purposivism and the rule in *Heydon's Case* is underlined by the fact that it is quite common for the courts still to speak in terms of mischiefs. Strictly speaking, however, there are three points of distinction between the mischief rule and purposivism.

First, as *Heydon's Case* itself makes clear, the mischief rule applies only where there is a gap in the common law, whereas purposivism clearly applies whether the area covered by the enactment was previously within the domain of common law or statute law.

Secondly, and more importantly, purposivism is merely one aspect of the modern emphasis on the importance of context, and therefore can be regarded as having evolved from literalism, in contradistinction to *Heydon's Case*, which pre-dated literalism.

Thirdly, according to Lord Diplock in *Black-Clawson International Ltd v Papierwerke Waldhof-Aschaffenburg AG* [1975] 1 All ER 810, the rule in *Heydon's Case* was originally intended to restrict the scope of the court's inquiry to the four corners of the Act itself, whereas purposivism as currently practised clearly allows reference to various extrinsic materials, and may even allow reference to *Hansard*. (See pages 303–6.)

The power of purposivism

The power of the purposive approach to interpretation can be illustrated by three widely different cases, dealing with the law relating to landlord and tenant, the law relating to majority verdicts in Crown Court trials, and the law relating to adoption.

*Kammins Ballrooms Co Ltd v Zenith Investments Ltd* [1970] 2 All ER 871 involved the scheme of security of tenure for business premises under Part II of the Landlord and Tenant Act 1954. Briefly, the statutory scheme requires that a tenant who wishes to retain the tenancy of premises on the expiry of the existing tenancy should ask the landlord to grant him a new one. If the landlord refuses to comply, the tenant can then apply to the court where the matter will be resolved. In the context of this procedure, s. 29(3) of the Act provides that 'no application ... shall be entertained unless it is made not less than two nor more than four months after ... the making of the tenant's request for a new tenancy'. In *Kammins*, the tenant's application to the court was made outside the statutory period, but the House of Lords held that this did not necessarily invalidate it. Lord Diplock acknowledged that:

> 'Semantics and the rules of syntax alone could never justify the conclusion that the words "*No* application ... *shall be* entertained *unless*" meant that some applications should be entertained notwithstanding that neither of the conditions which follow the word "unless" was fulfilled.' (Original emphasis.)

Nevertheless, this seemingly strange conclusion could be reached by way of the purposive approach. Lord Diplock pointed out that the purpose of the Act was to persuade landlords and tenants to proceed by agreement wherever possible, and that the time limit in question had been enacted for the protection of landlords. It followed that landlords should be entitled to waive compliance with the time limit if they so wished. (The fact that, in the event, this particular landlord was held not to have waived compliance is irrelevant to the principle of interpretation.)

The purposive approach may prevail even over the conventional willingness of the court to give the benefit of the doubt to defendants in criminal cases by construing statutes strictly in their favour, as illustrated by *R v Pigg* [1983] 1 All ER 56. The point in issue was the validity of a conviction for rape. Under s. 17(2) of the Juries Act 1974, a majority verdict shall not be accepted unless 'the foreman of the jury has stated in open court the number of jurors who respectively agreed to and dissented from the verdict'. In *Pigg*, the foreman indicated that ten jurors had agreed to convict and the clerk of the court then said 'ten agreed to two of you'. The foreman made no reply, and therefore there had been a contravention of the plain words of the statute. Lord Brandon approached the matter thus:

> 'If the foreman of the jury states no more than that the number agreeing to the verdict is ten, it is nevertheless a necessary and inevitable inference, obvious to any ordinary person, that the number dissenting from the verdict is two. True it is that the foreman of the jury has not said so in terms as the 1974 Act, interpreted literally, requires. In my opinion, however, it is the substance of the requirement ... which has to be complied with, and the precise form of words by which such compliance is achieved, so long as the effect is clear, is not material.'

It is interesting to note that in *Pigg*, the Court of Appeal had felt bound by its own decision in *R v Reynolds* [1981] 3 All ER 849, where the charge involved the less emotive offence of shoplifting. It seems reasonably clear that the peculiarly abhorrent nature of the offence in *Pigg* brought an inarticulate major premise into play in the House of Lords, and that that premise was sufficient to induce the House to depart from the plainest of plain statutory words.

In *Re X (A Minor) (Adoption Details: Disclosure)* [1994] 3 All ER 372, the Court of Appeal was considering the Adoption Act 1976, which, together with regulations made under the Act, requires the Registrar-General to maintain the Adopted Children Register which is open to public inspection and includes, *inter alia*, the names, addresses and occupations of adopting parents. The case involved a child whose natural mother suffered from a personality disorder which made her prone to aggressive and violent behaviour, such that there was reason to fear for the safety of both the social workers in the case and the child itself. The Registrar-General's duty to maintain, and allow inspection of, the register was expressed in absolute terms. Nevertheless, the court concluded that it would be proper to make an order requiring that, until the child became an adult, the Registrar-General must obtain the leave of the court before disclosing any of the registered details relating to that adoption. This conclusion was justified on the basis that the paramount consideration in adoption cases is always the welfare of the child.

On the evidence of cases such as *Kammins*, *Pigg* and *Re X*, you may think that purposivism is objectionable on the constitutional ground that it transfers to the courts a degree of power which ought properly to reside in Parliament. However, there are two reasons why this objection appears to be misconceived.

First, a modern understanding of the relationship between Parliament and the courts (see Chapter 19) reveals a functional partnership (albeit one between senior and junior partners) which is inconsistent with the simplistic notion that Parliament is supreme and the courts are simply subordinate. Secondly, in *R v Broadcasting Complaints Commission ex parte Owen* [1985] 2 All ER 522, May LJ said:

> 'Whilst ... it is clearly legitimate to adopt a purposive approach and hold that a statutory provision does apply to a given situation when it was clearly intended to do so, even though it may not apply on its strict literal interpretation, nevertheless I do not think that the converse is correct and that it is legitimate to adopt a purposive construction so as to preclude the application of a statute to a situation to which on its purely literal construction it would apply.'

In other words, purposivism is a technique for extending the application of statutory principles rather than restricting them, and so may be seen as a technique for promoting the efficacy of the rules which Parliament has enacted, rather than for frustrating them.

### 18.4.3　Identifying the purpose

The modern practice of preferring interpretations which promote statutory purposes over those which do not do so requires that the statutory purpose should be identifiable, although there is clearly nothing new in this, since the same point arises whether we speak in terms of *mischiefs* or *purposes*. The traditional view was that in many cases the intention was contained in the words which Parliament had used. As we have already seen (at page 256) Lord Tindall CJ said, in the *Sussex Peerage Case* (1844) 8 ER 1034: 'If the words of the statute are in themselves precise and unambiguous, then no more can be necessary than to expound those words in their natural and ordinary sense. *The words themselves alone do, in such a case, best declare the intention [or purpose] of the lawgiver*'. (Emphasis added.)

However, where the purpose is not clear from the words of the statute there are the makings of a problem, since, as Lord Halsbury LC said in a contract case of roughly similar vintage to the *Sussex Peerage Case*:

> 'It appears to me to be arguing in a vicious circle to begin by assuming an intention apart from the language of the instrument itself, and having made that fallacious assumption to bend the language in favour of the assumption so made'. (*Leader v Duffy* (1888) 13 App Cas 294.)

Two points arise. First, although for some purposes there are significant differences between the interpretation of statutes and contracts,

Lord Halsbury's comment is equally valid in respect of any instrument, including a statute. Secondly, although Lord Halsbury's assertion that the assumption as to intention will be fallacious may not always be true, his essential point about circularity remains sound.

It is clear that preambles (in those rare cases where they exist), long titles, short titles, marginal notes and headings may be used as indicators of the legislative purpose (see pages 291–6), as may pre-Parliamentary, Parliamentary and post-Parliamentary materials (see pages 297–307). However, you may well think it would be helpful if Parliament made explicit statements of purpose within statutes themselves. The matter is usefully discussed in the report of the Renton Committee on *The Preparation of Legislation* (1975):

'11.7 Among the advocates of statements of purpose are those whose task it is to pronounce or advise on the effects of legislation: members of the judiciary, practising lawyers, and teachers of law. The draftsmen themselves are less enthusiastic. First Parliamentary Counsel takes the view that "in many cases the aims in the legislation cannot usefully or safely be summarized or condensed", and that "there may be a temptation to call for something which is no more than a manifesto, and which may obscure something which is otherwise precise and exact". He also points out that "detailed amendments to a Bill after introduction may not merely falsify the accompanying proposition but may even make it impracticable to retain any broad proposition". The Parliamentary Draftsman for Scotland adopts the same view: apart from certain special circumstances, he says "the Act should in general explain itself". New Zealand's Chief Parliamentary Counsel told us that preambles were rare in public Acts in New Zealand; purpose clauses, forming part of the text of the Act, were sometimes used, but were not thought to aid comprehension. Professor Reed Dickerson thinks that "most purpose clauses are quite unnecessary"; that general purpose clauses tend to degenerate into pious incantations ... such as ... the one in a recent ecology Bill, which in substance said "Hurray for Nature!", but that "in prefatory language in individual sentences such as *For the purpose of this*, or *For the purpose of that*, or *In order to do this*, you may have an economic, focussed purpose statement that is of some use".

'11.8 We agree that statements of purpose can be useful ... A distinction should, however, be drawn between a statement of purpose which is designed to delimit and illuminate the legal effects of the Bill and a statement of purpose which is a mere manifesto ... the latter kind should in our view be firmly discouraged ... and we should not like to see a reversion to the archaic use of preambles as a means of declaring or justifying the objectives of public Bills. The preamble can be valuable as a means of reciting facts, such as the terms of a relevant treaty. But when a general statement of purpose is appropriate, we think it should be contained in a clause in the Bill. This has advantages at the Parliamentary stage, since a purpose clause can be amended (or omitted) exactly like any other clause. Preambles are subject to special rules. For the reasons we have given, we think that purpose clauses can be helpful, but that they should be used selectively and with caution.'

It must be said that, on the whole, this aspect of the *Renton Report* has had little effect on the practice of English statutory drafting, although there are notable exceptions, such as s. 17 of the Courts and Legal Services Act 1990, which introduces Part II of the Act. The first subsection of the section provides:

> 'The general objective of this Part is the development of legal services in England and Wales (and in particular the development of advocacy, litigation, conveyancing and probate services) by making provision for new or better ways of providing such services and a wider choice of persons providing them, while maintaining the proper and efficient administration of justice.'

One matter which sometimes arises is whether the legislative purpose is to be assessed subjectively or objectively. According to Aharon Barak (a former President of the Supreme Court of Israel), the subjective purpose of an enactment is the purpose which the author of the text had in mind at the time of writing, while the objective purpose is the purpose which the text has at the time when it is being interpreted. More particularly, the objective purpose is identified by reference to aims which the text was intended to achieve. In *Purposive Interpretation in Law* (English translation, 2005), Barak argues that the subjective purpose will carry more weight in relation to recent statutes, as well as to statutes which deal with specific problems and those which lay down rules. On the other hand, he argues that the objective purpose will carry more weight in relation to older statutes, as well as to statutes which deal with general principles or codifications and those which enact standards.

Although of relatively little practical relevance to the English legal system and its unwritten constitution, it is worth noticing that, when interpreting constitutions, Barak argues that the objective purpose should generally be given greater weight, while recognizing that the subjective purpose may usefully be prioritized when resolving conflicts between objective purposes. (Also see page 327 for the topic of *change of meaning with the passage of time*, for examples of cases in which the courts have applied updating constructions in the light of changed circumstances.)

Finally, at the level of practical politics, it is worth remembering that although it may be obvious that statements of purpose will be useful aids to interpretation, their exclusion from the body of a Bill may in some cases facilitate its enactment, by allowing individual members of Parliament to persuade themselves that the Bill means what they want it to mean and so vote for it with a clear conscience.

## 18.5 The problem of statutory nonsense

Although there are cases in which simple literalism and purposivism may produce diametrically opposed results, both techniques will always have at least one thing in common: they will both assume that the enacted words do have some meaning. However, from time to time situations arise where the enacted words are meaningless.

In *Lyde v Barnard* [1835–42] All ER Rep 690, the provision under consideration was s. 6 of the Statute of Frauds Amendment Act 1828. The section dealt with certain situations where one person made a 'representation or assurance ... to the intent or purpose that ... [an]other person may obtain credit, money, or goods upon, ...'. Although the drafting of this provision was plainly defective, the judges disagreed as to what had gone wrong, and what had been intended. Gurney B had no doubt that the word 'credit' should be inserted after 'upon'. Lord Abinger CB, on the other hand, thought that 'upon' should be deleted, on the basis that the draftsman had probably written 'thereupon' and then crossed it out in a careless fashion, so that the typesetter had thought that it was only the first syllable which was to be omitted.

Some examples of statutory nonsense appear never to have received the benefit of judicial comment. Section 11(5) of the Landlord and Tenant (Rent Control) Act 1949 referred to s. 6 of the Furnished Houses (Rent Control) Act 1946, whereas the content of the 1946 Act made it obvious that the reference should have been to s. 7 of the Act. The Queen's Printer simply altered the text of subsequent printings of the 1949 Act.

Similarly, s. 22(3) of the Artisans and Labourers Dwellings Act (1868) Amendment Act 1879 required that, where mortgage loans were made in accordance with the Act, the mortgage document should be 'in the form set forth in the Third Schedule hereto'. There was no Third Schedule to the Act, nor was there any form of mortgage anywhere else within the Act. Parliament corrected the error with an amending Act the following year.

Now that the courts are much less literalistic, express corrections may not be felt to be necessary unless additional enacted material is required. Section 10(2) of the House of Commons Disqualification Act 1975 provided for the repeal of the enactments 'specified in Schedule 4 to this Act'. The Act contained no Schedule 4, but Schedule 3 was headed 'Repeals' and is plainly what the drafter of s. 10(2) intended. This particular embarrassment was removed from the statute book when the Statute Law (Repeals) Act 1977 repealed, *inter alia*, both s. 10(2) of, and Schedule 3 to, the 1975 Act.

The examples discussed above may be interesting, but they are not particularly amusing. This deficiency may be remedied by referring to the original version of the Canadian Marriage Act (c. M50: Revised Statutes of Manitoba 1970), dealing with the publication of the banns of marriage, which made provision for the situation where the parties were 'in the habit of attending whorship at different churches'. (Quoted by Megarry, *A Second Miscellany-at-Law*, 1973, p. 183.)

## 18.6 Are there any 'rules' of interpretation?

Having concluded our survey of meanings, mischiefs and purposes, it is appropriate to ask whether it is sensible to speak of 'rules' of interpretation at all. You may well conclude that the word 'rules' implies a degree of rigidity and precision, and therefore a predictability of outcome, which is simply not present in practice. As Lord Reid said in *Maunsell v Olins* [1975] 1 All ER 16:

> 'They are not rules in the ordinary sense of having some binding force. They are our servants, not our masters. They are aids to construction: presumptions or pointers. Not infrequently one "rule" points in one direction, another in a different direction. In each case we must look at all relevant circumstances and decide as a matter of judgment what weight to attach to any particular "rule".'

This comment provides a valuable reminder that problems of interpretation, in common with other tasks in legal method, will often involve balancing competing arguments, and deciding which one is to be preferred in the context of the instant case. It may also prompt you to develop the habit of thinking about interpretation in terms of *techniques*, or *principles*, or *approaches*, rather than *rules*. However, even such a distinguished commentator as Francis Bennion still refers to a basic rule of interpretation, together with sub-rules, even though (as we shall see at page 285) he expressly accepts the need to weigh and balance various factors.

## Summary

- It is wrong to assume that words always have plain meanings.

- Nevertheless, the practice of statutory interpretation in the 19th century developed largely along the lines of simple literalism.

- However, the pre-19th century technique of interpreting statutes in the light of the mischief which they were intended to cure did not die out entirely, and was sometimes used to mitigate the worst excesses of simple literalism.

▷ The mischief-based approach has developed into the modern approach known as *purposivism*, under which the starting point is to consider the purpose of the statute in question.

▷ Where statutes literally do not make sense, either Parliament will correct the error or the courts will do their best with the defective text if called upon to do so.

▷ Strictly speaking, there are no *rules* of statutory interpretation. It is more helpful to think in terms of *techniques*, *principles* and *approaches*.

## Exercises

1  Why is it wrong to assume that words always have plain meanings?

2  What is the relationship between the *mischief rule* and the *purposive approach* to statutory interpretation?

# Chapter 19

## The idea of legislative intention

Introduction

The courts and commentators often use phrases such as 'the intention (or will) of Parliament'. Indeed, for many years *Maxwell on the Interpretation of Statutes* defined 'statutes' as being simply 'the will of the legislature'. (See, for example, 11th edn, 1962, p. 1.) Similarly, in *Ealing London Borough Council v Race Relations Board* [1972] 1 All ER 105, Lord Simon said: 'It is the duty of a court so to interpret an Act of Parliament as to give effect to its intention'. On the other hand, it is not difficult to find statements, from both academic and judicial sources, which are sceptical about both the existence of 'the intention of Parliament' and (if it does exist) its relevance to the process of statutory interpretation.

Bell and Engle, for example, say that the phrase is 'not so much a description as a linguistic convenience' (*Cross, Statutory Interpretation*, 3rd edn, 1995, p. 28), while, according to Lord Reid, in *Black-Clawson International Ltd v Papierwerke Waldhof-Aschaffenburg AG* [1975] 1 All ER 810: 'We often say that we are looking for the intention of Parliament, but that is not quite accurate. We are seeking not what Parliament meant but the true meaning of what they said'. Support for Lord Reid's point may be found in *Hilder v Dexter* [1902] AC 474, where Lord Halsbury declined to give judgment as to the meaning of the Companies Act 1900, on the ground that he had drafted the Act:

> 'I have more than once had occasion to say that in construing a statute I believe the worst person to construe it is the person who is responsible for its drafting. He is very much disposed to confuse what he intended to do with the effect of the language which in fact has been employed. At the time he drafted the statute, at all events, he may have been under the impression that he had given full effect to what was intended, but he may be mistaken in construing it afterwards just because what was in his mind was what was intended, though perhaps it was not done. For that reason I abstain from giving any judgment in this case myself.'

In short, it is impossible to imagine a modern English court adopting the view expressed by Hengham CJ in 1305, when he rebuked counsel thus: 'Do not gloss the Statute; we understand it better than you do, for we made it'.

Nevertheless, despite the problems which are inherent in the concept of the intention of Parliament, it can be said to serve a constitutional role, as Lord Simon emphasized in *Stock v Frank Jones (Tipton) Ltd* [1978] 1 All ER 948, when he said:

> 'In a society living under the rule of law, citizens are entitled to regulate their conduct according to what a statute has said, rather than by what it was meant to say, or by what it would have otherwise have said if a newly considered situation had been envisaged.'

Similarly, an American commentator has said:

> 'Of course we use a fiction if we speak of the legislature as if it were a being of one mind. But so durable a fiction endures because it has a use validated by experience. This formula reminds all who deal with a statute that they are operating in a field of law in which they are not free to define public policy simply according to their own judgment.' (Hurst, *Dealing With Statutes*, 1982, New York, p. 33, quoted in Bell and Engle, *op. cit.*, p. 29.)

The variety of reactions provoked by the idea of the intention of Parliament provides a clear indication that it is a topic deserving close consideration. However, bearing in mind Lord Watson's comment that '"the intention of the legislature" is a "very slippery phrase"' (*Saloman v Saloman & Co Ltd* [1897] AC 22), it may be as well to approach the concept cautiously by recognizing that there are different types of intention, not only in legislation but also more generally.

## 19.2 Different types of intention

### 19.2.1 Direct and indirect intentions

It is clearly not always realistic to assume that all intentions, even when they are of a single person, are of the same type. For example, I may have both a *direct intention* and an *indirect intention* (or *motive*). The difficulty is that, even if the direct intention is readily apparent, it may well be that the indirect intention is not. For example, a husband and wife may share a direct intention to save a specific sum of money, but one of them may be thinking of spending it on a new car while the other is thinking of spending it on a holiday.

### 19.2.2 Particular and general intentions

In the context of legislative drafting and interpretation, it is useful to draw a corresponding distinction between *particular intention* and *general intention*. (See the Law Commission's Report on *The Interpretation of Statutes*, 1969, Law Com No 21.) According to this usage, *particular intention* applies to the meaning of the words enacted in a statute, while *general intention* applies to the purpose underlying the enactment of those words.

Furthermore, bearing in mind the fact that legislation in complex societies will typically be produced by multi-member legislatures, it is obvious that the problem of multiple intentions is likely to arise. For example, a shared particular intention to increase taxation may well reflect varying general intentions, such as a desire to curtail the level of activity in the domestic economy, and a desire to increase the level of public spending.

Additionally, in terms of practical politics, the intention of the individual member of the legislature may have other dimensions beyond the narrowly legislative context. In a democratic system, for example, securing re-election may be the prevailing general intention motivating everything which the individual member does. This may lead to voting on legislative proposals according to the member's perception of public opinion, without any intention whatsoever as to the legislative effect of that vote. Alternatively, the member may have no intention beyond toeing the party line, as a matter either of political commitment, intellectual indolence or as a means of currying favour with the party leaders. W S Gilbert's account of how Sir Joseph Porter became First Lord of the Admiralty illustrates a combination of the second and third possibilities:

'I always voted at my party's call,
And I never thought of thinking for myself at all.
I thought so little they rewarded me,
By making me the Ruler of the Queen's Navee!'

(*HMS Pinafore*, Act I)

The fact that individual members of a legislature may have different general intentions raises a crucial problem. How can a body such as Parliament be said to have an intention when, being made up of many members rather than being a natural person, it cannot have a mind?

It is tempting, therefore, to abandon the idea of intention, and think in terms of what words are *understood* to mean, rather than what they are *intended* to mean. This leads to a consideration of the *speaker's meaning* theory of interpretation.

## 19.3 The speaker's meaning theory

According to the speaker's meaning theory, legislation is an act of communication in which the legislature transmits its meaning to the judges and to anyone else who uses statutes. Superficially attractive though this theory sounds, it is difficult, if not impossible, to sustain in the face of the problems which it generates. The starting point is that, in a corporate sense, there can be no speaker. An individual may choose his own words, albeit with greater or lesser felicity according to his degree of linguistic sophistication. In this context the choice of words is part and parcel of the thought process itself: 'Having a thought and choosing words to represent that thought are not two separate activities'. (Dworkin, *Law's Empire*, 1986, p. 315.)

However, where legislative bodies are concerned, individual members cannot honestly say that the legislative product consists of them expressing themselves in their own words. In reality, individual members are limited to adopting, or rejecting, the words of someone else, who will typically be an apolitical drafter:

> '[The member] is ... not like someone choosing to communicate some thought or idea or wish. He occupies a position intermediate between speaker and hearer. He must decide what thought the words on the paper before him are likely to be taken to express and then decide whether he wishes that message to be sent ... given the only realistic alternative of sending no message at all ... he treats the document, not himself or any other person, as the author of the message he agrees to send.' (Dworkin, *op. cit.*, p. 322.)

If we attempt to avoid this difficulty by deeming the legislature to be the speaker for the present purposes, there remains the difficulty of identifying the legislature's collective membership. To be logical, in many cases this would have to be done not only as at the date of the statute's enactment, but also for the duration of each succeeding legislature which allows the statute to continue in force without amendment.

For example, the Offences Against the Person Act 1861 remains, well over a century later, as the major statute defining crimes of violence. In a sense, therefore, every Parliament since the one which enacted it can be taken as having tacitly approved its continuation in force. Therefore the membership of those Parliaments is relevant, if the speaker's meaning theory of interpretation is to be taken seriously.

Of course, you may respond that the argument about the continued existence of a statute being evidence of a continuing legislative intention is thoroughly artificial, because in reality many statutes continue in existence by default, without successive Parliaments giving them any thought whatsoever. While this may be true in some cases, it is inconceivable that a statute like the 1861 Act, which is interpreted by the courts on a daily basis, could have been allowed to remain in force unless successive Parliaments had been (rightly or wrongly) substantially satisfied with its operation.

The speaker's meaning theory has, therefore, led us down a blind alley. The best solution is to return to the ideas of particular and general intention, in order to formulate a model which will accommodate both, while also being realistic and constitutionally acceptable. The model which achieves all these objectives may be summed up in one word: *delegation*.

## 19.4 Particular intention: delegation to the drafters

Since Parliament itself cannot speak, it must necessarily delegate to drafters the task of formulating the words to be enacted. It goes without saying that drafters may, and indeed as responsible and effective technicians should, have coherent intentions at least at the level of what they intend their words to mean. It also goes without saying that delegation to the drafter is not absolute and uncontrolled, since the legislature may amend or reject Bills which are submitted to it. This aspect of the delegation model is, therefore, both realistic and constitutionally acceptable.

## 19.5 General intention: delegation to the judges

### 19.5.1 Introduction

When Parliament enacts a statute it realizes that it cannot hope to foresee all possible eventualities. As Payne says:

> 'The proper office of a judge in statutory interpretation is ... that of a junior partner in the legislative process, a partner empowered and expected within certain limits to exercise a proper discretion as to what the detailed law should be.' (*The Intention of the Legislature in the Interpretation of Statutes* [1956] *Current Legal Problems* 96.)

Even this model of partnership is too weak for some commentators. For example, MacCallum says:

> 'The judgment of ... persons ... authorized by the legislature may stand for the judgment of the legislature ... Thus our discovery of what these persons intended in attempting to ... interpret the language ... so as, in their judgment to achieve what the legislature wanted to achieve, is a discovery of intentions that the legislature stood behind, wished us to attend to, wished us to regard as authoritative as their own – indeed wished us to regard as their own. These intentions may therefore be taken as, and in fact are, the intentions of the legislature.' (*Legislative Intent* (1966) 75 Yale LJ, 754, reprinted in *Essays in Legal Philosophy*, 1968, ed. Summers.)

While neither of these passages contains the word *delegation*, they both clearly embody the idea that Parliament may be taken to be delegating to the judges the task of identifying and formulating the general intention which underlies a particular piece of legislation. However, this analysis appears to create a circular difficulty. How are the judges to exercise the discretion which Parliament has given them, otherwise than by reference to the concept of the general intention of Parliament – which is precisely what they are being required to identify in the first place.

In a simple case, of course, where the language of the statute is clear and explicit, the problem can be glossed over for, as Lord Tindal CJ said in *Warburton v Loveland* (1832) 2 D & Cl 480, 'in that case the words of the statute speak the intention of the Legislature'. In more difficult cases, however, it will be necessary to look elsewhere.

Dworkin, whose *policies* and *principles* are discussed at page 6, provides a promising solution, namely the idea of *political integrity*.

**19.5.2**   The idea of political integrity

*Introduction*

If it is self-evident that the state as a political entity ought to act consistently through the formulation, adoption and application of a coherent body of principle, there is no difficulty in accepting Dworkin's proposition:

> 'We have two principles of political integrity: a legislative principle which asks lawmakers to try to make the total set of laws morally coherent, and an adjudicative principle, which instructs that the law be seen as coherent in that way, so far as possible.' (*Op. cit.*, p. 176.)

It follows that, when exercising their discretion, judges should look to the coherence, or integrity, of the legal system as a whole: a decision which promotes that integrity is, in a real sense of the word, *better* than one which detracts from it. If there are disputes as to what the promotion of coherence actually requires in terms of a decision in a specific case, judges must, in the final analysis, simply make up their own minds. A judge

> 'must rely on his own judgment ... not because he thinks his opinions are automatically right, but because no one can properly answer any question except by relying at the deepest level on what he himself believes.' (Dworkin, *op. cit.*, pp. 313–14.)

He accepts that a judge's personal beliefs will by no means always be objectively reasoned:

> 'Any judge will develop ... a fairly individualized working conception of law on which he will rely ... in making ... judgments ... and the judgments will then be, for him, a matter of feel or instinct rather than analysis.' (Dworkin, *op. cit.*, p. 256.)

Furthermore, he argues that a judge's beliefs are unlikely to be highly idiosyncratic, because 'most judges will be like other people in their community', and any judge who does happen to possess unusual opinions should nevertheless adopt whatever solutions 'show the community's record in the best light'. (*Ibid.*)

However, although the idea of political integrity is attractive, it may not necessarily to prescribe clear solutions in all cases, as an example will show.

### Political integrity in operation

In *Harrogate Borough Council v Simpson* (1986) 2 FLR 91, Miss Simpson and Mrs Rodrigo were a lesbian couple who regarded themselves as husband and wife. They lived in a house owned by Harrogate Borough Council. The tenancy, which was in the sole name of Mrs Rodrigo, was a periodic one and was what is technically known as a 'secure tenancy'. The cohabitation lasted approximately two-and-a-half years, until Mrs Rodrigo died. The council obtained a county court order for possession of the house against Miss Simpson, who then appealed to the Court of Appeal.

The relevant parts of s. 30 of the Housing Act 1980 stated:

'(1) Where a secure tenancy is a periodic tenancy and, on the death of the tenant, there is a person qualified to succeed him, the tenancy vests by virtue of this section in that person ...

'(2) A person is qualified to succeed a tenant under a secure tenancy if he occupied the dwelling-house as his only or principal home at the time of the tenant's death and either (a) he is the tenant's spouse; or (b) he is another member of the tenant's family and has resided with the tenant throughout the period of twelve months ending with the tenant's death.'

The relevant part of the definition of 'family' was to be found in s. 50(3): 'A person is a member of another's family ... if she is his spouse ... or if they live together as husband and wife'. Although the argument for Miss Simpson referred to a line of apparently similar cases decided under the succession provisions contained in the Rent Act 1977 and its precursors (which are discussed at page 328) her appeal failed. Watkins LJ felt that the Rent Act cases were clearly distinguishable because they all involved heterosexual couples:

'If Parliament had wished homosexual relationships to be brought into the realm of the lawfully recognized state of a living together of man and wife for the purpose of the relevant legislation, it would plainly have so stated in that legislation, and it has not done so ... It would be surprising in the extreme to learn that public opinion is such today that it would recognize a homosexual union as being akin to a state of living as husband and wife. The ordinary man and woman ... would in my opinion not think even remotely of there being a true resemblance between those two very different states of affairs.'

Why did Watkins LJ not conclude, instinctively or otherwise, that adjudicative integrity requires homosexual and heterosexual couples to be treated in the same way in relation to security of tenure? The answer lies in his appeal to the views of the 'ordinary [i.e. heterosexual] man and woman'. In other words, even if ordinary people might feel initially that all couples should be treated equally in terms of security of tenure, they would give greater weight to the cultural preference for heterosexuality over homosexuality.

Putting this in Dworkinian terms, the decision can be justified on the basis of adjudicative integrity, by saying that society promotes heterosexuality over homosexuality, because the former is the basis of the family unit and reinforces both social stability and cultural values. Furthermore, this case was decided at a time when the law was inclining somewhat against homosexuals, as evidenced by s. 28 of the Local Government Act 1988, which introduced a general prohibition on local authorities intentionally promoting homosexuality, and a specific prohibition on the teaching in maintained schools of 'the acceptability of homosexuality as a *pretended* family relationship'. (Emphasis added.)

However, times change, and at least some judges change with them, as the case of *Fitzpatrick v Sterling Housing Association Ltd* [1997] 4 All ER 991 (CA) and [1999] 4 All ER 701 (HL) shows. Two men had lived together for 18 years in a flat, of which one was the tenant. The men enjoyed a 'longstanding, close, loving and faithful, monogamous, homosexual relationship'. When the tenant died, the question was whether his partner could inherit the tenancy under the Rent Act 1977 (as amended). More particularly, if the survivor was a *member of the tenant's family* he would have been entitled to an *assured tenancy*, but if he was the tenant's *spouse* he would have been entitled to a *statutory tenancy*, which would have been more advantageous than an *assured tenancy*.

Although the decisions in *Fitzpatrick* and *Simpson* involved different statutes and, therefore, in accordance with first principles (see page 238) no binding precedent existed, the issue of principle was plainly the same in both cases. All three judges in the Court of Appeal were clearly sympathetic to the survivor. Thus Roch LJ said that to allow the survivor to succeed 'would ... be consistent not only with social justice but also with the respect accorded by modern society to those of the same sex who undertake a permanent commitment to a shared life'. Nevertheless, both he and Waite LJ concluded that it was a matter more suited to consideration by Parliament rather than the courts. On the other hand, Ward LJ, in a dissent which Roch LJ described as 'interesting and elegant', had no such constitutional qualms:

'To exclude same-sex couples from the protection of the 1977 Act proclaims the inevitable message that society judges their relationships to be less worthy of respect, concern and consideration than the relationship between members of the opposite sex. The fundamental human dignity of the homosexual couple is severely and palpably affected by the impugned distinction. The distinction is drawn on grounds relating to their personal characteristics, their sexual orientation. If the law is as my Lords state it to be, then it discriminates against a not insignificant proportion of the population who will justly complain that they have been denied their constitutional right to equal treatment under the law.'

He concluded his judgment thus:

'I have not reached this decision lightly. In truth, it has caused me a great deal of anxiety. I have worried that I have gone too far. If it is a matter for Parliament, and not for me, I hope that Parliament will consider it soon. I have endeavoured to reflect public opinion as I see it, but I am very conscious that public opinion on this topic is a continuum and it is not easy to see where the line is to be drawn. As Bingham MR said in *R v Ministry of Defence ex parte Smith* [1996] 1 All ER 257 at 263 [in which the Court of Appeal upheld the legality of excluding homosexuals from the armed forces], "A belief which represented unquestioned orthodoxy in year X may have become questionable by year Y and unsustainable by year Z."
'I have come to the clear conclusion that *Harrogate Borough Council v Simpson* was decided in year X; Waite and Roch LJJ, for reasons with which I could well have agreed, believe us to be in year Y, whereas I have been persuaded that the discrimination would be thought by the broad mass of the people to be so unsustainable that this must now be year Z. To conclude otherwise would be to stand like King Canute, ordering the tide to recede when the tide in favour of equality rolls relentlessly forward and shows no sign of ebbing. If I am to be criticized – and of course I will be – then I prefer to be criticized, on an issue like this, for being ahead of the times, rather than behind the times. My hope ... is that I am in step with the times.'

Two points may be noticed in passing. First, Ward LJ approved Dworkin's comment (*op. cit.*, p. 348) that '[the judge] interprets not just the statute's text but its life, the process that begins before it becomes law and extends far beyond that moment ... [the judge's] interpretation changes as the story develops'.

Secondly, just as the climate of opinion which gave rise to the enactment of s. 28 of the Local Government Act 1988 formed part of the contemporary context of the decision in the *Harrogate* case, so s. 145 of the Criminal Justice and Public Order Act 1994, which reduced the age of consent for homosexual acts between consenting males from 21 to 18, may have contributed to the sympathy expressed, although not the decision made, by the majority of the Court of Appeal in *Fitzpatrick*. Subsequently, by the time the House of Lords heard the appeal in April 1999, it was known that a private member's amendment to the Bill which became the Crime and Disorder Act 1998, and which would have further reduced the age of consent to 16, was passed by the House of Commons but rejected by the House of Lords (as a House of Parliament). The Commons did not press the issue on the understanding that the proposal would return as a government measure, and in December 1998 it did so, in the form of the Sexual Offences (Amendment) Bill. Once again, however, although the Bill passed through the Commons easily enough, it was defeated in the Lords in April 1999. The same Bill was then reintroduced into the Commons in the next session of Parliament, and was passed in February 2000. On this occasion, the Lords did not reject the Bill, but did amend it by providing differential ages of consent depending on the nature of the homosexual act. Since this amendment amounted to a defeat for the purposes of the Parliament Acts 1911 and 1949, the government proceeded to obtain the Royal Assent without the Lords' approval, under the procedure created by those Acts.

Thus when *Fitzpatrick* reached the Appellate Committee of the House of Lords, it was abundantly plain that both the government and the Commons were sympathetic to at least some degree of homosexual law reform, and that final outcome was a foregone conclusion. In the context of an atmosphere of this type, it may not be surprising that the appeal was allowed, albeit only by a majority of 3:2. More particularly, having carefully emphasized that their decision was authoritative only in relation to the provision before the House, the majority held that although the surviving partner could not be the *spouse* of the deceased tenant, he could be a *member of his family*. Curiously, however, he went on to draw a distinction which is at best subtle and and at worst mere sophistry:

'It is accordingly not necessary to consider the alternative question as to whether by 1999 the meaning of the word in the Act of 1920 needs to be updated. I prefer to say that it is not the meaning which has changed but that those who are capable of falling within the words which have changed.'

The House of Lords returned to the issue of homosexual partners' rights of succession to tenancies in *Ghaidan v Mendoza* [2004] 3 All ER 411. On this occasion, taking the final step beyond *Fitzpatrick*, the House held (by a majority of 4:1) that, for the purposes of the Rent Act 1977, a homosexual partner may be more than merely a *member of the tenant's family*, and may fall within the meaning of the word *spouse* (and would, therefore, inherit the more advantageous *statutory tenancy*, rather than the less advantageous *assured tenancy*). More particularly, the House held that there was no reason to exclude the survivors of stable, homosexual relationships from the statutory protection which would clearly have applied to the survivors of identical heterosexual relationships; and that, therefore, the denial of that protection constituted unjustifiable discrimination against homosexuals.

The House was not bound by *Fitzpatrick* because that decision predated the interpretative obligation imposed by s. 3 of the Human Rights Act 1998. (Section 3, which is discussed at page 325, requires courts to read and apply legislative provisions in such a way as to make them compatible with Convention rights under the Act, where it is possible to do so. The Convention rights which arose for consideration in *Ghaidan* are contained in articles 8 and 14 of the ECHR, relating respectively to respect for the home and the grounds on which discrimination is prohibited – see Appendix 3 for the full text of both articles.)

In passing, and continuing the contextual nature of the foregoing discussion, *Ghaidan* was decided after the general climate of legislative opinion in relation to gay and related rights had moved on in at least three respects. First, the Local Government Act 2003 had repealed s. 28 of the Local Government Act 1988. Secondly, the Sexual Offences Act 2003, which had largely replaced the Sexual Offences Act 1967, had totally abolished the offences of buggery and gross indecency between consenting male adults. Thirdly, the enactment – on July 1, 2004 – of the Gender Recognition Act 2004, which enables transsexuals to obtain legal recognition of their acquired gender, was imminent. (The decision in *Ghaidan* was handed down on 21 June 2004.)

### 19.5.3   Does the delegation model give the judges too much power?

It may be argued that acceptance of the delegation model of statutory interpretation places excessive power in the hands of judges. Certainly, some judges feel that public confidence in the independence of the judiciary may be put at risk if the effect of judicial decisions is to amend statutes which the judges feel to be injurious to the public interest. In *Duport Steels Ltd v Sirs* [1980] 1 All ER 529, this unease moved Lord Scarman to complain that the use of open-ended expressions, such as conduct 'in contemplation or furtherance of a trade dispute', in politically sensitive statutes, such as the Trade Union and Labour Relations Act 1974, 'will bring the judges inevitably into the industrial arena exercising a discretion which may well be misunderstood by many and which can damage confidence in the administration of justice'.

Although it is possible to sympathize with Lord Scarman as to the practical consequences, it is important to emphasize his point that the danger arises from a misunderstanding. More particularly, it is clearly established that delegation in English law consists of a sharing, rather than a transfer, of power. In *Huth v Clarke* (1890) 25 QBD 39, a local authority appointed an executive committee, which in turn appointed local subcommittees to deal with diseases of animals. When the sub-committees took no action under the Rabies Order 1887, the executive committee itself made appropriate regulations. Following a conviction for an offence against the regulations, the question arose as to whether the executive committee had retained the power to make the regulations. The High Court held that the power had been retained, and that giving the delegate authority to act on behalf of the delegator did not involve a transfer of all the delegator's powers.

Moreover, delegation can be revoked. In *Manton v Brighton Corporation* [1951] 2 All ER 101, a councillor had been appointed to three committees of the local authority. Following allegations of misconduct by the councillor, the local authority decided he should no longer serve on any of the committees. The High Court held that a local authority can revoke the authority of any of its committees as a whole, and therefore it could revoke the authority of individual committee members.

In the present context, therefore, the idea of delegation explains how the courts acquire the extensive discretion which they undoubtedly possess in cases of statutory interpretation. On the other hand, the doctrine of the legislative supremacy of Parliament remains as a long-stop, ensuring that the courts acknowledge the possibility that sufficiently plain words may compel them to reach a particular conclusion. Additionally, as the cases discussed at page 208 show, Parliament can enact legislation to annul the effect of judicial decisions which offend Parliament's view of what the law either is or ought to be.

### 19.5.4  Conclusion

In short, therefore, the model of delegation to the judges is both realistic and constitutionally acceptable. The fact that it does not prescribe outcomes to individual cases merely reinforces the underlying theme of this book, that legal method is a creative activity and not a mechanical one.

## Summary

▸ It is commonplace to encounter references to phrases such as *the intention of Parliament*, but there is doubt as to what (if anything) such phrases mean, and in any event the rule of law requires that the courts apply the meaning of what Parliament said, rather than giving effect to what Parliament meant to say.

- Individuals' intentions may be classified as *direct* and *indirect*. An individual may have multiple intentions, and in the case of multi-member legislatures this possibility is even more obvious.

- In the legislative context it is more helpful to think in terms of *particular* and *general* intentions, but even these concepts cause difficulties.

- The superficially attractive idea of regarding the legislature as a speaker which communicates its meaning to an audience does not survive critical analysis.

- The most useful analysis of the concept of *particular intention* lies in the model of *delegation to the drafters*.

- The most useful analysis of the concept of *general intention* lies in the model of *delegation to the judges*.

## Exercises

1 Distinguish between *particular intention* and *general intention* in the context of legislation.

2 How (if at all) can the model of *delegation to both the drafters and the judges* be reconciled with the constitutional requirement that Parliament should retain control of the legislative process?

# Chapter 20

# Modern statutory interpretation in practice

## 20.1 Introduction

As we saw in Chapter 17, the technique which we labelled *simple literalism* is seriously defective and no longer characterizes the judicial approach to statutory interpretation. In the words of Francis Bennion, one of the leading contemporary commentators on statute law and statutory interpretation and a former Parliamentary Counsel: 'nowadays, a legislative drafter ... never intends the literal rule to be adopted.' (*Understanding Common Law Legislation: Drafting and Interpretation*, 2001, p. 44)

As we also saw, there is a greatly increased perception of the significance of the context within which words are used and, more particularly, of the purpose underlying the enactment. The contemporary approach is, therefore, sometimes called either *contextualism*, or, more usually, *purposivism*, but the alternative label of *enlightened literalism* is also useful, because it recognizes the evolutionary development of the modern approach, while at the same time clearly differentiating it from its predecessor.

Obviously the key to understanding any approach which may be labelled *contextual* lies in being able to identify the context. Before examining this matter in more detail, however, we will consider the basic rule of interpretation and emphasize the proposition that the meaning of an ordinary word of the English language is a matter of fact (see also page 235) and then contrast ordinary words with technical ones.

## 20.2 The basic rule of interpretation

Bennion formulates the basic rule of modern interpretation thus:

> 'It is taken to be the legislator's intention that an enactment shall be construed according to the numerous general guides laid down for that purpose by law; and that where these conflict (as they often do) the problem shall be resolved by weighing and balancing the interpretative factors concerned.' (*Op. cit.*, p. 84.)

Pausing only to notice that this observation fits very well with the idea of *delegation to the judges* (see pages 276–83), you will recall that we have already considered the importance of the 'weighing and balancing' process to which Bennion refers. However, the point is so fundamental that it is worth reinforcing it in Bennion's own words:

> 'Contrary to what is often said, the court does not select any one of these many guides and then apply it to the exclusion of the rest. What the court does (or should do) is take an overall view, weigh all the relevant interpretative factors, and then arrive at a balanced conclusion.' (*Ibid.*)

The remainder of this chapter will consist of formulating and discussing the major factors which go into the balancing exercise.

## 20.3 Ordinary and technical meanings

The basic proposition that the meaning of an ordinary word of the English language is a question of fact for the tribunal of fact has already been discussed (see page 235). However, there remains the possibility that the court may give a technical meaning to an apparently ordinary word or phrase, as in *Fisher v Bell* [1960] 3 All ER 731, where the contract lawyer's understanding of the phrase 'offer for sale' was preferred to the ordinary meaning. Similarly, in *Knocker v Youle* [1986] 2 All ER 914, the court held that the term 'interest' in s. 1(1) of the Variation of Trusts Act 1958, which deals with interests 'whether vested or contingent', must be given its technical, legal meaning, otherwise the words 'whether vested or contingent' would not make sense. The technical context which gives special meanings to words need not be legal. In *Prophett v Platt Brothers & Co Ltd* [1961] 2 All ER 644, the wording in question was 'fettling of metal castings'.

Clearly, therefore, the question arises as to how ordinary and technical meanings are to be distinguished from each other. The truth of the matter is that there is no acid test, and the courts are quite happy to preserve an element of uncertainty in order to give themselves a degree of flexibility. Nevertheless, some guidance was offered by Lord Simon in *Maunsell v Olins* [1975] 1 All ER 16:

> 'Statutory language, like all language, is capable of an almost infinite gradation of "register" – i.e. it will be used at the semantic level appropriate to the subject matter and to the audience addressed (the man in the street, lawyers, merchants, etc.). It is the duty of a court of construction to tune into such register and so to interpret the statutory language as to give it the primary meaning which is appropriate in that register (unless it is clear that some other meaning must be given in order to carry out the statutory purpose or to avoid injustice, anomaly, absurdity or contradiction). In other words, *statutory language must always be given presumptively the most natural and ordinary meaning which is appropriate in the circumstances.*' (Emphasis added. See page 261 for an explanation of the concept of *linguistic register*.)

Since modern interpretation emphasizes the meaning of the words in the context within which they are used, it is obviously of the first importance that we should be able to identify the elements which make up that context. It is convenient to consider this topic under two headings: *matters of language*, which apply to all linguistic communication, and *matters of law*, which take account of the specific problems of interpretation which arise from the technical nature of statutes.

## 20.4 Analysing the context: matters of language

### 20.4.1 Dictionaries

It may seem obvious that the courts should rely heavily on dictionaries for guidance as to the meanings of words, but in fact they are seldom much use in statutory interpretation. In *Re Attorney-General's Reference (No 1 of 1988)* [1989] 1 AC 971, the House of Lords had to decide whether a person who came into possession of certain information, without making any effort to do so, could be said to have 'obtained' that information for the purposes of the Company Securities (Insider Dealing) Act 1985. The House of Lords answered this question in the affirmative, on the basis that within the statutory context under consideration, Parliament must have intended the word 'obtained' to be given a wide meaning which was, in effect, synonymous with 'received'. Lord Templeman cited with approval the following passage from the speech of Lord Upjohn in *Customs and Excise Commissioners v Top Ten Promotions Ltd* [1969] 1 WLR 1163:

> 'It is highly dangerous, if not impossible, to attempt to place an accurate definition upon a word in common use; you can look up examples of its many uses if you want to in the *Oxford Dictionary* but that does not help on definition. The task of the court in construing statutory language such as that which is before your Lordships is to look at the mischief at which the Act is directed and then, in that light, to consider whether as a matter of common sense and everyday usage the known, proved or admitted or properly inferred facts of the particular case bring the case within the ordinary meaning of the words used by Parliament.'

The emphasis on 'the mischief at which the Act is directed' seems to indicate that the best occasion for using dictionaries arises when the court is seeking the meaning of a word at the time the Act was passed, in which case it may be worth consulting a contemporary dictionary. However, before relying on even contemporary dictionaries, it is worth considering the possibility that the meaning of the words may have changed with the passage of time. (See paragraph 20.8, below.)

### 20.4.2 The immediate textual context

As we saw at page 238, the cases of *Newman v Lipman* [1950] 2 All ER 832 and *Burgess v McCracken* (1986) 150 JP 529 illustrate perhaps the most fundamental principle of all interpretation (whether or not within a legal context), namely that the meaning of a word is governed by the context in which it is used. Although the point is of general application, it is so basic to the process of statutory interpretation (and yet so easily overlooked) that it is worth considering some more examples by way of reinforcement.

In *Foster v Diphwys Casson Slate Co* (1887) 18 QBD 428, the relevant statute provided that explosives could be taken into a mine only if they were contained in a 'case or canister'. The question for the court was whether a cloth bag was sufficient. The court held that, in context, what was covered were containers of the same strength and solidity as 'canisters', and that therefore a cloth bag did not comply with the statute.

A specific instance of the importance of the immediate context lies in those provisions where specific words precede general words. Thus, for example, in *Re Stockport Ragged, Industrial and Reformatory Schools* [1898] 2 Ch 687, the phrase 'cathedral, collegiate, chapter or other schools' in the Charitable Trusts Act 1853 was held to be limited to schools associated with the Church of England, because this was the uniquely distinguishing feature of *cathedral* schools, *collegiate* schools and *chapter* schools. In other words, the general words were interpreted as applying only to other schools of *the same class* as those identified by the specific words. (The Latin phrase *ejusdem generis* means *of the same class*, and is very widely used by lawyers when speaking of this aspect of interpretation.) In general terms, therefore, and adopting the words of McCardie J in *Magnhild SS v McIntyre Bros & Co* [1921] 2 KB 97:

> 'The only test seems to be whether the specified things which precede the general words can be placed under some common category. By this I understand that the specified things must possess some common and dominant feature.'

In other words, it is not sufficient that the unspecified thing is like one, or other, or even all of the specified things: they must all possess a common characteristic which is sufficiently basic to justify classifying them together as a class (or *genus*).

By way of further example, in *Wood v Commissioner of Police for the Metropolis* [1986] 2 All ER 570, the statutory definition of 'offensive weapon', namely 'any gun, pistol, hanger, cutlass, bludgeon, or other offensive weapon' was held not to apply to a piece of broken glass which had just fallen out of the defendant's front door. The court said the definition was to be confined to articles *made* or *adapted* for use for causing injury to the person, therefore the fact that a particular object merely had the *potential* for such use was not sufficient to bring it within the scope of the statutory definition.

Similarly, in *R (Lord Chancellor) v Chief Land Registar (Barking and Dagenham London Borough Council, interested party)* [2005] EWHC 1706 (Admin), [2005] 4 All ER 643, the provision related to the transfer of 'property, rights or liabilities'. Rejecting the view that the word 'property' should be limited to physical property, Stanley Burnton J said that, in the context of this particular provision, 'it would be anomalous to construe "property" as meaning something physical, when there is a clear non-physical genus'.Another aspect of the importance of the immediate context when identifying meaning lies in the common sense proposition that if you list a number of things as being relevant, it is reasonable to assume that you mean to exclude anything which you do not mention. A classic example can be found in the well-known case of *Shylock v Antonio* (reported by William Shakespeare in *The Merchant of Venice*, Act IV, Sc. 1). Shylock was seeking to enforce a bond given by Antonio, under which Antonio was to forfeit 'a pound of flesh' if he defaulted. In argument before the court, Antonio's advocate says:

'This bond doth give thee here no jot of blood;
The words expressly are "a pound of flesh":
Then take thy bond, take thou thy pound of flesh;
But, in the cutting it, if thou dost shed
One drop of Christian blood, thy land and goods
Are, by the laws of Venice, confiscate
Unto the state of Venice.'

A more modern (and authoritative) illustration of the principle may be found in *R v Cuthbertson* [1980] 2 All ER 401, where the Misuse of Drugs Act 1971 enabled a court to order the forfeiture of a defendant's property following conviction for 'an offence under this Act'. The defendant was convicted of *conspiracy* to contravene the 1971 Act. Although this was undoubtedly an offence, it was not created by the 1971 Act, and therefore he had not been 'convicted of an offence under this Act'. Accordingly, the House of Lords held that there was no power to make a forfeiture order.

A final aspect of the relevance of the immediate textual context is known as either the *rank principle* or the *rule of rank*:

'Where a string of items of a certain rank is followed by residuary words, it is presumed that the residuary words are not intended to include items of a different rank'. (Bennion, *Statutory Interpretation*, 4th edn, 2002, p. 1067.)

The operation of this principle, which it must be admitted is seldom encountered in practice, may be illustrated by *Casher v Holmes* (1831) 109 ER 1263, where the court said that a provision imposing excise duties on 'copper, brass, pewter, and tin, and all other metals not enumerated' would not apply to gold and silver, because they are of a higher rank than the metals which are listed. In more modern times, the phrase 'an officer or examiner of the court or some other person' in RSC Ord 39, r 4(a) was said not to apply to a judge, partly because of the rank principle, and partly because another rule included judges as well as officers, examiners and other people. (*Re Brickman's Settlement* [1982] 1 All ER 336.)

### 20.4.3　Reading an Act as a whole

The statement that an Act should be read as a whole may, when expressed in this form, appear to be a specifically legal proposition. However, in reality, an exactly similar proposition could be made with equal force in the context of any other document, and therefore the proposition may legitimately be discussed as a matter of language.

In *Courtauld v Legh* (1869) LR 4 Exch 126, Cleasby J said: 'It is a sound rule of construction to give the same meaning to the same words occurring in different parts of an Act'. Without wishing to detract in any way from the general soundness of this statement, there are occasions where the same word may have different meanings even within a single section, let alone within a single Act. Two examples will suffice.

The first, and classic, example is s. 57 of the Offences Against the Person Act 1861, which provides: 'Whosoever being married shall marry any other person during the life of the former husband or wife ... shall be guilty of felony'. In *R v Allen* (1872) LR 1 CCR 367, the court held that someone who is already married to one person cannot marry anyone else, and therefore the section must mean 'whosoever being validly married shall go through a ceremony of marriage ...'.

Secondly, s. 2(1) of the Law of Property (Miscellaneous Provisions) Act 1989, provides: 'A contract for the sale ... of land ... can only be made ... by incorporating all the terms ... in one document or, where contracts are exchanged, in each'. In *Commission for the New Towns v Cooper (GB) Ltd* [1995] 2 All ER 929, the Court of Appeal pointed out that although 'exchange of contracts' is the expression used both in practice and by the statute to describe the process whereby there is an exchange of signed documents containing the terms which the parties have agreed, where this practice is adopted there is in law no contract until exchange has taken place. It follows that the documents which are exchanged cannot accurately be called 'contracts', and therefore the subsection uses the words 'contract' and 'contracts' to mean two different things.

Quite apart from matters of interpretation, there may be other reasons for reading an Act as a whole. *Lloyd v McMahon* [1987] 1 All ER 1118 involved an action by the District Auditor against certain members of Liverpool City Council who delayed making a rate until well after the start of the relevant financial year, thus causing substantial financial loss to the council. (The rates were a form of local taxation raised by local authorities.) There was no statutory provision prescribing any cut-off date by which a rate had to be made, but the court, having read the Act as a whole, identified the right of domestic ratepayers to pay their rates by ten monthly instalments. The court concluded, therefore, that at the very latest the rate must be made in time to enable this right to be exercised.

A particular problem with reading an Act as a whole arises where the Act has been amended. Does the context consist of the whole Act as originally passed, or the whole Act in its amended form? In *Attorney-General v Lamplough* (1878) 3 ExD 214, the Court of Appeal held that the appropriate context was the Act as originally passed. Similarly, in *R v Greater Manchester North District Coroner ex parte Worch* [1987] 3 All ER 661, even though *Lamplough* was not cited, the High Court came to the same conclusion, with Slade J saying:

> 'The original s. 21(2) [of the Coroners (Amendment) Act 1926] is no longer law, since it has been replaced by s. 23(3) of the Births and Deaths Registration Act 1953. Nevertheless, the original subsection is admissible in construing the section as a whole and, in our judgment, throws light on its construction.'

## 20.5 Analysing the context: matters of law

### 20.5.1 Introduction

Having considered some matters which arise in the use of language generally, as well as in statutory interpretation, we can now turn to some more specifically legal matters. Bearing in mind the fact that we are constantly looking for the meaning of the words in the context within which they are used, it will be useful to begin by analysing the structure of statutes, since this will establish the most immediate context, before considering a variety of other matters beyond the statutory text itself.

### 20.5.2 The anatomy of a statute

*Preambles*

Where there is a preamble to a statute it will recite the reasons why the statute was passed. However, modern drafting practice in relation to

Public Bills has almost entirely dispensed with the use of preambles, although they still appear in Private Bills, and therefore in Private Acts. It follows that their status for the purposes of interpretation is relatively insignificant in quantitative terms. Nevertheless, in those cases where preambles are encountered, their status is clear.

According to Lord Normand in *Attorney-General v Prince Ernest Augustus of Hanover* [1957] 1 All ER 49, 'It is only when it conveys a clear and definite meaning in comparison with relatively obscure or indefinite enacting words that the preamble may legitimately prevail'. In practice, however, a preamble may prevail even over enacting words which are plain. Thus, for example, the preamble to the Life Assurance Act 1774 indicates that the statute is intended to deal with 'a mischievous kind of gaming', and the terms of the Act itself provide that life policies are unlawful unless they name the people whose lives are covered. In *Siu Yin Kwan v Eastern Insurance Co Ltd* [1994] 1 All ER 213, the Privy Council held that the Act was irrelevant where the facts arose within the commercial context of insurance, agency and insolvency, and had nothing to do with gaming.

The idea that something may resolve an ambiguity but not create one occurs elsewhere within statutory interpretation. Additionally, however, it carries echoes of certain techniques which the courts use when handling precedents. For example, as we saw at page 159, there may be situations in which the changed circumstances principle may justify the exercise of the power to distinguish earlier cases, although that power clearly exists independently of that principle.

### Long titles

Long titles are much more important than preambles in practice, since all modern statutes have them. Moreover, as the leading cases show, they have much the same effect in practice. For example, in *R v Galvin* [1987] 2 All ER 851, Lord Lane CJ, speaking of the Official Secrets Act 1911, and its predecessor of 1889, said:

> 'One can have regard to the title of a statute to help resolve an ambiguity in the body of it, but it is not, we consider, open to a court to use the title to restrict what is otherwise the plain meaning of the words of the statute simply because they seem to be unduly wide.'

In *Black-Clawson International Ltd v Papierwerke Waldhof-Aschaffenburg AG* [1975] 1 All ER 810, Lord Simon took the view that where a long title provides 'the plainest of all guides to the general objectives of a statute', there can be no justification for restricting its use to cases of ambiguity. Further evidence of the utility of long titles may be found in *Firstpost*

*Homes Ltd v Johnson* [1995] 4 All ER 355, where the Court of Appeal was concerned with the Law of Property (Miscellaneous Provisions) Act 1989, the long title of which recited the intention of making 'new provisions' with respect to contracts for the sale of land. Balcombe LJ could see 'no justification for retaining the old law on what constituted a signature under the Statute of Frauds [1677] or s. 40 of the 1925 [Law of Property] Act, and every reason for consigning it to the limbo where it clearly belongs ...'.

It is fortunate that the same principle applies to preambles and long titles, because some judges have difficulty in distinguishing one from the other. In *Ward v Holman* [1964] 2 All ER 729, Lord Parker CJ, while stating the principle, spoke of the 'preamble' to the Public Order Act 1936, although even the most cursory glance at the first page of that Act reveals that there is no preamble. Indeed, judicial confusion is not always limited to preambles and long titles. In the *Firstpost Homes* case, Balcombe LJ even managed to describe the *long* title as the *short* title, which is the category to which we now turn.

## Short titles

The short title is almost always found towards the end of the statute. The leading case is *Re Boaler* [1915] 1 KB 21, where it was acknowledged that the short title is part of the Act, and as such the court can and should consider it. However, it is by definition a *short* title and therefore, as Scrutton LJ said, 'accuracy may be sacrificed to brevity'. Moreover, particular care should be taken when dealing with the short titles of old Acts. Before 1896 it was not the practice for Acts to have short titles, but the Short Titles Act of that year conferred short titles on many older Acts. However, all the short titles were not necessarily appropriate, so that, for example, the short title of the Criminal Procedure Act was given to a statute passed in 1865 which dealt with both criminal and civil procedure.

## Headings and marginal notes

A glance at any substantial statute will reveal that the text is broken down under a number of *headings* (also known as *cross-headings*) which appear between groups of sections. Additionally, until 2001, the statutory text was accompanied by *marginal notes* (also known as *side-notes* or *shoulder notes*), which, obviously enough, appeared in the margin. Parliamentary Counsel discontinued the use of side-notes in 2001 when the Office adopted new desktop publishing software. Consideration of how this software should be customized in order to meet the very specific needs of Parliamentary Counsel led to the conclusion that the sort of material which had previously been included by way of side-notes could equally well be included by way of headings to each section.

From time to time there have been *dicta* to the effect that headings and side-notes are irrelevant to the process of interpretation, on the basis that they are inserted by the drafter and are never subject to debate by Parliament. (See, for example, *Re Woking UDC (Basingstoke Canal) Act 1911* [1914] 1 Ch 300 where Phillimore LJ described them as being 'inserted not by Parliament nor under the authority of Parliament, but by irresponsible persons'.)

However, it is clear that statements such as this are based on judicial ignorance of the process of statutory drafting, and there has long been a general consensus that headings and marginal notes are relevant to the process of interpretation, 'provided that we realize that they cannot have equal weight with the words of the Act'. (Lord Reid in *Director of Public Prosecutions v Schildkamp* [1969] 3 All ER 1640.) More particularly, the courts have often accepted as being authoritative Upjohn LJ's view that

> 'while the marginal note to a section cannot control the language used in the section, it is at least permissible to approach a consideration of its *general purpose* and the *mischief* at which it is aimed *with the note in mind.*' (Emphasis added. *Stephens v Cuckfield RDC* [1960] 2 QB 373.)

The general consensus received the unqualified approval of the unanimous opinion of the House of Lords in *R v Montila* [2005] UKHL 50, [2005] 1 All ER 113:

> '[33] It is not true that headings and sidenotes are inserted by 'irresponsible persons', in the sense indicated by Phillimore LJ. They are drafted by Parliamentary Counsel, who are answerable through the Cabinet Office to the Prime Minister. The clerks, who are subject to the authority of Parliament, are empowered to make what are known as printing corrections. These are corrections of a minor nature which do not alter the general meaning of the Bill. But they may very occasionally, on the advice of the Bill's drafter, alter headings which because of amendments or for some other reason have become inaccurate: Bennion, [*Statutory Interpretation,* 4th edn, 2002], p 609 ... When the Bill is passed, the entire Act is entered in the Parliamentary Roll with all its components, including those that are unamendable. As Bennion states at p 638, the format or layout is part of an Act.
>
> '[34] The question then is whether headings and sidenotes, although unamendable, can be considered in construing a provision in an Act of Parliament. Account must, of course, be taken of the fact that these components were included in the Bill not for debate but for ease of reference. This indicates that less weight can be attached to them than to the parts of the Act that are open for consideration and debate in Parliament. But it is another matter to be required by a rule of law to disregard them altogether. One cannot

ignore the fact that the headings and sidenotes are included on the face of the Bill throughout its passage through the legislature. They are there for guidance. They provide the context for an examination of those parts of the Bill that are open for debate. Subject, of course, to the fact that they are unamendable, they ought to be open to consideration as part of the enactment when it reaches the statute book.'

'[35] … It has become common practice for their Lordships to ask to be shown the explanatory notes when issues are raised about the meaning of words used in an enactment.

'[36] The headings and sidenotes are as much part of the contextual scene as these materials, and there is no logical reason why they should be treated differently.'

## Schedules

Although some comments may be found which suggest there is some significance in the distinction between the main (or operative) part of an Act and a Schedule to an Act, in reality the distinction is purely a matter of form and not of substance, as Bennion explains:

'It is often convenient to incorporate part of the operative provisions of an Act in the form of a Schedule. The Schedule is often used to hive off provisions which are too long or detailed to be put in the body of the Act. This does not mean they are unimportant.' (*Statutory Interpretation*, 4th edn, 2002, p. 574.)

Judicial authority to the same effect may be found in the judgment of Brett LJ, in *Attorney-General v Lamplough* (1878) 3 ExD 214:

'A schedule in an Act is a mere question of drafting, a mere question of words. The schedule is as much part of the statute, and is as much an enactment, as any other part.'

## Transitional provisions

A statute which amends an existing statute may well contain provisions which regulate the transition from the old scheme to the new. These transitional provisions will be found towards the end of the statute, and their substance is not uncommonly contained in Schedules. For example, the provisions of the Magistrates' Courts Act 1980, which amended the procedure to be followed by a magistrates' court when committing a defendant for trial at the Crown Court, came into force on 6 July 1981. A Schedule to the Act contained transitional provisions relating to proceedings which had begun before 6 July.

## Definition sections

Definition sections, which are commonly found towards the end of statutes but towards the beginning of statutory instruments, contain provisions of two types. First there are those which simply state that the defined terms shall 'mean' whatever the provision states them to mean. Secondly, there are those which state that the defined terms shall 'include' whatever the provision states them to include. In cases falling within the latter category the words will have not only their special statutory meaning but, according to Lord Selborne LC in *Robinson v Barton-Eccles Local Board* (1883) 8 App Cas 798, they will also possess their 'ordinary, popular and natural sense whenever that would be applicable'. In other words, this category does not enact definitions in the strict sense of the term, since it is in the nature of a definition to restrict, rather than simply to illustrate, the meaning of a word.

Definition sections generally include a form of words to the effect that the definitions they contain shall yield to a contrary intention within the main part of the Act, although some drafters omit these words on the basis that they are no more than a statement of the obvious. In addition to specific definition sections, the Interpretation Act 1978 will often be relevant. The provisions of that Act which are most commonly relied upon are reproduced in Appendix 2.

### Commencement sections

Commencement sections are generally found towards the end of statutes. Section 4 of the Interpretation Act 1978, whose ancestry can be traced to the Acts of Parliament (Commencement) Act 1793, states that, where provision is made for an Act or part of an Act to come into force on a particular day, it comes into force at the beginning of that day; and that, where no such provision is made, an Act comes into force at the beginning of the day on which it receives the Royal Assent. The limited degree of retrospectivity inherent in this provision appears to cause no injustice in practice, and is in any event a marked improvement over the pre-1793 position, when Acts took effect from the beginning of the Parliamentary session in which they were passed (see *Latless v Holmes*, which is discussed at page 209).

Section 4 of the 1978 Act is seldom relevant in practice, because statutes commonly state that they will come into force either on a particular future date, or on the expiry of a stated period after they receive the Royal Assent, or on whatever day may be appointed by the appropriate Secretary of State, who will usually be empowered to make a commencement order by way of a statutory instrument. Appointed days and commencement orders are frequently used when the successful implementation of an Act depends on things such as setting up administrative machinery, appointing staff, making delegated legislation, and so on. In *R v Secretary of State for the Home Department ex parte Fire Brigades*

*Union and Others* (1995) 7 Admin LR 473, the House of Lords decided that a power to make appointed day and commencement orders puts the relevant Secretary of State under a continuing obligation to consider whether the time is ripe for a relevant order to be made, and therefore it is unlawful for a Secretary of State to make a decision which will effectively preclude the making of such an order.

It is common for different parts of the same Act to come into force on different days, and it is not unknown for provisions to be amended, or even repealed, before they come into force.

### 20.5.3 Reference to extrinsic materials

Having surveyed the anatomy of a statute, we must now consider how far beyond the actual text a court may go when seeking to establish the context within which the statutory words are to be understood. In other words, what use can the court make of extrinsic materials? The answer to this question depends on analysing extrinsic materials into three different categories: pre-Parliamentary materials, Parliamentary materials and post-Parliamentary materials.

#### Pre-Parliamentary materials

Pre-Parliamentary materials, such as reports of Royal Commissions and committees of various kinds, are useful because, according to Lord Halsbury in *Eastman Photographic Materials Co Ltd v Comptroller of Patents* [1898] AC 571, there is 'no more accurate source of information' as to the mischief at which the Act was aimed. In *Assam Railways and Trading Co v Commissioners of Inland Revenue* [1935] AC 445, Lord Wright emphasized that in the *Eastman* case Lord Halsbury had been speaking only about the mischief, not the meaning, and in *Letang v Cooper* [1964] 2 All ER 929, Lord Denning MR pointed out that identifying the mischief 'does not help very much, for the simple reason that Parliament may, and often does, decide to do something different to cure the mischief'.

The case of *Black-Clawson International Ltd v Papierwerke Waldhof-Aschaffenburg AG* [1975] 1 All ER 810 requires careful consideration. The Foreign Judgments (Reciprocal Enforcement) Act 1933 resulted from the report of a committee under the chairmanship of Greer LJ. The House of Lords disagreed as to the use to which the committee's report could be put. Lord Reid and Lord Wilberforce took the established line that the report could be used only for identifying the mischief, but Lord Simon and Viscount Dilhorne thought it could also be used in relation to identifying the meaning of the statutory words. In this situation, the views of the fifth member of the House, Lord Diplock, are particularly important, even though he thought that the meaning of the provision in question was plain anyway, and therefore did not need to consider the report for either purpose. Nevertheless, he did deliver the following *dictum*:

'Parliament, under our constitution, is sovereign only in respect of what it expresses by the words used in the legislation it has passed.

'This is not to say that, where those words are not clear and unambiguous in themselves but are fairly susceptible of more than one meaning, the court, for the purpose of resolving – though not of inventing – an ambiguity may not pay regard to authoritative statements that were matters of public knowledge at the time the Act was passed, as to what were regarded as deficiencies in that branch of the existing law with which the Act deals. Where such statements are made in official reports commissioned by government, laid before Parliament and published, they clearly fall within this category and may be used to resolve the ambiguity in favour of a meaning which will result in correcting those deficiencies in preference to some alternative meaning that will leave the deficiencies uncorrected. The justification of this use of such reports as an aid to the construction of the words used in the statute is that knowledge of their contents may be taken to be shared by those whose conduct the statute regulates and would influence their understanding of the meaning of the ambiguous enacting words.'

Although this *dictum* appears to give a majority in favour of using reports as an aid to identifying meanings, at least in cases where there is ambiguity, this is not the general understanding of the courts. In *R v Allen* [1985] 2 All ER 641, where the Court of Appeal had declined to look at a report of the Criminal Law Revision Committee, Lord Hailsham LC described the use of reports for identifying the mischief only as being 'the present practice'. Similarly, in *R v Broadcasting Complaints Commission ex parte British Broadcasting Corporation* (1995) 7 Admin LR 575, Brooke J cited *Black-Clawson* in support of the view that he was entitled to consult the pre-Parliamentary history of a statute 'to help [him] identify the mischief', while *Pepper v Hart* (which is discussed at page 303) meant that *Hansard* was available 'to assist [him] in interpreting any ambiguity in the Act, particularly in relation to the parliamentary intention behind' the section under consideration.

In *British Leyland Corporation v Armstrong Patents Co Ltd* [1986] 1 All ER 850, the House of Lords referred to the report of the Gregory Committee on Copyright, which had preceded the Copyright Act 1956. Lord Templeman took the traditional line when he said: 'Thus s. 9(8) of the Copyright Act 1956 was defective to achieve the intended purpose'. Similarly, Lord Edmund-Davies said:

'I do not know what Parliament intended to do. Assume, as one reasonably may, that the Gregory Report was available to the legislators in 1956, and one will still have no knowledge of how far they intended to implement any of its recommendations when legislating as expansively as they did. We may think they could, and should, have done better, but that is by the way.'

However, the restriction on using pre-parliamentary materials to identify only the mischief is subject to an exception where the court is considering reports of the Law Commissions, which may be used even to interpret the meaning of a statute. *R v Horseferry Road Metropolitan Stipendiary Magistrate ex parte Siadatan* [1991] 1 All ER 324 dealt with the concluding words of s. 4(1) of the Public Order Act 1986, which creates an offence where certain things are done

'with intent to cause [a] person to believe that immediate unlawful violence will be used against him or another by any person, or to provoke the immediate use of unlawful violence by that person or another, or whereby that person is likely to believe that such violence will be used or it is likely that such violence will be provoked.'

The issue was whether 'such violence' in the last line of the provision meant *any* unlawful violence, or only *immediate* unlawful violence. Watkins LJ quoted the Law Commission report (Law Com No 123 (1983)) which preceded the Act:

'*Fear of violence and provoking violence*
5.43 The offence requires that each defendant use threatening etc, words or behaviour which is intended or is likely (a) to cause another person to fear immediate unlawful violence, or (b) to provoke the immediate use of unlawful violence by another person.'

Deciding the case on the basis that the report made it plain that only immediate unlawful violence was meant, Watkins LJ said: 'That the Parliamentary draftsman, when drafting the last part of s. 4(1), did not achieve the same clarity and precision is, we think, most regrettable'.

The question of whether the court can compel advocates to cite pre-Parliamentary reports is considered at page 211. The use of international conventions as pre-Parliamentary materials is considered at page 320, in the context of the presumption of compliance with international law.

Finally, from the Parliamentary session beginning in 1998, the established practice of issuing an Explanatory Memorandum and Notes on Clauses, was discontinued, and a new form of pre-Parliamentary material, known as *explanatory notes*, was introduced. The new material is intended not merely to replace the old, but also to

'extend and improve it. The notes will be made available alongside the Bills when they are first published ... updated when Bills move from one House to the other and updated finally at Royal Assent ...

'Like the present explanatory memoranda, the notes will not constitute
legislative text and will not be amended or passed by Parliament. They will be
prepared by the department responsible for the Bill ... [and] ... by explaining
the key points of legislation in non-technical language and setting out relevant background material, can assist the reader to understand legislation ...

'... it is for the courts to decide what attention they should pay to them.'
(Lord McIntosh of Haringey, answering a question on legislative drafting,
HL Deb, January 21, 1998, col 1600.)

In *R (S) v Chief Constable of South Yorkshire* [2004] UKHL 39, [2004] 4 All
ER 193, Lord Steyn dealt with the status of explanatory notes thus:

'[4] ... Explanatory notes are not indorsed by Parliament. On the other hand,
in so far as they cast light on the setting of a statute, and the mischief at which
it is aimed, they are admissible in aid of construction of the statute. After all,
they may potentially contain much more immediate and valuable material
than other aids regularly used by the courts, such as Law Commission
reports, government committee reports, Green Papers and so forth.'

However, it is important to remember that, once an Act has come into
force, the decisions of the courts are the definitive guides to its
meaning.

As well as being available in hard copy, the explanatory notes are
published on the internet in the Bills and Legislation section of
www.parliament.uk.

### Parliamentary materials: the use of Hansard

As a matter of first impression it may seem obvious that *Hansard*, as the
official record of Parliamentary proceedings, should be available to the
courts when interpreting statutes, on the basis that the Parliamentar-
ians who debated a Bill before it became an Act may well have said what
they intended it to mean. However, two bundles of arguments have
traditionally been deployed against this proposition. One bundle of
arguments is constitutional, the other purely practical.

One of the constitutional arguments for saying that the courts should
interpret statutes without reference to *Hansard* relies on the doctrine of
the separation of powers (see page 69). This argument proceeds on the
basis that it is the function of the legislature to make the law and the
function of the courts to interpret and apply it. As we have already
noted (page 272), in *Black-Clawson*, Lord Reid said: 'We often say that we
are looking for the intention of Parliament, but that is not quite accurate. We are seeking not what Parliament meant but the true meaning
of what they said'.

For nearly two centuries the House of Commons itself raised an additional constitutional argument, to the effect that using *Hansard* could, at

least potentially, constitute a breach of art. 9 of the Bill of Rights 1689, which provides, in modernized spelling, 'that the freedom of speech and debates or proceedings in Parliament ought not to be impeached or questioned in any court or place out of Parliament'.

Admittedly, in practice the Commons often gave permission for the use of *Hansard* in response to specific requests, and therefore it was not altogether surprising that, on 31 October 1980, the House passed a resolution giving general leave for reference to be made to *Hansard* in court. Obviously, however, this resolution did nothing to invalidate Lord Reid's point in *Black-Clawson*, nor did it address the other bundle of traditional arguments, namely those based on considerations of sheer practicality.

Turning, therefore, to the practical arguments, the views of Lord Reid are once again significant. In *Beswick v Beswick* [1967] 2 All ER 1197, his Lordship pointed out that *Hansard* is not always easily available, and therefore allowing its use would be expensive in terms of both time and money. Furthermore, in many cases *Hansard* would not help, containing as it does a multiplicity of views as to what a Bill may, or should, mean or not mean. However, in *R v Warner* [1968] 2 All ER 356, which turned on whether a particular offence was one of strict liability or whether *mens rea* was required, Lord Reid was prepared to acknowledge the possibility of an exception to the exclusionary principle if the case were such that referring to *Hansard* would almost certainly solve the problem of interpretation which was before the court.

Certainly the House of Lords did not consider the Commons' resolution of 1980 to be of overriding significance. When Lord Denning MR admitted that he had referred to *Hansard* while formulating his judgment in the Court of Appeal, five Law Lords unanimously declared that he had been wrong to do so and that neither advocates nor judges should refer to *Hansard*. (*Hadmor Productions Ltd v Hamilton* [1982] 1 All ER 1042.)

However, the 1980 resolution does appear to have had some effect, at least to the extent of creating a more relaxed atmosphere in the courts. The starting-point is *R v Secretary of State for Trade and Industry ex parte Anderson Strathclyde plc* [1983] 2 All ER 233, where Dunn LJ acknowledged that, while the courts could use *Hansard*, both the extent of that use, and the weight to be given to it, were 'entirely at large'. In *Brind v Secretary of State for the Home Department* [1991] 1 All ER 720, the House of Lords referred to *Hansard* in order to identify the Home Secretary's reasons for preventing both the British Broadcasting Corporation and the Independent Broadcasting Authority from broadcasting certain types of material relating to Northern Ireland. Furthermore, their Lordships appear to have seen nothing odd in what they were doing, since the use of *Hansard* was accompanied by neither apology nor explanation.

Perhaps more startling, from the traditional point of view, was the case of *Pierce v Bemis* [1986] 1 All ER 1011. When deciding whether the sunken ship *The Lusitania* was 'derelict', Sheen J not only allowed counsel to cite, but also himself cited, *Hansard* in order to explain how the provision which became s. 72 of the Merchant Shipping Act 1906 came to be enacted. On the other hand, in *Church of Scientology v Johnson-Smith* [1972] 1 All ER 378, Browne J said that a plaintiff, who was suing a Member of Parliament for libel in respect of comments made in a television interview, could not refer to *Hansard* in order to prove malice on the part of the defendant.

In addition to the cases involving purely domestic law, it seems that special considerations may arise where Community Law is involved. The case of *Pickstone v Freemans plc* [1988] 2 All ER 803 involved the construction of a statutory instrument which was introduced as a consequence of a decision by the European Court of Justice to the effect that the United Kingdom had failed to comply with a specific requirement of Community Law. The House decided to read the instrument as if it contained certain words which were not actually there. By way of justification, Lord Templeman said:

> 'The draft of the 1983 regulations was not subject to any process of amendment by Parliament. In these circumstances the explanations of the government and the criticisms voiced by members of Parliament in the debates which led to approval of the draft regulations provide some indications of the intentions of Parliament.'

The remainder of Lord Templeman's speech included a passage from *Hansard*. Lord Oliver acknowledged that the decision involved

> 'a departure from a number of well-established rules of construction. The intention of Parliament has, it is said, to be ascertained from the words which it has used and those words are to be construed according to their plain and ordinary meaning. The fact that a statute is passed to give effect to an international treaty does not, of itself, enable the treaty to be referred to in order to construe the words used in other than their plain and unambiguous sense. Moreover, even in the case of ambiguity, what is said in Parliament in the course of the passage of a Bill cannot ordinarily be referred to to assist in construction. I think, however, that it has also to be recognized that a statute which is passed in order to give effect to the United Kingdom's obligations under the EEC Treaty falls into a special category and it does so because, unlike other treaty obligations, those obligations have, in effect, been incorporated into English Law by the European Communities Act 1972.'

Given that the courts have in fact been referring to *Hansard* for many years, albeit normally for purposes other than those of statutory interpretation, the case of *R v Governors of Haberdasher Aske's Hatcham Schools ex parte Inner London Education Authority* (1989) 153 LG Rev 809, is instructive on the approach which they should take towards the words which they find. In considering, *inter alia*, a Parliamentary answer given by a junior Education Minister, Glidewell LJ indicated that the courts should assume that people meant what they said:

> 'I cannot accept that we should interpret the Parliamentary answer as being in some sort of code: in other words that we should interpret the Ministers who say they have not yet made up their minds ... as meaning that they have made up their minds.'

The use of *Hansard* in the specific context of statutory interpretation came before the House of Lords in *Pepper v Hart* [1993] 1 All ER 42, which is now the leading case. The facts concerned the quantification of the liability of certain income tax payers in respect of benefits which were to be treated as part of their emoluments. The taxpayers were schoolmasters at an independent school, and their children were being educated at the school under a concessionary fee scheme which resulted in them paying some 20 per cent of the normal fees. At all relevant times the school had spare capacity, and therefore the question arose as to whether the taxpayers' liability should be based on the difference between the amount which the taxpayers paid and the marginal cost which the school actually incurred in educating the taxpayers' children, or on the difference between the amount which the taxpayers paid and the full cost which the school incurred in educating the taxpayers' children, including an apportionment of overheads. Section 63 of the Finance Act 1976 was capable of bearing either meaning but, when the provision was going through Parliament, the Financial Secretary to the Treasury had made it plain that the government intended the words to bear the meaning which was favourable to the taxpayers.

Delivering the leading speech, Lord Browne-Wilkinson, having canvassed all the relevant arguments and authorities, said:

> 'I therefore reach the conclusion, subject to any question of Parliamentary privilege, that the exclusionary rule should be relaxed so as to permit reference to Parliamentary materials where (a) legislation is ambiguous or obscure, or leads to an absurdity; (b) the material relied upon consists of one or more statements by a minister or other promoter of the Bill together if necessary with such other Parliamentary material as is necessary to understand such statements and their effect; (c) the statements relied upon are clear.'

The echo of Lord Reid in *Warner* is clear. Expressing his conclusion on the Parliamentary privilege aspect of the matter, Lord Browne-Wilkinson said:

'I trust when the House of Commons comes to consider the decision in this case, it will be appreciated that there is no desire to impeach its privileges in any way. Your Lordships are motivated by a desire to carry out the intentions of Parliament in enacting legislation and have no intention or desire to question the processes by which such legislation was enacted or of criticizing anything said by anyone in Parliament in the course of enacting it. The purpose is to give effect to, not thwart, the intentions of Parliament.'

Although the decision in *Pepper v Hart* is clear, it is worth noticing that Lord Mackay LC dissented in principle on the *Hansard* point, while being able to concur on the substantive point by using conventional means of interpretation. Lord Mackay accepted that using *Hansard* would not breach the Bill of Rights 1689, but based his dissent simply on the practical issue that reference to *Hansard* would be time-consuming and therefore expensive, and it would not be until the time and the money had been spent that the parties would know whether it had been worthwhile. Bearing in mind, therefore, the public interest in containing the cost of litigation, the Lord Chancellor declined to be a party to a decision which could substantially increase those costs. (In passing, it is worth noticing that the Lord Chancellor is the government minister with responsibility for legal aid, so the propriety of his participation in this decision was questionable in terms of the constitutional doctrine of the separation of powers.)

Lord Oliver was unimpressed with the argument based on increased costs, saying: 'I do not, for my part, consider that the relaxation of the rule... will lead to any significant increase in the cost of litigation or in the burden of research required to be undertaken by legal advisers'.

Turning to the case-law on the application of *Pepper v Hart*, it is necessary to consider how the courts decide whether an ambiguity exists in a particular case. Although a judge may take a robust view of the matter, as Millett LJ did when he declared that the meaning of s. 56(4) of the Taxes Management Act 1970 was 'too plain for argument' (*Petch v Gurney* [1994] 3 All ER 731), it is clear that some judges may not regard their own opinions as being necessarily decisive of the matter. In *Restick v Crickmore* [1994] 2 All ER 112, Stuart-Smith LJ considered there was no ambiguity in the relevant provision, but nevertheless said:

'Perhaps it may be said that the difference of judicial opinion between the judges in the courts below and this court shows that there is an ambiguity (see *Chief Adjudication Officer v Foster* [1993] 1 All ER 705 at 717 *per* Lord Bridge of Harwich).'

When applying *Pepper v Hart*, the courts will not go behind the statement which is reported in *Hansard*. In *R v Secretary of State for Foreign and Commonwealth Affairs ex parte Rees-Mogg* [1994] 1 All ER 457, the court was invited to disregard a ministerial statement which had been made on the advice of the Attorney-General, as that advice was demonstrably wrong. Lloyd LJ said that this argument, 'would, if correct, undermine the utility of *Pepper v Hart* in every case in which it would otherwise apply. Ministers act on advice. It cannot make any difference whether the source of the advice is made explicit'.

As the decision in *Pepper v Hart* has become more deeply embedded in the law, the courts have started to take a more relaxed view of it in various ways. For example, where it is doubtful whether the criteria in *Pepper v Hart* are satisfied, the court may be willing to permit a citation provided the other side does not object. (See *Richardson v Pitt-Stanley* [1995] 1 All ER 460.)

The courts have even referred to *Hansard* without mentioning *Pepper v Hart* at all, as illustrated by Lord Mustill's lengthy references to a speech of the Minister of State at the Home Office, relating to the Bill which became the Criminal Justice Act 1991. (See *Doody v Secretary of State for the Home Department* [1993] 3 All ER 92.)

A statement in Parliament as to the meaning of an existing Act is not within the *Pepper v Hart* principle (*Hillsdown Holdings plc v Pensions Ombudsman* [1997] 1 All ER 862), but where an existing provision is replaced by one expressed in different words, the absence of any Ministerial indication that a change in the law is intended may result in the court attaching no significance to the change of wording (*Berkovits v Grinberg (Attorney-General Intervening)* [1995] 2 All ER 681).

The House of Lords has subsequently seen the danger which only Lord Mackay LC perceived in *Pepper v Hart* itself, namely that references to *Hansard* may cost more than they are worth. More particularly, in *Melluish v BMI (No 3) Ltd* [1995] 4 All ER 453, Lord Browne-Wilkinson, giving the only substantial speech, emphasized that only statements specifically related to the provision in question could be brought within *Pepper v Hart*, and that where attempts were made to introduce other material:

> 'judges should be astute to check such misuse of the new rule by making appropriate orders as to costs wasted. In the present case, if it were otherwise appropriate to order the taxpayers to pay the costs of this issue, I would advise your Lordships to disallow any costs incurred by the Crown in the improper attempt to introduce this irrelevant Parliamentary material.'

Pausing only to comment that the possibility of wasted costs orders is discussed at page 27, it will be apparent that Lord Browne-Wilkinson's comment could easily be applied more widely to cases where the material in *Hansard* was relevant to the provision before the court, but nevertheless did not assist in the process of interpretation.

In *Three Rivers District Council v Bank of England* [1996] 2 All ER 363, the High Court said that a purposive approach to statutory interpretation, which it accepted as being generally appropriate, is particularly important when the court is seeking a construction which is consistent with a Community obligation. More particularly, in these circumstances, reference to Ministerial statements in *Hansard* is permissible in order to identify the purpose of a statute, even though the criteria specified in *Pepper v Hart* may not be satisfied.

By way of comment on the desirability of the rule in *Pepper v Hart*, it must be conceded that the traditional argument based on the Bill of Rights is unconvincing, but this still leaves the other constitutional arguments, as well as the practical ones. More particularly, the decision seems to be taking the legal system down a road which leads to government according to the intentions of the executive as understood by the executive, rather than government according to the enactments of the legislature as interpreted by the courts. As such, it is a significant step away from constitutional orthodoxy, and towards what may be termed, in Lord Hailsham's memorable phrase, 'elective dictatorship'. However, this objection could be met by adopting the view expressed by Lord Hope in *R v A (No 2)* [2001] 2 WLR 1546 (acknowledging his debt to Lord Steyn's article *Pepper v Hart: A Re-examination* (2001) 21 OJLS 59), that

> 'strictly speaking ... [*Hansard*] is available only for the purpose of preventing the Executive from placing a different meaning on words used in legislation from that which they attributed to those words when promoting the legislation in Parliament.'

This way of looking at the matter, which has led Bennion to coin the term *executive estoppel* (see *Pepper v Hart and Executive Estoppel* (2006) 170 JPN 167), provides a useful insight. However, if this approach is followed through, it would be at least arguable that one consequence would be to make *Pepper v Hart* relevant to the intepretation of any given statute only while the government which was responsible for the enactment of that statute is still in office.

Finally, at a purely practical level, *Practice Note* [1995] 1 All ER 234 requires parties who intend to introduce *Hansard* into argument, whether in reliance on *Pickstone v Freemans plc* or *Pepper v Hart*, to provide the court and the other parties with advance notice, in the form of copies of the extracts on which they propose to rely, together with a summary of the arguments they propose to raise.

*Post-Parliamentary materials*

It is commonplace to find that government departments who bear responsibility for administering, or supervising the administration of, particular areas of law will issue guidance to their own officials and to the public.

At one time it was held that such guidance could not even be cited in argument, on the basis that a judge who knows what the official view is will find it practically impossible to come to a conclusion uncoloured by that view. (See *London County Council v Central Land Board* [1958] 3 All ER 676.) However, the modern practice is for such guidance to be citable, and to be given whatever weight the court thinks it deserves. For example, in *R v West Dorset District Council ex parte Poupard* (1987) 19 HLR 254 (and, on appeal, (1988) 20 HLR 295), which is discussed at page 5 in the context of inarticulate major premises, Balcombe LJ referred to a *Guidance Manual* issued by the relevant government department, without giving any indication that he was aware of any reason why he should not do so. Nevertheless, the unofficial nature of such guidance must always be borne in mind. In *R v Wandsworth London Borough Council ex parte Beckwith* [1996] 1 All ER 129, Lord Hoffmann, giving the judgment of the House of Lords and having referred to a statement contained in a Local Authority Circular which purported to explain the statutory duty of local authorities to provide residential care for the elderly, said that 'the opinion of the Department is entitled to respect, particularly since I assume that the Act was drafted upon its instructions. But in my view this statement is simply wrong'.

## 20.6 Presumptions

### 20.6.1 Introduction

The courts have regard to a number of principles which they call *presumptions*. Although there is no universally accepted list of these principles, nor of the way in which each one should be formulated, there is a large measure of agreement as to most of them, and the major ones can be dealt with relatively easily. As a preliminary, though, it is important to note that all the presumptions will always give way to a clear contrary intention, and also that they can conflict not only with each other but also with the other principles of interpretation. Such conflicts clearly give the courts considerable leeway in interpretation.

### 20.6.2 Presumption against injustice

The presumption against injustice is the most basic presumption and all the others can be regarded as sub-formulations of it. It may be illustrated by *Coltman v Bibby Tankers Ltd* [1987] 3 All ER 1068. Section 1(3) of the Employer's Liability (Defective Equipment) Act 1969 provides that, for the purposes of that Act, 'equipment' 'includes any plant and machinery, vehicles, aircraft and clothing'. In the High Court, Sheen J held that a worker injured in a ship had a remedy under the Act even though ships are not mentioned in the definition, because it would be unjust to differentiate between accidents in, say, aircraft and ships. A majority of the Court of Appeal reversed the decision, but the original decision was unanimously reinstated by the House of Lords, where Lord Oliver said:

> 'The purpose of the Act was manifestly to saddle the employer with liability for defective plant of every sort with which the employee is compelled to work in the course of his employment, and I can see no ground for excluding particular types of chattel merely on the ground of their size or the element on which they are designed to operate.'

### 20.6.3 Presumption against absurdity

The presumption against absurdity may be illustrated by *Jones v Conway & Colwyn Bay Joint Water Supply Board* [1893] 2 Ch 603, which concerned the statutory right of a company which was supplying water to lay mains through other people's land. The court held that this right could be exercised before the water was supplied, because it would be absurd to say that water had to be supplied before the necessary mains had been laid.

### 20.6.4 Presumption against retrospectivity

Although the doctrine of binding precedent operates retrospectively (see page 133) there is a strong presumption that statutes are not retrospective.

At one time the courts drew a distinction between matters of procedure and matters of substance, with the presumption against retrospectivity applying only to the latter. However, this changed with the decision of the Privy Council in *Yew Bon Tew v Kenderaan Bas Mara* [1982] 3 All ER 833, where the facts involved the limitation period in respect of a personal injuries claim. (Limitation periods are regarded as being procedural, not substantive, because they only affect the exercise of the right to bring proceedings, and not the existence of the right in the first place.) Under a law enacted in 1948, the limitation period was 12 months. An accident happened in April 1972, and therefore the limitation period expired in April 1973. However, in June 1974 the 1948 law was amended so that the limitation period became three years. In the instant case, proceedings were begun in March 1975, so the action was clearly statute-barred if the original limitation period applied, but not if the new one did. The procedural nature of the provision did not prevent the Privy Council from holding that the action was statute-barred, on the basis that the purpose of the amendment was to extend limitation periods which had not yet expired, and to extend those which would arise in the future. Putting it the other way round, the purpose of the provision was not to deprive potential defendants of defences which they already had, because to do so would be unfair.

For many years, the decision in *Re A Solicitor's Clerk* [1957] 3 All ER 617 was commonly cited as a classic example of the way in which the presumption against retrospectivity operates. Under the Solicitors Act 1941, the Law Society could prohibit solicitors from employing clerks who had been convicted of theft of property belonging either to their employer or to their employer's clients. The Solicitors (Amendment) Act 1956 changed this so that the ownership of the property became irrelevant. In 1953 a clerk was convicted of theft in respect of property which belonged neither to his employer nor to his employer's clients, and therefore at that stage his employment could not be prohibited. In 1957 the Law Society prohibited the clerk's employment. The court held that this would not be giving retrospective effect to the 1956 Act because, although the prohibition referred to something done in the past, it did not affect what had been done in the past. Despite the court's argument, you may find it difficult to avoid feeling that the conclusion of the case really was retrospective.

However, in *Secretary of State for Social Services v Tunnicliffe* [1991] 2 All ER 712, it is clear that issues of alleged retrospectivity may need to be approached from the standpoint of specific individuals, rather than in more abstract terms. The facts were that the Secretary of State had power to recover welfare benefits which had been paid in error. Until 6 April 1987, the exercise of the power was subject to different tests according to whether the benefit in question was means-tested or not, with repayment of non-means-tested benefits being subject to a test of due care and diligence on the part of the claimant, and means-tested cases being subject to a test of misrepresentation and non-disclosure by the claimant. From that date the two systems were reconciled by making the test of misrepresentation and non-disclosure common to both types of benefit. The question arose as to which test should be applied after 6 April 1987 in respect of overpayments occurring before that date. The Court of Appeal held that the test which had become universal should be applied. From the point of view of the presumption against retrospectivity, the significance of the case lies in the judgment of Staughton LJ:

> 'A good illustration of the difficulty is afforded by *Re A Solicitor's Clerk* ... From the point of view of the clerk, that was in my view plainly retrospective legislation if he was caught by it: a new disability was imposed in respect of his sins in the past. So far as any employer was concerned, however, I would not say that the legislation was retrospective. It regulated whom he might employ in the future ... it will be apparent that I have doubts about the decision.
>
> 'In my judgment the true principle is that *Parliament is presumed not to have intended to alter the law applicable to past events and transactions in a manner which is unfair to those concerned in them, unless a contrary intention appears*. It is not simply a question of classifying an enactment as retrospective or not retrospective. Rather it may well be a matter of degree – the greater the unfairness, the more it is to be expected that Parliament will make it clear if that is intended ...
>
> 'On the whole I reach the conclusion that the retrospective aspect of [the new Act] is not *so* unfair to recipients of benefit, or some of them, as to require greater clarity than Parliament has used.' (Emphasis added.)

The House of Lords approved this approach in *L'Office Cherifien des Phosphates and Another v Yamashita-Shinnihon Steamship Co Ltd: The Boucraa* [1994] 1 All ER 20. More particularly, Lord Mustill, delivering the principal speech, said:

> 'Precisely how the single question of fairness will be answered in respect of a particular statute will depend on the interaction of several factors, each of them capable of varying from case to case. Thus, the degree to which the statute has retrospective effect is not a constant. Nor is the value of the rights which the statute affects, or the extent to which that value is diminished or extinguished by the retrospective effect of the statute. Again, the unfairness of adversely affecting the rights, and hence the degree of unlikelihood that this is what Parliament intended, will vary from case to case. So also will the clarity of the language used by Parliament, and the light shed on it by consideration of the circumstances in which the legislation was enacted. All these factors must be weighed together to provide a direct answer to the question whether the consequences of reading the statute with the suggested degree of retrospectivity is so unfair that the words used by Parliament cannot have been intended to mean what they might appear to say.'

The Court of Appeal's decision in *Antonelli v Secretary of State for Trade and Industry* [1998] 1 All ER 997, provides a useful example of a situation in which the possibility of substantial individual hardship was held to be justified in the public interest. More particularly, the issue was whether the Director General of Fair Trading's statutory power to ban people with certain types of convictions from carrying on estate agency work could be exercised in respect of convictions imposed before the statute which conferred the power had been passed. Holding that it could be so exercised, the court said that, having regard to the purpose of the Act, it would be 'quixotic' to suppose that Parliament intended that the public should be protected against an estate agent who was convicted a week after the Act came into effect but not from one who was convicted a week before it did so. The court accepted that severe hardship could arise from the exercise of the power to ban on the ground of a past conviction, but pointed out that the Act merely made conviction a precondition of the exercise of the banning power, with the Director General of Fair Trading then having to decide whether, in all the circumstances, the conviction rendered an individual unfit to carry on estate agency work.

The presumption against retrospectivity may have startling consequences, as illustrated by the case of *Re Barretto* [1994] 1 All ER 447. The Drug Trafficking Offences Act 1986 gave the court power to make a confiscation order in respect of the proceeds of drug trafficking, and in January 1990 such an order was made against Barretto, who was also sentenced to 20 years' imprisonment. The court found that Barretto had benefited to the extent of approximately £600,000 from drug trafficking, but that only about £287,000 was realizable, and therefore the order was made in the latter figure, with three years' imprisonment in default of payment. In 1991 the Criminal Justice (International Co-operation) Act 1990 came into effect. One purpose of the Act was to allow the amount specified in confiscation orders to be increased where additional assets subsequently came to light. In the present case, substantial subsequent assets did come to light after the 1990 Act had come into force, and therefore the question arose as to whether the sum specified in the original order could be increased. The Court of Appeal held that the application of the presumption against retrospectivity meant that no increase was possible. Sir Thomas Bingham MR acknowledged that:

'Many would think that on the present facts there would be nothing unfair in stripping Mr Barretto of the fruits of his criminal activity which he did not disclose in January 1990 even if this means relying on a law enacted later. But the court is here concerned with fairness in a more particular sense. A defendant is not to be substantially prejudiced by laws construed as having retroactive effect unless Parliament's intention that they should have that effect is plain. The blackest malefactor is as much entitled to the benefit of that presumption as anyone else. Parliament has not displaced the presumption in this case and it would not be fair to treat it as having done so however strong one's disapproval of Mr Barretto's conduct.'

One crucial consideration was that the 1986 Act was expressly retrospective, and it would have been easy for the 1990 Act to have been expressed in similar terms if retrospectivity had been intended. (It is worth noticing that the result of this case would have been different if the court had given primacy to the presumption against gaining advantage from wrongdoing, which is discussed at page 322.)

**20.6.5** Presumption of strict interpretation of penal provisions

*Introduction*

A convenient statement of the presumption that penal provisions should be construed strictly in favour of the person who is liable to be penalized is contained in the judgment of Brett J in *Dickenson v Fletcher* (1873) LR 9 CP 1:

> 'Those who contend that a penalty may be inflicted must show that the words of the Act distinctly enact that it shall be incurred under the present circumstances. They must fail if the words are merely equally capable of a construction that would, and one that would not, inflict the penalty.'

Of course, the presumption that penal provisions shall be interpreted strictly is nothing more than a presumption; and, as such, it will not necessarily determine the outcome of every case where there are two credible interpretations of a penal provision with varying degrees of strictness. For example, in *R v James* [2006] EWCA Crim 14, [2006] 1 All ER 759, the Court of Appeal was faced with a 3:2 decision of the House of Lords in *R v Smith (Morgan)* [2004] 4 All ER 289, giving an interpretation of s. 3 of the Homicide Act 1957 which favoured the defendant, and a 6:3 decision of the Privy Council in *Attorney-General for Jersey v Holley* [2005] UKPC 23, [2005] 3 All ER 371, giving an interpretation which was adverse to him. Despite the fact that the presumption of strict interpretation of penal statutes, and the conventional requirements of the doctrine of binding precedent, both indicated a decision in favour of the defendant, as we saw at page 170 in the context of the weight to be given to Privy Council decisions, the Court of Appeal adopted the interpretation which was adverse to the defendant.

A common source of difficulty arising from this principle is the presumption that *mens rea* is a necessary ingredient of statutory offences.

*The presumption that mens rea is a necessary ingredient of statutory offences*

The common law requires two elements to be present before a defendant may be convicted of a crime, namely an *actus reus* and a *mens rea*. The *actus reus* is the guilty act, and the *mens rea* is the guilty mind or intention. Many statutes also require both elements to be essential preconditions to the imposition of criminal liability. For example, the offence of theft under the Theft Acts 1968–78 requires both the appropriation of property belonging to someone else (the *actus reus*) and the dishonest intention that that person should be permanently deprived of the property (the *mens rea*). However, a problem arises where a statute which creates an offence is silent as to the need for *mens rea*. Is the silence to be explained on the ground that liability is to be strict and no *mens rea* is necessary? Or is it to be explained on the ground that the requirement of *mens rea* is so basic that Parliament was confident that the courts would imply the need for it to be proved, without any express provision being necessary?

The short answer is that the courts will normally presume that Parliament expected *mens rea* to be a precondition of guilt, and accordingly they will refuse to convict in its absence. However, it is important to remember that this is only a presumption, and the possibility of rebuttal must always be borne in mind.

Before examining the operation of the presumption more closely, we must distinguish the concept of *mens rea* from the principle that ignorance of the law is no excuse. The distinction may be illustrated by returning to the Theft Acts 1968–78. If I appropriate property belonging to you, I commit the *actus reus*, but if I genuinely believe that the property is mine (and therefore that I am entitled to take it) I will not be acting dishonestly, so there will be no *mens rea*, and I am not guilty. On the other hand, if I appropriate your property, being dishonest and intending to deprive you of it permanently, I am guilty even if I know nothing of the criminal law and do not know that what I am doing is an offence.

Returning to the topic of strict liability, the classic starting point is *Sherras v de Rutzen* [1895] 1 QB 918, where Wright J said:

'There is a presumption that *mens rea*, or evil intention, or knowledge of the wrongfulness of the act, is an essential ingredient in every offence; but that presumption is liable to be displaced either by the words of the statute creating the offence or by the subject-matter with which it deals, and both must be considered.'

In *Sweet v Parsley* [1969] 1 All ER 347, Lord Diplock said 'it is contrary to a rational and civilized criminal code ... to penalize one who has performed his duty as a citizen to ascertain what acts are prohibited by law ... and has taken all proper care to inform himself of any facts which would make his conduct unlawful'. Even more succinctly, in *Lim Chin Aik v R* [1963] 1 All ER 223, the Privy Council said: 'It cannot be inferred that the legislature imposed strict liability merely in order to find a luckless victim'.

However, it must be remembered that, in common with all the other presumptions of statutory interpretation, the presumption that *mens rea* is a necessary ingredient of statutory offences may be rebutted. It is useful to approach the topic of rebuttal by applying the two-fold classification which we have already encountered (in *Sherras v de Rutzen*) to the effect that rebuttal may arise from either the words or the subject-matter of the statute, although it will be necessary to add a gloss to the first of these two possibilities.

Although express words showing that no *mens rea* is necessary will genuinely rebut the presumption, it is much more common in practice to find the enactment of a specific formula expressing what the *mens rea* is to be. In these cases, it is more accurate to say that the presumption has become redundant, rather than that it has been rebutted. The example of the Theft Acts illustrates a specific formula, namely 'dishonestly ... with the intention of permanently depriving'. Innumerable other provisions indicate the need for *mens rea* by incorporating words such as 'knowingly', 'intentionally' and 'wilfully'. Unfortunately, however, although words such as these clearly indicate the need for *mens rea*, they do not always make clear precisely what the prosecution must prove, with the word 'wilfully' often causing particular difficulty.

In *Arrowsmith v Jenkins* [1963] 2 QB 561, a campaigner for nuclear disarmament found a crowd had assembled round her while she held a public meeting on the highway. The crowd obstructed the highway. Upholding her conviction for *wilfully* obstructing the highway without lawful authority or excuse, Lord Parker CJ said:

'If a person, without lawful authority or excuse, intentionally as opposed to accidentally, that is, by an exercise of his or her free will, does something or omits to do something which will cause an obstruction or the continuance of an obstruction, he or she is guilty of an offence.'

In other words, once the defendant had wilfully done the act of holding the meeting, her liability for the ensuing obstruction was strict.

Similarly, in *Cotterill v Penn* [1936] 1 KB 53, a defendant was convicted of wilfully killing a house pigeon even though he believed that the bird which he shot was a wild pigeon. His act of shooting was wilful: therefore he was guilty.

This difficulty encountered in these cases could easily be avoided if the courts were to give full weight to Lord Diplock's opinion that, in order to give the word 'wilfully' any effect beyond excluding mere accidents, it ought to be understood as implying a requirement of proof of knowledge of something beyond the mere doing of the act itself. (*R v Sheppard* [1980] 3 All ER 899.)

Turning to the second basis for displacing the presumption, namely the subject matter of the offence, the leading case is *Gammon (Hong Kong)*

*Ltd v Attorney-General for Hong Kong* [1984] 2 All ER 503. The issue was whether it was an offence of strict liability to contravene the Hong Kong equivalent of the English Building Regulations, which prescribe standards aimed at ensuring the quality and safety of buildings. Holding that contravention was an offence of strict liability, the Privy Council said:

'(1) There is a presumption of law that *mens rea* is required before a person can be guilty of a criminal offence; (2) the presumption is particularly strong where the offence is "truly criminal" in character; (3) the presumption applies to statutory offences, and can be displaced only if this is clearly or by necessary implication the effect of the statute; (4) the only situation in which the presumption can be displaced is where the statute is concerned with an issue of social concern, and public safety is such an issue; (5) even where a statute is concerned with such an issue, the presumption of *mens rea* stands unless it can also be shown that the creation of strict liability will be effective to promote the objects of the statute by encouraging greater vigilance to prevent the commission of the prohibited act.'

The reference in *Gammon* to offences which are 'truly criminal' in character is intended to distinguish between offences involving turpitude, conviction in respect of which therefore involves some moral stigma, and offences which are sometimes referred to as being merely 'regulatory'. Regulatory offences are said to be those where a statutory prohibition is imposed in the public interest, and is enforced by means of a penalty imposed on conviction. (The Trade Descriptions Act 1968 was regarded as being within this category in *Wings Ltd v Ellis* [1984] 3 All ER 577, where the House of Lords was concerned with an inaccurate holiday brochure.) In practice, however, this distinction is seldom very satisfactory, because enforcement by means of a penalty imposed on conviction is usually a sign that the prohibition involves a matter of social concern. It can be argued, therefore, that contraventions of such prohibitions must involve turpitude, and that as a result they can properly be stigmatized as being genuinely criminal.

Nevertheless, it is clear that the courts are influenced by their perception of the seriousness of the conduct which constitutes the *actus reus*, even though the degree of seriousness may not always be immediately apparent to the untutored eye. For example, in *R v St Margaret's Trust Ltd* [1958] 2 All ER 289, the defendant finance company unknowingly contravened a Hire Purchase Order which required substantial minimum deposits where goods were bought on hire purchase. Holding the offence to be one of strict liability, Donovan J said:

'The object of the order was to help to defend the currency against the peril of inflation which, if unchecked, would bring disaster on the country. There is no need to elaborate this. The present generation has witnessed the collapse of the currency in other countries and the consequent chaos, misery and widespread ruin. It would not be at all surprising if Parliament, determined to prevent similar calamities here, enacted measures which it intended to be absolute prohibitions of acts which might increase the risk in however small a degree. Indeed, that would be the natural expectation. There would be little point in enacting that no one should breach the defences against a flood, and at the same time excusing anyone who did it innocently.'

Strict liability was also held to exist in *R v Wells Street Magistrate ex parte Westminster City Council* [1986] 3 All ER 4. Section 55 of the Town and Country Planning Act 1971 created an offence of doing certain works to buildings which were listed as being of special architectural or historic interest. The court held that the defendant could be convicted even without knowing that the building was listed, because protection of the national heritage is a serious matter. On the other hand, in *Sweet v Parsley* the House of Lords held that the owner of a house could not be convicted of being concerned in the management of premises used for drug-taking when she did not know that her tenants were taking drugs. In other words, her lack of *mens rea* was vital.

However, by way of further contrast, it is useful to consider the House of Lords' decision in *Pharmaceutical Society of Great Britain v Storkwain Ltd* [1986] 2 All ER 635. Under s. 58(2) of the Medicines Act 1968 it was an offence to dispense certain drugs on a forged prescription. The House held that a pharmacist committed the offence even without knowing, and without reason to believe, that the prescription was forged. Lord Goff, with whom the other four Law Lords agreed, laid heavy emphasis on the fact that various other provisions of the Act created offences which expressly required *mens rea*, and therefore it was reasonable to suppose that the absence of any requirement of *mens rea* from s. 58(2) was intentional. The logical force of this is clear, and thus it is probably safe to assume that *Storkwain* has overruled that part of *Sweet v Parsley* in which Lord Reid said: 'It is ... firmly established that the fact that other sections of the Act expressly require *mens rea* ... is not in itself sufficient to justify a decision that a section which is silent as to *mens rea* creates an absolute offence'. Furthermore, Lord Reid's use of the expression 'absolute offence' must be treated with caution. The topic under discussion is *strict* liability, not *absolute* liability. The distinction is important because in all the cases we have considered the defendant intended to do something – such as shooting a pigeon, undertaking building works, lending money on hire purchase, allowing a tenant to occupy premises, or dispensing drugs – even though in each case the intention was accompanied by a degree of ignorance as to at least some element of the surrounding circumstances.

The need to balance a number of conflicting contentions when deciding whether an offence is one of strict liability may be illustrated by *B (A Minor) v Director of Public Prosecutions* [2000] 1 All ER 833. The issue was whether the offence of inciting a child under the age of 14 to commit an act of gross indecency, contrary to s. 1 of the Indecency with Children Act 1960, had been committed where the defendant honestly but mistakenly believed the child to be over the age of 14. The House of Lords accepted that the purpose of the provision was the protection of young girls from sexual abuse, which Lord Steyn acknowledged was 'unquestionably a great social evil'. On the other side of the argument, however, the House accepted that the provision penalized a very wide range of conduct, including, again in the words of Lord Steyn, 'any sexual overtures between teenagers if one of them is under 14', and that conviction would seriously stigmatize the defendant. Furthermore, the draft Criminal Code Bill, prepared by the Law Commission in 1989, had provided that a mistaken belief as to the age of the victim could be a defence in relation to certain sexual offences, and therefore there was no general consensus that imposing strict liability was necessary in order to protect children in sexual matters.

Overall, having regard to these and other considerations, the House concluded that the balance of competing arguments justified the conclusion that the absence of an honest belief as to the victim's age was an essential element of the offence. In other words, the presumption that *mens rea* is an essential element in statutory offences had not been rebutted, and therefore it was for the prosecution to prove that the defendant did not honestly believe that the victim was over 14.

The House of Lords returned to the presumption of *mens rea* in *R v K* [2001] 3 All ER 897 in the context of the offence of indecent assault on a girl under the age of 16, contrary to s. 14 of the Sexual Offences Act 1955. The decision was to the same effect as that in the previous case, but on this occasion the House emphasized that the honest and mistaken belief need not be reasonable, while acknowledging that the more unreasonable a belief is, the easier it will be to disprove that the defendant honestly held it.

Finally, the courts may be less ready to find strict liability in cases where members of the general public are liable to be convicted than in cases where it is only members of some defined, and self-selected, group who are at risk. As Lord Diplock said in *Sweet v Parsley*:

> 'Where penal provisions are of general application to the conduct of ordinary citizens in the course of their everyday life, the presumption is that the standard of care required of them in informing themselves of facts which would make their conduct unlawful is that of the familiar common law duty of care.

But where the subject-matter of a statute is the regulation of a particular activity involving potential danger to public health, safety or morals, in which citizens have a choice whether they participate or not, the court may feel driven to infer an intention of Parliament to impose, by penal actions, a higher duty of care on those who choose to participate and to place on them an obligation to take whatever measures may be necessary to prevent the prohibited act, without regard to those considerations of cost or business practicability which play a part in the determination of what would be required of them in order to fulfil the ordinary common law duty of care. But such an inference is not lightly to be drawn, nor is there any room for it unless there is something that the person on whom the obligation is imposed can do directly or indirectly, by supervision or inspection, by improvement of his business methods or by exhorting those whom he may be expected to influence or control, which will promote the observance of the obligation.'

### 20.6.6    Presumptions relating to 'and' and 'or'

Recurrent problems in statutory interpretation arise from the use of 'and' and 'or'.

The normal usage of 'and' is *con*junctive, so that it joins two things in such a way that they become one. According to this usage, therefore, a provision which makes it an offence to do *A and B* will not be committed by a defendant who does only *A* or only *B*. Similarly, the normal usage of 'or' is *dis*junctive, so that it separates two things in such a way that they become alternatives. According to this usage, therefore, a provision which makes it an offence to do *A or B* will be committed by a defendant who does only *A* or only *B*.

However, there is ample authority to show that both the conjunctive and disjunctive meanings are only presumptions, which may be rebutted where the context so requires. One example of each situation will suffice.

Taking first a case in which 'and' was held to have been used *dis*junctively, in *R v Oakes* [1959] 2 All ER 92, the court was faced with s. 7 of the Official Secrets Act 1920, which provided that 'any person who attempts to commit any offence under [the Official Secrets Act 1911] or this Act, or solicits or incites or endeavours to persuade another person to commit an offence, or aids or abets *and* does any act preparatory to the commission of an offence under [the 1911 Act] or this Act ...' was guilty of an offence. (Emphasis added.) The appellant, who had been convicted of an offence solely on the basis that he had done an act preparatory to the commission of an offence under the 1911 Act, argued he should have been acquitted because he had not also done one of things listed before the 'and'. Dismissing the appeal, Lord Parker CJ treated the 'and' as being disjunctive, even though it came after a string of 'or's which were clearly disjunctive, since any other meaning would be 'unintelligible'.

Turning to the 'or' problem, in *Fowler v Padget* (1798) 101 ER 1103, the court had to interpret the provision of the Bankrupts Act 1601 under which a trader committed an act of bankruptcy if he left his dwelling-house 'to the intent, *or* whereby his creditors ... shall or may be defeated or delayed'. (Emphasis added.) The problem was that if the first 'or' was read *dis*junctively, a perfectly solvent trader who went out of his house, entirely legitimately and without giving any thought whatsoever to his creditors, would commit an act of bankruptcy if, during his absence, a creditor called to collect payment of a debt, because the trader's absence would mean that payment to the creditor was delayed. However, as Lord Kenyon CJ put it, 'by reading the word "and" for "or" ... which is frequently done in the construction of legal instruments *where the sense requires it,* all difficulty will be removed'. (Emphasis added.) In other words, there would be an act of bankruptcy only if the trader was absent with the intention of defeating or delaying his creditors.

### 20.6.7    Presumptions relating to consolidating and codifying statutes

Before looking at the presumptions relating to consolidating and codifying statutes, it is necessary to distinguish *consolidation* from *codification.*

*Consolidation* is the process whereby all the existing statute law on a particular subject is brought together into one Act, or into a small group of Acts. It is a technical matter, designed to make the law more accessible, and is generally not intended to change the law, although, as we saw at page 250, some minor changes are permitted.

*Codification* must be approached with a little more caution, because the term has two distinct usages. In English Law (as opposed to the civil law systems of mainland Europe) the term 'code' is used to mean a statute, or a small group of statutes, containing all the law (and not merely all the statute law) on a particular subject. This is quite distinct from the concept of codification in civil law jurisdictions, where a code is a basic but comprehensive statement of basic principles of law embodied in the legal system. Of course, we are concerned with the English usage.

While codifying statutes will, in common with consolidating ones, improve the accessibility of the law, they will also introduce changes. This distinction underlies the difference in approach to the interpretation of the two types of statute. In *Beswick v Beswick* (see page 301) Lord

Reid pointed out that those who are responsible for presenting a consolidation Bill to Parliament must certify that it contains no substantial changes in the law, and thereafter a Committee checks the Bill to see that this is so. It follows from this that the courts are entitled to presume that a consolidating Act does not change the law. It also follows that previously decided cases can be good authority in relation to the meaning of a subsequent consolidation Act, although in *Farrell v Alexander* [1976] 2 All ER 721, Lord Wilberforce, Lord Simon and Lord Edmund-Davies all said that, if the meaning of a consolidation Act was clear, there was no need to refer to decisions on the previous statutes. In passing, it is also interesting to note that neither Lord Wilberforce nor Lord Simon was particularly attracted to the idea that, when Parliament re-enacted a form of words which had previously been interpreted by the courts, it necessarily followed that Parliament was endorsing the correctness of the courts' interpretation.

In *Bank of England v Vagliano Brothers* [1891] AC 107, Lord Herschell LC, speaking of a codifying statute, said:

> 'I think the proper course is, in the first instance, to examine the language of the statute, and to ask what is its natural meaning, uninfluenced by any considerations derived from the previous state of the law, and *not* to start with enquiring how the law previously stood, and then, assuming that it is intended to leave it unaltered, to see if the words of the enactment will bear an interpretation in conformity with this view. If ... treated in this fashion it appears to me that its utility will be almost entirely destroyed and the very object with which it was enacted will be frustrated. *The purpose of such a statute surely was that on any point specifically dealt with by it, the law should be ascertained by interpreting the language used, instead of, as before, by roaming over a vast number of authorities.*' (Emphasis added.)

(When reading this quotation, it is important to realize that the italicized *not* governs the whole of the remainder of the first sentence.)

**20.6.8    Presumption of compliance with international law**

The case of *Fothergill v Monarch Airlines Ltd* [1980] 2 All ER 696 is authority for the proposition that Parliament will be presumed to have intended to comply with international law. In many cases this presumption will involve the use of international agreements as aids to statutory interpretation.

*Ellerman Lines Ltd v Murray* [1930] All ER Rep 503 clearly established that a relevant international Convention could be used in order to resolve an ambiguity, even though on the instant facts the House of Lords concluded that the meaning of the enacted words was plain beyond doubt. More recently, however, it has become clear that recourse may be had to treaties as an aid to interpretation without first having to identify an ambiguity. As Lord Denning MR said, in *Salomon v Commissioners of Customs and Excise* [1966] 3 All ER 871: 'I think we are entitled to look at [a Convention], because it is an instrument which is binding in international law; and we ought to interpret our statutes so as to be in conformity with international law'.

It is immaterial whether the Act specifically refers to the Convention in question, and of course the court may have to read a text in some language other than English. Lord Wilberforce stated the correct approach in *Fothergill*:

'My Lords, as in *Buchanan (James) & Co Ltd v Babco Forwarding and Shipping (UK) Ltd* [1977] 3 All ER 1048, I am not willing to lay down any precise rule ... The process of ascertaining the meaning must vary according to the subject-matter. If a judge has some knowledge of the relevant language, there is no reason why he should not use it; this is particularly true of the French or Latin languages, so long languages of our courts. There is no reason why he should not consult a dictionary, if the word is such that a dictionary can reveal its significance; often, of course, it may substitute one doubt for another ... In all cases he will have in mind that ours is an adversary system: it is for the parties to make good their contentions. So he will inform them of the process he is using, and, if they think fit, they can supplement his resources with other materials, other dictionaries, other books of reference, textbooks and decided cases. They may call evidence of an interpreter, if the language is one unknown to the court, or an expert if the word or expression is such as to require expert interpretation. Between a technical expression in Japanese and a plain word in French there must be a whole spectrum which calls for suitable and individual treatment.'

*Fothergill* is also authority for the proposition that, in interpreting an international agreement, it is legitimate to consult preliminary documentation, or *travaux préparatoires*, provided: 'First that the material involved is public and accessible, and secondly, that the *travaux préparatoires* clearly and indisputably point to a definite legislative intention.' (Lord Wilberforce.)

There will, of course, be no need to rely on the presumption in relation to Convention rights under the Human Rights Act 1998 (see Chapter 6).

**20.6.9** Presumption of compliance with Community law

In the words of Lord Diplock, when considering the need to avoid conflicts between English law and Community law:

'It is a principle of construction of United Kingdom statutes ... that the words of a statute passed after the Treaty has been signed and dealing with the subject matter of the international obligations of the United Kingdom, are to be construed, if they are reasonably capable of bearing such a meaning, as intended to carry out the obligation, and not to be inconsistent with it.' (*Garland v British Rail Engineering Ltd* [1982] 2 All ER 402.)

Subsequently, as we also saw, the *von Colson principle*, as clarified in *Marleasing SA v La Comercial Internacional de Alimentacion SA* [1992] 1 CMLR 305, requires national courts to interpret national law in such a way as to accord with Community law whenever possible. In this connection it is also useful to emphasize that, as we saw at page 229, the Community is formally committed to the legal protection of fundamental rights.

Sometimes, of course, there will be no need to invoke this presumption, because there is no conflict, or apparent conflict, between English law and Community law. Indeed, the two relevant provisions of both systems may be identical, as will happen where the English drafter has used the 'copy-out' method of transposing a Directive into English law. (Copy-out is exactly what it says: the drafter may simply copy out the relevant provisions of the Directive and incorporate them into a piece of English legislation.) Although copy-out is an obvious way of avoiding conflict, its use is not always appropriate. For example, the Directive may say nothing at all about the means to be adopted in achieving its objective, in which case copy-out will obviously produce a defective result. In other cases, there may already be English provisions governing the subject-matter covered by the Directive, in which case the least disruptive amendment may be achieved by conventional drafting, rather than by copy-out. However, even where the Directive is self-contained and there is no pre-existing English law, it does not follow that copy out will always be appropriate, because the Directive may deal with concepts and use terminology which require redefinition or translation in order to produce a result which fits into English law.

---

**20.6.10**     Presumption against gaining advantage from wrongdoing

*Re Sigsworth* [1934] All ER Rep 113 provides a classic example of the common sense presumption that people should not be allowed to profit from their own wrongdoing. Section 46 of the Administration of Estates Act 1925 provides that on an intestacy, the deceased's property 'shall be distributed' in accordance with the section. The court held that, where a son had murdered his mother, s. 46 did not apply, because otherwise he would inherit her property and therefore profit from his own wrongdoing.

In cases such as *Re Sigsworth* the presumption against gaining advantage from wrongdoing is particularly strong, and indeed the Forfeiture

Act 1982 refers to 'the forfeiture rule', which it defines as 'the rule of public policy which in certain circumstances precludes a person who has unlawfully killed another from acquiring a benefit in consequence of the killing'. A rule of public policy is clearly rather more than a mere presumption of interpretation. Nevertheless, the Act gives the court power to modify the effect of the rule where 'the justice of the case' so requires, and gives a Social Security Commissioner a corresponding power in respect of social security benefits. Curiously, the court's power does not apply to cases of murder, but there is no such restriction on the power of a Social Security Commissioner.

*Re Sigsworth* involved the court looking backward to the actual conduct of an individual, and preventing financial gain on the part of the wrongdoer. It is apparent, however, that neither of these elements is essential. The court may also look forward, on the basis of an intelligent estimation of likely future conduct, and apply the presumption in order to frustrate the illicit attainment of some non-financial goal which is nevertheless subjectively valuable.

Under s. 51(1) of the Adoption Act 1976, the Registrar-General is under a duty to give applicants who have been adopted certain information which will enable them to obtain certified copies of their birth certificates, which will in turn, of course, enable them to identify their natural mothers. This duty is stated to be subject to the satisfaction of certain conditions specified in the Act but otherwise it is couched in absolute terms. In *R v Registrar-General ex parte Smith* [1991] 2 All ER 88, Smith had been adopted while he was still a baby. While serving life imprisonment for murder, he killed another prisoner, saying that he believed his victim to be his adoptive mother. He was convicted of manslaughter and sent to a secure mental hospital. He then applied to the Registrar-General under s. 51(1) of the 1976 Act. The Registrar-General took medical advice and refused to issue the information, fearing that Smith would do harm to his natural mother.

The Court of Appeal held as a rule of public policy that, even when Parliament has enacted statutory duties in apparently absolute terms, there is a presumption that there was no intention either to enable people to benefit from serious crimes committed in the past, or to assist them to commit serious crime in the future.

**20.6.11**  Presumption against binding the Crown

The practical significance of the presumption that statutes do not bind the Crown lies in the fact that for the present purposes 'the Crown' includes all the departments of central government. (*Town Investments*

*Ltd v Department of the Environment* [1977] 1 All ER 813.) The presumption can be rebutted either by clear words to that effect, or by necessary implication.

Where there is a statutory provision to the effect that the Crown is bound, it will usually be found towards the end of the statute, along with provisions containing the short title, and dealing with the commencement and the territorial extent. The case of *Bombay Province v Bombay Municipal Corporation* [1947] AC 58 shows that the doctrine of necessary implication will be applied strictly, and it must be shown that the purpose of the statute would be wholly frustrated if the Crown were not bound. Thus, for example, in *Cooper v Hawkins* [1904] 2 KB 164, it was held that the driver of a Crown vehicle was not bound by a statutory speed limit. (Subsequent Road Traffic Acts have expressly bound the Crown.)

In *Lord Advocate v Dumbarton District Council and Another* [1990] 1 All ER 1, the House of Lords surveyed the authorities dealing with this presumption and categorically reaffirmed the existing doctrine. The Ministry of Defence coned off part of a road to facilitate work on the perimeter fence of a defence installation. A private operator doing this would have needed the consent of the roads authority and the local planning authority, but the Ministry took the view that it did not require these consents. When the authorities took enforcement action, the Ministry applied for judicial review, conceding that it had no right to do what it had done, but nevertheless arguing that it was not bound by the statutes. The issue was stated by Lord Emslie in the First Division (i.e. a Scottish Court):

> 'It is not suggested that the Crown has any right whatever to occupy and erect structures and obstructions upon ... the public road. It is not contended, accordingly, that the application to the Crown of the provisions ... would encroach in any prejudicial way upon the Crown's rights, interests or privileges. The question to be answered is whether upon a proper construction of the statute it can be affirmed that the Crown meant to be bound by the particular provisions. In order to answer that question it is essential to determine whether there is ... a special rule of construction which applies to the construction of all statutory provisions when the issue of Crown immunity has to be resolved, or whether ... the special rule of construction only applies when the statutory provisions in question would bind the Crown to its prejudice.'

In the House of Lords, Lord Keith, giving the only substantial speech, said: 'It is preferable, in my view, to stick to the simple rule that the Crown is not bound by any statutory provision unless there can somehow be gathered from the terms of the relevant Act an intention to that effect'.

## 20.7 The Interpretative Obligation under s. 3, Human Rights Act 1998

Section 3(1) of the Human Rights Act 1998 provides that 'so far as it is possible to do so, primary and subordinate legislation must be read and given effect in a way which is compatible with the Convention Rights'. However, even statutory provisions dealing with interpretation must themselves be interpreted, so the question arises: *what does this provision mean*? It will be instructive to approach this question by considering a selection of early decisions, which mainly involve Convention rights under art. 6 (the right to a fair trial) and art. 8 (respect for private and family life, the home, and correspondence), although one of the selected cases also involves art. 14 (non-discrimination) in one case. (The full texts of all these articles are set out in Appendix 3.)

In *R v A (No 2)* [2001] 2 WLR 1546, the House of Lords held that, in order to protect a defendant's Convention right to a fair trial, s. 3(1) of the 1998 Act required the court to read in certain words which were not, in fact, present in s. 41 of the Youth Justice and Criminal Evidence Act 1999. More particularly, although the scheme of s. 41 was intended to protect complainants in rape cases from having their sexual histories put before the court (except in certain very limited circumstances), the House nevertheless held that a trial judge must retain an overriding discretion to admit such evidence where its exclusion would prejudice the fairness of the defendant's trial. In *Ghaidan v Mendoza* (which is discussed more fully below), Lord Millett, accepted the propriety of this exercise thus:

> 'The House supplied a missing qualification which significantly limited the operation of the statute but which did not contradict any of its fundamental features ... The qualification which it supplied glossed but did not contradict anything in the relevant statute ... If [the qualification] had been expressed it would not have made the statute self-contradictory or produced a nonsense.'

According to this approach, which seems, on a careful reading of all the cases, to reflect the received wisdom of the House of Lords generally, the key issue can, therefore, be simply stated: *how and where is the line between glossing and contradiction (or interpretation and legislation) to be drawn?*

In *Re S (Minors) (Care Orders: Implementation of Care Plan)* [2002] 2 All ER 192, the s. 3 issue was whether the court could read new procedural requirements into the Children Act 1989, in order to safeguard the Convention rights contained in art. 6 and art. 8. More particularly, the House reversed a decision of the Court of Appeal which would have effectively empowered the courts to supervise the way in which local authorities implemented care orders made under the Act. The House said that the Court of Appeal's decision was contrary to a fundamental principle of the Act to the effect that the courts should not become so involved; and that, therefore, the court had crossed the boundary between interpretation and legislation. (The crucial distinction between *Re A (No 2)* and *Re S* is that the House of Lords thought that applying a Convention-compliant interpretation in the former would not contradict a fundamental principle of the relevant legislation, while in *Re S* it would do so.)

In *R (Anderson) v Secretary of State for the Home Department* [2002] 4 All ER 1089, the House was concerned with s. 29 of the Crime (Sentences) Act 1997, which gave the Home Secretary power to fix the punitive element of a mandatory life sentence. A seven-member House of Lords, putting the case in the same category as *Re S*, held that although the section was incompatible with the art. 6 Convention right, the court had no power to read and give effect to it in such a way as to limit the exercise of the Home Secretary's power so that he or she could not exceed the period recommended by the trial judge and the Lord Chief Justice, because this would amount to amending, rather than merely interpreting, the Act. Accordingly, the House held that the most it could do was to make a declaration of incompatibility under s. 4 of the 1998 Act. (See page 104 for declarations of incompatibility.)

However, as we have seen throughout this Part of the book, the dividing line between legislating and interpreting is by no means always sufficiently clear-cut to be unequivocally identifiable. In *Ghaidan v Mendoza* [2004] UKHL 30, [2004] 3 All ER 411 (which is also discussed at page 281) the issue was whether a surviving homosexual partner could be the *spouse* of a deceased tenant, for the purposes of succeeding to a statutory tenancy under the Second Schedule to the Rent Act 1977. The majority of the House had little or no difficulty in using s. 3 to provide an affirmative answer to this question, and thus safeguard the survivor's Convention rights under art. 8 and art. 14. On the other hand, Lord Millett (who had no difficulty agreeing with the majority that to exclude the survivor from the definition of *spouse* would not only contravene his Convention rights but would also be unacceptable in modern society), nevertheless dissented as to the result. The basis of his dissent was simply that only people of opposite sexes could be each other's spouses; and that a court which held otherwise would be amending, rather than merely interpreting, the statute; and that this would, of course, fall outwith the scope of s. 3.

When a court reads words in to a statute in order to produce a Convention-compliant result, Lord Nicholls, in *Ghaidan v Mendoza*, said that 'the precise form of words read in for this purpose is of no significance. It is their substantive effect which matters'. Although at first sight this may seem to be a distinction without a difference, the essential point is that detailed amendment of precise statutory language requires equally precise language. This is fundamentally different from ascribing meaning to words, which is the essence of interpretation.

One type of situation in which the court will feel not feel able to identify and apply a Convention-compliant interpretation is illustrated by *Bellinger v Bellinger* [2003] UKHL 21, [2003] 2 All ER 593. The issue was whether a male and a male-to-female transsexual could validly marry each other. The problem was that under s. 11(c) of the Matrimonial Causes Act 1973, a marriage was void unless the parties were 'respectively male and female'. The House of Lords held that, despite the s. 3 obligation, it was not [ossible to interpret s. 11 (c) in such a way that it would comply with the Convention rights contained in art. 8 (respect for private and family life) and art. 14 (non-discrimination). More particularly, the House contented itself with a declaration of incompatibility, because any other decision would have ramifications in areas of law as varied as pensions, national insurance, inheritance and financial provision and access to children following divorce, to name but a few; and only comprehensive legislative intervention by Parliament could cope with such a wide range of matters. It would be totally impracticable to rely on piecemeal provision in a succession of judicial decisions spread over many years. (In passing, it may be noted that legislative action did follow quite swiftly, in the form of the Gender Recognition Act 2004.)

With the exception of cases such as *Bellinger*, it is difficult to formulate a clear principle as to the limits of the interpretative obligation under s. 3, but it appears to be the case that *no linguistic ambiguity is necessary* before it can be said to be *possible* to interpret a statutory provision in such a way as to make it compatible with Convention rights under the 1998 Act. All that is necessary is that it should be *constitutionally* possible to do so, in the sense that the court must remain on the right side of the dividing line between interpretation and legislation. The difficulty, as the disagreement between the majority and Lord Millett in *Ghaidan* so clearly illustrates, is to know where that line is to be drawn in each case.

## 20.8 Change of meaning with the passage of time

### 20.8.1 Introduction

The classical doctrine of statutory interpretation is that the meaning of an Act does not change with the passing of time. In the late 19th century case of *The Longford* (1889) 14 PD 34, an Act dating from the time of

William IV prohibited the bringing of any 'action' in 'his Majesty's courts of law' against certain shipowners, unless one month's notice had been given. The question was whether a particular kind of case, referred to technically as an Admiralty action *in rem*, was within the prohibition. In the Court of Appeal Lord Esher said:

> 'The first point to be borne in mind is that the Act must be construed as if one were interpreting it the day after it was passed ... the word "action" ... was not applicable when the Act was passed to the procedure of the Admiralty Court. Admiralty actions were then called "suits" or "causes"; moreover, the Admiralty Court was not called and was not one of His Majesty's courts of law.'

Simple and straightforward though this appears to be, the reality is rather more complicated, as can be seen from two groups of cases. The first deals with security of tenure legislation and the other deals with technological developments arising after the passing of an Act.

### 20.8.2　The problem of social change

Since the Increase of Rent and Mortgage Interest (Restrictions) Act 1920, the law has given security of tenure to a member of a tenant's family who was residing with the tenant at the time of the tenant's death. In *Gammans v Ekins* [1950] 2 KB 328, the facts were that a Mr Ekins lived with a Mrs Smith, who was the tenant of the house concerned. On her death in 1939, Mr Ekins claimed to be a member of her family. The Court of Appeal rejected his claim. Asquith LJ said: 'To say of two people masquerading... as husband and wife (there being no children to complicate the picture) that they were members of the same family seems to be an abuse of the English language'.

Only a few years later, however, in *Hawes v Evendon* [1953] 1 WLR 1169, the Court of Appeal decided that the survivor of a non-marital relationship was a member of the tenant's family, although in this case there were children, so the comment of Asquith LJ in the previous case was not directly applicable. Subsequently, in *Dyson Holdings Ltd v Fox* [1975] 3 All ER 1031, the Court of Appeal returned to the same problem, but this time without the complicating factor of children. Although their Lordships did so with differing degrees of enthusiasm, all three held that the surviving common law wife was a member of the tenant's family. On the basis that times change and the meanings of words change with them, it was held that *Gammans v Ekins* should not be followed because the word 'family' in 1939 had not borne the same meaning as it did in 1961, which was the date of death in the present case. Similarly, in *Watson v Lucas* [1980] 3 All ER 647, the Court of Appeal held that a family exists if the relationship looks like a marriage in the old sense of a lifelong union rather than one which is merely temporary or casual.

However, as we saw at page 278–82, the courts have experienced some difficulty in deciding whether the modern approach should be extended to include the survivors of homosexual relationships.

### 20.8.3 The problem of technological change

In some cases the changes are technological rather than social, but from the point of view of statutory interpretation both the problem and the solution are substantially the same.

First, in *Barker v Wilson* [1980] 2 All ER 647, the High Court had to decide whether microfilm was within the meaning of a 'bankers' book' for the purposes of the Bankers' Books Evidence Act 1879. Section 9 of the Act defined 'bankers' books' as including 'ledgers, day books, cash books, account books and all other books used in the ordinary business of the bank'. Holding that microfilm could be a bankers' book, Bridge LJ said:

> 'The Bankers' Books Evidence Act 1879 was enacted with the practice of bankers in 1879 in mind. It must be construed in 1980 in relation to the practice of bankers as we now understand it. So construing the definition of "bankers' books" and the phrase "an entry in a banker's book", it seems to me that clearly both phrases are apt to include any form of permanent record kept by the bank of transactions relating to the bank's business, made by any of the methods which modern technology makes available, including, in particular, microfilm.'

Secondly, in *Re Attorney-General's Reference (No 5 of 1980)* [1980] 3 All ER 816, the Court of Appeal decided that a video cassette was an 'article' within the meaning of s. 1 (2) of the Obscene Publications Act 1959: 'In this Act "article" means any description of article containing or embodying matter to be read or looked at or both, any sound record, and any film or other record of a picture or pictures'. In dealing with the submission that, when the Act had been passed, videotapes were scarcely beyond the experimental stage, the court accepted that ordinary words should be construed 'in the ways in which they would have been understood by ordinary literate persons at the material time, namely in 1959'. Despite the traditional tone of this statement, the court was nevertheless able to come to a conclusion which allowed the law to keep pace with technology, because:

> 'If the clear words of the statute are sufficiently wide to cover the kind of electronic device with which we are concerned in this case, the fact that that particular form of electronic device was not in the contemplation of Parliament in 1959 is an immaterial consideration.'

Thirdly, in *Royal College of Nursing v Department of Health and Social Security* [1981] 1 All ER 545, the House of Lords had to decide what s. 1(1) of the Abortion Act 1967 meant when it referred to a pregnancy being 'terminated by a registered medical practitioner'. The proceedings began when the Royal College applied for a declaration that a circular issued by the Department was wrong as a matter of law. The circular purported to give advice as to the state of the law on abortion and, in particular, as to the extent to which nurses and midwives could lawfully participate in termination. The legal difficulty arose because when the Act was passed only surgical techniques of abortion were medically accepted in cases where the mother was three months pregnant or more, and therefore there was no question of anyone other than a registered medical practitioner performing the operation. From 1972 onwards, however, a new technique became available, involving two stages. First, a registered medical practitioner introduced a catheter and a cannula into the mother's body. Secondly, the registered medical practitioner gave instructions to the nursing staff who then introduced abortifacient drugs into the body, through the catheter and cannula. The registered medical practitioner remained available for consultation throughout.

The House of Lords divided three to two, with the minority holding that under these circumstances it was the nursing staff who were terminating the pregnancy because it was they who actually introduced the abortifacient drugs. The majority, however, held that Parliament had envisaged that abortions within the Act would be team efforts, as is the case with most hospital treatment. It followed that, provided a registered medical practitioner prescribes treatment, and remains in charge throughout the time the treatment is being administered, the pregnancy has been 'terminated by a registered medical practitioner'.

### 20.8.4　Conclusion

Clearly the pragmatic approach which emerges from the cases we have just considered makes it difficult to the point of impossibility to reconcile the *Longford* principle with current judicial reality.

# Summary

- Simple literalism in statutory interpretation has been replaced by the approach known as contextualism or purposivism or enlightened literalism.

- Bennion formulates the basic rule of statutory interpretation as being that the legislator intends an enactment to be construed according to the general guides laid down for that purpose and that conflicts shall be resolved by weighing and balancing the various factors involved in each case.

⯈ The court may have to choose between ordinary and technical meanings.

⯈ Many matters which are commonly regarded as being principles of statutory interpretation are in fact simply matters of language in general.

⯈ In particular, any statute should be read as a whole in order to establish the context of the words in question.

⯈ However, in addition to matters of language in general, certain specialized principles are necessary because of the legal and constitutional context of statutory interpretation.

⯈ There are various presumptions of statutory interpretation. However, these may conflict with each other and with other principles of interpretation.

⯈ The courts may be willing to provide updating constructions to take account of social and technological changes since a statute was passed, where they are satisfied it is appropriate to do so.

## Exercises

1  'The court which interprets a statute has more power than the Parliament which enacted it.' Discuss.

2  Read the fictitious Act which is set out below, and answer the questions which appear beneath it. You must make the following assumptions:

A: The Act is neither a consolidating nor a codifying measure.
B: There are no other Acts *in pari materia* with the Act, nor are there any relevant provisions of European Community Law.
C: The Act was passed as a result of a Report by a Committee set up by the Department of Trade.
D: The Act was passed two years ago.

TRAVEL AGENTS REGISTRATION ACT
*An Act to provide for the registration of travel agents and tour and charter operators.*

Be it enacted etc., etc.

Travel Trade Registration Council
1(1)  There shall be established in accordance with this section a Travel Trade Registration Council (hereinafter referred to as 'the Council'), which shall consist of a chairman appointed by the Secretary of State for Trade and Industry (hereinafter referred to as 'the Secretary of State'), and such other members (not exceeding ten) as the Secretary of State may appoint, being persons appearing to him to

have knowledge and experience of the requirements of the travelling public and of the interests of travel agents and of tour and charter operators.

(2) The Council may from time to time fix the quorum required at its meetings and regulate its own procedure.

(3) The Council may employ such officers and servants as it thinks fit.

Register of Travel Agents and Tour and Charter Operators

2(1) It shall be the duty of the Council to prepare and maintain in accordance with the provisions of this Act a Register of travel agents and tour and charter operators (hereinafter referred to as 'the Register'), which shall be open to inspection by the public during business hours and on such terms as the Council with the approval of the Secretary of State may determine.

(2) No person shall carry on business as a travel agent or tour or charter operator unless his name and address are included in the Register, and any person carrying on business in breach of the provisions of this subsection shall be guilty of an offence under this Act; Provided that this subsection shall come into force three months after the passing of this Act.

(3) A person carrying on business as a travel agent or tour or charter operator at any time before the last foregoing subsection comes into force, or proposing at any time thereafter to commence such a business, may apply to the Council on the prescribed form; and subject to the conditions of registration mentioned in the next following section, the Council shall cause his name and address to be included in the Register.

(4) A person whose name and address are included in the Register shall notify the Council when he ceases to carry on business as a travel agent or tour or charter operator; and on such notification his name and address shall be removed from the Register.

Conditions of Registration

3(1) The conditions of registration referred to in the last foregoing section are as follows:

(a) that the applicant is able to satisfy such criteria as to his financial solvency as the Secretary of State may from time to time prescribe; and

(b) that the applicant has, and declares himself to have, in force such a policy of insurance as may be approved by the Secretary of State.

(2) If any person makes or signs any declaration under the last foregoing subsection which is untrue in any material particular, he shall be guilty of an offence under this Act.

4(1) It shall be the duty of any person whose name and address are included in the Register to notify the Council forthwith of any change of circumstances such that, if he were to apply again for registration, he would be unable to comply with conditions specified in the first subsection of the last foregoing section.

(2) If any person fails to comply with the requirements of the last foregoing subsection, he shall be guilty of an offence under this Act.

## Cancellation of Registration

5(1) Without prejudice to the duty imposed by the last foregoingsection upon persons whose names and addresses are included in the Register, the Council may at any time require information from such persons relating to their suitability to be so registered.

(2) If the Council is satisfied that a person whose name and address are included in the Register is no longer able to comply with the conditions specified in s. 3(1), the Council may either:

    (a) invite that person to request that his registration shall be cancelled forthwith; or

    (b) where such an invitation is either not issued, or is issued and refused, cancel the registration.

## Expenses of the Council

6(1) The prescribed form shall require applicants for registration to state their annual turnover to the nearest £1000.

(2) The expenses of the Council shall be met by a levy set by the Secretary of State and expressed as a percentage of the annual turnover of persons whose names and addresses are included in the Register.

## Penalties and Proceedings

7(1) A person guilty of an offence under this Act shall be liable:

    (a) on summary conviction to a fine not exceeding £1000; or

    (b) on conviction on indictment to a fine not exceeding £10,000.

(2) No proceedings for an offence under this Act may be initiated except by, or with the consent of, the Director of Public Prosecutions.

## Interpretation

8 In this Act the following expressions have the meaning assigned to them respectively, that is to say:

'charter operator' means a person who arranges or provides travel facilities for sale to organizations, societies, or other groups, but not to individual customers;

'holiday accommodation' means temporary accommodation in hotels, boarding houses, other dwellings or caravans;

'prescribed form' means such form as the Secretary of State shall prescribe;

'tour operator' means a person who arranges, on a large scale, travel or holiday facilities for sale either directly or through travel agents, to individual customers;

'travel agent' means a person who carries on business arranging or providing holiday accommodation for members of the public.

## Short Title, Commencement and Territorial Extent

9(1) This Act may be cited as the Travel Agents Registration Act.

(2) Without prejudice to section 2(2), this Act shall come into force at the expiration of one month after the day on which it is passed.

(3)   This Act does not extend to Scotland or Northern Ireland.

QUESTIONS

(a) For what purposes, if any, would the courts be able to refer to the Report of the Committee which preceded the Act?

(b) Must each person appointed to the Council have comprehensive 'knowledge and experience of the requirements of the travelling public and of the interests of travel agents and of tour and charter operators', or is it sufficient that the Council as a whole should have such knowledge and experience, with individual members each having only one kind of knowledge and experience?

(c) Jason, who is registered for the purposes of the Act, has an insurance policy which satisfies the Secretary of State. However, as a result of an error by his bank, the annual premium is not paid. The insurance company decides that, in accordance with the terms of the policy, Jason no longer has insurance cover. When Jason discovers what has happened, he immediately pays the premium and the company reinstates his cover. Naturally, Jason did not initially know of the non-payment of the premium, and accordingly he did not notify the Council under s. 4(1). Has Jason committed an offence under s. 4(2)?

(d) Would the definition of 'holiday accommodation' include (i) a camp site where holiday-makers pitch their own tents; and (ii) a camp site where permanently pitched tents are let to holiday-makers?

**3**   *The Carriage of Dangerous Substances by Road Act*

Following a road traffic accident in Manchester, in which serious spillage of nuclear waste occurred, a committee established by the Department of the Environment recommended the creation of a scheme of licensing to control the movement of nuclear waste by road.

The (fictitious) Carriage of Dangerous Substances by Road Act has now been passed, under which 'any person who transports, or causes or permits the transport of, any dangerous substances by road, through any city, town or other place' commits an offence, unless each local authority through whose area the transport is to take place has first 'issued a licence in writing', permitting the transport to take place.

While the Bill which became the Act was being debated in Parliament, a Minister of State at the Home Office said the intention was that the Act should be enforced strictly and the courts should bear in mind their responsibility to protect the public.

On the basis that

- the Act is neither a consolidating nor a codfying one;
- the Act has been brought into force; and
- there are no other relevant provisions of either English or EC Law, apart from the cases containing the general principles of English statutory interpretation;

discuss the likely attitude of the courts to the following cases, assuming that no licences have been issued in respect of the situations given in (a), (b) and (c):

(a) Tom drives a lorry carrying nuclear waste through Ambridge, a village in the Cotswolds.

(b) Dick drives a lorry carrying cigarettes through Nottingham.

(c) Harry drives a lorry carrying poisonous chemicals through Leicester. His employer had sent Harry to collect a load of waste paper, but as that load was unavailable, Harry picked up the chemicals instead. (Harry was acting within the scope of his employment in substituting one load for another.) (You should consider the position of both Harry and his employer.)

(d) Before transporting a load of nuclear waste through Birmingham, John telephones the local authority, one of whose officials tells John that he is filling in the relevant form of licence as they speak, and that it will be in the post that evening. Immediately after the telephone conversation, John sets out with his load.

# Chapter 21

## Legislative interpretation in the European Court of Justice

**21.1** Introduction

Historically it may have been legitimate to characterize the principal distinction between common law and civil law styles of interpretation in terms of the contrast between simple literalism and purposivism. Also historically, the matter was of largely academic interest, since very few practitioners of English law would ever come across laws originating from civil law jurisdictions. However, the reception of Community law into English law has meant that the civil law style of interpretation as practised by the Court of Justice (which, for the present purposes, includes the Court of First Instance, as it did in Chapter 15), is now of immediately practical importance to English lawyers. As Lord Denning MR said in *Bulmer (HP) Ltd v Bollinger SA* [1974] 2 All ER 1226:

> 'It is apparent that in very many cases the English courts will interpret the Treaty themselves.... Beyond doubt the English courts must follow the same principles as the European court. Otherwise there would be differences between [the member states] ... '

Perhaps fortunately, the English judiciary's widespread conversion to purposive interpretation means that the gap between the two styles of interpretation has narrowed very considerably. Nevertheless, it is worth giving some attention to the Community law style of interpretation, and this chapter will do so. As a preliminary, however, it may be useful to offer some general observations on those characteristics of Community law which have the greatest influence on how it is interpreted.

**21.2** Characteristics of Community law which are relevant to its interpretation

First, Community legislation is drafted in several languages, and, since all the texts are equally authentic, all must be taken equally into account.

'When a single decision is addressed to all the Member States the necessity for uniform application and accordingly for uniform interpretation makes it impossible to consider one version of the text in isolation but requires that it be interpreted on the basis of both the real intention of its author and the aim he seeks to achieve, *in the light in particular of the versions in all [the official] languages.'* (Emphasis added. *Stauder v City of Ulm* [1969] ECR 419.)

In *R v Customs and Excise Commissioners ex parte EMU Tabac srl* [1998] *The Times*, 9 April, the Court emphasized once again the equality of all the official language texts. The essence of the case was that a company's business consisted of obtaining orders, from private individuals resident in the United Kingdom, for cigarettes which it then bought in Luxembourg and imported into the United Kingdom on behalf of those individuals. The company wished to argue that the cigarettes were exempt from duty in the United Kingdom, because they had been bought duty-paid in the EC and privately imported for personal consumption. The key to this argument lay in the application of the Latin maxim *qui facit per alium facit per se,* which may be translated as 'a person who does something through an agent is doing that thing himself'. In other words, the company's argument was that, as a matter of law, its activities were those of the individuals on whose behalf it was acting. On a preliminary reference from the Court of Appeal, the Court accepted that the maxim is common to the legal systems of many member states, but nevertheless rejected its relevance to the present case. One ground for the Court's reasoning was that the Greek and Danish texts of the Directive in question both clearly precluded the involvement of agents. More particularly, the Court rejected an argument that, because Greece and Denmark represented only five per cent of the Community's population as a whole, and their languages were not easily understood by the nationals of other member states, it followed that those texts should be disregarded.

Secondly, Community law has its own terminology and employs its own concepts, and every provision of Community law must be interpreted in the light of Community law as a whole.

'It must ... be borne in mind that even where the different language versions are entirely in accord with one another, that Community law uses terminology which is peculiar to it. Furthermore, it must be emphasized that legal concepts do not necessarily have the same meaning in Community law and in the law of the various Member States.

'Finally... every provision of Community Law must be placed in its context and interpreted in the light of the provisions of Community Law as a whole, regard being had to the objectives thereof and to its state of evolution at the date on which the provision in question is to be applied.' (*CILFIT v Ministry of Health* [1982] ECR 3415.)

The point may be illustrated by the decision of the Court of Appeal in *Rosgill Group Ltd v Commissioners of Customs and Excise* [1997] 3 All ER 1012, concerning Council Directive (EEC) 77/38 on the harmonization of turnover taxes. Speaking of art. 11A(1) of the Directive, which defined the taxable amount as 'everything which constitutes the consideration which has been ... obtained', Morritt LJ commented that 'the word "consideration" must be approached as a matter of Community law' which meant that the correct approach was for the court 'to ascertain whether there is "a direct link" between the relevant supply and that which is alleged to be consideration for it'. In other words, the doctrine of consideration developed by the English law of contract was nothing to the point.

Thirdly, and in some ways most importantly, although the Treaties contain the fundamental provisions on which the Community's legal order is based, when it comes to Regulations, Directives and Decisions, the Community knows no doctrine of legislative supremacy. For example, the Court may quash Community legislation which contravenes the general principles of Community law (see Chapter 15). By way of further example, art. 253 [ex 190] EC provides that 'Regulations, Directives and Decisions ... shall state the reasons on which they are based ...'. The Court explained the multi-faceted purpose of this provision in the *Brennwein Case (Germany v Commission)* [1963] ECR 63.

> 'In imposing ... the obligation to state reasons ... art. 190 is not taking mere formal considerations into account but seeks to give an opportunity to the parties of defending their rights, to the Court of exercising its supervisory functions, and to member states and to all interested nationals of ascertaining the circumstances in which [the Treaty has been applied].'

It follows that when the Court is deciding whether to quash a provision because its statement of reasons is insufficient to comply with the article, it will ask itself whether the opportunities set out in *Brennwein* have genuinely been made available. However, the stringency of the test which the Court applies will vary with the type of act in question. For example, Regulations are legislative measures of a general character, and therefore will require less specific reasons than Decisions, which are issued to named addressees, and where, therefore, a higher degree of specificity can reasonably be expected.

## 21.3 The teleological approach to interpretation

Although the practice of statutory interpretation in the English courts has become increasingly purposive since the Second World War (see page 263), there are nevertheless degrees of purposivism. The English courts have generally moved towards a relatively conservative version in which the court seeks to identify what it calls 'the intention of the legislature', even though, as we saw in Chapter 19 this apparently simple concept is far from straightforward.

The European Court of Justice, in common with the courts of the Communities' original members, draws on a different legal tradition from that which produced the common law. Within the continental tradition, which traces its origins back to Roman law, a more dynamic form of purposivism, known as the *teleological* approach, has been commonplace. It is not surprising, therefore, that this is the approach which the Court of Justice has adopted when seeking to turn the legislative texts of the Communities into a working legal system:

> '[The Court] tries to give the provision an interpretation which fits in with the general scheme of the instrument ... [but] ... beyond this the Court makes little attempt to establish the actual subjective intention of the authors of the text ... One reason for disregarding the subjective intention of the authors of the text is that, in the case of an agreement reached after hard bargaining, there may be no common intention – only an agreement on a form of words. A more important reason is that the Court prefers to interpret texts on the basis of what it thinks they should be trying to achieve; it moulds the law according to what it regards as the needs of the Community.' (Hartley, *The Foundations of European Community Law*, 9th edn, 2003, p. 75.)

More particularly, 'one of the distinctive characteristics of the European Court is the extent to which its decision-making is based on policy ... This may be summed up in one phrase: the promotion of European integration'. (*Op. cit.*, p. 80.) Some examples may be useful.

First, in the leading case of *van Gend en Loos v Nederlandse Administratie der Belastingen* [1963] ECR 1 (which is also discussed at page 82) the Court said:

> 'The objective of the EEC Treaty, which is to establish a common market, the functioning of which is of direct concern to interested parties in the Community, implies that this Treaty is more than an agreement which merely creates mutual obligations between the contracting states. This view is confirmed by the preamble to the Treaty which refers not only to governments but to peoples. It is also confirmed more specifically by the establishment of institutions endowed with sovereign rights, the exercise of which affects member states and also their citizens.'

On the basis of this, together with a close consideration of the details of the case itself, the Court concluded:

> 'It follows ... that, according to the spirit, the general scheme and the wording of the Treaty, art. 12 must be interpreted as producing direct effects and creating individual rights which national courts must protect.'

Thus the basic doctrines of the supremacy of Community law, and its direct effect, flow from the Court's adoption of the teleological approach to interpretation.

Secondly, in *Broekmeulen* [1981] ECR 2311, a Dutch national who had received his medical education in Belgium was refused permission to practise in The Netherlands, on the ground that he lacked a year's training in general medicine, which all Dutch nationals were required to have by Dutch law. The Court held the requirement of the year's training to be contrary to Community law, because nationals of other member states were not required to have it. The Court held that freedom of movement of persons, the right of establishment and the freedom to provide services, all of which are guaranteed by the EC Treaty and fundamental to the Community, could not be fully achieved if a member state could discriminate against one of its own nationals who had exercised his Community law right of freedom of movement in order to pursue his education in another member state.

Thirdly, the case of *Polydor v Harlequin Records* [1982] ECR 329 dates from the period when there was a Free Trade Agreement between the Community and Portugal, which was then only an aspiring member. The relevant terms of both the Agreement and the EC Treaty were substantially the same, and yet the Court held that records which could have been freely imported into the United Kingdom from another member state, without obtaining the copyright owners' consent, were not similarly exempt under the Agreement. The Court's reasoning was that the Community's ultimate aim was to unite national markets into a single market which would have the characteristics of a domestic market, whereas the aim of the Agreement was simply to remove certain barriers to trade.

Pursuit of the purpose of a provision may lead the Court to adopt what amounts to a somewhat restrictive version of the principle of interpretation which may be illustrated by cases such as *R v Cuthbertson* [1980] 2 All ER 401 (see page 289). But, in *Meroni & Co* [1957–58] ECR 157, the Court said that what it called 'an argument in reverse' is possible only where 'no other interpretation appears appropriate and compatible with the provision and its context and with the purpose of the same'. In other words, such arguments are available only as a last resort.

However, without in any way intending to cast doubt on the primacy of the teleological approach to the interpretation of Community law, it would be wrong to suggest that the Court of Justice is entirely free from textual constraints.

## 21.4 Literal meaning, clear meaning and legal meaning

As Advocate-General Mayras explained in *Fellinger* [1980] ECR 535, there may be a distinction between the 'literal meaning' and the 'clear meaning' of a provision:

> 'Where a literal interpretation of a rule of written law leads to an unreasonable or unjust result is it permissible for the Court to look for another interpretation which avoids that result? In my opinion, one may be guided on this by general principles of interpretation and by the case-law of the Court.
>
> 'The distinct roles of the legislator and the judge within a national legal system have been elegantly described by Portalis:
>
> > "There is the art of the legislator just as there is the art of the judge, and they are not alike. The art of the legislator lies in seeking for each issue those principles which are most beneficial to the common weal; the art of the judge lies in putting those principles into practice, in developing them and extending them by applying them wisely and rationally to individual cases; in studying the spirit of the law when its letter is slave and rebel and of transgressing through a spirit of servility."
>
> 'In accordance with the distinction drawn by that eminent jurist, this Court may not substitute its discretion for that of the Community legislature; when the meaning of the legislation is clear it has to be applied with that meaning, even if the solution prescribed may be thought to be unsatisfactory. That is not to say, however, that the literal construction of a provision must always be accepted. If such construction were to lead to a nonsensical result in regard to a situation which the Court believed the provision was intended to cover, certain doubts might properly be entertained in regard to it. In other words, the clear meaning and the literal meaning are not synonymous. *There have been many cases in which the Court has rejected a literal interpretation in favour of another which it found more compatible with the objective and the whole scheme of the legislation in question.*' (Emphasis added.)

More particularly, a word is to be given its ordinary legal meaning, unless the context otherwise requires. In *Netherlands v Commission* [1979] ECR 245, a Regulation dealing with the so-called butter mountain provided for butter which had been in store for more than four months to be sold to the intervention agency, which would then resell the butter in the export market. The resale had to be within 30 days of the sale to the agency. An issue arose as to whether the 30-day period ran from the conclusion of the contract of sale to the agency, or from the time the butter left the store. The date of leaving the store was held to be irrelevant, because there was 'no reason why the term "sale" ... should be given a meaning different to that which it has in ordinary legal language'.

When seeking to identify the meaning of a provision which has been amended or replaced, the Court may consult the original text, because a change of wording raises a presumption of a change of meaning. In

*Simon v Court of Justice* [1961] ECR 115, employees who lived more than a certain distance from their place of work were eligible for separation allowances. An early Regulation had spoken in terms of living 'within a radius of 25 km', but its successor spoke merely in terms of 'distance'. Simon's journey to work was 26 km by road and 29 km by rail, but less than 25 km as the crow flies.

> 'If the word "radius" had replaced the word "distance" in the article, the scope of the amendment would have been clear, for the authors of the new provisions would have obviously had the intention of choosing between the two possible interpretations of the former wording that which related to the concept of distance as the crow flies.'In the present case, however, it is the reverse which has happened.
>
> 'The very fact of having replaced in the present case the word "radius" by the word "distance" clearly shows that the authors of the article wished to reject the concept of "as the crow flies" (a concept which was clearly expressed by the word "radius") and that they wished on the other hand to adopt the concept of "journey" by road or railway ...
>
> 'It must also be observed that [the provision] does not prescribe precisely the method of calculating the distance (by road or rail or the shortest of these two ways).
>
> 'If the drafting is defective there is nothing to prevent selecting by means of interpretation the most reasonable criterion, that is to say, that of the shortest distance either by road or by rail of a normal journey.'

**21.5** Retrospectivity

The extent to which the Court's decisions have retrospective effect is discussed at page 227.

## Summary

▷ Since the English courts have generally moved towards the purposive approach to interpretation, the gap between English and European styles of interpretation has been reduced, and is now more a matter of degree than of kind.

▷ Community legislation is drafted in several languages, and all the texts are equally authentic.

▷ Community law has its own terminology and employs its own concepts.

▷ The Community knows no doctrine of legislative supremacy, and therefore the Court of Justice may quash Community legislation.

▷ The Court's approach to interpretation is teleological, being based on the objectives of the Community as a whole, as well as the general scheme of the instrument which is subject to interpretation.

▶ An interpretation deduced from the absence of an express statement may be acceptable, but only as a last resort.

▶ The Court of Justice may draw a distinction between the *clear meaning* and the *literal meaning* of a provision. A word is to be given its *ordinary legal meaning*, unless the context otherwise requires.

▶ Where a provision has been amended or replaced, the original can be consulted, because a change of wording raises a presumption of a change of meaning.

## Exercises

**1** What particular problems of legislative interpretation arise from the nature of the European Community?

**2** What (if anything) is the difference between the European Court of Justice and the English courts in their approach to *ordinary* and *legal* meanings?

# Law reports and journals (some useful references)

(A comprehensive listing of current references is included in each monthly part of *Current Law*.)

AC (formerly App Cas) = Appeal Cases (Law Reports)
ACD = Administrative Court Digest (the re-titled Crown Office Digest)
Admin LR = Administrative Law Reports
All ER = All England Law Reports
All ER (EC) = All England Law Reports (European Cases)
Anglo-Am = Anglo-American Law Review

BLR = Building Law Reports

Ch (formerly ChD) = Chancery (Law Reports)
CJQ = Civil Justice Quarterly
CLY = Current Law Yearbook
CMLR = Common Market Law Reports
CMLRev. = Common Market Law Review
COD = Crown Office Digest (to end of 2000); also see ACD (Administrative Court Digest)
Co Law = Company Lawyer
Con LR = Construction Law Reports
Conv (ns) (or Conv. or Conveyancer) = Conveyancer and Property Lawyer (New Series)
Cox CC = Cox's Criminal Cases
Cr App R (or CAR) = Criminal Appeal Reports
Cr App R (S) (or CAR(S)) = Criminal Appeal Reports (Sentencing)
Crim LR = Criminal Law Review

DLR = Dominion Law Reports (a Canadian series)

EBLRev = European Business Law Review

ECR = European Court Reports
EG = Estates Gazette
EGLR = Estates Gazette Law Reports
EHRR = European Human Rights Reports
ELRev = European Law Review
ER = English Reports

Fam = Family Division (Law Reports)
Fam Law = Family Law
FCR = Family Court Reporter
FLR = Family Law Reports
FSR = Fleet Street Reports
FTLR = Financial Times Law Reports

Harv LR = Harvard Law Review
HLR = Housing Law Reports

ICLQ = International and Comparative Law Quarterly
ICR = Industrial Cases Reports
ILJ = Industrial Law Journal
Imm AR = Immigration Appeals Reports
IRLR = Industrial Relations Law Reports
ITR = Industrial Tribunal Reports

JBL = Journal of Business Law
JP = Justice of the Peace Reports
JPL = Journal of Planning and Environment Law (formerly Journal of
    Planning Law)
JPN = Justice of the Peace Journal (abbreviating 'Journal' to 'N' may
    seem rather odd. The explanation is that this periodical was origi-
    nally known as 'Justice of the Peace Newspaper', and the 'JPN'
    abbreviation has survived even though it is now commonly
    referred to as 'Justice of the Peace Journal' by way of contradistinc-
    tion to 'Justice of the Peace Reports' – see 'JP')
JR = Juridical Review
JSPTL = Journal of the Society of Public Teachers of Law
JSWL = Journal of Social Welfare Law

KB = King's Bench (Law Reports)
KIR = Knight's Industrial Reports

LGR = Local Government Reports

LG Rev = Local Government Review (renamed as *Local Government Review Reports* in November 1993, and absorbed into the *Justice of the Peace* in 1996)
LJ = Law Journal
Ll Rep (formerly Lloyd's Rep ) = Lloyd's List Reports
LQR = Law Quarterly Review
LS = Legal Studies
LS Gaz = Law Society's Gazette
LT = Law Times

Med LR = Medical Law Reports
MLR = Modern Law Review

New LJ = New Law Journal
NILQ = Northern Ireland Legal Quarterly
NZLR = New Zealand Law Reports

OJ = Official Journal of the European Communities
OJLS = Oxford Journal of Legal Studies

P (formerly PD) = Probate (Law Reports)
P & CR = Property and Compensation Reports (formerly Planning and Compensation Reports)
PL = Public Law

QB (formerly QBD) = Queen's Bench (Law Reports)

RPC = Reports of Patent, Design and Trade Mark Cases
RTR = Road Traffic Reports

SJ (sometimes given as Sol Jo) = Solicitors' Journal
SLT = Scots Law Times
Stat LR = Statute Law Review
STC = Simon's Tax Cases

TLR = Times Law Reports

US = United States Reports

WLR = Weekly Law Reports

Yale LJ = Yale Law Journal

# Extracts from the Interpretation Act 1978

This material is copyright and is reproduced with the permission of Her Majesty's Stationery Office.

The words appearing in **bold type** immediately after the section numbers are the marginal notes of the Queen's Printer's text.

EXTRACTS FROM THE
INTERPRETATION ACT 1978

General provisions as to enactment and operation

3 **Judicial notice** Every Act is a public Act to be judicially noticed as such, unless the contrary is expressly provided by the Act.

4 **Time of commencement** An Act or provision of an Act comes into force –

(a) where provision is made for it to come into force on a particular day, at the beginning of that day;

(b) where no provision is made for its coming into force, at the beginning of the day on which the Act receives the Royal Assent.

Interpretation and construction

5 **Definitions** In any Act, unless the contrary intention appears, words and expressions listed in Schedule I to this Act are to be construed according to that Schedule.

6 **Gender and number** In any Act, unless the contrary intention appears –

(a) words importing the masculine gender include the feminine;

(b) words importing the feminine gender include the masculine;

(c) words in the singular include the plural and words in the plural include the singular.

7 **References to service by post** Where an Act authorises or requires any document to be served by post (whether the expression 'serve' or the expression 'give' or 'send' or any other expression is used) then, unless the contrary intention appears, the service is deemed to be

effected by properly addressing, pre-paying and posting a letter containing the document and, unless the contrary is proved, to have been effected at the time at which the letter would be delivered in the ordinary course of post.

8 **References to distance** In the measurement of any distance for the purposes of an Act, that distance shall, unless the contrary intention appears, be measured in a straight line on a horizontal plane.

9 **References to time of day** Subject to section 3 of the Summer Time Act 1972 (construction of references to points of time during the period of summer time), whenever an expression of time occurs in an Act, the time referred to shall, unless it is otherwise specifically stated, be held to be Greenwich mean time.

...

11 **Construction of subordinate legislation** Where an Act confers power to make subordinate legislation, expressions used in that legislation have, unless the contrary intention appears, the meaning which they bear in the Act.

### Statutory powers and duties

12 **Continuity of powers and duties** (1) Where an Act confers a power or imposes a duty it is implied, unless the contrary intention appears, that the power may be exercised, or the duty is to be performed, from time to time as occasion requires.

(2) Where an Act confers a power or imposes a duty on the holder of an office as such, it is implied, unless the contrary intention appears, that the power may be exercised, or the duty is to be performed, by the holder for the time being of the office.

13 **Anticipatory exercise of powers** Where an Act which (or any provision of which) does not come into force immediately on its passing confers powers to make subordinate legislation, or to make appointments, give notices, prescribe forms or do any other thing for the purposes of the Act, then, unless the contrary intention appears, the power may be exercised, and any instrument made thereunder may be made so as to come into force, at any time after the passing of the Act so far as may be necessary or expedient for the purpose –

(a) of bringing the Act or any provision of the Act into force; or

(b) of giving full effect to the Act or any such provision at or after the time when it comes into force.

14 **Implied power to amend** Where an Act confers power to make –

(a) rules, regulations or byelaws; or

(b) Orders in Council, orders or other subordinate legislation to be made by statutory instrument,

it implies, unless the contrary intention appears, a power, exercisable in the same manner and subject to the same conditions or limitations, to revoke, amend or re-enact any instrument made under the power.

## Repealing enactments

**15 Repeal of repeal** Where an Act repeals a repealing enactment, the repeal does not revive any enactment previously repealed unless words are added reviving it.

**16 General savings** (1) Without prejudice to section 15, where an Act repeals an enactment, the repeal does not, unless the contrary intention appears –

(a) revive anything not in force or existing at the time at which the repeal takes effect;

(b) affect the previous operation of the enactment repealed or anything duly done or suffered under that enactment;

(c) affect any right, privilege, obligation or liability acquired, accrued or incurred under that enactment;

(d) affect any penalty, forfeiture or punishment incurred in respect of any offence committed against that enactment;

(e) affect any investigation, legal proceeding or remedy in respect of any such right, privilege, obligation, liability, penalty, forfeiture or punishment;

and any such investigation, legal proceeding or remedy may be instituted, continued or enforced, and any such penalty, forfeiture or punishment may be imposed, as if the repealing Act had not been passed.

(2) This section applies to the expiry of a temporary enactment as if it were repealed by an Act.

**17 Repeal and re-enactment** (1) Where an Act repeals a previous enactment and substitutes provisions for the enactment repealed, the repealed enactment remains in force until the substituted provisions come into force.

(2) Where an Act repeals and re-enacts, with or without modification, a previous enactment then, unless the contrary intention appears –

(a) any reference in any other enactment to the enactment so repealed shall be construed as a reference to the provision re-enacted;

(b) in so far as any subordinate legislation made or other thing done under the enactment so repealed, or having effect as if so made or done, could have been made or done under the provision re-enacted, it shall have effect as if made or done under that provision.

Miscellaneous

18 **Duplicated offences** Where an act or omission constitutes an offence under two or more Acts, or both under an Act and at common law, the offender shall, unless the contrary intention appears, be liable to be prosecuted and punished under either or any of those Acts or at common law, but shall not be liable to be punished more than once for the same offence.

...

Supplementary

21 **Interpretation etc** (1) In this Act 'Act' includes a local and personal or private Act; and 'subordinate legislation' means Orders in Council, orders, rules, regulations, schemes, warrants, byelaws and other instruments made or to be made under any Act.
(2) This Act binds the Crown.

Schedule I
(extracts)

'Commencement', in relation to an Act or enactment, means the time when the Act or enactment comes into force.

'The Communities', 'the Treaties' or 'the Community Treaties' and other expressions defined by section 1 of and Schedule I to the European Communities Act 1972 have the meanings prescribed by that Act .

'Month' means calendar month.

'Person' includes a body of persons corporate or unincorporate.

'Secretary of State' means one of Her Majesty's Principal Secretaries of State.

'Writing' includes typing, printing, lithography, photography and other modes of representing or reproducing words in a visible form, and expressions referring to writing are to be construed accordingly.

# Articles 2–12 and 14 of, and Articles 1–3 of the First Protocol and Articles 1 & 2 of the Sixth Protocol to, the European Convention for the Protection of Human Rights and Fundamental Freedoms 1950

Note: This Appendix covers the 'Convention Rights' referred to in the Human Rights Act 1998.

## SECTION 1

Article 2

1. Everyone's right to life shall be protected by law. No one shall be deprived of his life intentionally save in the execution of a sentence of a court following his conviction of a crime for which this penalty is provided by law.

2. Deprivation of life shall not be regarded as inflicted in contravention of this Article when it results from the use of force which is no more than absolutely necessary:

(a) in defence of any person from unlawful violence;

(b) in order to effect a lawful arrest or to prevent the escape of a person lawfully detained;

(c) in action lawfully taken for the purpose of quelling a riot or insurrection.

Article 3

No one shall be subjected to torture or to inhuman or degrading treatment or punishment.

Article 4

1. No one shall be held in slavery or servitude.

2. No one shall be required to perform forced or compulsory labour.

3. For the purpose of this Article the term 'forced or compulsory labour' shall not include:

(a) any work required to be done in the ordinary course of detention imposed according to the provisions of Article 5 of this Convention or during conditional release from such detention;

(b) any service of a military character or, in case of conscientious objectors in countries where they are recognized, service exacted instead of compulsory military service;

(c) any service exacted in case of an emergency or calamity threatening the life or well-being of the community;

(d) any work or service which forms part of normal civic obligations.

Article 5

1. Everyone has the right to liberty and security of person. No one shall be deprived of his liberty save in the following cases and in accordance with a procedure prescribed by law:

(a) the lawful detention of a person after conviction by a competent court;

(b) the lawful arrest or detention of a person for non-compliance with the lawful order of a court or in order to secure the fulfilment of any obligation prescribed by law;

(c) the lawful arrest or detention of a person effected for the purpose of bringing him before the competent legal authority on reasonable suspicion of having committed an offence or when it is reasonably considered necessary to prevent his committing an offence or fleeing after having done so;

(d) the detention of a minor by lawful order for the purpose of educational supervision or his lawful detention for the purpose of bringing him before the competent legal authority;

(e) the lawful detention of persons for the prevention of the spreading of infectious diseases, of persons of unsound mind, alcoholics or drug addicts, or vagrants;

(f) the lawful arrest or detention of a person to prevent his effecting an unauthorized entry into the country or of a person against whom action is being taken with a view to deportation or extradition.

2. Everyone who is arrested shall be informed promptly, in a language which he understands, of the reasons for his arrest and of any charge against him.

3. Everyone arrested or detained in accordance with the provisions of paragraph 1(c) of this Article shall be brought promptly before a judge or other officer authorized by law to exercise judicial power and shall be

entitled to trial within a reasonable time or to release pending trial. Release may be conditioned by guarantees to appear for trial.

4. Everyone who is deprived of his liberty by arrest or detention shall be entitled to take proceedings by which the lawfulness of his detention shall be decided speedily by a court and his release ordered if the detention is not lawful.

5. Everyone who has been the victim of arrest or detention in contravention of the provisions of this Article shall have an enforceable right to compensation.

## Article 6

1. In the determination of his civil rights and obligations or of any criminal charge against him, everyone is entitled to a fair and public hearing within a reasonable time by an independent and impartial tribunal established by law. Judgment shall be pronounced publicly but the press and public may be excluded from all or part of the trial in the interest of morals, public order or national security in a democratic society, where the interest of juveniles or the protection of the private life of the parties so require, or to the extent strictly necessary in the opinion of the court in special circumstances where publicity would prejudice the interests of justice.

2. Everyone charged with a criminal offence shall be presumed innocent until proved guilty according to law.

3. Everyone charged with a criminal offence has the following minimum rights:

(a) to be informed promptly, in a language which he understands and in detail, of the nature and cause of the accusation against him;

(b) to have adequate time and facilities for the preparation of his defence;

(c) to defend himself in person or through legal assistance of his own choosing or, if he has not sufficient means to pay for legal assistance, to be given it free when the interests of justice so require;

(d) to examine or have examined witnesses against him and to obtain the attendance and examination of witnesses on his behalf under the same conditions as witnesses against him;

(e) to have the free assistance of an interpreter if he cannot understand or speak the language used in court.

## Article 7

1. No one shall be held guilty of any criminal offence on account of any act or omission which did not constitute a criminal offence under national or international law at the time when it was committed. Nor

shall a heavier penalty be imposed than the one that was applicable at the time the criminal offence was committed.

2. This Article shall not prejudice the trial and punishment of any person for any act or omission which, at the time when it was committed, was criminal according to the general principles of law recognized by civilized nations.

Article 8
1. Everyone has the right to respect for his private and family life, his home and his correspondence.
2. There shall be no interference by a public authority with the exercise of this right except such as is in accordance with the law and is necessary in a democratic society in the interests of national security, public safety or the economic well-being of the country, for the prevention of disorder or crime, for the protection of health or morals, or for the protection of the rights and freedoms of others.

Article 9
1. Everyone has the right to freedom of thought, conscience and religion; this right includes freedom to change his religion or belief, and freedom, either alone or in community with others and in public or private, to manifest his religion or belief, in worship, teaching, practice and observance.
2. Freedom to manifest one's religion or beliefs shall be subject only to such limitations as are prescribed by law and are necessary in a democratic society in the interests of public safety, for the protection of public order, health or morals, or for the protection of the rights and freedoms of others.

Article 10
1. Everyone has the right to freedom of expression. This right shall include freedom to hold opinions and to receive and impart information and ideas without interference by public authority and regardless of frontiers. This Article shall not prevent States from requiring the licensing of broadcasting, television or cinema enterprises.
2. The exercise of these freedoms, since it carries with it duties and responsibilities, may be subject to such formalities, conditions, restrictions or penalties as are prescribed by law and are necessary in a democratic society in the interests of national security, territorial integrity or public safety, for the prevention of disorder or crime, for the protection of health or morals, for the protection of the reputation or rights of others, for preventing the disclosure of information received in

confidence, or for maintaining the authority and impartiality of the judiciary.

Article 11

1. Everyone has the right to freedom of peaceful assembly and to freedom of association with others, including the right to form and to join trade unions for the protection of his interests.

2. No restrictions shall be placed on the exercise of these rights other than such as are prescribed by law and are necessary in a democratic society in the interests of national security or public safety, for the prevention of disorder or crime, for the protection of health or morals or for the protection of the rights and freedoms of others. This Article shall not prevent the imposition of lawful restrictions on the exercise of these rights by members of the armed forces, of the police or of the administration of the State.

Article 12

Men and women of marriageable age have the right to marry and to found a family, according to the national laws governing the exercise of this right.

Article 14

The enjoyment of the rights and freedoms set forth in this Convention shall be secured without discrimination on any ground such as sex, race, colour, language, religion, political or other opinion, national or social origin, association with a national minority, property, birth or other status.

### ARTICLES 1–3 OF PROTOCOL 1 – ENFORCEMENT OF CERTAIN RIGHTS AND FREEDOMS NOT INCLUDED IN SECTION 1 OF THE CONVENTION

Article 1

Every natural or legal person is entitled to the peaceful enjoyment of his possessions. No one shall be deprived of his possessions except in the public interest and subject to the conditions provided for by law and by the general principles of international law. The preceding provisions shall not, however, in any way impair the right of a State to enforce such laws as it deems necessary to control the use of property in accordance with the general interest or to secure the payment of taxes or other contributions or penalties.

Article 2

No person shall be denied the right to education. In the exercise of any functions which it assumes in relation to education and to teaching, the

State shall respect the right of parents to ensure such education and teaching in conformity with their own religious and philosophical convictions.

Article 3
The High Contracting Parties undertake to hold free elections at reasonable intervals by secret ballot, under conditions which will ensure the free expression of the opinion of the people in the choice of the legislature.

## ARTICLES 1 & 2 OF PROTOCOL 6 – CONCERNING THE ABOLITION OF THE DEATH PENALTY

Article 1
The death penalty shall be abolished. No one shall be condemned to such penalty or executed.

Article 2
A state may make provision in its law for the death penalty in respect of acts committed in time of war or of imminent threat of war; such penalty shall be applied only in the instance laid down in the law and in accordance with its provisions. The State shall communicate to the Secretary General of the Council of Europe the relevant provisions of that law.

Note: The Human Rights Act 1998 does not confer the status of *Convention rights* on the rights covered by arts 16, 17 and 18. These articles provide, respectively, that arts 10, 11 and 14 do not prohibit restrictions on the political activities of aliens; that nothing in the Convention gives any right to do anything which would harm the rights which it protects; and that the restrictions contained in the Convention may be applied only for the purposes for which they are prescribed.

# Selected further reading

The field of potential further reading is so vast that this selection can be no more than indicative. It follows that readers who are pursuing formal courses of study should pay careful attention to the recommendations of their lecturers, which may vary from my suggestions. I have specified the editions which were current or imminent at the time of writing. However the essential point is that you should always use the latest available edition.

Where there is more than one title within a category, I have tried to list them in ascending order of difficulty.

## General Reading

For *Legal Method* generally, see:

*The Law Making Process*, by M. Zander, 6th edn, 2004, Cambridge University Press.
*Learning Legal Skills*, by M. Fox and C Bell, 3rd edn, 1999, Oxford University Press.
*How To Do Things With Rules*, by W. Twining and D. Miers, 4th edn, 1999, Cambridge University Press.

For a more theoretical approach to the nature of Law, see:

*Legal Theory*, by I. McLeod, 3rd edn, 2005, Palgrave Macmillan.
*Legal Philosophies*, by J. W. Harris, 2nd edn, 1997, Butterworths.

## Part 1: Ideas and Institutions

For a basic book on thinking logically in any context, see:

*Critical Thinking Skills: Developing Effective Analysis and Argument*, by Stella Cottrell, 2005, Palgrave.

For a description of the structure of the English Legal System, see:

*The English Legal Process*, by T. Ingman, 11th edn, 2006, Oxford University Press.

For the constitutional background, see:

*Constitutional and Administrative Law*, by J. Alder, 6th edn, 2007, Palgrave Macmillan.

For the European Community dimension, see:

*Textbook on EC Law*, by J. Steiner, L. Woods and C. Twigg-Flesner, 9th edn, 2006, Oxford University Press.
*EU Law: Text, Cases and Materials*, by P. Craig and G. de Burca, 3rd edn, 2002, Oxford University Press.

For the Human Rights Act 1998, see:

*Blackstone's Guide to the Human Rights Act 1998*, by John Wadham, Helen Mountfield, Anna Edmundson and Caoilfhionn Gallagher, 4th edn, 2007, Oxford University Press.

## Part 2: Case-Law and Precedent

In addition to the books cited on *Legal Method* generally, see:

*Precedent in English Law*, by Sir Rupert Cross, 4th edn, 1991, by J. W. Harris, Oxford University Press.
*Precedent and Law*, by J. Stone, 1985, Butterworths.
*Precedent in Law*, by L. Goldstein (ed.), 1987, Oxford University Press.

## Part 3: Legislation and Legislative Interpretation

In addition to the books cited on *Legal Method* generally, see:

*Cross: Statutory Interpretation*, by J. Bell and Sir George Engle, 3rd edn, 1995, Butterworths.
*Statutory Interpretation*, by J. Evans, 1988, Oxford University Press.
*Understanding Common Law Legislation: Drafting and Interpretation*, by F. Bennion, 2001, Oxford University Press.
*Craies on Legislation*, Daniel Greenberg, 8th edition, 2004, Sweet & Maxwell.
*Purposive Interpretation in Law*, by Aharon Barak, English translation 2005, Princeton University Press.
*Statutory Interpretation*, by F. Bennion, 4th edn, 2002, Tottel.

For the standard text on legislative drafting, see:

*Legislative Drafting*, by G. C. Thornton, 4th edn, 1996, Tottel.

And for a more radical approach, see:

*Legislative Drafting: A New Approach*, by Sir William Dale, 1977, Butterworths.

## The Lighter Side

For three books in which a vast amount of learning is not only carried lightly but also deployed deftly in the simultaneous achievement of entertainment and instruction, see:

*Miscellany at Law*, by R. E. Megarry, 1955, revised impression 1958, Stevens.
*A Second Miscellany-at-Law*, by R. E. Megarry, 1973, Stevens.
*A New Miscellany-at-Law*, by R. E. Megarry, edited by Bryan A. Garner, 2005, Hart Publishing.

# Index

**A**

Academic questions, non-justiciability of  18
Acts of Parliament – *see* Statutes
Adjectival law – *see* Procedural law
Administrative tribunals  58
American Realism  3
Analogy, reasoning by  11 *et seq*
Appeal
  distinguished from judicial review  33
  permission to  58
  rights of  58

**B**

Bill of Rights 1689  66
Brandeis briefs  216

**C**

Changed circumstances – *see* Precedent
*Cessante ratione cessat ipsa lex* – see Precedent
Civil law
  meaning of  30 *et seq*
  purpose of  31
Common law
  meaning of  23 *et seq*
  remedies at  25 *et seq*
Computer databases  121
Convention rights
  declaration of incompatibility with  104
  meaning of  100 *et seq*
  statement of compatibility with  105
County Courts
  judicial personnel in  48
  jurisdiction of  48
Court of Appeal
  judicial personnel in  54

  jurisdiction of  52 *et seq*
  leapfrog over  56, 203
  precedent in  193 *et seq*
Criminal law, purpose of  31
Crown Court
  judicial personnel in  47
  jurisdiction of  46 *et seq*

**D**

Damages  25 *et seq*
Deduction, reasoning by  11 *et seq*
Delegated legislation, constitutional status of  68

**E**

Equity
  origins and nature of  24 *et seq*
  remedies in  25 *et seq*
European Communities (and Union)
  Charter of Fundamental Rights  93, 230
  Commission of  75
  Council of the European Union  75
  Court of First Instance of  78
  Court of Justice of
    composition of  77
    jurisdiction of  78
    precedent in  224 *et seq*
    preliminary references to  78
    principles of law in  226 *et seq*
    teleological interpretation in  338
  distinction between European Community and European Union  74
  Parliament of  76
European Community law
  decisions  85

direct applicability of 80 *et seq*
direct effect of 80 *et seq*
directives 83 *et seq*
national sovereignty and 86
principles of 226 *et seq*
regulations 83
European Convention for the Protection of Human Rights and Fundamental Freedoms 8, 93 *et seq*, 229
European Court of Human Rights composition of 93
precedent in 94
procedure in 98
European Court of Justice – *see* European Communities (and Union)
European Union – *see* European Communities (and Union)

**F**
Fact
distinguished from law 34 *et seq*
establishing matters of 39 *et seq*
meaning of ordinary word as a question of 35, 236, 286
Fundamental rights 93 *et seq*, 229

**H**
High Court
judicial personnel in 51
jurisdiction of 49 *et seq*
precedent in 205 *et seq*
House of Lords
appeals and appellate committees of 55 *et seq*
judicial personnel in 56
jurisdiction of 55 *et seq*
precedent in 172 *et seq*
Human rights – *see* Fundamental rights

**I**
Induction, reasoning by 10 *et seq*
Injunctions 28

**J**
Judicial decision-making, political element in 20 *et seq*
Judicial notice 39
Judicial review, distinguished from appeal 33
Justice, relationship with law 15 *et seq*

**L**
Law
distinguished from fact 34 *et seq*
reform of through precedent 208 *et seq*
perceived strengths of 208 *et seq*
perceived weaknesses of 210 *et seq*
Law reports
citability and status of 117 *et seq*
delay in publication of 120
editorial discretion in compilation of 119 *et seq*
Legal practice and legal scholarship 13 *et seq*

**M**
Magistrates' courts
judicial personnel in 45
jurisdiction of 44

**N**
Neutral citation of cases 116 *et seq*

**O**
*Obiter dictum* distinguished from *ratio decidendi* 148, 160 *et seq*

**P**
Parliament
intention of 272 *et seq*
direct and indirect 273 *et seq*
particular and general 273 *et seq*
legislative supremacy of 61 *et seq*
origins and evolution of 63

*Per incuriam* – *see* Precedent
Periodicals, status of 110 *et seq*
Political integrity 277 *et seq*
Precedent, doctrine of 129 *et seq*
   *cessante ratione cessat ipsa lex* –
     *see* changed circumstances
   changed circumstances 159
   horizontal dimension of 168
   *per incuriam* 157 *et seq*
   prospective overruling 140
   *res judicata*, distinguished from
     131 *et seq*
   retrospective effect of 133 *et
     seq*
   vertical dimension of 163 *et
     seq*
   whether law or evidence of law
     144 *et seq*
   *see also* County Courts; Court of
     Appeal; European Court of
     Justice; High Court; House of
     Lords; *Obiter dictum*; Privy
     Council; *Ratio decidendi*
Private law 32
Privy Council, judicial committee
   of
   judicial personnel in 57
   jurisdiction of 57
   precedent in 168 *et seq*
Procedural law 33
Processes, validity of 9
Proof, varying standards of 40 *et
   seq*
Propositions, truth of 9
Public law 32

**R**
*Ratio decidendi*, concept of 148 *et
   seq*
   descriptive and prescriptive
     versions 150 *et seq*
   multi-judge courts in 153 *et
     seq*
   techniques used in handling
     155 *et seq*
Royal prerogative 64 *et seq*
Rule of law 61

**S**
Separation of powers 69 *et seq*

Specific performance 28
Statutes
   citation of 121 *et seq*
   codifying 319
   commencement of 296
   consolidating 250, 319
   drafting of 241 *et seq*
     Law Commission's Report
       on 273
     Parliamentary Counsel,
       role of 244 *et seq*
     Renton Report on 246,
       249, 251, 267
     Tilling's Rules for 252 *et seq*
   interpretation of
     contextualism 285
     definition sections 295
     dictionaries 7, 287, 321
     *ejusdem generis* principle 288
     enlightened literalism – *see*
       contextualism
     implied exclusion 289
     extrinsic materials,
       reference to 297
       Parliamentary materials
         300 *et seq*
       post-Parliamentary
         materials 307 *et seq*
       pre-Parliamentary
         materials 297 *et seq*
     golden rule of 257 *et seq*
     Interpretation Act 1978
       296, 347 *et seq*
     linguistic register,
       importance of 261
     mischief rule of 260 *et seq*
     presumptions of 307 *et seq*
     purposive approach to
       263 *et seq*
     rank principle 289
     schedules, status of 295
     simple literalism,
       inadequacy of 256 *et seq*
     social change, problem of
       328 *et seq*
     statutory nonsense 269 *et
       seq*
     technological change,
       problem of 329 *et seq*
Statutory inquiries 58 *et seq*

Subsidiarity   230
Substantive law   33
Syllogistic reasoning   7

**T**
Textbooks, status of   110 *et seq*
Treaties, status of   79